One Day in October

Forty Heroes, Forty Stories

Toby

ONE DAY IN OCTOBER

Forty Heroes, Forty Stories

YAIR AGMON • ORIYA MEVORACH

TRANSLATED BY
Sara Daniel

The Toby Press

Yair Agmon and Oriya Mevorach
One Day in October: Forty Heroes, Forty Stories

First English Edition, 2024

The Toby Press
An imprint of Koren Publishers Jerusalem Ltd.

POB 8531, New Milford, CT 06776-8531, USA
& POB 4044, Jerusalem 9104001, Israel
www.korenpub.com

© Koren Publishers Jerusalem Ltd., 2024
Cover design: Studio Dov Abramson

The publication of this book was made possible through
the generous support of *The Jewish Book Trust.*

ISBN 978-1-59264-688-3

Printed in the United States

Dedicated in honor of all of the heroes of October 7th
who, on Israel's darkest day, revealed glimpses of light
through their heroism, selflessness, and courage, exemplifying
what it means to be truly responsible for one another
and reawakening our fundamental value of unity.

As members of the South African Jewish community,
we are inspired by the acts of bravery
of all the heroes in this book,
among them

Captain Daniel Perez Hy"d

In dedicating this book,
we hope that Daniel's legacy of bravery,
along with the other heroes featured in this book,
will serve as an eternal testimony to the events of that day
and inspire all those who read it to unite
and build a better tomorrow.

Contents

Preface I
Why This Book?

For Israelis, the seventh of October 2023 was the day the world turned upside down. Thousands of Hamas terrorists – cruel, bloodthirsty, heartless, and full of hate – crossed the border and slaughtered and mutilated and burned and raped and kidnapped men, women, and children, from the very young to the very old. It was the darkest day in the history of the State of Israel. Within a single morning, Israelis turned from proud citizens into persecuted refugees.

Twelve hundred people were murdered; two hundred and fifty-one were taken hostage. Many thousands were wounded. Millions locked themselves inside their safe rooms, frightened for their lives. Terror struck – with great force and without mercy – and we were left gasping, anxious, and broken.

All this took place on one day in October. Within less than twenty-four hours, history came knocking, and the State of Israel was changed forever. This was the largest, most brutal massacre of Jews in a single day since the Holocaust. The country was filled with grieving parents and siblings, widows and orphans. Social media exploded with posts desperately seeking missing loved ones. Thousands of people from the communities near the Gaza Strip had to flee from their homes and become refugees. This was Israel's saddest moment, its lowest moment, its weakest moment. And the scars from that dark day – both physical and emotional – will haunt our people forever.

But out of the pillars of smoke and rivers of blood, heroes rose up – heroes and heroines. They emerged from the shelter of their homes, charged into the inferno, and fought like lions to save lives. They snatched the wounded from the jaws of death, dragged the helpless from the battlefield, huddled in their safe rooms to protect month-old babies; threw themselves on grenades to save others; emptied their wallets to pay off terrorists; carried little children out of a hellscape of shot-up and burned cars, and hugged shell-shocked soldiers in the middle of battle.

They are heroes. Like the heroes of old, like the heroes of the Bible, the stuff of stories and legends. Confronting the sadness and loss and depths of hell, they give us hope and inspiration and the chance to tell another kind of story.

On that day, countless heroes risked and sacrificed their lives for their people, for their brothers and sisters and children and future children and the future of the State of Israel. It is this courageous story that we wish to share with the world.

Our journey finding stories of strength and courage from the seventh of October started with the simplest of searches. We started looking for heroes, and within less than a day and a half, we found ourselves inundated with them. Hundreds and hundreds of unbelievable stories. How is it possible that so many regular people – just normal civilians going about their lives – rushed fearlessly into the killing fields to fight evil?

This is mass heroism, both individual and collective. This is heroism that came from every sector of the country – the heroism of women and men; of children, teens, adults, and the elderly; of religious and secular, of Jews and Arabs, of all colors and ethnicities; of Russian Jews,

Ethiopian Jews, Bedouins, Druze, and foreign workers – people of all kinds and all walks of life. Together, they saved countless lives.

In other words, the book you now hold in your hand is only a rivulet of a sweeping torrent of heroism. There are many stories that we missed, heroes who wouldn't – or couldn't – speak; some are still catching their breath and piecing their own stories together. We could produce another dozen volumes of incredible stories of courage from that cursed day. Perhaps we yet will.

The mystic Rabbi Nachman taught that even in the depths of concealment, even during the darkest, lowest, most miserable of moments, there is a hidden spark of exalted divinity, of profound Godly truth. The modern Israeli poet Leah Goldberg insisted that even during the bleakest days, we can dream of forgiveness and kindness, and we can delight in the feel of bare feet treading on soft grass. Taking its cue from both of them, *One Day in October* is a small, earnest attempt to see the good that emerged within the torment and to rejoice in the sweetness of the light.

This book documents all kinds of heroism, in the broadest and most generous sense of the word. There are stories of classical heroism, of the courage under fire of those who faced off against terrorists. But there are also stories of a different heroism. Of an elderly man who sits on the couch and awaits terrorists as a decoy to save his family. Of a midwife who turns her home into a field hospital. Of a surveillance soldier who spends months trying to sound a warning. Of volunteers who struggle to preserve the honor of the slain. All of them are heroes of human dignity who were true to the spark of sanctity within them.

Until now, we've used the plural form; now I, Yair Agmon, want to add something personal. When war broke out around Gaza on the seventh of October, my reserve unit didn't call me up for duty, and I sank into a deep depression. For long weeks I remained home in Tel Aviv, listless with shame and frustration, paralyzed by existential fear. All my friends were called up for reserve duty while I was left behind, with children who were too frightened of the sirens to fall asleep at night.

For long weeks, I was stuck in a black and bitter place. Then, miraculously, thanks to my dear co-author Oriya, the opportunity to work on this book presented itself. At first I was sure that I wouldn't be able to do it. I could hardly breathe, let alone read.

But then I began to read the stories, and each successive story made it a little easier to breathe. The stories gave me moments of consolation, boosts of resilience. Even though they were set in the midst of the horror, they all uncovered veins of light that pulsed through that day of darkness.

This book lifted me out of depression. I fell in love with the people I met through these stories, with their hearts, and with their values. Their stories are "a still, small voice" that soars above the noise and turmoil. These heroes don't know it, but they saved my life too.

July 2024

Preface II
How?

From this book's inception, we felt that it was important to hear stories straight from the people who experienced them, with as few filters as possible. Here is how we worked on this book with our dedicated team, step by step.

The first stage was to create an initial database of stories of heroism from October 7th. There were hundreds, all of them accounts of true heroes.

The second stage was to choose the heroes whose stories we wanted most to tell. Diversity was important to us. We aimed for a wide range of settings, of acts of heroism, and of people, in the hope of giving the broadest possible picture of the heroism and courage that transpired on that day.

The third stage was to track down and approach potential interviewees.

The fourth and most important stage was to go out and meet our heroes and interview them. In cases where the heroes were no longer among the living, we spoke with those closest to them. Each story was told over the course of an interview lasting between one-and-a-half and two-and-a-half hours, and each story was long and detailed. The purpose of these meetings was not only to get the story, but also to get to know the person behind each story, to delve into the intricacies of the human experience, and to ensure that each narrative reflects the tastes, scents, and longings of the person whose story it tells.

Some of the heroes of October 7th are minors. These interviews were conducted by an experienced therapist, Michal Kurnedz, in the presence of an adult family member or friend of the minor's choice.

The fifth stage was to transcribe each interview.

The next stage was to render these transcripts into narratives. With slow, careful, meticulous editing, we shaped each interview into a clear, concise, accessible piece of prose. We were faithful to the transcripts and to the hero's own language and inner world – maintaining their rhythms of speech, repetitions, and exclamations, sometimes at the cost of grammar and syntax, all in order to preserve the interviewee's authentic voice. We did our utmost to portray our heroes accurately and to capture their essence as people. We attempted to investigate "what makes a hero." We strove to describe the actual sequence of events as accurately as possible and how the hero was feeling at each moment. We tried our best to convey the darkness and misery of that black day as delicately as possible alongside the light, beauty, and human greatness that lit up that darkness. We tried our best to tell the whole story.

Finally, at the end of the writing process, we showed each story to its respective hero, who graciously corrected, commented, and helped us perfect it.

A full list of those who contributed to the preparation of this book can be found in the acknowledgments. To each of them our deepest thanks.

Map of the Gaza Envelope

MAP INFORMATION

The information on the map on the following page is based on a combination of official and unofficial sources. We used government reports, including the Bituah Leumi and IDF websites; private initiatives that mapped out and documented the events of the massacre; newspaper reports; and interviews with members of first response teams.

In the event of disparities between different accounts, we relied on the more meticulous account. Similarly, we gave more weight to first-person testimonies than other reports.

It is possible that we made mistakes, and we apologize sincerely if we did. The fallen heroes are forever in our hearts and we have attempted to tell their stories to the best of our abilities.

This list of main sources is arranged according to the extent of use:

- https://yuval-harpaz.github.io/alarms/oct_7_9.html
- https://www.edut710.org/
- https://www.710360.kan.org.il/5
- https://www.kan.org.il/content/kan-news/defense/558406/
- https://laad.btl.gov.il/Web/He/HaravotBarzelWar/Default.aspx
- https://www.idf.il/נופלים/חללי-המלחמה

Location	Murdered	Hostages	Length of time (hours or days)
Alumim (kibbutz)	31	3	2 days
Be'eri (kibbutz)	134	33	2 days
Ein HaShelosha (kibbutz)	4	0	2 days
Erez (kibbutz)	1	0	27 hours
Erez Checkpoint	10	7	10 hours
Holit (kibbutz)	15	6	13 hours
Kerem Shalom (kibbutz)	5	0	2 days
Kfar Aza (kibbutz)	64	19	2 days
Kissufim (kibbutz)	17	1	21 hours
Kissufim Outpost	32	0	15 hours
Magen (kibbutz)	3	1	2 days
Mavki'im Junction	1	0	1 hour
Meflasim (kibbutz)	1	0	7 hours
Meflasim Junction	47	7	3 days
Mivtahim	15	0	3.5 hours
Nahal Oz (kibbutz)	16	6	9.5 hours
Nahal Oz Outpost	66	11	13 hours
Netiv HaAsara	19	0	14 hours
Nir Am (kibbutz)	2	1	20.5 hours
Nir Oz (kibbutz)	31	86	9 hours
Nir Yitzhak (kibbutz)	7	8	14 hours
Nirim (kibbutz)	5	8	7 hours
Nova Music Festival	364	44	7.5 hours
Ofakim	52	0	2 days
Patish	0	0	0
Poga Outpost	15	0	6 hours
Pri Gan	5	0	2 days
Psyduck Party	17	0	10 hours
Re'im (kibbutz)	18	4	2 days
Re'im Base	8	0	11 hours
Sderot	56	1	2 days
Sha'ar HaNegev Junction	31	0	3 days
Sufa (kibbutz)	3	0	11 hours
Sufa Outpost	11	0	14 hours
Talmei Yosef	1	0	1 hour
Urim Base	8	0	9 hours
Yakhini	7	0	12 hours
Yated	0	0	2 days
Yesha	3	0	1 hour
Yiftah Outpost	8	0	12 hours
Zikim Base	22	0	7 hours
Zikim Beach	18	0	8 hours
Unspecified	–	5	–

Khan Yunis

Egypt

Rafah

Q = Locations of major occurrences in the book

= Other places attacked on October 7th

Kibbutz
Kerem Shalom

Mavki'im Junction

Zikim Beach
Zikim Base

Yiftah Outpost
Yad Mordechai Junction

Netiv HaAsara

Kibbutz Erez

Route 232

Highway 34

Kibbutz Nir Am
Sderot
Sha'ar HaNegev Junction
Meflasim Junction

Jabalya

Gaza City

Kibbutz Kfar Aza

Nahal Oz Outpost
Yakhini
Kibbutz Nahal Oz

Gaza Strip

Kibbutz Alumim

Poga Outpost

Netivot Junction

Kibbutz Be'eri

Highway 25

Nova Music Festival

Re'im Junction

Kibbutz Re'im

Kissufim Outpost
Kibbutz Kissufim

Israel

Re'im Base
Kibbutz Ein HaShelosha

Kibbutz Nirim

Psyduck Party
Nir Oz Outpost
Patish
Kibbutz Nir Oz
Urim Junction
Ofakim
Maon Junction
Urim Base

Kibbutz Magen

Sufa Outpost
Kibbutz Nir Yitzhak
Yesha
Mivtahim
Kibbutz Sufa
Kibbutz Holit

Pri Gan
Yated
Talmei Yosef

~ 5 km | 1 : 150,000 ~

You Hold the Door; I've Got the Baby

Shaylee Atary's Story

Age 35

Kibbutz Kfar Aza

Yahav and I met in acting school, and from the day we met until our final moment together, we never stopped arguing about who fell in love first. I always insisted that he hit on me; he always said that I hit on him. Maybe both of us were right.

I started a course of study in Nissan Nativ Acting Studio in Tel Aviv some time after I had been sexually assaulted. I was very, very damaged and closed off. What I didn't know at the time was that Yahav had gone through trauma of his own; in 2008 he went through something that changed him forever. He was in the kibbutz in Kfar Aza when a mortar shell fired from Gaza suddenly landed out of nowhere. There were no bomb shelters back then, no Red Alert sirens, and the bomb fell and killed his best friend Eyal's father, Jimmy Kedoshim, while Yahav was nearby in the yard; Yahav was the first to see him. Sometimes he would tell me about that moment when a human being became a corpse right before his eyes. He was twenty-two years old at the time, a young man, and all his faith in this world just shattered.

I remember that during the first year of study, he performed Meir Ariel's song "Erol" as a monologue, and he was so charismatic. I remember watching him as he stood there, lit up by this yellow spotlight, and I remember thinking, "Who is that?" and also, "Wow, he's talented." Little by little, we found ourselves working together all the time. Writing together. That was the foundation of our relationship: we were partners who loved to create art together.

Later that year, he asked me to do a scene from *Romeo and Juliet* with him. After rehearsal one night we were tired and put our heads down on this musty old mattress there, and I looked into his eyes, and something suddenly changed. I saw something that made me feel at home. Later, I learned that it was a pivotal moment for him too, when he looked into my eyes. Sometime during rehearsal of that scene, we kissed.

⊱

It was a while before we became a real couple. I think he was a little frightened by all his feelings. I would tell him that I loved him, and he would say, "I don't know if I can," I'd tell him, "Okay, but I know you love me," and he'd say, "I don't know if we'll make it together," and I'd say, "It's okay, you'll go and come back. It doesn't matter, okay? You can go and come back." Like, I was absolutely confident that he loved me; I don't know why. I knew that he loved me deep inside. I just trusted our love. I told him, "If you need time to understand that, take it." I knew he'd come back.

In 2016 I was in a terrible car accident. My left leg was broken badly in several places, and I had head trauma. I was in rehabilitation for over a year. I was in a wheelchair for a very long time; all the surgeries failed. I still have a disability and a pain disorder, and I have to walk with a cane. I can do almost everything, but slowly.

At first I was embarrassed to leave my house with a cane. I preferred to limp along even if it hurt. But then I found myself leaving the house less and less. Until one day, Yahav said to me, "Sweetie, what are you trying to prove? Let's go buy you canes in every color!" And we really did that. We went on a hunt for quality canes. We bought me a purple cane, a gold cane, a blue cane. I had every kind of cane you can imagine; I even had one of those canes with a carved head on top, like some kind of villain.

One evening, we were at home in Jaffa eating pasta – pappardelle – and I was sitting in my wheelchair. Then, while we're eating, Yahav just whips out this little box and opens it, and there's a ring inside. My mouth is full of pappardelle, and I didn't even manage to swallow, and I said "yes" with my mouth full. That was a few weeks after the doctors had told me that I'd probably never be able to walk again; that there was a miniscule chance, but only with another operation that was very risky. I think that Yahav chose to propose to me just then, in the midst of my despair, to give me the strength not to give up, so that I'd give the surgery a chance. Also, he wanted to marry me, I guess.

After my accident, we started going to Kfar Aza more and more. Everything there is much more accessible for wheelchairs; it was very comfortable for me, and Yahav started falling back in love with his kibbutz. Back then, after his trauma, he would work in the field with his father; the earth just healed him, he said. He started talking about raising our kids on the kibbutz, next to their grandma and grandpa. At first I was against it – not because of the security risks there, being so close to the Gaza border, but because I was afraid I'd be bored, that I wouldn't find work. I said to him, "I don't want to. I have this vision: I see myself sitting next to some grubby screen door, nursing a baby and just sad." And Yahav said to me, "I actually have a different vision: I see us sitting in the yard with a joint, with this little bare-bottomed boy next to us, running through the sprinklers." I sat quietly for a moment, imagining it. I said to him, "That actually sounds like a good vision to me." That's how we decided to move.

We lived here for two and half years, a little more. It really was a dream. We're both filmmakers, directors, actors. We made four movies in those two years. He worked nearby in Sapir College, in the School of Audio and Visual arts, as production manager, and I edited films. I worked on a lot of projects from southern Israel. People would come from the big cities in central Israel to work with me in little Kfar Aza.

Yahav's last movie, *Kibbutz Legend*, is a full-length feature that he filmed right here in the kibbutz, with a lot of people from Kfar Aza.

3

Iris Haim acted in the movie too. Her acting was fantastic. I still can't bring myself to look at the footage. So many people who appear in that movie, lots of the extras, were murdered or taken hostage. We filmed several scenes in the kibbutz dining hall; it's totally shot up now. I'll edit it someday. But not now. Not yet.

❧

Yahav's grandfather died a few days before the massacre. On Friday morning, the sixth of October, we buried his grandfather in the kibbutz cemetery. I remember thinking to myself at the funeral: Wow, what a beautiful place to be buried; it's all so green with all the leaves and trees. Yahav spoke at the funeral; he loved his grandfather very much and spoke about how much he meant to him. At the end, he said to him, "Farewell, my friend. We'll meet again!" It scared me, that he said "we'll meet again" – I didn't get why he said that.

That evening, we had a family dinner with everyone who was observing the shiva week of mourning, and everyone wanted to see our daughter, Shaya, who was just a month old, and Yahav held her and walked around and showed her off to everyone, so that everyone would see his baby. Our baby.

On the way home, along the paths in the dark, Yahav and I talked about how special it was, and I remember saying to him, "Whoa, sweetie, the best thing we ever did was moving to the kibbutz," and Yahav said, "Whoa, totally," then kept talking about something else. That was how we felt. We both felt good about our lives. We felt that we were in the right place at the right time.

❧

At six-thirty the next morning we woke to Red Alert sirens and crazy booms. I've never heard so many explosions in my life. I was still in this meditative kind of state, half asleep, because I was waiting for Shaya to wake up for her bottle. I was in shock. I ran to the shelter, and Yahav was already there; he had already started closing the window, and then he closed the door. Our shelter window doesn't really lock because there's no latch. Our home is in the old neighborhood, where the houses are older and the shelters don't really lock.

Soon after, we started getting all these messages – the kibbutz has been infiltrated, lock your doors, stay in your homes. Just then Yahav realizes that our dog Buckley isn't there. So he says to me that he's going to get him, and I scream at him, "You're not going to get him!" I was scared for him to go out; I didn't want him to get killed. But he didn't listen to me; he just went out and looked for Buckley and brought him inside. Buckley usually barks a lot, but he was startled by all the explosions, and he just sat there quietly. I was really scared. I started praying, and crying, and praying, and crying, and when Buckley saw that I was crying, he came over to me and started licking my tears. To this day, he still licks my tears.

Not much time passed before we started to hear shooting. Just a little at first. And motorcycles. Then we hear voices coming closer, voices getting louder, shouting and laughing, greeting each other, "*Ta'al, ta'al* – come in, come in" in Arabic. And we realize that they're coming closer, and we start motioning to each other in sign language. Not saying a word. We motioned to each other and made an agreement, barely whispering: "You hold the door; I've got the baby." We didn't think they'd come in through the window; we thought they'd enter the house and try and open the door inside.

Then the metal window railing opened. They forced it open, and bright light flooded the room. The shelter was dark and closed before that, and there was suddenly daylight coming in. A terrorist's hand groped around inside, a big, terrifying hand. We were both facing the window. I was behind Yahav, and Shaya was in my arms. There wasn't really time; the terrorist was already in the room, but Yahav still turned to me for one last, brief look. Not a real goodbye. He just signaled to me with his head to run away. His eyes were blank, as if he realized that this was it, this was the end.

If words could describe what he said to me with that look, it would have been something like, "I'm sorry, sweetie." And then he just turned back to the window, opened the handle on the glass and grappled with the terrorist to keep the metal railing closed. The last thing I remember is how his pelvis shifted as he fought against the terrorist.

He was this slim, almost skinny guy, and his hips moved as he fought. That's my last memory of him.

≫

Yahav stayed in the shelter, and I went outside holding Shaya, and I turned left on the path. If I had turned right, I would have run straight into the terrorists; I turned left by sheer luck. Then I started to run. I was barefoot, without a phone on me, in my pajamas, with that disposable underwear, the kind you wear after you have a baby. I ran, and at one point I felt all this shooting around me; it was a noise I'd never heard before, this sort of buzzing, whistling kind of sound, and I realized that I'd die if I kept running along that path, so I ducked into some bush next to my neighbor's bamboo fence. And I heard them calling after me "*Ta'al, ta'al!* Come, come!" with these whoops of joy, like there was some kind of prize to kill me and Shaya.

I couldn't run quickly because of my leg, so I kept running through the bushes, then I started knocking on doors, and all the houses were locked. I ran from house to house, from yard to yard, but it was all locked, and I was too scared to shout, "It's Shaylee" in case the terrorists heard me, because they were still so close. At some point I realized that I had nowhere to go, so I hid in a small vestibule between my neighbor Yardena's screen door and her front door. Shaya was somehow still sleeping; I prayed that she wouldn't wake up. I prayed and waited there until I couldn't hear the terrorists' footsteps anymore. I peeked through the screen and saw that the terrorists weren't there, so I got up and kept running and knocking on doors and windows.

And at some point I realized that no one was going to open up for me, so I found some little garden shed and went inside and closed the door. It was a wooden storage shed. I looked for something sharp and I remember I found a hammer and another long tool, some kind of chisel. So I held the hammer in one hand and hid the chisel in my pajamas. There was a washing machine in the shed, and I hid behind it and put some kind of planter over Shaya, and her little feet poked out from underneath. So I put another planter over us, and these bags of sand and fertilizer. And I prayed that she wouldn't start crying.

I tried pretending that this was all happening to someone else; I tried imagining that I was a character in a Holocaust movie. A character in an extermination camp, hiding her baby in one of those bunk beds. It's not me right now. We're in a movie. This helped me calm down; it helped me not to allow the fear to paralyze me. And right then, when I had a second to breathe after I had made us a hiding place, it started to hit me – where I was, what was happening. I was dying to cry out to the heavens, but I couldn't let anyone hear me. I was dying to scream. I felt trapped inside my body, and I screamed a silent scream without making a sound.

There were constant explosions and shouts from the terrorists outside. They were happy. Afterward, some people said that they were drugged, but that wasn't my impression. No. They weren't out of it. They ran after me and my month-old baby with excitement, with joy. They *chose* to shoot at me and Shaya. I heard them. They knew what they were doing; they made a choice.

After some time in the shed, Shaya started crying. She didn't like it when I settled down in the shed because she was used to falling asleep to movement. I let her suck on my finger and hoped that she'd calm down. It worked for a few minutes, but she woke up hungry. She hadn't eaten since four a.m. Her crying got louder, and I heard shouts from outside; I sensed that they would be happy to find me. I realized that if I stayed there, I was done for. I had to go outside.

Outside the shed there was a lawn, a huge one, and I knew that I had to cross it to get to the next row of houses. I tried knocking at a door, but no one opened up; so I had no choice but to cross the lawn. I peered through the bushes and saw that on the other side of the lawn, one of the houses there had a laundry room, and the door was open. I decided to run there. I went out of the bushes and starting running, running for my life as fast as I could. Don't look back, don't look back; run run run. I reached the laundry room. When I got there I heard someone whispering to me from the window: "Come in, come in!"

It was Zuli's voice, and it was Zuli and Liron's house. My guardian angels. They have three kids. The house was all locked down, and

Zuli guarded the door with his handgun. When I went in, his son was terrified of me. He saw me, this big adult holding a hammer, and he started screaming; I guess he thought I was a terrorist. I said to them, "I'm sorry, I'm sorry! I didn't know where to go." I saw their three kids, and I said to Liron, "I'm sorry I brought her; I'm so sorry I brought her here" because I knew that in that situation, when everyone has to hide and keep quiet, a baby was like a ticking bomb. I thought that I would be the death of them all.

I was so apologetic. I said to Liron, "They were in our bedroom, they came in from the window, they killed Yahav, they murdered him. I didn't know where to go!" And Liron said to me, "It's all okay, you did exactly what you had to do. They killed my sister, too."

To this day, Liron is saved on my phone as "Liron My Guardian Angel." I'll never forget what they did for me. They let me and Shaya in, knowing full well what could have happened to them because of us. Liron already knew that her sister and brother-in-law were dead; that their little girl was taken hostage; she understood exactly what it meant to let us into their shelter.

For twenty-seven hours I was there with her and with Zuli, and with their three kids in the shelter. Twenty-seven hours with a hungry baby. I wasn't breastfeeding, I was never able to nurse her after she was born. Every time she cried, I apologized, and Liron kept saying, "You don't have to apologize."

Twenty-seven hours in the shelter. We became a sort of little family. The kids and I played all these games with Shaya – as if we opened a little daycare. Liron was on her phone and kept trying to send messages for someone to rescue us. Zuli was out of the shelter a lot; he patrolled the house with his gun. The little kids helped me with the baby. They stroked her and held her and made sure that I had toilet paper to keep her clean because I didn't have any diapers for her. They were truly wonderful.

At one point – I don't remember exactly when, it's all a big blur – Zuli came into the room. He turned off the light and said, "Okay guys, we have to go to sleep; we have a long day ahead of us. I don't think the army will come until tomorrow morning." He told us to go to the bathroom, not to flush, and we took turns and went back to the shelter. Then Zuli took this board from one of the kids' beds, wedged it under the door handle, covered himself with a blanket, and said, "Come on guys, go to sleep! Good night!" He made us feel safe. I saw him and said, "Oh, okay, let's go to sleep." Later on, Zuli told me that he had seen dozens of terrorists walking around outside with RPGs; he understood that a handgun wouldn't be much help and decided that we might as well all go to sleep. At least we'd be quiet.

At one point, while we were sleeping, we heard people come into the house. They shouted, "IDF! IDF! We've come to rescue you!" But Zuli motioned to us to keep quiet. We were lucky that somehow Shaya was quiet just then. Liron and I tried to make out if they were speaking in Hebrew or Arabic. They walked around the house with these heavy footsteps. They somehow missed the door to our shelter, then they simply left the house. Liron and I didn't understand why they didn't come to rescue us if they were really the IDF. Only a few days later, after we were rescued, Zuli told us that they had definitely been terrorists.

The hours dragged on and on and on, and I kept thinking about Yahav. Is he still alive? What's going on with him? There was some kind of rumor on the Whatsapp group that he was wounded and then rescued, but I couldn't calm down. He was always on my mind, and I asked him not to die. I said to him in my heart, "Sweetie, sweetie, you can't do this to me, you can't do this to me!" But from the outside I just looked like a woman rocking her baby.

Shaya was getting weaker; she was becoming limp and apathetic. She breathed in a lot of smoke because the house next to us had been set on fire. I remember watching her, noticing that she was becoming less alert, less responsive. It was a very frightening moment, feeling that your child isn't responding to you. Liron kept trying to reach out to everyone possible to rescue us – she sent messages to the army, to the Shin Bet, to our families, friends, everyone.

Suddenly it was morning. I remember hearing birds outside the shelter. Birds! It was the strangest thing in the world; I'll remember it for the rest of my life. Amid all the shooting and explosions there was suddenly birdsong. And a few hours later, they came to rescue us. Soldiers,

I don't know from which unit, called Liron on the phone and told her that they're outside, so we opened the shelter and went outside, straight into these armored military vehicles. I remember that out of all twenty-seven hours in the shelter, the hardest part was actually leaving it. I began to cry. The kids tried to calm me down. They said, "Look, Shaylee, the army is here. There's nothing to be scared of anymore," but they didn't realize that I was crying because I was leaving *them*. Because I knew deep in my heart that this was the last time in my life that I would feel like I had a family.

When I left the house, I saw burnt homes all around us and terrorists lying dead on the ground, and I told myself not to look. And I really did stop looking. I just kept my eyes closed until we were out of the kibbutz, and I hugged Shaya, and I prayed to God. At the gas station outside Kfar Aza an army doctor checked Shaya. She was in poor condition; she had red bags under her eyes, and she was barely responsive. We had to take Shaya to the hospital.

From Kfar Aza we drove to Netivot in an army vehicle. From Netivot they took us in an ambulance to Soroka Hospital in Beersheba. Only then, only on those drives when I saw all the overturned cars through the window, burnt cars, and bodies and more bodies; only then did I understand what had happened. Only then did I realize just how many terrorists had come in and how many people were killed. I hadn't had a phone all day; even at the beginning, when Yahav realized what was happening from all the messages they sent on the kibbutz WhatsApp group, he didn't tell me anything. He kept it from me so that I wouldn't be even more stressed. When we arrived in Soroka doctors pounced on the baby. Her medical report said that she was crying without tears, she was so dehydrated. She was given oxygen for two days to clear all the smoke she inhaled from her lungs.

The battles in Kfar Aza continued for three days. They only managed to retrieve Yahav's body three days later. Until then it wasn't clear if he was hurt or missing or taken hostage. I looked for him in every possible place. I felt that I was going crazy. I had seen him fighting; I saw how his narrow hips struggled against the terrorist. They had shot at me and the baby; there was no reason they wouldn't shoot at him as well.

But then came the news. The moment I understood that's it, he's dead, I screamed, and I couldn't get up off the floor. They said to me, "Shaylee, come to the living room. Come, sit with us in the living room," but I didn't want to get up. I was a rag; I was broken; I couldn't get off the floor. But then Shaya cried, and without thinking I just got up, took her to the changing table, and changed her diaper. Then I made her a bottle, and without noticing I sat down in the living room like everyone had wanted.

Then I asked Yahav's mother, "Michal, do you think that I can retrieve sperm from him even though he's a civilian, not a soldier?" I knew that they performed sperm retrieval on soldiers; I didn't know if the procedure was available to civilians as well. It turns out that you can, but you need a court order; it's a whole procedure. The problem was that there was no time for any protocol; there's a very short window of opportunity from the moment of death until the sperm is no longer viable. And Yahav's body had already been lying there for too long until they found him. But his vision of a little bare-bottomed boy running through the sprinklers didn't leave me. I had to try; I had to keep our family going, and I had already seen what Shaya had done for me when I couldn't get off the floor. She was the only one who managed to lift me up.

So I started making a lot of noise; I reached out to the press and to social media to see if we could cut through all the bureaucracy, I did as much as I could, but in Yahav's case it was too late. The wonderful doctor from Assaf HaRofeh Hospital who performed the procedure told me, with a heavy heart, "The sperm is no longer viable. But you did everything you could." Yahav's body lay there for three days in the heat of our burned-out house. There was nothing left to save. But what the doctor said stayed with me: I had done everything I could. Only then, when I understood that there was no more sperm from him, when I understood there was nothing left to do, when Shaya was okay, when I knew where Yahav was, and that his sperm was no longer viable – only then, when I had nothing else I had to take care of, did I begin to mourn.

An analysis of the scene showed that Yahav had fought the terrorists to the last moment; when he held down the metal railing, they threw explosive charges and grenades into our bedroom and burned down the house while he was still inside. Yahav fought his instincts to run outside and stayed inside to keep them from coming in. The soldier who found Yahav told me that they had found his body next to Shaya's stroller – he had used the stroller to block the door that led to our bedroom. It touched me that he had died that way, next to a baby stroller; like, how optimistic is that, to think that a baby stroller could keep out the seventy terrorists that were outside our window.

Yahav sacrificed his life so that Shaya and I could save ourselves. He went up to the window and fought the terrorists to give us time to run. I think about that moment a lot, the moment that he chose to go up to the window. It helps me when thoughts start running through my head, thoughts like, why didn't I say to him, "Don't be a hero! Come escape with me!" – because I know deep in my heart that he would have done it all over again. Because that was Yahav. He would give everything for the people he loved. And he wanted so badly to be a father. It feels to me like that's all he ever wanted in this life. And the fact is that Shaya and I are alive now. Thanks to him, we're still alive.

I think he must have realized that I wouldn't be able to run so fast because of my legs, so he tried to hold them off. Even afterward, after we had left, he could have run outside. I left all the doors open for him. But he chose to stay behind and fight. It's as if he told himself, "It's either me or my baby." He loved Shaya so much, he loved me so much, he loved us too much.

Right now, our daughter Shaya is the only thing that interests me. She's the only thing that makes me feel good. She lights up my life. Each time I break down, every time I crash, she reminds me that she's here. Her diapers ground me; her bottles keep me tethered to reality. She also isn't judgmental; she doesn't understand my tears. She can watch me cry and then suddenly break out into a huge smile. And that smile, that smile so far removed from reality, brings a smile to my face too.

We had an agreement, Yahav and I. We had an agreement, there in that room, when the terrorists broke in: "You hold the door; I've got the baby." That was our agreement. We each had our job. And that's still what's going on. He's still holding the door. He'll be holding that door for the rest of my life. And I've still got the baby. And as long as I'm here with the baby, I'll never let my light go out. With all the trauma I endured, I have to keep going, I have to find my optimism, I have to find reasons to live. I saw him sacrifice his life for mine. We had an agreement. "You hold the door; I've got the baby." So I'm keeping our agreement. And that agreement is what keeps me alive.

The other day, a good friend asked me: "Tell me, Shaylee, if you could be someone else who didn't go through everything you went through; if you could live a different life, would you do it? Would you switch places with them?" I thought about it for a second, then I answered, "No. I would rather live through this pain another thousand times."

Because if I were someone else, I wouldn't have met Yahav, and I wouldn't have had thirteen wonderful years with him, thirteen years that were larger than life. If I were someone else, I wouldn't have been gifted with such a love story; I might have gone through life without ever knowing such love. It doesn't matter how terrible what I went through was; I'm still grateful to have gone through it. I'm still grateful. I'm grateful that I saw him standing there under that yellow spotlight, so talented and goodlooking; I'm thankful that I saw into his soul when he was Romeo and I was Juliet. That I found my home in his eyes. I had a great love, a love larger than life. I have a daughter, and her name is Shaya. And that's my story now in this world.

The Miracle of the Jar of Vaseline

Daniel and Neriya Sharabi's Story

Ages 23 and 22

As told by Daniel Sharabi

◉ *Nova Festival*

I've been through a lot in life. A lot of situations. I grew up in an Ultra-Orthodox family – my father became religious before he married my mother. My brother Neriya and I went to an Ultra-Orthodox school, but when I was in eighth grade I started to feel that it wasn't really me, that it wasn't my path in life. All that obligation, with everyone breathing down each other's necks. I don't know – it wasn't what I wanted from life. And then, after a few incidents, they just kicked me out of school, then out of more than one. Okay, so that's my journey. You know, I believe that everyone has their own relationship with God. Even if that means doing all the religious rituals – handwashing, making *kiddush,* and eating a holiday meal – then going out to a trance party 'til the next morning.

The trance scene has tons of ex-religious guys; tons, it's a known thing. Maybe it's because it's all so free, no inhibitions, finally, finally, nothing holding you back! When you're on the dance floor, no one's looking at you, no one's judging you; everyone's smiling, loving; they're just there to have a good time. Every so often I hit the party scene to let go a little, to unwind, to let loose and lose control however I want, as much as I want. To do what I want and maybe to feel like a kid again. Everyone has this kid inside them, and when they're feeling good, it comes out a little.

So I've been part of this nature party and trance scene for a long time now, and I never go alone. Five of us went to the Nova Festival together: me, my brother Neriya, who's about a year younger than me, our cousin Shalev, Yosef, and Karin. Yosef is my best friend in the world; we dormed together in school and were in the army together, in the Givati Brigade. Karin is a very good friend of Yosef's, and of mine too; she's like our sister. She had just broken her leg, so she came to the party with a cast – but she danced like a queen! With the cast on!

No way do I go out without my guys; I need them with me. 'Cause the moment we're together, the moment that we're this group of people that it feels so much fun to be with, so good for me to be with – when we cut loose together, my brother, my cousin, on the dance floor, I feel this pure joy. When you're dancing together with someone you love so much, you just become a better person.

Nova is an amazing festival; it's just wild. I've never seen anything like it in this country: almost forty-five hundred people were there in a few different areas they laid out. The party was from Friday night to the next day, so tons of people slept over in the campgrounds so that they could get up and dance in the sunrise. To bring in the sun.

It's Shabbat morning; we're in the campground. The sun is just starting to rise, and we leave our tents. It was a crazy sunrise; I'll never forget it. Okay, so we go to the dance floor; we're dancing and feeling the joy when suddenly the music stops. We don't really get what's happening, then someone looks up and shouts, "Missiles!" And we see, we actually see the whole sky become grey and white, smoky, with actual explosions, and I begin to see the missiles going up from the direction of Gaza, and I see the whole sky filling up with streaks.

Then all the emergency exits were opened. I've never seen emergency exits opened before. We start making our way toward the emergency exits – me, Neriya, Shalev, Yosef, and Karin, and the booms don't stop, they don't stop, and we start moving faster and faster until we break into a run. And everyone around us is running like crazy; people start cutting in from the sides, cutting in from here, from there, and there's this moment when we stop next to the security area, and I hear on the security guard's radio: "They shot Hassan's son! They shot Hassan's son," who's one of the security guards. Then I understood that there's shooting. That terrorists are here.

So we start running around, shouting, "There's shooting, there's gunfire! Run away, there are terrorists!" We keep running, and suddenly I hear a friend of mine from home, a good friend, calling me: "Daniel, come, come! Come here, we need a medic; someone's been shot!" He knows that I was trained as a combat medic. So we run over with him, and he takes me to this girl who's been shot, and there are two guys helping her, Ben and Itai. The wounded girl was lying under some car, and Ben and Itai are sitting with her, like, to calm her down, so I go up to them and say, "I'm a medic; I'm here to help!" And I see that she's been shot three times, once in the thigh and twice in the back; it's just insane.

I treat her with a tourniquet so that we can evacuate her; there's an ambulance about seven hundred meters away. Someone brings us a stretcher, then we lift her up and start running with the stretcher – me, Yosef, Ben, Itai, Neriya, and Shalev – we run like crazy, and there's shooting everywhere. We run toward the ambulance, and the girl is conscious the whole time, poor thing, and the stretcher's bouncing because we're running out of sync, and we're telling her, "We're almost at the ambulance." We see the ambulance and get to it – and it's locked. There's no one there, and it's just locked.

So we're like, Okay, we'll take her to the control center. There was this medical control center at the festival, with a doctor and equipment and everything, but there was no way to take her there on the stretcher; we had no chance. And suddenly Bar shows up. Bar is one of the security guards there; he brings his golf-cart, and we lift her onto it and drive with him and drop her off at the control center. We wanted to go right back to where the party was, to bring more wounded people, when suddenly one of the cops starts shouting at us, "Terrorists! Terrorists!" and we see a pickup truck full of terrorists! And they start spraying bullets at us; it must be five hundred rounds a minute, and there's nowhere to take cover so we start to run.

So we're running, dodging between cars, and suddenly we see a car, a Kia Picanto, and hide behind it. But they saw us, they spotted us, so they fire at the Kia, too, and we must, must run. So me and Neriya get up and run out of there, and I look back for a second and see Yosef standing there behind the Kia, and he's looking right and left like he's not sure what to do, and I shout to him, "Yosef, run for it! Run!" and then he ducks down behind the Kia, and boom! The Kia's hit by an RPG.

Neriya says that that was the first time he ever saw me terrified. Both of us are bent over on the ground from the shock of the RPG, and he sees me getting up, turning around, and he realizes that I'm about to run over there to Yosef, and he grabs me and pulls me back down to the ground and says, "Daniel, listen! Yosef is dead. You're not going there! There's no way I'm going home without you. And there's no way you're going home without me. I understand that you want to go back to Yosef, but there's nothing to go back to. If you turn back, you'll be killed on the spot, and then I'll be killed too, because I'm not going back without you." That's what he said to me.

From there, we started running for our lives, and suddenly we see a tank on the shoulder of the road. By that point our group had split up; it was just me and my brother Neriya. When we saw the tank, we both decided that we had to get in there; that was what we had to do. So we both go into the tank, and inside it we see a dead soldier. That was Ariel Eliyahu, may God avenge his blood. Later, after the whole thing, we discovered that it was actually the tank of Ido Somech, the tank driver who saved lots and lots of people, but he had already left before we went in. So we were there on our own.

At that point I want to try and get the tank moving, but you know, I'd never driven a tank before! So I try and play around with the controls, but the tank doesn't move, won't move, so I try the tank's two-way radio, but I realize that they don't hear me on the other side, so I call all kinds of people that I know, but no one knows how to tell me how to start a tank. And suddenly I say to myself, I'll call my grandfather – he knows!

So I call him, and I say, "Hi Grandpa, good morning! How do you start a tank?" and he's like just waked up so he says to me, "Good morning Daniel!" And then I realize that he's seventy-four years old and I'm not going to stress him out, not even a drop, so I say to him, "Good morning Grandpa! I love you! Have a happy holiday!" and I hang up.

Well, the tank isn't moving, so we start looking for weapons. There had to be some kind of weapon there, there had to be! But we open up everything, and in the weapons compartment all we see are prayer books and Bibles. No weapons. So Neriya asks the dead soldier's forgiveness and searches him for a weapon but doesn't find anything. Looking back afterward, we understood that there was no ammunition left because they had used it all to fight the terrorists. And in the meantime, we suddenly begin to get hit with heavy artillery aimed at the tank. Serious barrages. So we can't exit the tank, but we also can't return fire because we had nothing, no ammunition. Zilch.

Then Neriya stops everything, and I hear him talking – he's talking to God, and he says, "God, I don't know why You did everything You did! I'm not getting into Your considerations! I don't get into things I don't understand! But I do know that there's a soldier here who was murdered for You, for Your people, and I did everything I could, God. I got into that tank, and now it's on You!" And he starts shouting, "Now it's Your turn! Give me a weapon! I don't care how, God! You give me a weapon!"

And just as he finishes talking – I swear, it happened the second he stopped talking – he looks down at the dead soldier who was there with us, and there's a rifle strap right next to the soldier's shoe. I swear to God, that's what happened.

Neriya couldn't climb out of the tank while he was holding the rifle, because there were tons of bullets flying right over the turret. So we decided that I'd get out first, then he'd throw me the rifle, then he'd come out. And that's what we did, but when he was climbing out of the tank I was already outside, and I discovered two things. First, there were like thirty people hiding under the tank! So if we had managed to start the tank, God forbid – I don't even want to think about it. And the second thing I discovered was that the rifle was jammed. It didn't work.

So Neriya gets out of the tank and opens the rifle's chamber, and we see that it's full of sand. What we needed was oil. But where were we going to get oil? There was no way we could climb back into the tank; it was under heavy fire, so where were we going to find oil? Then I see all the girls hiding behind the tank, and I remember that sometimes girls bring Vaseline to nature parties because their lips get dry from the wind. So I shout out, "Does anyone have Vaseline?" and someone comes up to me and takes out this tiny tub of Vaseline from her pocket – and I think no way would it be enough. But it was like the Hanukkah story, the miracle of the jar of oil – we had the miracle of the jar of Vaseline!

So the rifle started working again, and we begin to return fire! By this point, I had called the whole army to come help us – I called up my whole Givati battalion, but the army only got to us much, much later, and we were on our own there for hours.

At some point I managed to reach my officer in the army reserves, Yoni, the deputy commander of my company. I describe the situation to him, and he tells me what to do. He tells me to shoot into the bushes so they don't surprise us from there; later, he tells me to shoot a bullet every sixty seconds so they know there's someone there with a weapon. He was in Tel Aviv when I called him, and as he's talking to me, he picks up a bunch of guys in his Mazda, and they make their way to us. But they only got to us five hours later. Yoni stayed on the line with me for five hours. Five whole hours.

After a while, we managed to get hold of a MAG heavy machine gun, which is already a more serious weapon. One guy, Daniel Ben Guzi, climbed up on the tank and brought down the MAG mounted there. So, he was on the MAG, Neriya had the M-16 rifle, and I'm on the line with Yoni directing the fight, and we're using the tank for cover. We were all trained by the army, we all knew military tactics, but let's just say that the fighting was more freestyle, more Sharabi style, ha!

The Miracle of the Jar of Vaseline

❧

At nine-forty, we started getting hit by brutal fire. It was very tough. They were closing in on us, and there were a lot of them, and they wanted to take us down and finish us off. And then an RPG exploded right near us – they shot it at a car that was next to the tank – and everyone there got hit by shrapnel. Everyone including us. My cousin Shalev got shrapnel in the arms and forehead; I have two pieces of shrapnel in my arm; Neriya was hit by shrapnel in the hand, and he lost a piece of his finger.

That was when all the screaming started – disorder, chaos, panic; everyone just lost it. All thirty people hiding behind the tank, all of them are injured, and all of them are crying, and all of them are screaming, and suddenly I hear myself yell at them: "Quiet! Everyone! Quiet!!!" And it got quiet. And then I said to them, "Listen! Some of us are wounded, and some of us are fighting. Everyone else – pray!"

And they did it. They started praying; they started saying, "*Shema Yisrael*," and reciting psalms. I'll never forget it. And there were two Arabs there with us, Bedouins, and they also prayed together with us. And I prayed too. I'll never forget it as long as I live.

And Neriya's bleeding from the finger, so I make a tourniquet for him, and we go back to fighting, but the MAG gets jammed. Another Vaseline treatment from the miracle jar, and the MAG goes back to work. And that's how we took down that band of terrorists that came at us. We finished them off. And that's how it went on – every half an hour another band of terrorists would come, and we'd take them down. With one MAG and one M-16, we wiped out band after band. Later on, we also took their Kalashnikovs, and we also captured some of the injured terrorists alive.

At this stage, there were still thirty people behind the tank, all of them wounded, and I was the only medic. And I had no equipment at all, so I began to improvise. I tore people's shirts to use as tourniquets, I used empty magazines and branches for splints. What am I supposed to do? Improv, Sharabi-style. One of the guys with us was hit so badly that his arm was nothing but bone and vein; his whole arm was open, so I make him a tourniquet like six times, but it keeps falling off because there was nothing for it to catch onto. Actually, that guy is alive and well today, and his arm is better. Unbelievable.

They even brought me a soldier with bullet wounds in his back. And I know from my medic course that a bullet wound in the back is a suspected spinal injury, and just then I noticed someone clearing stuff out of his car to make room and he's taking out these IKEA closet parts. So I took one of the shelves – it was this 1.5 meter wooden board – and lay the soldier down on the ground without any stretcher and used the board as a splint for his back. Thank God, that soldier is alive and well today.

Neriya and I lived to tell the tale. You know, I don't know why we survived when so many didn't. Our friend Karin Journo, the one who danced with her cast on – that was her final dance. She never came back from that party. Ben and Itai and the injured girl that we dropped off at the control center – we found out later that they were all murdered there. Bar Kupershtein, the security guard who helped us evacuate the girl with his golf-cart, is held hostage now in Gaza. Yosef Haim Ohana, my best friend in the world, we thought he was dead, but we found out later that he was taken to Gaza too. I can't begin to grasp it.

After the forces finally came, after we finally felt safe, I remember standing there next to those terrorists that we captured. And I look at them sitting there, and I say to myself, I know exactly what they did to us, and I can see on their faces the people they murdered, the people they tore apart, the people they burned, and I just kicked one of the terrorists sitting there. Boom, a strong kick, and he kind of flies to the ground. And at that moment I understood something, I understood something deep about life.

I mean, with that kick I felt so powerless. I kicked him, and I felt so miserable. That kick didn't do anything to him; it didn't change anything, didn't move anything. I gave him a kick, and it didn't pay back even a fraction of what we suffered; it didn't even touch it. Then I understood. I understood that the only thing I can do now, the only thing that I can do against their evil – is to do good. Good every bit as powerful as the pain and evil. That's the only way to take revenge. That's the victory, the best revenge. And that realization, honestly, that was one of the greatest insights I ever had in my life.

A month after it all happened, Neriya and I flew to the US for a speaking tour. We started a non-profit called "For the Survivors and the Wounded" and started to raise money, and we've already begun to pay for treatments for the survivors of Nova, to help them in all kinds of ways. That's what we're continuing to do now; it's a type of calling. Because, basically, at that moment when I stood in front of that terrorist, at that moment I understood, I *decided*, to be a light. To shine a little light wherever I go. No matter what's around me, I will be a light. That's what I promised myself. To be a light. And I try to keep that promise every single day.

The Power of Motherhood

Tali Hadad's Story

Age 48

📍 *Ofakim*

I'm a kindergarten teacher. I worked in a kindergarten for twenty-two years, thank God. I opened a religious daycare, I got my master's, but that's it, I've had enough. I've been retired for three years now. I'm at home, I have high blood pressure, high cholesterol, knee pain, so I haven't been doing much – I'm doing nothing, really. I'm trying to find myself, trying to figure out what to do. I've always envied people who love what they do. I haven't found it yet – who I am, what I am, who Tali is.

The father of my children is quiet, kind of shy. We're married, yes, but we're opposites. I'm a loner. I like my alone time. We're great partners, we have wonderful children, our home runs like clockwork, no one works together better than we do. It all works.

A lot of things have happened to me this past year. Spiritual things, inner things. I've let myself be guided by the universe, by reality. At night, in bed, I've heard voices, felt someone speaking to me – I know that they're speaking to me, but I don't know what they want from me. I've felt this way a long time. Then it all happened.

Sabbath morning, six-thirty. A siren goes off. My son Itamar and his girlfriend, who slept upstairs, go down to the safe room. I don't like the safe room, but eventually I go too. Itamar is texting with his commander. He's just finishing up his officers course; it was the last week of the course, and from the messages we understand that there's some kind of attack going on, there are terrorists. We all go into the living room, Itamar takes his gun, and I open the door and tell him, "Go sweetheart, go baby, go do your job – you're a commander, run, go, this is your moment!"

And he goes out, and his girlfriend is watching him and sobbing, and I calm her down, "It's his job; this is what he's been training for." And that's when I decide – I don't know what comes over me – I put on my sneakers and start running after him, after Itamar. I run fast, not along the main road but along the alleyways and down small paths, and I reach the biggest playground in the neighborhood. That's when I suddenly register that there are something like seven terrorists with vests and guns and heavy weapons marching toward the buildings with raised weapons. I also hear shooting coming from somewhere else, not there, and I suddenly know – I feel – that that's where Itamar is, caught up in that firefight.

So I start running again – it's hard for me to run – and I reach somewhere else, where the battle is. It's a mess, chaos, shooting and screaming, police, terrorists, and citizens with guns, and I start shouting to them, "You're strong! Don't be afraid! Kill them!" to encourage them, to raise morale, because not everyone was fighting. Not at all – some of them were terrified, standing frozen in place. And I know that my Itamar is there but I'm not sure where, and I'm the only one without a weapon there – except for two Ultra-Orthodox men who were passing through and had no idea what was going on. I yelled at them too: "Get out of here, get out, there are terrorists here!" and I'm there in my pajamas and sneakers, a complete mess, barely even awake.

Soon after, I'm not sure how long, I hear people shouting that there are wounded, there are dead, and time goes by, and where are the ambulances, where are they, what's going on here? And someone said that the ambulance came but they took gunfire, and they aren't sending any more ambulances, and I realize that there's no one to evacuate the wounded;

there's no chance of evacuation, because they shot up the only ambulance in Ofakim, and time is ticking away but no one is coming. A total mess.

There was this guy with a gun there, and I couldn't believe it – he had a gun, he said he was a doctor, but he was doing nothing. So I said to him, "Listen, man, you're not doing anything with your gun – you should either give it to someone here, or fight," and he was like, "No, they're paging me from Soroka Hospital," so I said to him, "Go, go away, you coward" – that's what I said to him, I'll never forget it. And he got into his car and took someone who was wounded with him and drove away. It made me so mad that he had a gun but instead of fighting he drove away.

That was when I made my decision. I turned to someone there – we had this moment of karmic connection – and I said to him, "Listen, I'm going to get my car to evacuate the wounded"; he nods and says to me, "Go, you hero of Israel!" I started running, I crossed the whole square and the playground and got home, and my daughter, who was home and heard me shouting, ran outside and brought me the keys. I was completely out of breath, huffing and puffing. I got into the car and started driving toward the wounded, and suddenly I see Itamar on the road, and I see that Itamar is wounded.

I look at him, and he's like, "Mom, what are you doing here?" and I say to him, "I came to get you guys," and that was it; the people there put him in the car, along with others who were wounded, and I realize that he's been hit in his stomach and is losing blood, and I have to save him. I drive toward the urgent care station that was set up at the entrance to the city, and I bring him in along with the other casualties who were with us. We were the first ones to get there.

So I go to the doctor there and tell him, "This one has an abdominal injury; it's urgent, take him to the hospital," and I go and take Itamar's gun and say to him, "Itamar, I'm not coming with you. Take care of yourself. You're brave. Mommy will be back later, but now I have to go and pick up more casualties," and he moves his head, he kind of nods at me, like, "Okay."

So I get back into the car to get more of the injured, and I'm doing 120 kilometers per hour the whole way, and there are gunshots and speedbumps and the car is jumping and flying – it's still banged up from those drives – and I bring in more wounded and go back and bring more wounded and go back, three times in a row. I evacuated twelve casualties in all, including my son. A lot of the wounded are Russian and can't even speak Hebrew – it's an immigrant neighborhood. When I go back for the fourth time there are no more wounded, so I stop there and leave the car running in case there are any more people that need evacuating.

I gave the gun to a soldier who was there – at first I didn't want to give it to him; it's my son's gun and I wanted to keep it, but then he said to me, "I'm a soldier in a commando unit; give me the gun, I'm in Duvdevan," and I believed him and gave him the gun, and he ran off and I stood there. I later learned that he was killed – he had a jam; Itamar's gun got jammed.

And that's it; soon after that a military helicopter arrived, and I realized that I was finished there; there was nothing else for me to do. So I got into my car and drove home, and I told my husband and the kids who were home what had happened, and we packed things up and went to be with Itamar in the hospital.

I wasn't scared. Not for myself and not for Itamar. I didn't think about it. I was in a good state of mind. No bad thoughts. My daughter's ringtone is this new song called "Good thoughts, good thoughts," and that's just how I was. I had good thoughts the whole time, and I did good things. My son wasn't killed; he's going to have surgery, and he'll be okay. I believed in the world, in the Creator of the world; it was all good vibes. I don't know, it was just right. I had the right thoughts. I left Itamar there, and it was the right thing. I told myself the whole time, I won't get hurt, it's all good, nothing bad will happen. Nothing bad will happen.

I'll tell you something else. I didn't really want to say it because I don't want people thinking I'm some kind of nutcase or anything like that. But when Itamar was fighting, when there was shooting, there was this moment when I stood there in the street and raised my hands, as if in victory. And I thought, I won't put my hands down; I felt that as long as I kept my hands up, my child was winning. I felt like I was doing it for him, and I'm not all that religious at all – my faith in God is simple, normal – but I felt like I was in some kind of trance, that something had taken hold of me, that someone was controlling me, and I was doing something supernatural. What kind of a mother says to her son, "Take your gun and go fight"?

෴

Itamar is okay, thank God; he's out of the hospital. And many people were saved. But there are so many terrible stories about this war. Terrible things. And I always wonder, as a believer, how I'm supposed to make sense of it all. Throughout history, I think, we see that someone always pays a price. There's no way around it. Someone always pays a price – whether it's the story of the Exodus from Egypt, or the Purim story, or the Chanukah story – some were saved and some were killed. There's no guarantee that God will protect everyone. Someone always pays the price. The Holocaust too. There's always a price.

And this price is the pain we suffer, and that's how we're measured. Everyone got hurt – religious, secular, rich, poor, but the question is: When the blood cries out to us, how do we respond? Ultimately, we're being tested now, and the test is how much of a family we really are. It's amazing to see how everyone is all fighting together, how we're all recruited to the cause. We are brothers and sisters.

And it might also be that all the feminine power, all the power of motherhood, all this resilience, is good for our people. Do you remember that woman, Vicki Knafo, who led marches and fought on behalf of the single mothers? She brought this message of feminine power, about how strong we women are. They say that the redemption will come "in the merit of righteous women." History is filled with strong women, and I'm part of history. Maybe we need to strengthen our power of motherhood; not necessarily feminine power, but the power of motherhood.

Every woman has power; in every home, the mother is the one who leads the way, who sets the tone, who wields the strength within the home. It's all written; I'm not making anything up. The homemaker is the one who makes the home what it is, and we need to appreciate how strong that is, how powerful it is, even on the battlefield. We are there too; I was there too. I'm just a simple woman. Who am I? Just a retired kindergarten teacher. I've been a homemaker for three years now; I'm not working, I'm not a captain in the army, I'm not a commander, I'm no one, really. So if I did what I did, then surely every woman should understand the kind of strength she has inside her.

The Exact Opposite of All Those Hero Stories

Shlomo Ron's Story

Age 85

As told by Shlomo's niece, Irit

 Kibbutz Nahal Oz

I'm related to Shlomo through his wife Chanaleh. Shlomo and Chanaleh met on the kibbutz. They basically founded it – Chanaleh moved there from Kvutzat Kinneret at age twenty-two, and Shlomo came before her from Tel Aviv to found the kibbutz with his Nahal group. That's how they met, then got married, lived there, and raised three kids right on the border.

If we're here to talk about heroism, I think they were heroes long before October 7th because it was *always* dangerous there; there were always attacks. They used to call it *"Fedayeen,"* and then "infiltrations," and they were always under threat, but they never left. Even in recent years, when all the missiles started, and the mortar bombs, and all the different threats, and lots of families with young children left – they never left! Most of the old kibbutz families never left. They stayed and felt safe there, very safe.

This is a book about heroes, but Shlomo and Chanaleh weren't those tough hero types or warriors, not at all! They were gentle, tender souls who loved culture and art. Chanaleh was a kindergarten teacher in Nahal Oz for years; you would always see her, so sweet, leading a trail of little kids, little kibbutzniks. Shlomo was always curious, always interested in everything. It was fun to share things with him; he'd ask all these questions and tell stories of his own. He was a deep man; talking with him was much more than small talk or joking around; it was conversation on deep subjects.

And he was an actor, Shlomo, a good one. He always had the lead role in all the kibbutz plays; he loved acting, and in recent years he started painting, too. They were gentle, cultured souls, the exact opposite of all those hero stories, but at the same time, in spite of all that, they truly lived incredibly brave lives.

Then that Sabbath came along. Shlomo and Chanaleh have three kids, and that Sabbath – which was also a holiday – their two daughters came to spend the weekend with them. One daughter came from up north, from Rosh Pina, the other came all the way from Oxford, and the two daughters and the grandson all stayed in a tiny guest apartment adjacent to Shlomo and Chanaleh's place. It's usually empty; people only stay there when they come for the weekend.

Now, everything we know about that morning is based on what Marissa, Chanaleh's wonderful caretaker, told us. What happened is that the siren went off in the kibbutz. Shlomo and Chanaleh were eating breakfast with Marissa, the girls were still asleep in the guest unit, and sirens were old news to everyone – okay, fine, when the siren sounds you go into the safe room. But then, a few minutes later, they started hearing gunshots in the kibbutz, and an announcement on the loudspeakers said there was an infiltration – which had also happened before. That seems to be when Shlomo told Chanaleh and Marissa, "Go to the safe room; I'm staying out here." That's what he said.

This all happened within minutes, and the shooting was close – very close. Marissa told us that as they were closing the door to the safe room, she already saw the man who later shot Shlomo; he was right there in the entrance! Their porch has a big window with a view of the front, and Marissa could see the terrorist coming, and so could

Shlomo. When she and Chanaleh ran to the shelter they tried to call him to come in, but he refused to go. Instead of running with them, he went and sat down in the armchair. He said to Marissa, "Take Chanaleh into the safe room and close the door; I'm here, I'm not coming in," and he told Chanaleh, "The army will come soon, and everything will be okay," so that she wouldn't be scared.

Marissa took Chanaleh into the safe room and locked the door. It was all at the very last second; she barely had time to lock the door before the terrorists burst in and shot him, and that was it. They must have thought that he was alone there. And all this was taking place while his daughters and grandkid were just a few steps away, in the tiny apartment next to him, in this old shelter that doesn't even lock. They just sat there terrified and made sure everything was dark. They hunched down on the floor so that no one would see anything from the outside, and no one went in there that whole time. Hamas must have had some kind of intelligence map, some kind of plan and knew that the tiny apartment was always empty, so they didn't even go in there.

It's hard to know – no one really knows what was going through Shlomo's head at that moment – but Shlomo knew; he knew that his daughters and his grandson were there in the safe room in the apartment next door; he knew that his wife and Marissa were in the safe room in back; and he's an actor, a true actor. He must have said to himself, "I'm sitting here. I'll sit here in my chair, all calm, and let them shoot me." That's how I understand it.

That armchair is the most prominent thing in the room. He just sat there, not trying to hide or get into a closet or anything; he didn't even close the window! On the contrary, he purposely drew all the attention to himself… like an actor on center stage. He sat there in the chair – "Here I am, I'm right here, I'm not hiding," and since he wasn't hiding, the terrorists thought that he was the only one there. That he was just a lonely old man, sitting alone in his chair. So they shot him and moved on to the next house.

It's not like no one else came after the first terrorists. Marissa told us that for the rest of the day – they were only rescued at six-thirty that evening – dozens of others came in as well; they came in to loot the place, and they opened up the closets and looked for cash or jewelry or whatever, and it didn't occur to any of them to keep looking for more people there because Shlomo's act was so convincing: his lonesomeness, sitting there in the chair all by himself. That's how he saved his wife Chanaleh, Marissa, his daughters, and his grandson. That's it.

I think a lot about Shlomo's courage and how he died as a hero, but not in the usual way. He was a soft hero, a gentle hero. This gentle courage combines two extremes – courage on the one hand and gentleness on the other – and it's so different from all the usual hero stories. He was a man of culture, a man of letters; he read a lot and loved to converse. He was a family man. He didn't have a gun, nothing. He was a soft man, and Chanaleh is such a gentle woman, the most delicate thing in the world. Yet he still had this courage, the courage to sacrifice himself for others. His tenderness saved lives.

I think about him sitting there in his chair, eighty-five years old and still keeping his family safe the only way he could. His death is a perfect microcosm of his whole life. His death is the death of modest, humble people, of gentle heroes. They're real heroes, he and Chanaleh; they always talked about being the country's guardians by living on the border, never budging, never moving away. They never left the kibbutz, even during the hardest, most dangerous wars. All the people who lived there in the Gaza Envelope kibbutzim, they've been keeping the rest of us safe for years, and no one ever talks about it or notices it. What's been happening in recent years, all the anger and hostility toward the kibbutzim, it's all so unbearably painful.

I wanted say something on the subject of unity. In my eyes, everything that happened on October 7th – what we need to learn from it – is that we need to come together as one. I write about that on Facebook, and some of my friends respond so angrily. They write things like, "How can we unite with the Orthodox, with the settlers; all the budgets are used up on them; they're this and they're that." And I say, it's not easy to come together, but that's what we need! We have to unite! That's the moral of the story, and if we don't get that, it'll happen to us again. It's that simple.

A Generation of Heroes

Matan Abargil's Story

Age 19

As told by Matan's father, Arik

⚲ *Kibbutz Nir Am*

We're a family with four children, and Matan is the youngest. When people ask how many kids I have, I get a little stuck because I have four but one was killed, so what am I supposed to say? I've learned to answer that I still have four children. I don't say that I have three children and one who was killed, no! I say, "I have *four*, but one is no longer with us." That's the answer that I give. That's how I feel most comfortable talking about Matan.

Matan was born on the festival of Shavuot, on the day the Torah was given at Sinai. That's why we called him Matan, which means "giving." And he was taken from us on Simchat Torah, the day we celebrate the Torah. It's one of those things that only hits you afterward, in retrospect. Only later do you connect the dots. And on the same day that he was killed, his cousin Avraham was killed too, at the Nova Festival. Their grandmother lost two grandsons on the same day. They were buried two hours apart. Avraham was buried in Jerusalem, on Mount Herzl; my son was buried in Hadera. It was a blow for our family, a terrible blow.

When Matan was little, his older brothers – who are much older than him – would play rough with him. Even then, I could see that he was something else. First of all, he wasn't scared of them – he'd take them both on at once. Fearless! They'd pounce on him, kick him, choke him, twist his arms and legs, but I wouldn't get involved. I'd let it go and watch from the side, and he would always fight back. They'd yell at him, "Give up!" and he'd yell back, "Never!" I'd watch him and mutter to myself, like, *Come on, just give it up already*, but he never would. There he was, buried beneath his brothers; they're piled on top of him, and he's all red, but he won't give in! In the end they'd let go of him, then he'd jump on them and try and beat them up. It was all in good fun, roughhousing, the way brothers do; it wasn't serious fighting. It was okay. That's how brothers bond.

❀

He had this pleasant way about him. You'd sit with him and see this quiet person in front of you; he wasn't one of those noisy kids, those trouble-makers. No. He was a quiet kid. Not shy but quiet – he was just taking it all in. It's difficult to explain. He had this sort of geeky look, with his round face and his glasses, but that was the opposite of what he really was.

In school, he wasn't one of the best students. Let's put it this way – he didn't exactly work the hardest. I mean, I didn't either, to put it mildly! Well, it's okay. But he was very well-behaved. He was always respectful to his teachers, and they all loved him. He was a polite boy, and he did whatever they asked. Whenever they asked for a volunteer, he was always the first to raise his hand.

This is what he was like: he'd go visit his grandmother, say, and he'd see that her grass was a little high, so he'd say, "I'll mow the lawn," and he'd just go and start the lawnmower without her even asking. He was like that in the army, too. Wherever he went, he would try to help people.

When he was about sixteen, something like that, he started play-ing around with the stock market, crypto, that kind of thing, all kinds of stuff I don't know anything about. He really got into it, he learned about it on the internet, listened to lectures about investments, and started play-ing with his money. He worked at a pizza store and invested his earnings; he would buy here and there, invest, lose money, make money, it didn't matter to him. He wasn't afraid! He had guts. Sometimes he'd come to me and say, "Dad, guess how much I lost today, just throw out a number," and I'd say, "Two hundred dollars," and he'd say, "Higher, higher, I lost eight hundred dollars today, but don't worry, I'll make it back!" He had guts. In the army, his commanders would come to him and say, "Here's twenty thousand shekel, invest it for me," but he wouldn't take it from them. He'd always say, "I'm prepared to risk my own money, but not other people's."

I remember, in basic training, one of the soldiers in his unit had a tough time. Matan really helped him out with all kinds of things, fixing up his equipment, things like that. That soldier couldn't really cope with basic training; he'd get punished every day. When everyone else got out for the weekend, he'd be kept back for three or four hours. So Matan felt bad for him and tried to help him however he could. He'd help him tie his laces and fasten his belt and vest whenever they had sudden wake-up drills, to help him out, to make it easier for him. He was really a good kid. He was pure gold.

Matan was stationed near the Gaza border that morning. He and his guys were on call; they were the first response team in case something happened at daybreak. "Ready at Dawn," they call it. They were a bunch of guys from the Golani Brigade with a Namer – that's a type of armored personnel carrier, an APC – and a team from the armored corps with a tank. They were all in full gear, of course, at six in the morning, and they were sitting there on call, joking around and drinking coffee, nothing unusual.

Then, all of a sudden, all these Kassam rockets started falling, and sirens started blaring, and they get a radio report of a sighting of an infiltration along the fence in the area of Nir Am. So of course they set off right away and drove to where the breach was supposed to be. They still had no idea that this was all part of something much bigger; at the time, no one explained to them that this was just one front of a major invasion all along the border. From their perspective, this was an infiltration of just two or three terrorists, so they're driving over to take them out, end of story. No big deal.

So they set out, but already on their way they saw a whole sea of terrorists coming at them – on motorcycles, on foot, in pickup trucks – and en route they begin fighting the terrorists, shooting at them – that's when their battle really began. His platoon commander up in the APC starts directing fire against the terrorists, and they shoot at them as they advance.

After that, they get to Kibbutz Nir Am, where there was a battle near the hatchery just outside the town. The terrorists were inside, so they exited the APC – the platoon commander, Matan, and two other soldiers – and went inside, into the battle zone. Matan was his commander's signalman; the commander told us later that Matan was in overdrive there – that's to say, he ran ahead, kicked the door open and burst in, gun blazing. He said he was, like, totally fearless. And the commander told him, Matan, calm down, hang back a little, don't get too gung-ho. But he really charged straight into the fray, made contact with the enemy, didn't think twice. Already there he was a hero.

After they finished clearing out the compound, the platoon commander received orders over the radio from the company commander to meet up with him at a certain point with two fighters. So the platoon commander decided to leave Matan with the APC because he trusted him and there were no other officers there; he thought very highly of him. He gave them orders to lay low behind some embankment and guard the APC. But as they were lying there, more terrorists suddenly started coming at them, dozens of terrorists. The guys were wide open, with no commanding officer, and they decided to get back into the APC and fight. They ran inside as the terrorists were closing in – there were thirty or forty terrorists there, something like that, and they surrounded the APC and started shooting missiles and throwing explosive charges at them. Within minutes, they had totally wrecked the APC, messed up its drive, immobilized it, and killed the radio. It was a really serious situation, something major.

So there they were, surrounded by terrorists, fighting for their lives; they had no other options. And the APC was getting blasted by anti-tank missiles, with serious explosions. At one point – this is what the soldiers who were there told us later – Matan climbed up to the top hatch of the APC and started firing at the terrorists. He stuck his head and his weapon out of the APC and started shooting at them.

At first, I didn't believe the story. I wanted to know what really happened, the real story. So I spoke to some more people who were there, and they all said the same thing. There was an experienced soldier there, a serious guy. And when he saw Matan climbing up and beginning to shoot, he said to himself, If this kid is going up there and shooting at them, who am I to stay down here? That's what convinced him to go up – he felt ashamed not to fight when he saw Matan's courage. So he also climbed up with his weapon and started shooting.

After a few minutes like that, Matan got shot in his hand, in the finger, and he went back inside the APC, and started changing his magazine, even though his hand was wounded. In the meantime, the other guy shooting up there, the older guy, was shot in the shoulder so he fell back inside, which left the upper hatch of the APC wide open and all the soldiers down below. And the terrorists there took advantage of that situation and threw two grenades into the APC.

The first grenade was either a gas grenade or a dud, it isn't clear, but the soldiers inside began to gag, to vomit, who knows what. But the second grenade thrown inside, Matan saw it coming, and the moment he saw it, he shouted, "Grenade!" and bent down to catch it. He tried to grab hold of it but something went wrong – this was all a matter of two or three seconds. I assume he meant to throw it back out or something, but then he must have realized that he didn't have enough time.

So he picked up the grenade with his right hand. Pressed it to his chest. Turned his back to them, to all the rest of his friends. And then the grenade exploded. And the explosion mortally wounded him, but he didn't die on the spot. His hand blew off, and the blast actually threw him backward on top of his friends. The medic there started to treat him, but his injuries were too severe. The guys told me later that he lay there dying for like seven or eight minutes, and among the last words he was able to say, he told them, "I did everything I could for my country and my friends." That's what he said.

They were there without a radio, the soldiers were, but one of them managed to use his phone to call his friend who was at home, explain to him what their situation was, and tell him that some of them were seriously wounded. Then they sent them a team of Border Police to rescue them because their APC was immobilized. Another APC reached them, and they transferred all the soldiers and wounded from one APC to the other. There's a YouTube clip of that rescue. One of the rescuers there from the police counter-terrorism unit, was killed during that rescue. His name was Roman Gandel, and he was a hero, too. Write that down – that he was a hero too.

For three days, we didn't know what had happened to our son. We couldn't reach him; no one could tell us where he was. Nothing. All the worst possible scenarios were running through my head: I thought, maybe they took him hostage; maybe he's wounded or something. We didn't know anything. And then, late Tuesday night, an officer came to break the news. As soon as he walked through the door I said to him, "The boy's gone, right?" Like that. I had already prepared myself for the worst; what else can you do? I asked him if there had been a positive identification: "Are you sure that it's him?" and he said, "Yes, there was a positive identification." Then I asked him if he knew how he had been killed, and he said, "I don't know what to tell you; I have no idea, I have no information about it, I can't tell you a thing."

And then suddenly, on Wednesday morning, my neighbor sends me a message with some post by one of the soldiers who had been with Matan in the APC, and he says to me, "Arik, look at what he wrote." I opened the link and saw that he had posted something about thanking God for sending him Matan, because he saved his life; he threw himself on the grenade and saved everyone's life, something like that. And he'll never forget him, and so on.

I read this and I can't believe it. I come to my kids and say to them, "Look, he threw himself on a grenade!" We were all in shock. I said to them, "Find me the person who wrote the post! Try to get ahold of him on Facebook, I don't know what." And they did, and I spoke with him on the phone, and I asked him to tell me the story. And that's how we understood what happened.

After Matan was killed, about six and a half weeks later, his battalion commander Tomer Greenberg was also killed in Gaza, and I went to his funeral in Jerusalem. After the funeral, as I made my way out, suddenly some young guy came up to me, dressed in civilian clothes, and says to me, "You're Matan Abargil's father, right?" and I said to him, "Yeah, who are you?" So he says to me, "I was his sergeant in basic training." "Nice," I said to him, "and were you there with him that day?" "No," he says, "but I want to tell you something you probably haven't heard from anyone else." I said to him, "What, tell me." It was intriguing, right?

So he says to me, "Listen, once we did this training exercise. The whole platoon sat in a classroom, you know, chairs, desks, learning something theoretical, and I went into the classroom with a grenade – not a real one – a dummy – and I stood in the middle of the classroom and threw the grenade. Just as an exercise. And everyone ran away when I threw the grenade – everyone ran away except for Matan. He threw himself on it. He knew that it wasn't a real grenade, but he did it, half joking, half instinct, I don't even know what to call it, you know what I mean?" That's what the guy says to me. "Everyone bolted, but he threw himself on the grenade. That says something about a person."

His friends who were with him in the APC, all of them were wounded by that explosion to one degree or another. We love them, all those friends, those brave warriors from the APC. They're like our children. We're so happy to see them recovering, coming back to themselves. One was on crutches, another in a wheelchair, but they're all okay by now. They're walking, they're in rehab, they've been through surgeries, they've had shrapnel removed. They're also getting psychological therapy; it's not simple, they've all been through one hell of an ordeal. But they're going to be okay. And thanks to Matan, they're alive.

I think that I'm dealing with it relatively well. The psychologist from the Ministry of Defense has come to speak with us a few times; even she said that I seem to be doing okay, I don't know, that the way I'm talking about it, the way I'm dealing with the whole story, is the right way. And my wife is okay, more or less. She has maybe taken it a little bit harder than I have.

But I do feel that my kids at home have become a little tighter. I mean, they're reaching out to each other a little more than they used to. It makes them look out for each other more. They went through something very traumatic that's given them, like, a different perspective on life; they appreciate more what they have. That's also something that Matan has left them, I think.

I saw some report on TV, and one of the soldiers there said that they, the soldiers of today, grew up on the heroic stories of the fighters of 1948, of Israel's War of Independence. And he said he thinks that in another forty, fifty years, they'll talk about this generation, of 2023, like we talk about the generation of 1948. They really deserve it, no doubt at all. These guys saved the country, no question. They saved our country. They're still saving it. They fight for us every day. Doesn't matter to them whether they're right-wing, left-wing, Arab, religious – nothing! And I think so too. I think not just Matan, but all these young guys – they're all heroes. It's a generation of heroes.

I Tried to Help as Much as I Could

Gali Eilon's Story

Age 15

⚲ *Kibbutz Kfar Aza*

I remember how a kite once fell into our yard and started a huge fire. Hamas did that for a while – they would send burning kites and balloons to start fires here in the Gaza Envelope. My brothers and I were at home with a babysitter at the time, and I was terrified. From that day on, I developed a lot of anxieties; I was really, really scared of fires. Really frightened. My dad saw my fear and tried to help me. He took me to speak to some people about it, but fear is something hard to get rid of. So, a few days later, he and Danny Nitzan and Shahar Aviani, the head of our civilian guard, took me to the kibbutz fire station, and we all went out together in the fire truck to put out fires.

That's what we did – we just went around the area putting out fires. Every time we saw one of those fire balloons fall, we'd go over and put out the fire before it had a chance to spread. We'd pour water on it, or if it was a bigger fire, we'd use the firehose and put it out from far away. Daddy put me in a situation where I had to cope with my fear. He helped me understand that it was up to us – it was in our hands. And that's how I got over my fear of fire.

If Daddy had just said to me, "Nah, Gali, it's not dangerous at all," if he had lied, I wouldn't have gotten over it. But he taught me that yes, fire is dangerous, but you can do something about it; it can be controlled if you respond in time, before it spreads. You can cope with fire. You can cope with fear. That's what my father taught me my whole life.

And that day, too, October 7th – it was one of those days where everyone did what they could to stop the fire from spreading. Everyone in Kfar Aza coped with their fear and did what they could. What would have happened if my dad had been too scared to go out and fight the terrorists that day? What would have happened if our soldiers had been too frightened to go out and fight? What would have happened if I had let my fear control me?

For as long as I can remember, they taught us that we have eight seconds to run to the safe room. For as long as I can remember, I learned to run as soon as I heard the Red Alert siren. A few weeks ago I was in the US – we went on a speaking tour to talk to Jewish communities there – and I started saying, "That day, we woke up to a Red Alert..." The Jewish Agency representative cut me off: "Gali, they have no idea what a Red Alert is. You have to explain it to them," and I said to her, "What do you mean?" and she answered, "They're not used to missiles falling on their houses. They don't have safe rooms in their homes. They don't need to take shelter from someone shooting missiles at them every week."

It was only then that it hit me that the way we live isn't normal. We shouldn't normalize it. First thing's first: long before October 7th, it was never okay that we all had to have safe rooms in our homes; it was never okay that we had to learn how to run every time they launch a missile at us. It isn't something that anyone should ever have to get used to.

Still, it was a good life in Kfar Aza. We'd come back from school and go to the kids' club, and we'd all play and hang out there until four p.m., then my friends would usually come over to my house. Our house was always full; I love having people over. Even now, my friends tell me how much they miss my house and the homey feeling it had. We would always go to my house, always.

Every Saturday my house was bursting with people. Everyone would come over for Grandma Yael's *jahnun* pastry. We're three siblings, and on Saturday morning all of our friends would come over, and we'd all hang out together all day long. I don't know. It's hard for me talk about it; it's hard for me to think about life in Kfar Aza before. It seems so far away, I hardly know what to say.

A little while ago they sent us a photo of the little creek in the kibbutz. It flows through the kibbutz only during the winter after the rains, and whenever it would get full, we'd go out to play there – we'd get all wet and make little paper boats and float them on the creek. My friends sent me photos from back then, and another photo, one of the creek today. In the first photo the creek is full of kids and life and joy. In the second photo, the creekbed is empty, and the houses beside it are all burnt out and destroyed. What is there to say?

The night before that Shabbat, I slept over at my Grandma Liora's house; she also lives in the kibbutz. At about six-thirty in the morning we woke up to a Red Alert, and we all ran straight into the safe room without taking too much with us. We didn't take bottles of water or food or chargers. We just came as we were, in our pajamas. We thought it would be over quickly, like it always was – just a few minutes and that's it. But this time, it wasn't like that. The sirens just didn't stop.

After a few minutes, I suddenly get a message from my brother Roei. He told us that terrorists had infiltrated the kibbutz, and Daddy was called up but says not to worry. "Just stay in the safe room and wait until they rescue you." That's what he said. My father is the commander of the kibbutz's civilian security response team. From what I heard, he ran straight to the armory to get a rifle – he was one of the first to arrive there – and he and his friend Ori Rousso went out right away to fight the terrorists. He didn't know then just how many terrorists they would be confronting. He must have thought it was only a few. He never could have imagined that hundreds of terrorists were attacking the kibbutz all at once.

From the armory, they went to Smadar and Ro'i Idan's house. From there, they could see the terrorists coming in on paragliders, landing in the kibbutz. Daddy kept updating all the members of the security response team about his status and what each one should be doing. Even after he was injured, he kept running things over the phone. He was still their commander; he still guided everyone through it. He also called his friend from Kibbutz Sa'ad and updated him about what was happening as he fought. From what I heard, this really helped them prepare over there, so that they could be on the alert against attack. Even after he was injured, he told his friends not to come to his rescue. He told them, "Close in on the enemy; engage their forces." That's what he said. And he kept fighting until he was killed.

At that point, I'm in my grandma's safe room, and I start getting all these messages from my friends saying terrorists are coming into their houses, breaking down their doors, and shouting in Arabic, and I don't know what to do about it. I mean, my best friends' lives are in danger, and they're crying out for help, and I'm just helpless. I see on Instagram that the head of our regional council, Ofir Libstein, has been killed, and he's the father of my good friend. That was the moment that I understood, "Wait, what? Oh my gosh, it's for real. People I know are actually being murdered. I really will never see Ofir again; I really will never see people that I know and love again." It didn't make sense to me that I was just sitting there in the safe room without the ability to do anything about what was happening outside. It was a really terrible feeling of helplessness.

Then we heard glass breaking, shattering inside the house. My aunt and uncle were holding onto the handle of the safe room door. And on the other side of the door we can hear people coming in, shouting in Arabic, heavy footsteps, and shooting, shooting inside our house. I just crawl under the bed together with my cousin Mika. I hide under the bed hoping that maybe they won't see me when they break into the safe room. And I'm shaking with fear.

After a few minutes like that, we hear the sounds of a gun battle right outside, shouting, a real battle, and the shooting is getting louder and louder. Until it stops. And then we hear voices in Hebrew, soldiers' voices. The soldiers knock on the door and say, "It's the IDF, we're from the Duvdevan unit!" And I suddenly felt that I could breathe again. We're not alone anymore. The soldiers are here.

When the door opened, there was tons of noise coming from the soldiers' radios, and I realized that they didn't know where the fighting was, where the injured were, where the terrorists were – and I realized at this point that it would do no good to keep hiding under the bed. So I came out of the safe room, went up to the soldiers, and said, "I can help you."

For some reason, I was the only one in my family who still had cell service there. And the soldiers went along with me. So I wrote on the kibbutz WhatsApp group: If there are terrorists where you are or if anyone is wounded, send me your location! I also sent a voice message, and a soldier also recorded a voice message introducing himself, so that people knew they could trust us and that he can help and that it was safe to send us information.

Then people started sending me updates about more and more people who were wounded, and more and more terrorists, and I started gathering all the information. I sent the soldiers maps of the kibbutz and showed them on the map where everything was happening, where the fighting was, where the terrorists were, where the wounded were, and the soldiers passed all the information on to their guys, who sent troops to help the casualties.

Some of the messages were brutal. Some people wrote, "They're shooting me," "They're burning down my house!" There were a lot of casualties. I passed on a lot of locations. I tried to send the soldiers to where they were needed. They basically conducted the whole battle for the kibbutz from my grandma's house. I must have sat with them for two hours. I tried to help as much as I could. An article that came out about it later said I was like an operations officer.

At one point the soldiers said they had to move on to a different place in the kibbutz, and I was scared. I was really scared to be left alone without them, and we really didn't want them to go, but we really couldn't just ask them to stay with us. So we went back into the safe room, closed the door, held it tightly closed, and hoped for the best. There was a power outage in the kibbutz, and the room was dark and didn't have air, and my cousin nearly fainted. And the whole time, I kept forwarding messages to the soldiers with updates and locations.

In the meantime the hours go by, another hour and another hour, and night falls, and no one comes. I see on WhatsApp that some of my friends were rescued, but we're still there in the safe room. I consider for a moment whether I should ask the soldiers to come rescue us – but then I saw that there was fighting going on in a neighborhood called "The Young Generation," so we sent the soldiers there. It was a tough decision. But we did what we had to do.

At one point, we suddenly hear explosions coming closer, and we hear terrorists coming in, and we hear them trying to open the door, and they're screaming *"Allahu Akbar!"* and my battery is dying, I'm down to one percent, and I write to the soldier who was with us before that there are terrorists at the door and that he should send forces because they're trying to come in and we're scared. Suddenly there was a crazy explosion outside, the house simply shook, and I was sure that that was it – I'm going to die. I texted my mom that I love her. And I closed my eyes and waited for it all to end.

At that point, my mom was at the gas station outside the kibbutz, where they evacuated all survivors. She told me later that everyone there was in shock, that no one seemed like themselves at all. There were soldiers with them there at the gas station, and they heard my mom saying that she was trying to get hold of Gali, that she couldn't find Gali. So they came up to her and asked, "Gali who?" and she explained to them that her daughter Gali is back in the kibbutz with her grandmother. And one of the soldiers jumped up and said, "That's *our* Gali!" and showed her my picture on WhatsApp. And she says, "Yes, that's my daughter." And he went, "What, she wasn't rescued yet?!" and my mom said, "No!" and they all jumped up – how come nobody rescued Gali?

So they sent us a rescue force, urgently. Suddenly we heard loads of shooting, loads of explosions. Shouting in Hebrew. Then infantry soldiers from Givati opened our door. They told us that there were terrorists in the house, and they had to evacuate us quickly so that they could eliminate them. They made us this kind of wall of soldiers, a sort of safe passage so that we could get through; they passed us from soldier to soldier, and I finally get out of the house, and I barely recognize the kibbutz. I didn't know where I was going because all the houses had been destroyed.

Altogether, we'd been in the safe room for over thirty-three hours. When we got out, they took us to the gas station as well. There, at the station, I found my mom and brothers, and we hugged and cried. But there were still plenty of reports on WhatsApp, so I went up to a soldier and said, "I can help you. There are still a lot of people in the kibbutz. Give me your number; I'll send you locations." So also from there, I kept forwarding people's locations.

At this point I was sure that my dad was wounded or taken hostage or something like that. I was sure that he would be back soon with a big smile to tell us everything that happened and how he fought. It took three days before they told us they'd identified his body, and it took a full week to officially confirm that it was really him.

I'm not a hero. I'm a survivor – *they* saved me. "Hero" is a very loaded term. I think that my father was a hero. There's no one more heroic than him, really. How he fought there against a hundred terrorists, he and the civilian security coordinator and all the guys in the security response team. They're my heroes. They were our light when we were in the darkness of the safe room. And Netta Epstein from my kibbutz, who saved his fiancée, who jumped on a grenade for her. He's a hero. They're heroes. I don't feel like I'm a hero. No.

My mom is the strongest. She's the strongest person in the world, and she keeps us all going. Being strong doesn't mean hiding your feelings. People think that being strong means that you're not allowed to cry or show weakness, but I disagree with that. I think that being strong means understanding the pain. Accepting the pain. And letting others help you cope with it all, and helping them cope with it, too. Someone in pain who can see other people's pain as well – that's someone with tremendous strength. And that's my mom.

She started a WhatsApp group for all the wives of the security response team, for all the widows who lost their partners that Shabbat. On that group, they all support each other; they lift each other up. It inspires me that she decided to do that. My mom is a hero.

We have such amazing people in the kibbutz. Even on that day, even when it was all going on, when I asked for locations – people would send me their friends' locations. Everyone was concerned about their friends. It was amazing to see it on WhatsApp, how everyone took care of each other. Even when I wrote that my battery was about to die, this girl who used to be my Scout leader wrote, "Gali, send me your location so I'll know where to fight for you!"

Even today, after it happened, there's this special kind of sensitivity within the kibbutz. Everyone can feel each other. If, say, I run into someone on the street, and they can tell that I need a hug, they'll just stop everything and give me that hug. You don't have to say anything. With the Kfar Aza community, I don't feel like I'm expected to talk. People just get me. We all just get each other.

It's so difficult for me to tell this story. It hurts to talk about it. I'm sick of it. Everyone is always telling me how important it is to tell my story, to talk about it, and that's why I'm telling it. But the truth is that I'm sick of doing it because it's "important." I just want some quiet.

Since October 7th, I don't wish anything for myself anymore. When I lose an eyelash, when I see a shooting star, I don't make a wish for myself. I just pray that no one else will have to feel what I'm feeling. Ever again. And I pray that all our hostages, people I grew up with, will all come back home safely, and that all our soldiers will come home safe and sound.

I know that I want to go back to the kibbutz. I want to go back to my home. But I want to feel safe there. I want to stop jumping at every loud noise. I don't understand how we reached this point – that a quiet, peaceful, safe life in my own home is only something to hope for. It should go without saying.

And I think a lot about my dad. He was always so proud of me. And he always taught me to do my very best. I hope he's still proud of me now, and I hope he knows that, whatever I do, I'm always thinking of him. I promise him that, with time, we'll rebuild the kibbutz he fought for. We'll build it all up again and start over, together.

If I Drive on Shabbat, I'm Driving to Save Lives

The Story of Ambulance #54
Emanuel Sakat, Avi Gian, and Avi Yudkowsky

Ages 36, 40, 22

As told by Emanuel Sakat

⚲ *Yakhini, Kibbutz Kfar Aza, Sderot*

I'm Emanuel Sakat, a volunteer for United Hatzalah Emergency Medical Service. I'm thirty-six, married to Tehilla, and we have four cute kids. We're Ultra-Orthodox but not hardcore – I served in the army, then spent a little time looking for myself, I guess, and only got married when I was twenty-five. I've known my wife Tehilla since she was twelve; I had a school friend, Yossi, and every year he and his father would go over to build a sukkah for Tehilla's father, who's disabled, and I'd often join them. Every time I came, I'd see her there, Tehilla, with two braids and a knockout smile and a dimple in her cheek, a one-of-a-kind dimple. It was impossible not to fall in love with her; there was no chance I wouldn't have wound up falling in love with her. But I didn't make a move back then. Years later, after we both grew up a little, matured a little, Yossi's father came over to me and said, "Say, maybe there's something you'd like to talk to me about?" At first I had no idea what he was getting at, then he said to me, "If you're interested in something serious, pal, maybe you should ask her out!" So we went out on a date, and it was amazing. We were married eight months later. She's pure gold, thank God.

Shabbat (the Sabbath) at home with my family is the great love of my life. We all help prepare for Shabbat together. Each kid has his or her own job: my son cleans up the living room and sets up the candles; my daughter washes the floor of the terrace; the little one makes sure that every bathroom has tissues for Shabbat; everyone does something to help get ready. And then, at the Shabbat table, we eat and sing and talk about the Torah, and the children tell stories, and after the meal we always bring a fruit platter to the table. We sit around, cracking nuts and sunflower seeds, and talk and play games all day long. Those are the most beautiful moments – no phones, no screens, no electronics at all on Shabbat, other than my Hatzalah walkie-talkie, which I keep with me when I'm on call. On that Shabbat I was on call, which is how I got the alert from our ambulance driver, Avi Gian.

Avi Gian, forty years old, married with six kids, is a good friend of mine from United Hatzalah. He's an incredible guy, and his dedication to people is out of this world. One day, while he's on shift, he happens to go into this apartment belonging to a family with a lot of kids, and he sees that the place is falling apart; he just happens to see it. So, after he takes the patient to the hospital, Avi – on his own initiative – rounds up a few guys, gets hold of some funding, frees up some time, and together, with their own hands, they turn that place from a dump into a freshly renovated home, with new fittings, everything brand spanking new. Avi's also the world's fastest ambulance driver. We always joke that he gets to the scene before the accident even happens.

That day, the third member of our team was another Avi, Avi Yudkowsky, age twenty-two. Avi's a DJ by profession; if I had to describe him with one word, it would be "generosity." That guy is all heart; he's pure kindheartedness. Every Wednesday he organizes a Torah study group: he spends a ton of money – from his own savings – and goes and picks up meat, and makes a whole barbecue for the guys. Then a rabbi comes and gives them a class; Avi arranges it all, and he does it with this modesty that's typical of him. He's just that kind of guy, who's happy when you're happy. When Avi's treating patients, he always makes them laugh. If you're ever hurt, Avi Yudkowsky is the medic you want to have around.

>❧

On Shabbat morning, Simchat Torah, Avi Gian calls me and says, "Listen, something's happening down south; missiles all morning." I say to him, "Avi, missiles in the south? That's why you're calling me?" It's true, when things start heating up down south, they usually send reinforcements, but I've never done a round there, so I said to him, "Avi, you've got the wrong number; I've never gone down south, it's not my normal job." And Avi says to me, "Emanuel, we're not talking about normal. Something's up."

Right after we hang up, boom, there's a missile-alert siren in Jerusalem, and I understand that the situation is definitely not normal. Since when are there sirens in Jerusalem? I get ready, go to the storeroom, get my helmet and ceramic vest, strap on my handgun – with two magazines, just in case – and grab two black T-shirts, so we don't show up in our Sabbath clothes. Meanwhile, Avi came to pick me up, along with the other Avi. I got into the ambulance, and we started driving south. Avi, Avi, and me.

On the way I said to Gian, "Avi, what's going on, talk to me, what do we know?" and he says to me, "We know nothing, Aaron called me and said that there might be terrorists in Sderot." Aaron is Director of Operations of United Hatzalah; he's the guy who decides who gets which call, and he also went down south that morning.

So we're driving along, and as we get further south, we see dozens of cars driving alongside us, racing forward in the same direction, south. Some are driving with their weapons pointing out the window, some in uniform, some out of uniform, but everyone is speeding, speeding, speeding south. And we're an ambulance, so we turn on the siren, but people are still passing us. We get to a red light and try to go through carefully, but everyone's running the red! No one stops. And the ambulance radio frequency is silent; no other ambulances have reached that sector yet. We understand that there's an abnormal situation, but we don't have the slightest idea what's going on. We didn't turn on the radio at any point; it was the Sabbath after all.

At Heletz Junction meanwhile they had set up a central assembly point for evacuating the wounded to hospitals; there was even a landing pad for helicopters. In theory ambulances weren't supposed to go past that point – they were ordered to stop there and wait for patients to arrive. Only bulletproof ambulances were allowed to go further. Magen David Adom has some bulletproof ambulances, but there weren't nearly enough for an event like this. Our ambulance wasn't bulletproof, of course.

When we reached Heletz Junction, they signaled for us to stop, but we kept going. Avi decided that we'd keep driving ahead. He said to me, "If I drive on Shabbat, I'm driving to save lives! I don't drive on Shabbat just to sit at Heletz Junction!" Half a minute later, the ambulance behind us informs the operation center that there's an ambulance driving past the assembly point, and the dispatcher starts screaming at us over the radio: "HELLO! STOP! Turn around this instant; don't go any farther!" So we stop for a moment, put on our protective gear, our bulletproof vests and helmets, and keep going. And the radio goes back on: "Ambulance 54! I told you not to go past Heletz Junction! Where do you think you're going??!!" So Avi Gian says to him, "We're on our way to someone wounded; we have a SWAT team with us. They're covering us and giving directions." The other Avi and I look at each other. We didn't have a SWAT team; we didn't have squat. But the dispatcher bought it for a few seconds. A minute later, he gets on again and says to us: "I get that you don't want to come back alive. Have a good day, friends!"

I really love our driver Avi, a close friend of mine, a really righteous guy. I realize now that we're putting ourselves in danger, and I say to myself, "Whoa. God and Avi get on okay. He won't let him die. Everything's gonna be all right." So we're driving along when suddenly, around two kilometers from the community of Yakhini, a bulletproof vehicle pulls up next to us and signals us to stop. Four guys get out of the car; they all have helmets, vests, weapons, and they shout to us, "We have a kid who's been shot in some house!" and they add that the area isn't a hundred percent safe yet, so we decide that Avi and Avi will stay behind for now in the ambulance, and I'll drive down there in their armored vehicle with all the medical equipment.

The guys in the vehicle are from the first response team in Yakhini. They're around fifty years old, and on the way, driving, they're just crying and crying. "How did they do this to us, how did they manage, how were we not prepared for this?" And I ask them, "What's up, what happened?" but they don't answer. We reach a house at the edge of the community, and they say to me, "This is the place. We'll cover you in a sec; you'll get out and run through the door," and I'm like, "Cover me? What are you talking about!" I didn't understand the situation.

So they cover me, and I open the door and run to the house. When I enter the house, I see it's a Yemenite family; I also come from a Yemenite family, and there was this smell of food warming up on the Shabbat hotplate, it reminded me of my grandmother's house, this amazing smell. I'm going out of my mind! I ask the people there where the wounded boy is, and they take me up half a flight of stairs and lead me into a bedroom. The room already smells like death. I see on the floor an eighteen-year-old kid lying in a pool of blood, and there are two adults next to him trying to resuscitate him.

I realize already then that we got there too late. There's not much else I can do for the boy, but on the other hand I don't have the heart to tell the family that he's dead. It's not my role; I'm not authorized to do that. I've never done it before in my life. So I start resuscitating, and I call the doctor and say to him, "Listen, the kid isn't responding, he's already been unconscious for a long time," and he says to me, "I know, I know, but try, okay? It's important."

After a little while, Avi Gian arrives and reads the situation, and he looks at me and says, "There are twenty bodies outside this community; come on, we have to move!" and I'm like, "What!!!" but Avi doesn't explain a thing. He turns to the mother and gently tells her that it's over; there's nothing left to do. Outside is hell, they need the ambulance, and we need to go. And the mother breaks down in tears, but she understands. We cover up the boy and go out. A few days later, we found out that the massacre in Yakhini took seven lives. One of them was Yonatan Hajbi. A beautiful eighteen-year-old boy, a saintly boy.

❧

On the way out of Yakhini, this civilian suddenly stops us and says, "Guys, there's someone hurt; he's in Sapir College and shot in the legs. Help him out; go get him!" We call the guy and speak to him – it's a young guy who escaped the festival, and he sends us a location at Sapir College. So we leave Yakhini, and good God, I can't describe the horror. All along the road, cars are stopped, with bodies outside them, it's awful. And I say to Avi, "Slow down for a moment, let's go by slowly; maybe someone here is still alive, maybe we can save someone," and we drive along slowly, passing between the bodies, but there's nothing alive, no one; everyone there was dead.

We keep driving, and my eye catches a soldier slumped in his car, dead, and my heart aches. It's the first time I've ever seen a dead soldier. We keep going, and we reach Sapir College and get on the phone with the wounded guy, "Where are you? We're here!" So we drive to the back gate of the college, and suddenly he shouts to us on the phone, "Here's an ambulance! Here's an ambulance! You're here!" and he's overjoyed! And there's this big commotion around him. But when we get to him, the gate is locked. Oh my God, the gate is locked.

We try to break open the gate, but we can't. And the young guy is waiting right there on the other side of the gate, and he has a bullet wound in the leg, but he doesn't give up; he says he'll crawl under the gate. And suddenly we hear a screeching noise and an army jeep pulls up next to us, and they carry out a soldier, and one of them shouts, "I have a soldier shot in the head! I need you to treat him!" So we load the guy onto a stretcher, and I bring him into the ambulance – he's still responding a little to pain – I take off the bandage they put on him, and I discover a severe head wound. Very, very severe.

At the same time, Avi is still trying to open the gate to get the guy out, and I scream to him, "Avi, drop everything this second; come, we're getting this man out; he's critically wounded, if we don't get him out of here, he has no chance!" Avi tells the guy behind the gate, "Listen, we'll come back, I promise you; right after I drop him off I'll come to get you." When he heard that, his face just crumpled. But he pulled himself together within a moment, got ahold of himself, and rushed back into the building.

We speed off with the wounded soldier to Heletz Junction, to the evacuation point. I'm with the soldier in the ambulance and start to give him respiratory assistance, but he keeps fighting me – it's a typical reaction for someone with a head wound; they're unsettled because of the oxygen deprivation. He's fighting me, I attach the mask to his face, he pushes me away; I try to hook him up to a manual resuscitator, but he breaks it. I pull another one out of my bag and say to him, "Don't worry!" and try to talk with him, get him to talk, What's your name and all that, but he isn't with it; he's thrashing around, boom, he breaks the second resuscitator as well. I see that we're about eight minutes away, and I say to Avi, "Listen, Avi, I have no way to treat him; the only thing to do is to get him out to hospital as quickly as possible, so don't touch the brakes, put the pedal to the metal!"

Whoa, did that ambulance fly. Avi reports on the radio that we have a patient with a severe head wound, and a mobile ICU team needs to be waiting for him there at Heletz Junction. We got to Heletz Junction within minutes, handed him over to the intensive care ambulance team waiting for him, and they sedate and resuscitate him on the spot.

After we dropped the soldier off at Heletz Junction, we headed back to Sapir College to keep our promise. This time, Avi Gian gets out and forces the gate; he breaks the gate open and drives the ambulance into the campus. That guy with the leg wound finally comes to us, along with another eight young people who had managed to escape from the Nova Festival. Everyone was okay except for the one hit in the legs, but they were all traumatized, in shock, crying; we brought them all into the ambulance and evacuated them to Heletz, too.

After we drop them off, Avi Gian drives back toward the south. We reach Sha'ar HaNegev Junction, and it's the same scene all over again: a car screeches to a halt next to us and drops off a girl who's been shot in the shoulder. We load her onto the gurney and turn back to Heletz Junction. On the way, another car cuts us off, motions to us to stop, and brings us a girl who's been shot in the leg. I treat the first girl, Avi Yudkowsky treats the second, and Avi Gian turns us around to take them to Heletz Junction.

And that's how it went; every time we pass by, driving back and forth, every single time, people bring us their wounded, and we drive them to the evacuation point, turn around, and come back. After we complete yet another evacuation, I say to Avi, "Remember that dead soldier we saw at the beginning, inside the car? I know he's dead, but come on, let's go get him." I was thinking that anyone who'd pass by there on the road would see a dead soldier. Oy, what that sight does to you; it pierces the heart, to see a dead soldier, and it lowers morale. Whoever was driving on that road now was in the line of duty and shouldn't see that sort of thing.

So we get back to the car with the soldier, and I get out of the ambulance and take a look at him. I see a young soldier with a *kippa* on and a wedding ring on his finger; just heart wrenching. We take his rifle and lay him down on the gurney. And we say, Let's check what his name is, we'll look through his pockets, and inform the authorities about him. And we see that the guy is just a corporal, recently enlisted, and we confirm that he's married. And we find a love letter folded up in his pocket. That did it; that just tore us up – like, it was on another level. Our hearts couldn't take it anymore. We didn't read that letter. We folded it back up, loaded him into the ambulance and drove him to where they evacuated the casualties.

Later on, we found out that this was Amit Guetta, a fighter from Maglan, an elite unit, a hero of Israel. He had only been married for two months; that was it. I read what his friends said about him, what a great person he was. He was a modest man but a lion just the same. He was, like, a brilliant guy, a top guy; he studied Torah full out. His wife says that he was a *tzaddik*. How, how is it that God takes the righteous ones?

❧

By the time we got back to Sha'ar HaNegev Junction, it was clear that this was a full-scale war. We had a few moments of quiet there, without anyone bringing us any wounded, then Gian starts thinking out loud.

"Where are they bringing the wounded from? We keep driving back and forth here, and all these cars and jeeps keep bringing us more wounded. Where are they all from? Where are they bringing them from; where are they coming from?" and without thinking twice, he answers himself, "Well, all those cars came from that direction. Okay, that's why we're here!" and we start driving toward the kibbutzim.

By now we've reached Route 232, the road that connects all the towns in the Gaza Envelope. When we begin driving on that road, we realize that everything we've seen until now was just a preview. What we saw there on that road – I'll never forget it as long as I live. Burnt out cars, burnt people, infant car-seats – total chaos. The image that I remember the most is this huge area there, like a large field, and people are just lying there, face-down in the dirt, dead. They ran away together, and the terrorists just shot them down. I really felt like I was inside a Holocaust movie.

So we move forward, and suddenly, we reach a checkpoint, grim-looking soldiers with their rifles out, and the soldiers shout at us, "Who are you? What are you doing here?!" and Gian says to them, "We're an ambulance crew!" So the soldier opens up the back of the ambulance and inspects it, looks it over; he can't believe that we're actually going in. And he says to us, "Guys, way to go. Really, way to go," and when he says that, I realize that he's emotional, the soldier. He shuts the ambulance doors and we drive on.

We reach the entrance of Kfar Aza, and we stop there. We can sense the war. We hear crazy explosions. We feel like we're in the actual battlefield. Around us we see lots of soldiers running with their guns drawn; they're going into Kfar Aza. Not a minute passes before a car bursts out of there at crazy speed. The whole car is coming apart, no door, full of shrapnel holes. It stops next to us; a commander gets out and takes out soldiers: "Cover this one, cover this one, this one goes to the ambulance, this one needs care" – he does triage: who's dead, who needs treatment, who can still walk. And we're the only ambulance there; there was no other way to evacuate them there, no other cars, nothing.

So we load all the wounded soldiers into the ambulance and bring them to Heletz Junction. It's already four in the afternoon. Gian sees Aaron there, the United Hatzalah Director of Operations, who's directing all the teams there. So he goes up to him and says, "Aaron, I need more ambulances at the entrance to Kfar Aza, I have lots of wounded there; I need more ambulances!" And everyone knows that Kfar Aza is an active war zone right now; there's actually house-to-house combat. But Aaron says to him, "No way, Avi; you're the only nutcase who's going in there! I'm not taking responsibility for you, but if anyone gets a scratch there I'll never forgive myself, so no one else is going in!" And I see Avi say to him, "Come over here for a minute," and he takes him aside, and they talk for a couple of minutes, and afterward they come back, and Aaron says to all the drivers there, "Guys, every ambulance follows Avi! Now!"

Afterward, we asked Avi Gian what he said to him. He told us that he came up to him and said, "Aaron, what are we here for? We're here to save lives. Are you really telling me that because there's a chance we'll get hurt, we're not willing to try and save people's lives? I'm telling you, there are people who need us, and I'm telling you that all the volunteers here are prepared to risk getting hurt just on the chance that we'll save them!" That convinced him to let the drivers go.

So we lead the way, and four ambulances follow. As soon as we reach the entrance to Kfar Aza, a tank comes out, driving crazy, scraping some army vehicles along the way. And he unloads a whole bunch of wounded people from inside, and we pack them in. All the ambulances that we brought along load the wounded on board and we take them to Barzilai Hospital.

When we get to Barzilai, a soldier accosts us; he goes up to Avi Yudkowsky and says to him, "I got a piece of shrapnel in my arm a few hours ago, but they treated me, and I have to get back to my team, urgently! Can I get a ride back with you?" We said, "Sure, why not?" On the way, we found out that he was a commando from Sayeret Matkal. So we drove south, and suddenly the soldier gets a phone call, talks for a few seconds, then says to us, "There's an exchange of fire at Sderot Police Station," and he asks us to make a U-turn and take him there instead, so we drive him to Sderot.

By the time we reached Sderot, it was already dark. The Sabbath was over. And we learned that a huge band of terrorists had barricaded themselves in the police station, and that a large counter-terrorism team was planning to go up on a fireman's ladder and break in there. A serious operation. We also heard that there were wounded to evacuate. When we got into the parking lot, the soldier said to us, "Turn off your lights! Hide behind the ambulance!" and the soldiers there were firing into the building, and then they motioned to Avi Yudkowsky to come with the gurney. They put a wounded cop down on the gurney, and they motioned to him to run back to the ambulance. And we actually loaded the cop into the ambulance and rushed him to the hospital.

We kept working there, evacuating the wounded, and from the moment the Sabbath ended, throughout all the long drives, Gian kept playing Moti Weiss's song, "We Don't Question our Father," a nice song, but he played the song on continuous loop, again and again and again, and at some point we say to him, "Avi, give us a break! How many times can we hear the same song?!" but Gian said to us, "It gives me strength," so we said to him, "If it gives you strength, then keep it on – when you're strong, we're strong."

We finished at one in the morning. The whole drive home, we were all lost in thought; each of us deep in his own thoughts, replaying all the images from that day, trying to process it all. We were quiet the whole way. Then suddenly, just before we got home, my father calls and says to me, "What's this I hear?! You drove down south! Are you normal? Why are you driving there and putting yourself in danger?" I'm just broken, broken to pieces, and I say, "Whoa, Dad, don't worry, we didn't go anywhere dangerous!" then all three of us burst into laughter; it was this laughter that just released everything from that day. It was the saddest laughter I've ever heard in my life.

A month later, they broadcast a segment about us on the news show "*Uvdah*," and one of the things that we told them was about the soldier with the head injury, the one who fought me and broke my resuscitators. After that program aired, three different families contacted us, all of them claiming that it was their son. They wanted to thank us and told us that, sadly, he didn't make it. Given his injury, I thought that made sense.

But then, three weeks after the item aired, we suddenly got another voice message: "I saw the show, and that's my son; he's alive!" As soon as I heard that, I called her and said, "Describe your son to me!" and she says to me, "My son described you to me! He talks about you all the time, and then he recognized you on that show! He remembers the whole thing; he thought you were kidnapping him, which is why he tried to fight you! And he's doing okay!" She sends me a video clip of him, and we see him there, and I know it's him! And my heart was just bursting, bursting! I'm looking at a man who, until a moment ago, I thought was dead, and suddenly I see that he's alive. That day I was the happiest man on earth.

We evacuated sixty wounded on that black Sabbath, and they all survived. Every single person who was alive when they boarded our ambulance is still alive today. I'm so glad to have been part of that. It was a historic event, and I'm grateful that I had the privilege to play a small part in the story and share it with others. I'll never forget that day; what happened on that black Sabbath must never be forgotten.

People tell me that I'm a hero, but I tell them not to look at me – what I did was small compared to what others did there. People were so brave, so resourceful. Even those who were wounded – we spoke with them in the ambulance and heard their stories, how they hid for hours, how they struggled to survive. They're the heroes.

Three miracles happened to us on that day, I think. First and foremost, God was watching over us; God was with us the whole time. Second, the Sabbath protected us. If we had turned on the radio, it would have lowered our morale; it would have broken us. And the third thing is that those degenerates didn't believe that every armed civilian would rise up and go out to fight. There were so many people that did just that. Everyone raced in. The terrorists didn't believe that every civilian with a weapon would come at them; they thought everyone would be afraid.

But the people of Israel are fighters. Everyone came to tear the terrorists apart. And that's the third miracle.

We always come together during tough times, our people. But even now the cracks are starting to show again. And my dream, really, is to keep this sense of unity all the time. I hope that we wake up. We have to realize that we need to stay united even during the good times. Because for now, we remember to come together only when we're down.

She Decided to Become a Fighter

Eden Alon Levy's Story

Age 19

As told by Eden's mother, Inbar

📍 *Zikim Base*

Eden was the smiliest baby. We chose her name after she was born: we saw this light in her eyes. She would just lie there, smiling, laughing, just delighted with every little thing, and we knew – Eden. She was the same when she grew up; we'd always joke about how she'd just crack up in the middle of the night. She had these fits of laughter – everything would make her laugh hysterically, and it was so contagious. We'd be like, "Eden, that's enough! We want to go to sleep!" Ha! No chance.

She was such an easy kid – maybe too easy. There was always this gap: she was so beautiful, so talented, with this special energy, but she was so modest; she never really wanted to stand out. She didn't like the spotlight; she never wanted too much attention; it would embarrass her. Eden danced for years and took voice lessons, and she sang so beautifully, but she would never sing for anyone, just her voice teacher; she would never record anything – that was her way. I remember how she'd sing in the shower sometimes – she'd blast music on full volume, run the water, and sing along in the shower; she sang so beautifully, and I'd stand outside the bathroom, listening.

When it was time for her to join the army, she decided to become a fighter. We didn't put any kind of pressure on her; it was entirely her decision. But she was never really sure of herself; she never said, "Yes, I'm great! I'll go! I'll do it!" Before her enlistment she started tryouts for a pilots training course, and each time that she made it to the next phase, she was so surprised: "I can't believe I passed; I don't understand how they let me through!" She was surprised every time, and she kept passing the next phase, and the next, and the next, and when her enlistment date came, she said, "I'm enlisting; I'm not waiting until I pass all the tryouts. I'll start, and we'll see what happens next." She continued tryouts during her training and passed them all – she was supposed to go to a week of intensive testing to be accepted into the pilots training course right after October 7th.

In the meantime, wherever she served, she always stood out. Her commanders in basic training already marked her for command, and at the end of her squad commanders course she was assigned as a basic training commander, which is considered very prestigious. That's what she wanted to do, and that's what they thought suited her because of her way with people, and because of her professionalism. Soon after she started as a commander in basic training, they wanted her to do an officers training course right away. Everyone who met her realized how amazing she was; she was the only one who didn't see it.

That Shabbat morning, at around seven o'clock, we heard that something was happening down south; Eden wrote in the family WhatsApp group: "They're bombing us." At first we thought she meant rockets, Red Alert sirens. We texted, "Take care of yourself." But then we saw that there was a terrorist infiltration, all that terrible news, and they started to show what was happening on TV. I tried calling her, but she only answered at eight, just for a second, and said, "Mom! They're shooting at me!" and hung up. The call went dead, and at 8:10 she wrote, "I love you."

Eden had been on guard duty at six a.m.; it was her shift. Zikim was a training base, so the soldiers were always on guard with one of the staff because the soldiers were all new; they'd only been in the army for a few weeks. When it all started, Eden sent the new soldier away, and they reinforced all the guard posts with staff members and sent all the new recruits into the shelters. Eden was assigned to the post nearest to the fence, nearest to Gaza.

There were dozens of terrorists that attacked the post with heavy fire; one of their snipers did very serious damage. He hit their company commander, Adir Abudi of blessed memory, and Or Moses of blessed memory, and Noa Ze'evi, who was shot in the head and miraculously survived, and a few other soldiers. A real battle broke out – Eden and a few other commanders against all the terrorists.

They managed – they really managed – to keep fighting for fifty-two minutes there, with very little ammunition and very few people. A heroic battle. The terrorists fired mortars at them, and RPGs and grenades, but the soldiers kept fighting – the soldiers kept shooting at them, and you can see how they kept sending messages, asking for more ammunition and reinforcements, and an hour later one terrorist managed to infiltrate the base; he was killed there on base after he hit one new recruit, Neriya, but except for him, all the soldiers on base survived; there was no massacre there, and no horror stories like you hear and see in other places, and that's all thanks to them. It's thanks to those heroes who fought so fiercely. It's thanks to my daughter Eden.

Eden was killed at the sentry post near the fence together with her commander Adar Ben Simon, and with Omri Fierstein and Yannai Kaminka, who were also staff members. From what we know, reinforcements only arrived at nine o'clock, gradually neutralizing the terrorists and evacuating casualties. But until nine they were there all by themselves. Heroes.

A few minutes before it was all over, before she died, it was important to her to tell us that she loved us. I'm glad that she saw and heard that we loved her too, that we were worried about her. We didn't get it at the time, of course; we kept trying to get ahold of her but couldn't. Around noon, one of her friends called my husband and told him she saw Eden's name on the list of soldiers who were taken to Barzilai Hospital.

My husband went straight to Barzilai and started looking for her, but they couldn't find her there, so we went to other hospitals because we saw that they had sent the wounded to different places, and we kept hoping to find her somewhere, and that she wasn't answering because she couldn't speak, but it was only after many hours at the hospital that we realized she had been there at Barzilai all along – in the morgue.

The funeral was on Sunday; it was a beautiful funeral, as Eden deserved. Her friends wrote lovely things about her; her brothers and sisters, even her younger brother Tamir – you can barely squeeze a "happy birthday" out of him – stood and spoke. We played beautiful songs she loved to sing and loved to listen to, and I thought to myself that at least she had enjoyed life, the way she lived. She had a good life, she lived powerfully, and she died in a heroic way. That's how I felt.

One of the staff who had collected the bodies was at the funeral. He told us that it looked like they were all sleeping; like they were just resting for a moment after such a crazy battle, out of ammunition, facing RPGs and grenades. She was just resting for a while, with a smile on her face.

We ask the same questions as everybody else. Where was everyone; where were the reinforcements; why did she have to fight for two whole hours all by herself? Where were the forces, where were the commanders, why wasn't there enough ammunition? A million questions, but none of it matters; none of it matters because they did their best, and their best was enough; their best was incredible.

When we sat shiva, the Jewish ritual of mourning, the father of the new recruit Eden had been guarding with at the very beginning came. He said that his son couldn't come, so he had sent his father to thank us. To thank Eden, who had saved his life. Later we heard that from many other people as well. We didn't know at first; we only realized later that they had saved around ninety new recruits! And there were all kinds of administration people there, and civilians as well, who had fled from the beach onto the base when the terrorists had landed from the sea, and the battle that Eden and her friends had fought there had prevented the terrorists from breaking into the base and killing them all.

Eden had this dream to get a tattoo of a manta ray, a kind of gliding fish. She loved that fish, I don't know why. At the end of August, we went on a family vacation in Eilat. It's rare to get everyone together like that because they're all grown up, and everyone is in the army and has their own stuff going on, but we managed to get the whole family together for a weekend in Eilat. It was there, at the Underwater Observatory Aquarium in Eilat, that Eden had seen those big manta rays, the fish she loves. She was just entranced by them, and she really wanted to get a tattoo of one, and we kept telling her, "Think it over; you're still young, it's too soon," so she didn't. And she never got one, so now her sisters and her younger brothers and I – we each got a manta ray tattoo in her memory.

We've been talking in our family about how Eden is the third generation of fighters in Gaza. My father fought in Commando Unit 101 in the fifties and was mortally wounded in Gaza. He got hit in the stomach seventy years ago; there's a Black Arrow monument there in the south – that's my father's story. My husband fought in a classified unit, and they were in Gaza, and he risked his life there on a daily basis. And our Eden is the third generation fighting in Gaza. Each one of them hoped they were making it so that the next generation wouldn't have to fight there anymore. I hope that this time was enough. Our Eden, our beautiful, brave shining angel – she, and many others, died so that we might live.

I Have Kids Waiting for Me at That Party

Yosif Zeadna's Story

Age 47

Nova Festival

Usually Yom Kippur, the Day of Atonement, is just for Jews, but in my opinion, from now on, October 7th – that black Sabbath – should be turned into a day like Yom Kippur. A Yom Kippur for all Israelis, not just for Jews! It should be for anyone who lives and breathes in the State of Israel – Arabs, Bedouins, Christians, Druze, or Jews – because we all went through it together; it's everyone's story. And it has to be a hard day, the one that we'll create. Just like you're not allowed to drive or eat on Yom Kippur, they need to make that day exactly the same thing. In my opinion, that's what has to be done. To make a new Yom Kippur in October, a Yom Kippur for all of us, not just for Jews.

Me, my name's Yosif, I'm forty-seven, and I live in a Bedouin town next to Rahat. I'm married with seven children and two grandchildren, a baby girl and a baby boy. But I look far too young to be a grandfather; you'd never guess, ha! Originally, I worked as a maintenance man, but twenty years ago I realized that I love the road, I love to drive, so I was drawn to work in transportation. I started driving all different kinds of people – school kids from communities here in the south, workers that have to get to their jobs in the kibbutzim, that kind of thing.

I'm Arab, Bedouin, Muslim, Israeli. And I'm proud to be Israeli! I really wanted my son to enlist in the IDF, but when he went to get tested, they deferred his enlistment, and deferred it again, and kept deferring it until he was twenty-five years old, and in the end they didn't let him join up. But I wanted it; I pushed him to go. A lot of our family served in the Police. We've got investigators, detectives, workers in the Ministry of Education, doctors, farmers. We're Bedouin Muslims. And we're also Israeli. We're also Israeli.

My oldest daughter is finishing up her nursing studies now, yes she is! I've invested a lot in her studies; I would have invested in my second daughter's studies, too, but I saw that she wasn't as serious, she wasn't really into it, so I said, "It's your decision." I'm not from the old generation, the old-fashioned generation; my girls are liberated and can get a proper education. I got them drivers' licenses too; my wife also drives. But they know the limits; there are certain limits. That's how our *hamula*, our clan, works.

Most of the young people from our *hamula* work in kibbutzim in the Gaza Envelope. If it had happened on a Wednesday, say, and not on Saturday, those Hamas pigs would have gone and killed my family too. But they still managed to kill my cousin, those pigs; they killed my friend; they took some of my family hostage. Of course, I didn't know that when I did what I did that day. Only later I found out what they did to us.

My story of the black Sabbath actually begins the night before. At eleven at night, I got a phone call from a group of young people who know me; they called and said, "Yossi, we want to go out to a party. Can you pop us over to the Nova Festival in Re'im?" I said, "Sure, why not?" So I came; first I picked up some young people from the town of Omer, and after that I picked up some young women from the town of Givot Bar, next to Rahat, and when those girls got in, I saw them and said to myself, Wow,

I don't believe it, I know these girls! I was their bus driver when they were in first grade; terrific girls, and now look at them, they've finished school, they're out of the army, they're going out to a party for fun. Nice.

We got to Nova, and I dropped them off, and I see that there are many, many young people there, thousands; it's a huge party. And suddenly I see my friend next to me, Abed al-Rahman Alnasasrah. He was there with his van – he's also a driver; he also drove a group of kids from the Beersheba area. And Abed says to me, "What do you think, what should we do?" It was already a quarter to one in the morning. We debated whether we needed to stay there, but in the end we said, "Let's drive home now; we'll meet back here at one p.m. tomorrow, and we'll bring these kids back home."

At six-something in the morning, my wife shows me that my phone is going crazy, messages, calls, non-stop, a mess, but I said to her, "Drop it, I'm not at work, it's Saturday, I don't have anything until one in the afternoon." But I see that my phone just won't stop, so I figure I should check it out. I pick up the phone and see the name "Amit Hadar" on the screen. Amit Hadar is the guy from Omer who hired me to drive him and his friends to the party.

I answer, "Yes, Amit?" and he shouts to me, "Yossi, save us!!" I said, "What happened, what happened?" and he says to me, "Sirens, missiles, there are even rumors about terrorists!" I didn't think twice; I got out of bed, pulled on my shorts; my hair was sticking up on end, haha! – and even though I'm the kind of guy that never goes out before having coffee, I gave up my coffee! I didn't even wash my face; I put on my flip-flops – not even shoes – dashed to my van, and I'm driving. I know that when there's no traffic, it's a twenty-five minute drive from my place to them.

I drive through the farming towns, reach Netivot, and I see missiles – the sky is full of missiles – and I'm like, whoa, something weird is going on here; I've never seen so many, and I keep going. I'm the kind of guy who gives it my all; when I start something, I see it through. I got up to Kibbutz Sa'ad, and I turn left at the traffic circle there to Route 232, and when I turn I see a lot of cars coming from the other direction, from Nova, speeding, cutting in front of each other, driving on the shoulder and all that, and everyone is waving their hands and signaling me with their lights like, "Go back, make a U-turn!" I said, "This isn't normal; something's up," and I kept driving; I kept going until I reached Be'eri.

When I got to Be'eri, this young man, Jewish, blocked me – he jumped out of his car with two girls and stood in front of my car, and I open the window and he says to me, "Bro, terrorists!!" and as he speaks I can hear gunshots coming from Be'eri. And they're shooting in our direction, for real, all this loud noise; it was the first time I've ever been scared for my life. I immediately jumped out of my car into a ditch there between the fence and the road, together with those guys. We lay flat on our stomachs, me and the guy and the two girls. And bullets are flying over our heads, coming from all directions, and I lift my head and can feel them flying right over me, and the guy says to me, "Bro, don't pick up your head, they'll kill you!" In the meantime, my group keeps calling me; they're saying, "Come pick us up from here, Yossi, get us out of here! Please, Yossi! Come now!" I'm about to leave, and again the young guy says to me, "Listen, don't stand up! What are you thinking; if you leave here you'll get shot!"

I said to him, "Bro, life is in God's hands; He gave me breath, He's the only one who can take it away. I have kids waiting for me at that party, and I have to get to them, and I'm going to save their lives." I got up out of the ditch, I stood up under fire, and I ran to my minibus and started driving again. Most of my Jewish friends call me "Yosif the Righteous," like Joseph from the Bible, so I said, Well, maybe it's time to do something righteous.

So I drive along the road there and get to where the party was, and I lift my head up – and that's when I see something that, I swear, I'll never forget for the rest of my life. Above the party, I see this paraglider with someone sitting in it, and the paraglider is this lemon yellow color, and he's making figure eights in the air, going back and forth, shooting at everyone from up there.

I said to myself, "Well, looks like this is the last day of my life," and I say out loud, "*La ilaha illa Allah, Muhammad rasul Allah!*" – there is no God but Allah, and Mohammad is his prophet. That's what Muslims say when they realize they're about to die. Because right then I knew – I made the decision – that either I was getting out of there with those kids, or I would die trying.

I get all the way up to the entrance of the party, and the gunfire has really heated up. I hear the bullets flying; I swear, they almost hit the car, and I'm on the phone with Amit, and he says to me, "I'm on my way! I'm coming!" and then I see them, I see my group of kids. And they sprint right into the car and say to me, "Let's go, drive!!" but then I look and see someone in the distance, and it looks like he's been hurt in the leg or something, so I say to them, "Bring him in here; let's fit in as many as we can!" My van is a fourteen-seater, but I packed thirty people inside.

I know the area well; I drive workers from Rahat to Kibbutz Re'im all the time. So I knew that if I would take the road, the terrorists would catch us. The best way to escape was through the fields. I immediately turned left – to my left – and drove through the fields there, and I see kids running, terrified, with no idea where to go, running in every direction, and there were screams, shouts, and I kept driving, I drove and drove and drove, and in my mirror I could see a lot of cars driving behind me, following me, because what happened there was that I basically opened up an escape route.

I left the door of the minivan slightly open in case we had to get out suddenly, and as I drive, I see this girl lying on the ground, and her friend is trying to pick her up, and she's alive but she can't walk; she's wounded in the leg, her right leg; they shot her. You couldn't even fit a pin in that minibus, but I stopped the minibus – there, under fire – and I shouted, "Guys, pick her up! Help her, pick her up!" So we picked her up, took her away under fire, and she started screaming and all that, maybe she thought we were kidnapping her, so we said to her, "There's nothing to worry about! We're getting you out of here! We're already in the van! In the fields! We're going to get out of here, don't you worry!"

❧

After that, as I'm driving, I see this pickup truck totally packed with terrorists, and there's a police patrol car next to the truck, and they're fighting, so we took a white shirt and waved it out the door and shouted to the cops that we're Israeli – we were scared that they'd misidentify us and shoot us. They understood and let us pass. We got out of there. I drove fast; I must have been doing a hundred and twenty kilometers per hour on that dirt road.

From there we drove to Urim Junction, and this cop suddenly stops me, and I shout to him, "I'm an Israeli citizen! I have wounded people here, I have to keep driving!" and he says to me, "The terrorists are already in Ofakim. You can't go through – the road is blocked. The closest place you can go is Kibbutz Tze'elim." I know the area and continue to Tze'elim. I go into the kibbutz, and there was a guard at the security post, so I come up to him and say, "I have two wounded people here, I have to get them to the infirmary, where's the infirmary," and he tells me, and we bring them there, and from there they took them to Soroka Hospital by ambulance, a different way, along a road where there weren't terrorists.

Bravo to Kibbutz Tze'elim. What they did there was amazing – there were like four hundred people in the kibbutz who had escaped from the party. The kibbutz gave us all food to eat and brought us chargers for our phones and offered showers to anyone who wanted, to wash away all the dust. Some people took showers and got mattresses; they even brought us cigarettes, everything. You know what else they did? They brought out a computer and had everyone write down their name and phone number and they posted it on Facebook so that their families would see that they had made it out alive, and that they had reached safety.

Amit Hadar says to me there, he says to me, "Yosif, come here, listen; I don't want you leaving me for a second! We're sticking together; we're attached, you hear? Just like there are screwed-up Arabs, there's bound to be some screwed-up Jew here. If someone hears you speaking Arabic, if someone hears your accent, he might think that you're a terrorist and kill you! Don't you leave my side!" I said to him, "No problem, I get it."

Suddenly this nice girl comes up to me; she's also from the kibbutz, and she says, "I'm looking for the minibus driver, the Bedouin, the one that the whole country's talking about; I bet it's you!" I said to her, "I don't know, it might be me, I guess it's me, I'm the only Bedouin Arab here; everyone else is Jewish." And she says to me, "You know what, come with me to my place here, in the kibbutz; you can sit in my living room, we have a TV, a shower, food, coffee; come stay with me until the Home Front Command comes and releases everyone." And I understood – she didn't want to say that she was scared for me because I was Arab. I said to her, "Listen, I appreciate your intentions, but I'm not leaving my group here. I picked them up from their homes in one piece, and I'm going to bring them back to their parents in one piece."

At three in the afternoon, the Home Front Command came and opened up a route through the Tze'elim army base to the Negev Junction. So I drove my whole group that way. I got back to Omer, I dropped them off, and the truth is that I didn't even notice that Amit took a picture of me. Afterward, he posted it to Facebook and wrote: "Thanks to this person, Yosif, we're alive!" and he added my number underneath. When I finally got home, I turned on the TV and I saw everything that happened, the whole mess, the burning, the children killed, and I said, "Oh my God, something crazy is happening here, and I was in it and made it out alive! How? How did I make it out alive?"

Jewish, non-Jewish, Hamas doesn't care. They killed Muslims too. There was this guy from Tel Sheva who told them that he was Muslim like them, and they said, "No! For us, you're even worse than a Jew!" and they killed him, the pigs. And there was this young Muslim woman who was driving with her head-covering on, and her husband was sitting right next to her, and they saw, they saw her with her head-covering; they saw she was religious, and they still killed her! Poor woman, she left behind seven or eight orphans. The oldest was just seven years old.

My cousin Abdul was on Zikim beach with his wife, and they murdered them too. According to our religion, Islam, in wartime soldiers are only allowed to kill enemy soldiers. Not old people, not children, not women! But they didn't go to war with soldiers; they went out and murdered and raped and killed everything that moved, whether Jewish or Arab or Thai, they didn't care! It's unbelievable, they act like animals. That's not how Muslims behave.

Hamas is still after me. A few days later, I get a phone call; I see the area code is 056, a Palestinian area code. So I answer, and a voice says to me in Arabic, "Are you Yosif Zeadna?" and I say "Yes," and he says, "Do you think that just because you saved thirty Jewish lives, we're not going to get to you?" and I said, "Excuse me, who is this?" and he answers, "I'm from Gaza."

By God, I don't feel comfortable repeating everything I said back to him, not very nice words, but one thing I did say was: "Listen, before anything else, I'm an Israeli citizen! And second, I'm a human being, and they're human beings too, the people I saved. Like any other human beings in this world, it's good that they're alive!" After that, the police blocked that number and told me to report any more conversations like that. To this day, I can't drive wherever I want because I know that there are some places where they could do something to me. There are people that don't like what I did. Bad people.

⁂

A few days after the whole story, I found out that some people from my family were taken hostage as well. A cousin of mine who's also called Yosif Zeadna – he and his daughter Aisha and his two sons Hamza and Bilal. They were all working in Kibbutz Holit, near Gaza. Hamas spoke with them in Arabic; they saw that she was wearing a head-covering; they saw they were Muslim, but they still took them all hostage. That's who they are. They have no God.

Aisha and her brother Bilal were released, but their father and brother are still there in Gaza now. Yosif is fifty-five years old, he has diabetes, he has to take insulin. Hamza is twenty-one, and he's suffered from migraines since childhood; he also takes medication for them. I don't know how they're coping with the conditions there; I don't know how they'll survive. I can't even think about it; my heart's burning on the inside. Burning on the inside.

⁂

And I can't forget my friend, Abed al-Rahman Alnasasrah! I must never forget what happened to him. I was supposed to meet him there that afternoon; we were going to bring our groups back home together. He was a real hero there, Abed; he also came with his van to save kids, but he came on the road, he didn't drive through the fields, and they murdered him, those pigs. They murdered him, and he was a hero, Abed. Write that down in your book. Write down his name so that they'll remember him. Truly, he was a holy man. He must never, ever be forgotten.

There are many Bedouins, many, many Bedouins who did things like that. The problem is that most Israelis only know about Bedouins from the news, but you can't judge a person without seeing them for yourself. When you go to the supermarket or the souk and there are a few bad apples or tomatoes on the top of a pile, you think that they're all bad, that they're all rotten, but no! There are good and bad Bedouins, and there are good and bad Jews; you have to see for yourself. You have to move the rotten potato to see what's going on underneath. Meaning, what the real story is.

For me, personally, there's no difference between an Arab, a Jew, and a Christian – we're all human beings. We're all one people, we live in the same country, and we have no other country. It's ours, for good and bad. Bedouins and Jews, we're brothers. Who's our father? Abraham is our father! And if people would think the way I think and see things the same way I see them, there would be no mess here in our country, none at all. Really, it would be paradise here. That's what I think.

Down to the Last Band-Aid

Amit Man's Story

Age 22

As told by Amit's sister, Mary

◉ *Kibbutz Be'eri*

We weren't surprised about Amit. It was no surprise. Two years ago there was a terror attack at a shopping center in Beersheba; the terrorist ran around with a knife and stabbed people. Amit was first on the scene. When she got there, the police wouldn't let her out of the ambulance; they said, "The terrorist hasn't been caught yet; he's still on the loose; you can't go out and treat the wounded," but she just pushed her way past them and said, "I don't care if the terrorist is still around; someone is bleeding because he stabbed her, and I'm going to help her," and she just ran out to treat her. She had this whole disciplinary hearing afterward. So when we heard about how Amit's life had ended, we weren't surprised. It was her life's mission, after all.

⁂

My name is Mary. I grew up with my four sisters in Netivot; Amit is the youngest. We're fifteen years apart in age, but we were very, very close. We grew up in a very loving home. We were each other's partners in everything. We have a strong bond. That's how we were raised. My sisters are my bedrock, and my mother is the glue that keeps us all together. My father died eight years ago of that terrible disease, cancer. He died after four painful, tortured years.

Amit had a special bond with my father. He was a wonderful father, out of this world, and Amit was his baby, his youngest daughter. They had a special connection. I think Amit was ten years old when my father got sick; she was very young. She watched him dying from a very young age. He was such a big, strong father, and she saw how he withered away before her eyes. We, the older sisters, got married during those years; we moved out, so my father and Amit became even closer because she never left his side. Even when he needed full-time care and couldn't get out of bed, she never left him. She would just sit there next to him, singing to him.

Singing was always her special gift from as early as I can remember her, since she was a baby. She was always singing. At home, in the shower, everywhere. She would sing for anyone who would listen. We have so many videos of Amit sitting next to my father when he was already really ill, singing to him. There's one video of her singing Sarit Hadad's song "I Was in Paradise" to him, and he's shushing everyone else because she's the only one he wanted to hear. She was his comfort.

During that time, during those years when Dad was sick, all these doctors and nurses would come to our house, but Amit never budged from his bed; she saw everything. Even when Mom would say, "Go outside, this isn't for you," she would say, "No, Mom, I want to see what they're doing to him, I want to make sure that he's okay, that he feels okay after the treatment." That's when her passion for medicine began, when she saw all those angels in white – that's what she called them, the angels who would come to our house and help her father live another day, survive for just a little longer. When she saw them from so close up – that's when she decided what she wanted to do in life.

That's how a little girl of twelve started reading about diseases and about medicine. She'd come home from school and draw on the windows in Dad's room with whiteboard markers. She'd draw him the heart and the human body, and all these things she was learning about. She dreamed of studying medicine and becoming a doctor. That was her dream: to become a doctor and save lives.

At twenty years old, Amit became a paramedic, and at the age of twenty-two she was the youngest paramedics course instructor in the whole country; she ran the Magen David Adom paramedics course in the southern district. You can barely grasp what a crazy achievement that is. We only appreciated it during the shiva, how impossible her accomplishment really was. It was only then that we appreciated how much she'd achieved in her short life, that little girl.

We woke up to the sound of sirens at 6:20 on Shabbat morning. We sent messages on our sisters' WhatsApp group, making sure everyone was okay. Amit wrote to us that she was in the safe room at home in Be'eri with Ofir. Ofir is her partner; he's a paramedic in the Magen David Adom station in Netivot. So when the sirens started in the kibbutz, Ofir says to her, "Amit, get ready quickly; we're going to Netivot," and she says to him, "No way, I'm not going to Netivot; I'm the paramedic on call here and I have to stay here." So he says to her, "You're crazy! Look at what's happening, all these sirens, all these booms; we're the closest to the border. Come with me; let's go to Netivot!" But she refuses; she says, "No way. If something happens, I have to be here." He realizes that she's not going to budge; he knows her too well, so he says to her, "Promise me you'll stay here in the safe room!" and she promises, and he closes the safe room door and drives away and miraculously manages to make it to Netivot, to the Magen David Adom station. We heard later that they did amazing things there; they saved a lot of people that Shabbat. And Ofir is calm because Amit promised to stay in the safe room. He had no idea that she left her apartment and ran to the dental clinic to treat people there.

At a quarter to seven Amit writes to us that the kibbutz is on alert for a terrorist infiltration; she was sure that they were talking about one or two terrorists. That's what she wrote. When she heard shooting, she realized there must be wounded people who needed medical attention, so she ran out to the kibbutz dental clinic to receive them and treat them. She met the kibbutz nurse Nirit there, and after an hour or two, they called Dr. Daniel Levy, a doctor who lives on the kibbutz, to come and help. Dr. Daniel is amazing; he didn't think twice, he ran straight there with all the shooting, and the three of them found themselves all alone in the dental clinic with barely any medical supplies, trying to treat patients who were severely wounded. Fighting to save lives.

The whole time, Amit was in touch with Magen David Adom. We heard all the recorded conversations later; you can hear her pleading with them, "Send ambulances! People are dying before my eyes!" She's describing their injuries, and she's describing how she's treating them, and how she's bandaging them up. They answer her, and it's heartbreaking to hear them, how direct they are: "Amit, love, it's all up to you. The security services aren't answering us, and there are no medical aid teams that can get to you. No ambulances, no helicopters. You're on your own; just do whatever you can."

And you can really hear how her tone changes during that conversation, on the recording; how her voice changes from a whole bunch of exclamation marks, "We need this! We need that!" to a different tone, a quiet tone of understanding and acceptance – that this is it, she's alone there, she's not going to get any help or any aid, and whatever happens, happens.

She treated patients there for hours, from the morning on. At some point, people all over the kibbutz start sending her WhatsApp messages, asking her advice: "Amit, they shot my father in the shoulder; what should I do?" and she answers them, "Do this, do that," or "Amit, I'm thinking about running out of my apartment!" and she answers, "No way! Move the closet against the safe room door and secure the door handle." She's like completely exhausted, wiped out, covered in blood, but she keeps on answering them, giving tips, giving advice, insisting on taking care of every single person in the kibbutz.

The hours drag on and on, and Amit watches as some of her patients die before her eyes; they die of severe gunshot wounds. She can't treat them. She tries, but she can't. And we keep sending her messages, begging her to tell us what's happening. At one point we write, "Amit, send us a photo of what's going on, we want to see you!" She sends us a selfie, and we can see the dark circles under her eyes. She has this half-smile, like she's forcing herself to smile for us, for her family, and mainly for Mom. Behind her, you can see this trail of blood, and the corridor is full of wounded people just lying there. Horrifying. Later, we found out that at the same time, she sent another photo of herself to her best friend Lital, and in that photo she's crying, sobbing, and she writes to her, "God, I'm so scared."

All through those hours of hell, two guys from the civilian security squad, Shachar and Eitan, are standing by the clinic door with very limited ammunition, taking out any terrorists that come close. Amit keeps writing us, "Thank God that Shachar and Eitan are here! Thank God that they're keeping guard!" At one point she records a message: "Wait, wait, wait, I hear another terrorist coming closer, that's it, I think this is the end," but a minute later, "Whoa, thank God, Shachar managed to take him out!" As far as she was concerned, Shachar and Eitan were her shield; they were the ones who kept her alive all those hours. She was taking care of the patients, and Shachar and Eitan were keeping her and her patients alive.

My husband Haim spoke to Amit on the phone a few times. Each time he said to her, "Amit, look around; see if you can see any way out. Maybe there's a window there, maybe there's a safe room, or a bush you can hide in," and he kept trying to find ways to save her. We also kept trying to convince her to run away, to hide, to pretend she was dead, anything, but we all understood something simple: Amit won't abandon her patients. She told us that over and over. She won't leave them alone in the clinic, no matter what. And we understand that she'll never run away.

At 1:55 in the afternoon, she sends us this insane voice recording that she somehow managed to make, and in it you can hear shooting and Amit shouting, "Shachar! No! Shachar! God, please make it stop, please make it stop!" and Shachar is yelling at the terrorists, "I'm not your enemy! I'm not your enemy!" but it doesn't help. The terrorists kill him.

What happened is that the ammunition of the civilian security team simply ran out, and the terrorists managed to overcome them. At this point, Amit writes to me, "That's it, they're here, there's a lot of them, they're here, I won't make it out." And the terrorists start throwing loads of grenades into the clinic, then Amit writes to us, "They killed them all, I'm the last one left." Dr. Daniel Levy, and Eitan Hadad, and Shachar Tzemach – they were all murdered. The only one who miraculously managed to survive was the nurse, Nirit. We only found this out later; Amit didn't know that Nirit had made it.

We understand that this is the end. We understand that the terrorists took over the clinic. My mother and I call her, certain that she won't answer, but somehow she does! She picks up the phone. We put her on speakerphone, and my mom screams, "Amit, Amit, what's happening to you, Amit?" And she says, "Mom, they shot me in the leg, they shot me in the leg, I'm not getting out of here, I love you all!" She answered the call just to say goodbye to us.

But we don't get it, we don't get what's happening, and we say to her, "What do you mean, they shot you in the leg? Where are you? Try and hide, lie underneath the bodies, cover yourself in blood!" But she knows that she isn't getting out of there. She says to us, "I'm not going to get out of here alive," then she starts asking my mother to forgive her. I have no idea why. She must have said it three or four times: "Mom, forgive me for everything, Mom, forgive me for everything. I love you, Mom, please forgive me for everything."

They only found her body two days later. The people who found her saw that her bag of medical supplies was empty, down to the last band-aid. There was nothing left in her bag. For hours she just treated and treated people until not even a single band-aid was left.

Later on, we realized that she had managed to make herself a tourniquet on her leg, because there was a tourniquet on her body when they found it. One of the patients Amit had treated managed to hide in a little closet in the kitchenette there, and he saw everything. He saw Amit raising her hands to the terrorists in surrender, trying to approach them, and they shot her in the leg, and afterward, after she had treated her leg with a tourniquet, they came back in and shot her again and again. They didn't leave her a chance.

In retrospect, we know she had two chances to save herself. Two different options, which we only found out about later. The first was to go to Netivot with Ofir, first thing in the morning, which is what any normal person would have done. But she insisted on staying in the kibbutz to treat the wounded. The second was, if you're already staying, then shut yourself up in the safe room. You know there are terrorists, you hear all the sirens and the booms and the insane missiles. According to the rules of Magen David Adom, if a paramedic's life is at risk, they're required to stay in the safe room. But she really decided, against all the rules, against all human instincts, just to run straight into the gunfire, straight into the inferno, straight into the thick of the battle. Why??!! We keep trying to ask ourselves why she made this choice when she knew that it might cost her her life. But I understand that from her perspective, there was no other option. Because if Amit had hidden and shut herself up in the safe room while there were wounded people in the kibbutz, when she was the paramedic on call, who is responsible for tending to the wounded, she never would have forgiven herself. Her whole life, all her love for medicine, for saving people, all those hours she'd spent volunteering for Magen David Adom, all those hours in the library reading medical books – it all came down to this day, to those moments.

She simply understood that there were people who needed her. They needed someone to save them. And from her perspective, if she could save just one or two or three people, then she had done what she had to do in this world. That was Amit.

⚕

Another patient who survived told us something. He was in the civilian defense unit and was severely wounded that day, and his friends took him to the clinic. Amit spent hours treating him there. When he was finally taken to the hospital he was unconscious, and when he woke up three days later, he told everyone there, "I won't breathe until I speak to Amit's family! Get me Amit's family on the phone!"

He called us from the hospital just moments after he regained consciousness, and he said to my mother, "Listen, your daughter saved my life. Without your daughter, I wouldn't be alive. She treated me, and I'm alive thanks to her." He described everything that had happened in great detail. He told us, "Even after all the equipment was used up, even when she had nothing left to treat me with physically, she placed a sheet under my head so I could rest on something soft, and she stroked my head, and she spoke to me calmly; she was my heaven." These are the very words he used: "In the midst of all that hell, Amit was my little piece of heaven, and thanks to her I'm still alive today; thanks to her I'm alive."

Amit was a flower plucked far too soon. She had so many dreams. One of them, the biggest one, was to become a doctor. She also dreamed of becoming famous, a singer, an actress. And she dreamed of becoming a mother, of getting married; God, she had so many dreams. But now, all that's left of all those dreams is her story. And her story is here in the world, and it'll be told for many generations to come. Because somehow, she became a symbol. In this war, with all this insanity, she became a symbol – a symbol of saving lives, of helping others, of goodness, of song, of light. A symbol of love for humankind. That's Amit.

To Die Free

Yotam Haim's Story

Age 28

As told by Yotam's mother, Iris

⊙ Kibbutz Kfar Aza

Yotam was born with an intestinal malformation. From the moment he came into this world, he struggled with releasing waste from his body. During the first year of his life, we had to help him with all kinds of interventions and treatments – difficult, painful treatments, almost daily. He had no way to object, no way to resist. That was how his life begin. The world was violent toward him from the very beginning.

Where I am now, at my stage of life, I make all the connections and can appreciate the meaning of it all, but back then, as a young mother of twenty-eight, I couldn't understand why it was so hard for him to filter the world. I remember him as a four-year-old, worried that the world would explode and that we wouldn't have anywhere to live, and we'd say to him, "Yotami, what are you talking about? Where did you get that idea?" The world was always a difficult place for him; he always said that everyone was bad; the smallest things would throw him off. He didn't understand the world.

He was a very bright, intelligent kid – unusually bright – but he didn't do well with structure. He was very anxious in elementary school; he assumed that kids didn't like him, that anyone who looked at him was about to hit him. So he'd hit them first. He had real issues with violence. The school provided him with an aide. Once they called me to come and pick him up after yet another incident. I couldn't believe I had to deal with it; I couldn't understand how this child, this pure soul, could behave like that.

In seventh grade he moved to a school for special education, Beit Ekstein, in the center of the country. The taxi ride each day was an hour and a half long; on the way home, the driver would buy him schnitzel. It was a school for kids with severe disturbances, and it really set him straight. They developed all his strengths and helped him cope. After a year there, he went back to school here in the Gaza Envelope; this time he fit in well, and did well, and we had a few calm years until he was seventeen, when his eating disorder began.

↣

It started with all kinds of minor medical issues, nothing too serious. We checked it out and did a whole bunch of tests; I'm a nurse, after all, so I could follow the medical aspects, but we didn't find any physical explanations. We then understood that it was something emotional, psychological. At that point, Yotam started working out all the time and lost a lot of weight – it was a very difficult time, a terrible time. Hospitalizations, discharges – if I ever had moments of absolute despair, it was then, during the anorexia years. I was so worried about him; his life was really in danger.

During that time, the one who really lifted him up was a guy called Nir Shohat, an amazing guy with incredible sensitivity toward people who are struggling. He had a sushi place in Sderot, "Sushimoto," and he really saw Yotam. Nir offered him a job and found something for him to do. He taught him how to fold dumplings and gave him a place to be, and he worked there for two years. That's how he ended up in Kfar Aza – he moved to the youth housing there, and he worked at the sushi place in Sderot. He slowly got better, slowly built himself up again.

Yotam had this tendency to go up and up and up and improve and get back to himself but then – boom, crash, he'd go to pieces all at once in a total breakdown. His whole life was like that, riding these waves. This past year he worked in agriculture with my husband Raviv, and he got back together with his band Persephore, a heavy metal band. He was their drummer. Persephore is the male version of Persephone from Greek mythology, the wife of the god of the underworld who kidnapped her from her parents and took her underground.

He had a lot of girlfriends, a lot of girls. Ever since he was killed, every other day someone writes to me and says, "I was his girlfriend." He had this thing with girls; he was always looking for a deep connection, but it never worked out. Sometimes he would fall for girls like him, with all these issues; then he would have to support them, and it was too hard for him. Sometimes he would go out with girls who were more normative, but then they wouldn't really get him. It was hard. Very hard. Every time he had a girlfriend, he was so happy; but then every time it was over, he'd sink into this depression, as if punched in the face.

A few days before he was taken hostage – two or three days actually – he was in such deep emotional distress. He didn't stop talking about death; he kept texting me, "Maybe I should just get it over with already." We had already tried everything by then, tests, medication, treatments, and Yotam didn't believe in any of it. He had already said to me, "Mom, nothing can help me; just stop, no one is going to help me," and I had decided – together with him – that my role was just to focus on the good in him, to see the light in him, to see his strengths, to see the best in him. Instead of being disappointed or giving up on him, I would do just the opposite: I would be proud of him and of his deep strength. That was the agreement we made just a few days before he was kidnapped.

My husband and I had a WhatsApp group with Yotam called "Winning." That was the point of the group: to encourage him, to show him that he was winning. On October 7th, at a quarter to seven in the morning, we started sending him messages on the group. I was in the safe room in our home near Sderot, under heavy fire, and Yotam was also in his safe room in his tiny apartment in Kibbutz Kfar Aza.

Yotam was supposed to play with his band that afternoon in Tel Aviv, but the concert was cancelled when the sirens started that morning, and Yotam was furious. He was furious that the concert was cancelled.

That's what was bothering him at the beginning. But soon after, he started sending more disturbing messages; he wrote, "There's shooting here; I'm getting my sushi knives out," and I joke back, "I have bleach spray here if you need it," and he writes back, "I'll take it." Soon after, he posts a video of him drumming; he uploads it to Instagram story and writes, "Terrorists on the kibbutz, and I'm drumming!" We didn't get it at first.

But his messages gradually got more and more frantic. He sent us a voice message: "They're shooting at my door, they're burning my house down, they're looting my house, I don't know what's happening, I hear people." He texted that he was suffocating, and we wrote back, "Crack open a window!" but he wrote back, "No, if I open the window they'll shoot at me from outside; they're right here between the houses." We were completely shocked! We just didn't get it; we didn't understand what was happening. It was terrifying.

Then, at a quarter to eleven, we lost contact with him. He wrote us that he was scared to go out, that everything had burned down. That was the last message he sent us. At the time, we were trying to find out what was happening; we tried calling hospitals; we sent messages on the Kfar Aza WhatsApp group. I tried reaching the soldiers that were on duty in the kibbutz, to see if they knew anything. And I kept telling myself that he's probably in the safe room, and as long as he's in the safe room it'll be all right because Yotam's strong; he'll last there for as long as he has to. Twenty hours, fifty hours, he'll survive there for as long as necessary.

After a week of searching and stress and terrible fear and anxiety, the army sent us a message that they had tracked down his phone in Gaza. Hedva, the young woman who was accompanying us through the whole process, told us not to get our hopes up; there had already been cases where the phone had been stolen and taken to Gaza but the body was found soon after. That was a time of terrible stress. I was terrified that they would discover his body; I hoped that he had been taken captive. I hoped that he was still alive. Two weeks later, it was indeed confirmed that he had been taken captive. People from the army came and told us; they didn't explain how they knew, they just said, "We know."

At that point we decided that we weren't going to sink into despair; we would rise up and get ahold of ourselves. What, should we just sit and wait? Let's take action; let's start doing things. So my husband pretty much went back to work; we adopted a dog; I started doing interviews; we traveled abroad for PR; we tried to remain active, to get up and take action after our initial shock.

Gradually, the puzzle of where he was and what had happened to him started coming together. At one point, they found the footage of his kidnapping. It was caught on the kibbutz security cameras: the footage showed him walking out on his own feet; it showed how they put him into a car, and he looked okay; he looked healthy and strong. Shirtless. The footage cheered me up – to see that he wasn't injured, to see that he looked strong. Later on, we got more information from a Thai worker who had been released in the hostage deal. He had been with Yotam for fifty days; he told us that Yotam was in good spirits; that Hamas provided him with painkillers; that he was together with Alon Shamriz, and that the two of them maintained good morale, that Yotam was always drumming on his body and singing with Alon. Wow, it was amazing to hear that.

Hamas put out a video soon after that; hardly anyone has seen it, it's a propaganda video of the hostages yelling at Bibi Netanyahu. We haven't seen it yet, but friends who saw it told us that Yotam addresses us in it, saying, "Mom and Dad, don't worry, I'm strong!" and from what I understand he looks very strong in that video, all lit up and powerful. That doesn't surprise me. Because I knew, I always knew, that I have a strong boy. So at the time I had a powerful feeling that he was going to be okay, that he would come out of there alive.

One day during Hanukkah, we got a phone call from Tom, my eldest son Tuval's partner. He's a spiritual type, and he says to me that he received a message. He says, "I had this dream, and in it I saw December 15th." I listen to him and think to myself, What does that have to do with anything? December 15th was that coming Friday, and there was no talk of any deal on the horizon. It sounded totally disconnected from reality to me; it didn't sound serious.

But just a few days later, on December 15th, at six in the evening, just after the Sabbath began, a whole entourage comes to the door: army officers, a policewoman, a social worker, a doctor, and Hedva bringing up the rear, crying bitterly. I understand that something terrible has happened. They come to me and tell me something that just doesn't register: "Yotam was killed by our own forces, together with two other hostages; they mistook them for terrorists." We hear it, and we all lose it. It was terrible; I've never cried like I did just then. I couldn't believe it, I couldn't believe it, I couldn't believe that had happened.

From what I understood, from what they told us, there was a battle between some soldiers from Golani and the hostages' guards; the soldiers happened to find them and thought they were terrorists; they had no idea that there were hostages there. The soldiers killed the guards and left, and Yotam and Alon Shamriz and Samer Talalka went outside to find the soldiers. They wandered through Shuja'iyya for five days – without weapons, without food, without water, without anything! But they somehow got by. Crazy.

That story was… oy, it devastated. Not just me – it devastated the whole country. The disparity between what we'd hoped for and what had happened; that sense of what should have been, what almost happened. It could have been such a happy end. I called Yotam "Moses" because, just like Moses, he almost reached the Promised Land, but at the last moment, he only saw it from the outside, and he died just as they reached the border. So many people came to the shiva crying, weeping, sobbing; they told us that they had heard about Yotam as they were eating dinner, and they told us how their mouths had fallen open in disbelief; the food just dropped right out of their mouths, and they couldn't stop crying. The whole country was broken by that story. Not just us. Everyone was broken.

One day during the shiva, a woman approached me and said, "Iris, I'm the wife of the commander of that battalion, and all his soldiers are completely devastated; none of them are functioning; they just want to die." I said to her, "No, I have to speak to them right now!" She said to me, "But they're in Gaza," so I decided to record a voice message for them. I took the phone and sent them a message, spontaneously – I didn't sit and plan it, or write it out, I just recorded whatever came out of my mouth, and this is what I said to them:

"Hi, this is Iris Haim, Yotam's mother, and I wanted to tell you that we love you, we love you very much, and we're not angry, and we're not judging, and what you did – with all the pain and regret – was probably the right thing to do at that moment. I beg you not to think twice when you see a terrorist; you have to kill him and not be afraid that you'll kill a hostage. And as soon as you can, please come here to us; we want to see you so much, to look you in the eye, and to give you a big hug."

And the soldiers came; they came as soon as they got out of Gaza. They came, these sweet soldiers with bowed heads, and they sat here with us, and we hugged them, and we told them that we weren't angry. We weren't there, we don't know what happened there, and we had heard about all kinds of tricks and ploys that Hamas tried in Gaza – how they would pretend to be hostages and speak in Hebrew, then attack. We weren't angry at them. We just hugged them, and we cried together, and we told them about our wonderful Yotam.

I wasn't angry. For some reason, there was no anger in me. Even when it comes to October 7th, I wasn't angry at the country, and I didn't say things like "They abandoned us" or "We were humiliated." I can't stand that kind of talk. I was disappointed, perhaps. The army shot him; it really was a terrible letdown. But I didn't have any anger. It was a mistake, and I don't get angry about mistakes. I also make mistakes, my children make mistakes, we all make mistakes, so I really wasn't angry. It was very sad for me. It's still very sad for me now because he's gone. But with all the pain and anguish, I'm not angry about what happened to Yotam.

✎

Yotam's is a very special story. He wasn't an ordinary person. His whole life was intense; his emotions were intense; his suffering was intense. His story is the story of a boy who came full circle. He died as he lived; he played with his death his entire life. It might sound like a cliché, but I feel like the fact that his story has become so famous, the fact that I'm now talking openly about Yotam's journey in life and my own – I hope that I'll be able to help other people who are struggling with mental illness and other mothers who are coping with what I had to cope with: a special child, a different child, a challenging child who doesn't fit into any framework, a child who experiences so much suffering in life.

The officer who informed us of Yotam's death told me that day, "I don't know how much you'll be able to process what I'm about to tell you, but your son is a hero, and what happened there – that's heroism!" And it's true, right then I had no idea what he wanted from me, but I feel it now: that there are so many different levels of heroism in this story.

First of all, before this story even started, before he was taken hostage, this was a boy who had to cope with so much every single day from the day he was born! Years of pain, of illness, of addiction, of intrusive thoughts. That was the first reason Yotam was such a hero: he had to cope with so much and overcome so much every day of his life.

After that, I think that the first few hours he passed in the safe room that morning – that's also heroism; the footage of how he was taken hostage, how he went out calmly, back straight, head held high, no shirt on. That's courage. He had such strength at that moment. And all the days he spent in captivity – seventy days! – without breaking, without falling apart, in good spirits. I can imagine him there in those tunnels, in the underworld, Persephore, singing songs, drumming on himself. And this was Yotam, who'd been talking about death his whole life.

Above all, I think about that decision he and Alon and Samer made to go out, to take a chance. They went around Shuja'iyya for five days and used spices they found to write on a sheet, and hung it up – wow! They didn't say, "We'll wait around for someone to save us." No, they decided to go out and fight, and take a chance, and die free.

At Yotam's funeral I called him a "partisan." I called him a partisan because what he did was the essence of partisanism. They went out of the ghetto and took their fate into their own hands. They had no weapons, no nothing, but they didn't just sit quietly and wait. I think that that act of Yotam's, his final act in life, was a message for us, clarifying to all of us, once and for all: "I'm strong, I'm capable! I chose to die a free man, not in prison, not in captivity! I took a chance; I fought for my life. This was the biggest fight of my life, and I won. I won big."

Killed on the Land He Loved

Uriel Avraham's Story

Age 27

As told by Uriel's wife, Hodaya

○ *Kibbutz Re'im*

riel's most distinctive quality was his humility; he was such a humble, modest person. Even at work, when he was often in charge of others, he never gave them the feeling that he was above them – on the contrary, he always kept his gaze down. Whenever he spoke to people, he always gave them the feeling that – I don't know, it's so hard to put it into words; he never raised his voice, he always spoke calmly, he was never angry at anyone; he was the kind of guy who'd walk into the elevator and say "Good morning" with his gaze down; he'd always say "thank you" on the bus or at the supermarket, he had this calm that surrounded him wherever he went.

In the army he was in the Yamas, the undercover tactical unit of the Border Police; he was only twenty-seven years old, and he'd already completed so many courses – a counterterror commanders course, this course, that course, and he finished them all with distinction. And he would always go to the end-of-course ceremonies by himself, he never even told me about them, he would just go and receive his certificate and come back; for some reason he found it kind of embarrassing for anyone to know that he had received all those certificates.

He always showed such respect to his father, to his parents. His father was a community rabbi; he would go to him, bow his head, kiss his hand, like in olden days; he would approach him with so much respect, with admiration; it's every parent's dream to have a son like that. And his parents admired him back; they were so proud of him, like a crown on their heads, even though he was sort of the Ashkenazi of his Ethiopian family – he didn't even like injera bread, ha! – but they were so proud that he was their son. And I was proud too; proud that he was mine, that he was my husband.

We met through his sister, thanks to his sister. I met her at a National Service meeting, I served in the Ministry of Defense's Department of Bereaved Families and Commemoration. I can't believe that now I'm one of those bereaved families, it's so surreal. I know the whole team there, all of them. Anyway, I worked there, and I got to know her, and she wanted to set us up, and that's what happened. I never imagined I'd marry an Ethiopian, but the truth is that I always knew that I wanted to marry someone dark and handsome.

When we first started dating, we met only once every two weeks; he was in the army, so we mostly talked on the phone. He was so shy! He was gentle, gentle, gentle, so quiet and delicate, and I'm such a different kind of person – I'm the opposite! I'm not calm and collected at all, I'm a total drama queen, so he really balanced me out, grounded me with his quiet confidence, with his stability and support. And I helped him open up just a little; I helped him loosen up a bit. We balanced each other out, each of us giving the other just what they needed.

He had these eyes, there was something so angelic in them, soulful, something you don't usually encounter; they were so pure, exuding something you don't see in just anybody. I remember that the first thing I told people about him was, "He has such good eyes, such good eyes," and it's not like I have this deep understanding about eyes, but you just couldn't miss them.

He proposed to me at the lookout point in Arad. He was born in Arad. That's where he proposed to me, in the quiet serenity of the desert. It was all simple and beautiful, and afterward we celebrated with a meal with friends, in their house; it was very moving. From the beginning, I knew that I wanted to marry him, I never had any doubts, I just knew, and I was always saying, "I want him to be the father of my children," I was just sure, absolutely certain.

We were blessed with two children, a girl and a boy. Halleli is three and a half, and Merom Rafael is nine months old now. He barely had any time with our baby, but he and Halleli – they were such a pair of lovebirds. He would pick her up from preschool and take her out for a walk; they'd buy ice cream and go to the woods near our house and sit there and come back, and she'd be covered in ice cream and she'd shout, "Mom! Me and Dad went to the woods, we got ice cream!" And whenever he'd come home she'd run to him like he'd been away for ages, like he was back from abroad! She'd run to him, like, "Daaadyyy!!!" and jump on him. They loved each other so, so much. They'd curl up together and fall asleep, their faces pressed against each other; they were just full of love for each other. You know that expression, "Daddy's little girl"? She was Daddy's little girl alright.

Six-thirty in the morning, sirens in Netivot. Uriel wasn't supposed to be on duty, but he got called up with the rest of his team. They were supposed to pick up gear in Beersheba – rifles, vests – but they didn't realize that it was a war; they didn't understand that yet. On the way, they start receiving messages from the guys in Ofakim – "Listen, they're shooting at us, there are terrorists here," so Uriel said to the friend who was with him, "Forget Beersheba, it'll take too long, let's go straight to Ofakim," so they only had their handguns.

He also called me from the road and said, "Listen, Hodaya, there are terrorists! Don't leave the house!" and I thought: There are probably one or two like the terror attacks in Judea and Samaria; they'll take them out right away – who could possibly have imagined that so many terrorists could come in from Gaza? Insane.

When they reached Ofakim they found themselves in a battlefield: loads and loads of terrorists had attacked in the old neighborhood; some policemen had already been killed, and some civilians; there were some terrorist bodies there as well. It was intense, and they started fighting, he and his friend and everyone who was with them. It became chaotic. There were so many policemen from so many different units, and Uriel took charge; he was like, "Wait, let's stop for a moment to understand what we're up against." And he started taking command – you guys go this way, we'll go that way. He stayed calm and tried to organize all the different forces.

There was a senior officer from Beersheba, really high-ranking, who was involved in the battle. He always loved Uriel; he always told him, "You're the crown jewel." He told me later, "Listen, Hodaya, when I saw that Uriel had come to fight with us in Ofakim, I felt so safe, like there was someone in charge, like a burden was lifted off my shoulders. I'm not ashamed to say it – I've been in the system for years, but when I saw Uriel there, I was so relieved; I just felt different!" That's what he said to me.

About an hour later the hostage situation started in town – it's the famous story about Rachel from Ofakim, whose home was taken over by terrorists, and who managed to appease and delay them by offering them coffee and cookies. The policemen realized that it wasn't about fighting anymore; it was all about negotiations, and then the negotiation team arrived. At the same time, a member of their unit showed up with all the gear – the vests, the rifles – right at the square beside Rachel's house. Right after he arrived, Uriel heard on the radio that there was fighting in Re'im, that there were a whole bunch of terrorists there, so he immediately said, "We're going to Re'im, there are people there who need us! We're going to Re'im!" He didn't hesitate for one moment.

So they drove to Re'im, five policemen in one car, and the whole way – it's a long drive – they see burnt cars and bodies along the road, terrible things, true horrors, and when they reached Re'im they parked far away and made their way on foot because they heard all the shooting and didn't want to be sitting ducks. There were a crazy number of terrorists next to the entrance to the kibbutz. There's this giant grassy area by the gate – by the way, Uriel and I loved that area, that's where all the poppies bloom just before spring. We loved to go and sit there with all the poppies, and Uriel would make us coffee and shakshuka there. That's where he was killed at the end, on the land he loved. It's so crazy.

What happened was that a battle started there, and the policemen split up and started making their way toward the kibbutz gate. There were so many wounded people there, and so many policemen had been hit. Uriel advanced, finding good vantage points, and as he fought, he saw that one of the policemen had been shot in both legs. Uriel told him, "I'm going to the car to get smoke grenades; we're too exposed here," but the wounded guy said to him, "No, don't go," so he stayed there and kept fighting.

At one point, I've been told, Uriel was hit between the shoulder blades. He crawled over to a hiding spot, next to some bush or tree, but even from there he kept shooting. His friend Arik was next to him and told me, "Hodaya, he was bleeding but he kept shooting! He kept shooting! He kept fighting to his very last breath!" After a few minutes like that, he realized that he was dying, so he said to Arik, to the friend who was with him, "Brother, tell my wife and kids and my family that I love them, and that I'll watch over them from above." Then, lying on his stomach, he said the *Shema Yisrael* prayer, and that was it. That was how he returned his pure soul to his Maker.

His friends, the ones who were there, who saw his head drop, started screaming then because Uriel was their light. They tried to get him out of there right away; six guys carried him together and started running with him, dodging bullets, and they brought him to the medic and tried to revive him, but it was no use, too late, he was gone, he was already up above, in heaven, and by the time they got to the first aid station in Urim there was nothing else to do; they just covered him with a sheet. So sad.

❧

Uriel is the name of an angel. According to tradition, Uriel is the name of the angel that walks ahead, in front of a person. I've felt that my entire life, that he was walking just ahead of me, leading me to a better place, and I still feel like that now. That he's with me, that he's walking with me. I recently told my psychologist that every day I fall even more in love with him, and it's hard, it's hard to love by myself, it's hard to love without holding each other, without living together, without him here beside me physically. I know I've been blessed by such a good life with him, we were so happy together. I was finishing up my master's degree, Uriel completed all these courses and was rising up the ranks, we have a daughter and son, thank God, and we have a home. I mean, such miracles, such blessings; what did we do to deserve such a good life?

Recently, I've been thinking about what happens when the Messiah comes, about the resurrection of the dead; I've been imagining him coming back to me. I'm not crazy; I'm just a simple person, and I'm a believer. I believe in redemption; I believe with all my heart. And everyone keeps telling me, "You're still young, everything's going to work out," but I want him, just him! I know that Uriel is in a good place in heaven, but I want him! What can I say? I'm still down here, I'm still the mother of his children down here, and I want the husband that he is, the person that he is, the father that he is. And I miss him so much, all the time. Even when he was still with us, I missed him often because he wasn't home much. But now it's different, and it doesn't end.

The kids help me, they save me. I draw so much strength from them, and they draw strength from me. It's mutual, and it gives me so much strength because I don't have to pretend to be happy with them. With them, I truly am happy. The smile they bring to my face, that stirring in my heart – it's real, not fake. The children are the greatest gift that my Uriel ever gave me. And I'll always have them, for the rest of my life.

The Least Average Person in the World

Guy Simhi's Story

Age 20

As told by Guy's mother, Orit

⊙ *Kibbutz Re'im*

My son Guy was a real hunk; all the girls wanted to be with him. Wherever he was, wherever he went, girls would just fall for him – he was always surrounded by girls! When he would dance at parties – this is what they told me – all eyes were on him: Simhi, Simhi, so good looking, so impressive. He just had this way with girls. He was a manly man, a strong, tough guy; he had an almost animal charisma. He wasn't much of a talker, he wasn't a clown, but he had this power; there was something very, very powerful about him. He was always powerful.

I remember, for example, how in the kibbutz when he was a little boy – when something happened, let's say someone hurt him, he wouldn't cry. No. He'd go home, wait for me, and even then, he'd ask me to go into a quiet room with him alone; only then, only there next to me, would he let himself cry. He had this kind of resilience from a very young age.

In high school he was king of the class. What is it they say? "The girls wanted him, and the boys wanted to be him." By twelfth grade he had a girlfriend, but he deliberately took a different girl to the prom, a friend of his. At the time, we didn't understand why he went with that friend; only after he was killed did we find out why. In ninth grade, there was this kid that was bullied, ostracized, and this friend stood up for him against the bullies. Ever since, her social status was a little shaky. Guy saw what was happening and said to her, "Don't worry, I'll make sure you're part of the group, I promise you – in twelfth grade I'll take you to the prom."

And he kept his promise! He took her to the prom, and they danced, and they were even voted prom king and queen. And that's Guy. That's Guy. On the one hand, he was the strongest, the most popular, the best looking, the toughest, but on the other hand, he also had this sensitivity toward others. And I think that the story of his death, of how he died, is another story that shows both of those sides: his great power and his great sensitivity at the same time.

And I remember that once, when his father Dedi was National Commissioner of Fire and Rescue Services, there were demonstrations outside our house. The Workers' Union would demonstrate here outside our house on Friday mornings. Guy, who was still in school then, would do this thing: he'd cut up a watermelon and go outside with his friends and give out watermelon to the demonstrators. It was summer, it was hot out, and he'd hand out watermelon to each one. People are demonstrating against his father, and he's giving them watermelon! They didn't know what to make of it. Suddenly they'd feel awkward. I'll never forget that.

Guy was always in motion, always happy, always doing things, meeting up with friends. He really lived life to the fullest in this dominant way, very, very dominant. When he sat down to eat, he'd pile his plate high with these crazy amounts of food; he would wolf it down like some animal, down to the last crumb.

He was a winner. Whatever he wanted, he would achieve. At first, he was interested in being an elite commando in Sayeret Matkal; he was set on it. He constantly trained and trained, his father Dedi would coach him for hours, and he would do bench-presses and chin-ups, so many reps; he just wouldn't stop. He passed the tryout for the Flotilla, the Navy commandos, and at the final interview they asked him if he was dead set on joining the Flotilla, and he told them, "No, I want Matkal," so they said to him, "Okay, goodbye." In the end, he didn't join Matkal but rather the Paratroopers commando unit.

We had our inside jokes, me and him. I would always tease him that he was "average," and it would drive him crazy because he wasn't average at all. He was the least average person in the world: he did everything to the max. But I'd tease him: you're average, you're just an average guy! During the shiva, I kept looking for a good photo of the two of us, but I could barely find any; in every photo, either I was sticking out my tongue or he was! We were always making faces; we have no normal pictures. He was such a happy kid.

Guy didn't rest for a moment. Not a moment! He always had something going on. On Friday before the Nova Festival, he went surfing in the morning, then he went to some party in the afternoon; he came back home for dinner, then he and his friends went out to another party! Two in one day. He and his friends from Gedera took two cars. They danced and had a good time all night. I think about that a lot, about what a great time he had on the last day of his life. Thinking about that comforts me.

And that's it; that's how it all began. Guy partied with his friends all night, and they danced together and had a good time, let loose. Then came the missiles. You can see it in the clips: they turned off the music, everyone threw themselves to the ground, and the sirens started there. Red Alert, it was a mess. When the sirens started, Guy took a group of friends with him and led them to Kibbutz Re'im.

Guy was born in Kibbutz Re'im and lived there until he was six, so he knew the whole area. He knew where to drive; he knew all the dirt roads. So instead of driving along the main roads, where everyone encountered the terrorists, he navigated through the fields until he reached the kibbutz. He led the way in his car, and a few cars followed behind him through the agricultural areas. He led them all to the house of a good friend of his from the kibbutz. And they all survived, everyone who followed him. They all survived.

At first they thought it was just missiles, sirens. No big deal, we're used to that. They went into the safe room in his friend's house – they all fit into that safe room – and waited for the sirens to end. But then they suddenly heard shooting outside, gunfire in the kibbutz. So Guy and his friend went outside to see what was going on. They started walking around the area just like that, without any weapons or anything – to investigate the situation, to see what was going on. That's a combat soldier for you. They weren't in uniform, they weren't in active service, they didn't have their weapons with them, but they were fighters, and they wanted to know whether there had been any infiltrations.

A few minutes later they understood; they realized that it wasn't just one or two terrorists; they saw dozens, dozens of terrorists, so they went back to the safe room where all their friends were. There were twelve of them there, and Guy told them to stay in the shelter and lock the door. And after that, Guy went back outside. He left his friend's house in his shorts and Lowa hiking boots with no weapon, with no nothing, to gather people who had run away from the party and were hiding in the mobile shelters. In Kibbutz Re'im, there are loads and loads of public shelters, shelters from missiles, scattered around everywhere because of all the Red Alerts there, and he just drove around and found them and told them, "Hi, I'm Simhi, follow me!" and they were in complete shock. All the kids hiding out there were in a state of shock; they weren't a hundred percent – I mean, they had been at a party that night, drinking and doing things, and they were really hysterical. Guy just found them and brought them out of it. He took responsibility for them.

They told me later, when they came to our shiva week of mourning, "He made us feel so safe that we just followed him! No one even thought twice; everyone just followed him." He led those people out of the public shelters to the safe rooms in the kibbutz. He saved about thirty people that day.

After that, he went back to the house where all his friends were. They were there for a few minutes, then they heard the terrorists coming closer – the terrorists were going from house to house, and they heard them coming. So Guy's childhood friend from the kibbutz brought his weapon, and he got ready for the terrorists. He said to Guy, "Guy, get into the safe room; you don't have a weapon!" Guy said to him, "No way I'm leaving you alone!" and they went out to the living room together and waited for the terrorists.

When the terrorists came, and when they tried to come inside, Guy just jumped on the first terrorist and strangled him with his bare hands, and his friend shot and killed him. Then another one came in, and Guy jumped on him, too, and his friend shot him. They managed to surprise him. But then the terrorists realized that whoever went into that house didn't make it out, so they started throwing grenades into the room. It seems that Guy was injured by the grenades. His friend managed to escape through the bathroom window. Guy also made it out that window, but he was already wounded. The grenades wounded him. And that was it; he was killed there. That was the end.

In the beginning, when the sirens started, we were still in touch with him. I called him to ask what was happening, and he said, "Everything is okay; we're in the safe room," but I know what kind of things he gets up to, so I said, "Okay, show me that you're in the safe room," so he sent me a picture of himself from there. That's the last photo we have of him. Later on, he spoke to Dedi and said to him, "Dad, there are terrorists here," and Dedi said to him, "Get into the safe room, close the door, and wait for the army to come. They'll come and kill them all." And Guy said okay, but we knew that there was no way he'd stay there without fighting.

At one point, a few hours later, Guy stopped answering our calls and messages, and we started to realize that something had happened to him. We tried calling people from the kibbutz to ask them what was going on. I even spoke to the kibbutz clinic, and they said he wasn't there.

We looked for him for hours trying to understand what was going on with him. It was the worst day of my life.

Dedi drove out to look for Guy in the hospitals; he went through them one by one and didn't find him, so he came back home. That evening, Guy's friends came over, the ones who had been with him in that hell, in the safe room with him, and they basically told us that Guy had been killed. At midnight, Dedi put on his uniform, took his gun, and drove to Kibbutz Re'im to bring Guy out of there. At the entrance to Re'im, they told him, "Listen, we're still under fire here; you can't come in," and he said to them, "Either you bring him to me right now, or I'm going in," so they brought Guy to him. He hugged him and kissed him, and stayed with him for about forty minutes until they took Guy away. I know that there are a lot of stories about people who didn't know where their children were, who didn't know if they had been taken hostage or burned to death; that some people didn't find out what happened. At least with Guy we knew what had actually happened.

Thousands of people came to his funeral. Thousands. Route 40 was completely backed up, up to the entrance to Gedera. And his shiva was a crazy week. It was the first week of the war, and the whole country was in shock. It was a really crazy week everywhere

I think a lot about everything he did that day. About his decision to go around the kibbutz without any weapons to save people from the public shelters. About his decision to jump on the terrorists with his bare hands. And I think about how Guy was such a fighter. He had the mind of a fighter. He was very strong, a powerful man. He'd always say, "I'm a bit of a psycho." I know that if he'd had a gun with him, this whole story would have ended differently. But he didn't have his gun with him. He did what he could do. He fought with what he had, using the mind of a fighter.

My son Guy was killed, and I'm trying to get back to myself. I'm trying. I'm trying to focus my energy, to do good, to help others. After Guy's death, I have nothing much to do, so I try to do good. I want Guy to

be remembered, I want them to remember the happy kid who liked to live it up, who insisted on living life to the fullest, on celebrating life and not wasting it. That's how he lived his life from the moment he was born to his final breath.

Ever since Guy was killed, we try to talk about unity. Guy saved people that he didn't even know, he sacrificed his life for his brothers and sisters – the people of Israel. So we talk about unity. Dedi spends hours on it every day. We just realize that this country has hit bottom, and from here what we need is to rise up. Unity is the lowest it's ever been. This low is what led to everything that happened to our army and to our country on the seventh of October.

So we're fighting for that unity among us. We work with the youth movements. We talk on the radio, on TV. We do what we can. We fight every day for a country that will be worthy of all those sacrifices, of all the soldiers and children and civilians and women and babies that were murdered here. So that we'll be worthy of Guy. It's really crazy, what happened to us. It's like the seventh of October was a harvest day, and they picked all the best kids in this country. If we want our country to be worthy of their terrible deaths, we need to talk about unity. If each one of us thinks, speaks, and acts for unity, then we'll be united. And we have to be united.

I Cried Because I Felt We Belonged, Too

Camille Jesalva's Story

Age 31

📍 *Kibbutz Nirim*

I've been working in Israel something like five years now. I'm thirty-one, a single mother from the Philippines – I have a little boy back in the Philippines, and I've been working here with Nitza for four years and a bit, something like that. Before her, I worked with other people, but they were so sick, so very sick, that they died within half a year. Before that, I worked in Dubai. The people there were a little tough, but I also got on with them; they respected me. I love people, I love working with people. I've loved everyone I've worked with, and I love Nitza as well.

Nitza is ninety-five years old, and she's so special. This is a woman who's had a lot of very special things in her life. She's been here in Israel from the beginning, and she was a soldier in Israel's War of Independence. I know, she told me, she was in Golani, in the 13th Battalion. She met her husband in the army, and they were together in Kibbutz Nirim for many, many years. Nitza has lived in Kibbutz Nirim for over seventy years! Her husband died a long time ago. I never knew him, but they have a beautiful, beautiful family – ten grandchildren and thirteen great-grandchildren. Nitza knows how to draw, she knows how to crochet;

when I first came, she taught me how to crochet too! But now Nitza isn't so well anymore, and also she can't hear so well.

Nitza and I, we live together in the same house. We have a big house: two bedrooms, two bathrooms, a living room, and a porch, and we have a big garden. I love Kibbutz Nirim, I love it so much; there are so many lovely trees, it's like paradise. I have everything I need there: we have a swimming pool, a dining room, and we have a grocery store, and we have good people – everyone says hello to everyone on the paths, and everyone I see smiles at me and says, "Hi, Shalom, good afternoon." For me, Nirim is like home; I feel loved and wanted there. It's my home in Israel.

On Friday afternoon, on the sixth of October, there was a big party – the kibbutz's seventy-seventh birthday. It was so nice that I said to Nitza, "It's the most beautiful party I've ever seen." There was dancing, and I got up to dance! It was the first time I ever danced in front of everyone. I don't have TikTok, and I don't make movies, but I danced, and afterward, in the clubhouse, they made this giant collage out of all these little photos of the kibbutz – flowers, people, activities. There was a photo of Nitza there, and there was also a photo of us, of all the women from the Philippines! When I saw that, I started crying. God, I cried because I felt we belonged, too.

And on the way home from the party Nitza and I were talking, and I said to her, "Nitza, it was so fun, it was so much fun," and I felt, I just knew, that when something so happy takes place, something bad is sure to follow. Yes, even back home, in the Philippines, I would say to my family that every time something happy takes place, just count a few hours or a few days, and something bad happens; that's why I'm afraid of being happy.

On the seventh of October, the Red Alert siren began at six-thirty in the morning. And Nitza, whenever there are sirens, goes to the bathroom first, and only then goes to the safe room. So we go into the safe room, and I'm sure it's a normal Red Alert like always, but the sirens go on and on, five minutes, thirty minutes, forty minutes of continuous Red Alert, and I say to her, "No, that's not normal." In the meantime we stay in the room, Nitza and I, and I do my job – she asks me for a lot of things: she's hungry, she wants to drink, to eat, cookies, she's confused, so I run out for her maybe four, five times to bring her things. And then they send out photos and announcements on the Nirim WhatsApp group that there are terrorists in Nirim, inside Nirim, and everyone writes, "Stay inside the safe room, stay inside the safe room," and suddenly the shooting begins. You could hear gunshots all over the kibbutz – I could hear it but Nitza couldn't, because of her poor hearing.

When I first heard the gunshots I thought it was the army, the Israeli army, coming to save us. So I said to her, "Nitza, everything's okay; the army is here." But after a few minutes, I understood. I hear that it's very heavy, the shooting, it's very violent, and I hear the terrorists shouting and screaming in Arabic, so I realized that it was Hamas.

Nitza asks me for the CPAP – it's an oxygen tube that helps her breathe – and I said to her, "Ms. Nitza, I got mixed up, it's not the army outside, it's terrorists, we can't leave the safe room." It took her a while to understand; she's an old woman, ninety-five years old, and she fell asleep, and woke up, and fell back asleep, and in the meanwhile terrorists are going from house to house and killing our neighbors, and Nitza is confused and asks for her CPAP again, and I say to her, "Please, not right now, please, please, not right now," I could hear the shooting already, but she couldn't hear it, and she got upset with me, and in the end I went out because I was afraid that they'd hear her and come.

I went out to the living room and looked for the device, and in the window I see Hamas running next to the house! There's only glass between us, and I saw burnt houses, and I heard shooting, chack-chack-chack, a lot of shooting. I ran back to the safe room and closed the door, and Nitza says to me, "Camille, can you bring me the moisturizing cream, can you put moisturizer on me," and I say to her, "No, Ms. Nitza, we can't go out," and I put the CPAP on her nose, and just then there's a blackout. They hit the electricity, so there was no electricity, and you need electricity for the CPAP, and it's dark. Nitza says to me, "The lights are out; there's no light!"

Nitza's son, Nimrod, writes and calls. It was such a mess, a huge mess, and Nitza said to me, "Put moisturizer on me," and I said, "Please no, not now," and she said to me, "Now, now!" So I went back out to the house, and I looked for moisturizer, and wipes, and a little medicine, and I went back inside and put moisturizer on her, and Nimrod said to me, "Camille, hold the door," so I ran to the door and held it closed. Not that my hand is much; it's nothing. If they wanted to they could easily open it, but I held the door, then I heard them in the house, I heard chack-chack-chack, I heard shooting in the living room, shooting! I heard them come in.

≫⊛

Nitza was sleeping at this point, she had fallen asleep, and her hearing isn't good, and I'm trembling and crying, crying behind the door. With one hand I'm holding the door and with the other hand I'm sending messages to my family, "I'm going to die now; send me a picture of my son Noah, send me a picture of Noah," and I pray to God, "I'm giving You my life, but Noah is still little; please watch over him."

Outside the door there's shooting, shooting, chack-chack, grenades, explosions, and I knew I was going to die, and suddenly Nitza woke up, she just woke up, she heard bombing, bombing, and she started shouting, and I jumped on her and covered her mouth and said to her, "Shhhh, Ms. Nitza, shhhhhh," and she's moving my hand and shouting "What!" She sees me crying and shaking, she sees my tears, and she understands from my expression, she sees on my face that we're in danger, and only then, finally, she understands that something is wrong, and only then she quiets down, only then.

Then they left. The first group. They simply left the house. And it was quiet, so quiet, as quiet as can be. And I'm praying, praying that I won't die, that they won't come back, and Nitza wants to talk to her family, so we call. Her phone is very old; every button makes a noise. It's so noisy, and I'm afraid that they'll come back, and Nitza can't hear anything, so she shouts, and I say to her, "Please, this isn't a good time for a conversation, Nitza," but she won't listen to me, so I take the phone and say to her daughter, "Please don't call, the army isn't here, there's no one here, we need to be quiet because I don't know what they can hear," and I close the phone and put it to the side. And Nitza understands me; this time she understands.

Afterward, another group of terrorists come, and another group, I hear it all through the door, and I hold the handle shut and pray, and kiss the photo of my son. The fourth time they came, they already came into the safe room, yes, Hamas are in the safe room with us. It was about ten-thirty in the morning, and I feel the door moving, and I hear them knocking, boom boom boom, and I know that they'll open it, so I get up and stand straight, and I don't know why, but I'm suddenly very calm, and I raise my hands and say to the man there at the door, "Hello sir."

Nitza hears him and wakes up again, and my hands are shaking – they shook like this. I look at the man, who has a big rifle in his hands, and I don't look at anything else but just look him in the eye. I know from Dubai that you have to look Arabs in the eye, and Nitza asks me right in front of him, "Camille, why didn't you close the door," and she asks him, the Hamas guy, she asks, "Why are you here, just leave us in peace, why are you here?" and to me she says, "Camille, why don't you close the door," and she says it sharply, and I see from the terrorist's face that he's angry.

And I thought, *Almighty God, Almighty God.* I was afraid that he was going to kill us, I was crying the whole time, and I said, "Please, Nitza, be quiet, please Nitza," and Nitza heard how my voice trembled. Only then was she quiet, and I looked at the man, and I said, "Please, mister, she's old, very old; please, mister, she doesn't understand; please, she's old." I knew some Arabic, but I thought it was better not to mix languages, so I said to him in English, "Please, sir, she's old; she doesn't understand anything. Please, sir, you can take anything, but not our lives, here – money, money, take it."

I took out my purse and I showed him all my money, and the man says to me, "Money money," so I give it all to him, my purse, and my phone, and I gesture to him to take everything, to take everything, "Please," and the man asks if there's anything more, so I go to my room and I give him all the money I have in the drawer, and I give him everything except for my passport and my ticket. I had a flight home on the ninth of October, just two days later, and the man saw the passport, and I said to him, "This is not – this I need to go home." And I wanted to go home so badly, home to see my son. And the man took everything, all the money, and he went to the other part of the room and looked around a little, touched things, and in the end he left the house, and I said to him as he went, I said to him, "Everything's okay sir, I'm closing the door now; thank you, thank you very much sir." Then I closed the door.

After he left, I started to cry. I cried so hard, I jumped right into Nitza's bed and hugged her so hard, and I felt that she was caring for me, like a baby, and for two hours I was there with her, hugging, and I'm shaking, shaking nonstop, and I looked at her, and I saw her face, and suddenly she seemed so beautiful to me, really, so sweet, she looked like an angel, and I said to her, "You're so beautiful! I love you!" Nitza cried too; she stroked me and held my hand so that I would stop trembling. And that's how we stayed for two and a half hours. Hugging. Nitza calmed me down; she made me feel safe.

Then, two and a half hours later, around two in the afternoon, after we had been alone for seven and a half hours, the army came. Suddenly I heard shouting, "Is anyone here? Is there anyone?" It was so frightening, the adrenaline made me jump. "I'm here, we're here!" and then they came, a woman, a woman from the army and a man, they saw us, and they were just in shock. That we were alive. They helped Nitza up because she can't walk, and they took us outside between the houses. Around us I see open cars, burning, on fire, and burnt houses, and a burst pipe, and I see soldiers hiding, I didn't understand why the army was hiding between the houses, then I heard bullets; there were bullets around us. They saved us, but they were still fighting there, the army and Hamas. The whole way there were bullets around us, and we fell a few times on the way, we fell in the mud, and there was shooting around us when we fell. I saw that Nitza was afraid, I could see it on her face, sweet Nitza, and I was so afraid for her, but we made it; the soldiers took us out of there, and we were saved.

Then after that they brought us to the clubhouse, and we were there all night. There were a lot of people there, a lot of old people, and that night Nitza was so kind; she helped me, she didn't raise her voice, she didn't get upset, she understood how lucky we were to be alive. And I also saw the big collage there from the party, the collage with all the people.

The next morning, they took us in army cars, and they brought us out, and I was afraid the whole way, I didn't know if they were kidnapping us, I didn't know what was happening, and only after we had gotten far away, I looked out of the window and saw the hills of Jerusalem. Only then I felt that I was safe, that I was okay, and that I would live.

They brought us to Yad HaShmona, a quiet place, very biblical. The people there are so religious; they talk about Jesus and study Bible, and again I felt like I was in paradise. Since I came here I cry all the time, and I say thank you to God for how He took me out from the valley of the shadow of death, from the darkest corner of the safe room, from a place of shooting and fire and Hamas – He took us out and brought us here to a little piece of heaven. It's the best place for us. We have a new life here.

That same day that we came to Yad HaShmona, Nitza's son Eshel called me. He's so nice, they're all especially nice, and he said to me, "Camille, how are you, what are your plans?" and I asked, "What plans?" and he said, "I know that you have a ticket; we'll take you to the airport, we'll find someone else to work with Nitza, I can take you to the airport right now."

And I said to him, "No, Eshel, I already cancelled my flight," and Eshel said, "What, why, Camille, no way, you don't have to cancel," and I said to him, "No way, how can I leave Nitza, how will she get by; if I leave her she might die." That's what happened every time I went home to the Philippines for a visit. Nitza would get sick, and the doctors don't understand her if I'm not there with her. She needs me. And Eshel said to me, "But what about your son and your family?" and I said to him, "I'll be okay, I'm staying with Nitza; don't worry."

She's my baby, Nitza, and I won't leave her, especially not now, when it's such a frightening time, when the whole family is frightened and the whole country is frightened, I won't leave her. I also promised her – not because of the war, even before the war, I promised Nitza, I said to her, "I won't leave you until your very last breath."

Like a Good Anarchist

Aner Shapira's Story

Age 22

As told by Aner's mother, Shira

◉ *Nova Festival*

When Aner was in elementary school, he suddenly decided to grow out his sidelocks, his *payot*. He let them grow long, way below his ears. He was the only one in his class with *payot*. Everyone made fun of him, of those *payot* of his. So I said to him, "Aner, are you sure that this is right for you? You know, everyone's making fun of them and all that; you really don't have to keep them." And he said to me, "What are you talking about, Mom! So what if they're making fun of me, let them laugh!" And now, when I look through the photo albums, I see him smiling there, a ten-year-old boy with over-the-top blonde *payot*, a kid who's saying to the whole world, including his parents, "There's nothing you can do. I'm my own boss."

That's how he was. He was his own boss, his own commander, his whole life. More than anything else, he couldn't stand injustice – he really couldn't stand it. If he saw a wrong taking place in front of him, he was simply incapable of keeping quiet. As early as elementary school, if someone would taunt someone else by calling them a "homo" or something like that, he'd pounce on them: "That isn't an insult; don't talk like that!" And if, let's say, kids would bully someone in his class, he would go up to them and say, "Whoever messes with him is also going to have to mess with me." That kind of thing happened all the time.

When he was in high school, for example, they'd go out on Thursday nights to hang out in the Mahane Yehuda market, and a lot of times he'd see the police cracking down on Ethiopians, or Sudanese, or foreign workers. Whenever that happened, he'd go up to the policeman and ask, "How come you're picking on those guys?" – he'd say it straight out – "But why specifically him? Is it because he's black? What did he do to you?" He didn't care that they were policemen; he didn't care that it might get him into trouble. That didn't matter to him. He was a real warrior for justice. Justice and equality, that was what occupied him his whole life. Whenever he encountered discrimination, racism, or homophobia, or any kind of injustice or injury to the weak, he would fight it.

He had a unique worldview. Anarchistic, even. Not a "let's tear it all down" kind of anarchy, but a philosophical, political, measured anarchy. The anarchism of someone trying to understand the world. He studied the topic; he read books about it, had long conversations about it with his grandfather. Aner believed that the human heart is innately good, and the natural inclination of a person living within society is to do good. If the foundation is good, if the stuff that people are made of is good, then there's no need to impose frameworks on them, like the police or the army or prison, or any kind of system that places limits on them. These systems are meant to protect society from evil, but what actually happens is that they often create evil instead. If we want the good to flourish, then it must not be disturbed; it must be given full freedom. That was his creed. That was what he believed in.

⤢

To be honest, I was sure that when he would be drafted to the army, it would bring out his rebellious side. I was sure that he would argue with his commanders, that he wouldn't understand the system, that he'd rebel. Like, what was the chance that a free-spirited, nonconformist kid was going to fit into a place that is all rules and hierarchy? But the fact is that he did fit in – he really fit in. In the end he was an outstanding soldier.

At every stage of his service, whenever someone could be awarded an "Outstanding Soldier" commendation, it was him.

At the end of basic training, he won "Outstanding Soldier," and they pulled him out; out of five hundred soldiers, they just pulled him out to join a commando unit. At the end of the commando training, he won "Outstanding Soldier" and was sent to the squad leaders course, and at the end of the course, he won "Outstanding Soldier" yet again. And all his soldiers, commanders, and friends said the same thing about him: as a soldier, he was simply in a league of his own, a cut above the rest. He was the strongest, the quickest, the most athletic, the most diligent, the most professional; he was always the best. He did every exercise wearing a ceramic vest even though you didn't have to wear a ceramic vest in training. But he would insist on it. He said that if war broke out, everyone would go out to battle wearing a ceramic vest, so you need to train with it to prepare properly for war.

Before his enlistment, he worked very hard so that he'd be able to give it his best, so that he would go as far as he possibly could. During his tryout for Sayeret Matkal, one of the most elite commando units in the IDF, he injured his knee. But he didn't give up; he worked hard at rehabilitation, waited a few months, went back to the same tryout – and dislocated his shoulder. Each injury lowered his physical profile, which limits combat options, but he was stubborn and rehabbed and worked out like crazy to get his profile back up.

But he wasn't a gung-ho militant type. That wasn't the story. He was a complex person. On the one hand, he had a worldview that was anarchistic, nonconformist, opposed to armies or any kind of hierarchy. But on the other hand, he understood that as long as people's lives depended on the army, he would give it his all and devote himself fully to the military system. That was Aner. Somehow, within his personality, all this complexity worked out.

Aner had two great loves in life. The first was his partner for the last three years of his life, Shelly. The moment they met, they fell in love, and from that moment on, their hearts beat to the same rhythm. They did everything together; they planned their future together; they had this fearless sort of love. A love larger than life. Shelly was Aner's first love.

And Aner's second love was music. Aner played the piano from the age of seven to the day he died. People who knew him would say to me, "How can it be that this guy, this athlete with muscles from here to America, sits down to play classical music with such sensitivity?"

In high school he started writing poems, too – brash, complex, authentic, sharp poetry, without any prettying up. Pure truth and justice. And at some point, he started putting the poems to music. He went from electronica to hip-hop, and from hip-hop to rap. He chose that genre for its defiance, its clear-headedness; music that takes a stand.

And all his siblings got into his love of music. Whenever he was working on something, he would call his third sister, and say, "Ayala, come for a second, come listen to something," and they'd sit down and close the door with their music – she played the piano. She was the first one he'd play his stuff for, and he'd ask her advice. And when his sister Tamara celebrated her bat mitzva, he wrote a song with her. She wrote the lyrics, and he put them to music, and together they created a song. Last year, when his little sister Hila was in second grade, she wrote this poem, just a few lines, and she put it to music too. He heard her singing it to herself at home, and right away he asked her, "Do you want me to record you?" They went into his bedroom, which, over the years, had become a sort of studio that he built for himself, and they just started recording! She sang, and he sang harmony and accompanied her. Soon, on his birthday, we're going to put out an album in his memory. That song of theirs will be on it.

Aner was the oldest of seven. He was their big brother, but I felt that he helped me raise them. I mean, I really felt that he played a big part in how they grew up. I would ask his advice about everything. Of course I also discussed everything with my husband, Moshe, but I really, really like analyzing things at length, talking and thinking things out, and Moshe wasn't always available for that, so I would talk things over with Aner a lot. And Moshe would hear us and say, "Whoa, guys, give it a rest!"

Aner rarely got out of the army for holidays, but this year he got out for both Yom Kippur and Simchat Torah. On Yom Kippur Eve he came over to eat the meal before the fast with us, and then he drove to the forest to retreat and meditate for the rest of the fast. He was alone in the forest for all of Yom Kippur, then came back after it ended. When he came back, he told me that on Simchat Torah he wouldn't be with us because he was going to something big down south, to some festival. We always talked about everything. I knew that at the time, he wasn't observing the Sabbath. I knew when he did observe the Sabbath, and I knew when he didn't observe the Sabbath. We would talk about everything.

His religious world was very complex. He was on a journey. Since high school, he had been clarifying this point for himself; he never came at it from a place of being anti-religious. He was just a person looking for some sort of truth. He was never fake; if something felt off for him, he just wouldn't do it. He never cut corners; he had integrity. But if he decided he was in, then he was in all the way, three prayers a day, a big skullcap, *payot*, and a beard. Above all, he was loyal to his truth; he was a man of truth.

So before that Sabbath of Simchat Torah, he told me that he wouldn't be home, and of course I was sorry to hear that because he was barely ever home. But I said to myself, "Okay, in a month he'll be finishing his army service. Wait a little longer, and he'll be home as much as you like." But then it became clear that his siblings would be home together for the holiday, so Aner said that if that's the case, then he'd stay for the holiday dinner that evening, and he'd only go to the festival after that. That was an amazing meal. Amazing. So much fun. We were all together, happy, an incredible atmosphere. I'll never forget that meal. And that was it; after the meal he left. He left his rifle at home. It was supposed to be a party out there. That's what it was supposed to be.

☙

At 6:20 in the morning, when all the shelling at the party began, Aner's platoon commander calls him and tells him that he has to go back to the base, and that he should urgently call up all his soldiers. Aner said, "No problem; I'm nearby, be there soon," and he phoned some soldiers he needed to call up, then he left the party to get to the base.

He and his friend Hersh and two girls hitched a ride together. But at the exit from the party, the deadly traffic jam had already started on the Road of Death, where everyone was massacred. So all the cars that were there made U-turns and drove in the opposite direction. But at that point, either because of the missile interceptions or because the terrorists were already shooting along the road, they stopped their car and went inside a small public bomb shelter at the side of the road.

The four of them went into the shelter at Re'im Junction, but they saw that it was already packed with twenty, twenty-five people. They were the last ones who got to the shelter. It's a tiny space, unbelievably small, about the size of a bus stop. It was really, really packed. And there were so many people there, all of them tense and sweating and stressed and panicked, and none of them knew what was going on. They were all in total shock.

The incident at the shelter – there are whole videos of what happened there because some of the people filmed it. We have a clip from the beginning of the incident, and you can really see Aner, you can see it through his eyes, and you can see how he goes in there and starts processing the information right away. I can see that he's standing there, sort of taking it all in, surveying the area, looking around, getting a grasp of what's happening. And then he basically takes command; he takes charge of the situation.

What he says to them there – this is what came out later from people who were there – is that a few seconds after he enters the shelter, he says to everyone, "Hi, I'm Aner Shapira, a soldier in the Nahal commando unit. Don't worry; everything is going to be all right. I've spoken to the army, and they're nearby – everything's going to be all right!" And one of the girls there at the back of the shelter says, "Wow, Aner, I'm so glad you came. You're making us feel so much calmer." That's how it went on for a few minutes: every time there's a boom and everyone crouches down, Aner calms them all down. That goes on for some time. Then they started hearing shooting outside. Terrorist gunfire.

Aner hears the shooting getting closer and closer, and he realizes that the terrorists want to overrun the shelter, so he picks up a beer bottle and breaks off the bottom and holds it by the neck. The shelter has this narrow passageway at the entrance, with the main shelter space behind it. Everyone else is hiding inside, crouching over each other in that space, and Aner goes to the front and positions himself by the entrance in that narrow opening. He stands there in the corner, just behind the opening, with the broken bottle in his hand, and he explains to everyone inside that he's going to attack any terrorist who tries to get in. He reassures them that as long as the terrorists can't get past the narrow passageway, they won't be able to hurt them, and he says to them, "If I don't succeed, if I get hit, then someone else has to try to do the same thing."

But then, instead of trying to break in, the terrorists start throwing grenades into the shelter. And Aner is by the entrance. So they throw a grenade, and he catches it before it explodes, and he throws the live grenade back outside. Then one of the kids who was hiding in the shelter panics and runs outside, and they shoot him to death. You can see it in the clip that's going around. The terrorists get closer to the shelter, and they stick their guns inside and start shooting, but they can't get in. They're clearly afraid of who's inside. Then they throw in a second grenade, and Aner throws that back outside too.

A few minutes pass, and the terrorists throw a third grenade inside. They go right up to the shelter entrance and throw the grenade inside. Aner again throws it back outside. Each time the terrorists run to the side because they don't want to get hit by their own grenade. After that they come back and throw a grenade for the fourth time, and Aner throws this one back at them, too.

They're not getting anywhere, and it's driving them crazy, so they shoot inside the shelter again. Another terrorist throws in a grenade, this is already the fifth, and Aner catches that too and throws it back outside. Again, grenade number six, and again Aner throws that back. But they don't give up. They shoot into the shelter again and at the same time throw a seventh grenade, but Aner throws that one back outside as well, and that grenade explodes right next to the terrorists. Seven grenades. Aner deflected seven grenades! So the eighth grenade that they throw, they throw right at Aner, and they make sure to throw it just a second before it explodes. And that's it; that's how Aner gets killed.

After the eighth grenade explodes, the shelter fills with smoke, and the terrorists go inside because there's no one to resist them any-more. They go inside and pull four people out, then they go back inside and shoot everyone. They take those first four captives to Gaza. By this point, Aner's friend Hersh Goldberg-Polin had already lost his hand; the grenade blew his hand off. They kidnapped Hersh like that, with his hand blown off, and they filmed the whole thing – those monsters – and posted it with no censoring and with no shame.

But because Aner delayed them and tired them out, the terror-ists ran away without confirming all the kills. They went in, sprayed bullets, and left; because of that, besides the four taken captive to Gaza, another eight people survived in that shelter. They were there for five or six hours, hiding under the bodies of those who were murdered until the army came to rescue them. When they finally came to rescue them, at two-thirty in the afternoon, the first thing they said was: "There's this guy, Aner Shapira, who took charge here; it's thanks to him that we're still alive."

Aner was a warrior for justice, a freedom fighter, a man of truth. Even in his final battle, no one told him what to do. He wasn't in uniform; he didn't have a weapon. Like a good anarchist, he was his own commander.

Not long ago, I was thinking about how he didn't even know most of the people in that shelter. But that didn't matter to him – ever since I can remember him, Aner was always deeply sensitive and responsible to others, to all people.

If Aner were to hear everything being said about him now, he'd go nuts. I'm one hundred percent sure that if he were to hear how moved everyone is by this story of his, it would make him crazy. From his point of view, he just did what needed to be done, that's all. He didn't think that his life was worth any more than anyone else's. He wouldn't have let anyone call him a "hero." Not any kind of hero. Ever since he was a little kid, he had this deep inner commitment to truth and to taking responsibility for others. And he was faithful to it until his very last moment. That's Aner.

I'm Going to Save My Boys

Eyal Aharon's Story

Age 53

📍 *Kibbutz Re'im*

When I was young, my father saw that when it came to religion, I wasn't exactly following in his footsteps. He was a *hazan,* a cantor, my father. He spent all day in the synagogue, but I wasn't into it, and my father said to me: "Listen. I have no problem with your decisions. In the end, it's all between you and God. But I have one request to make of you: love your neighbor as yourself. Be yourself, and love people. That's what I want from you."

When I joined the police force, he told me the same thing. He said: "Listen, your decisions affect people's lives. You can change someone's life completely – for better or worse – and I ask that you judge everyone favorably. Be a *mensch.*" When I was twenty-five years old, he died on me. Far too soon. It shattered my world. But ever since, I feel him with me wherever I go. On October 7th, too, when there were so many miracles, so many things that didn't make sense – people who looked on from the side said that it just didn't make sense, they asked me if I was wearing some kind of magic cloak, some kind of invisible shield – I'm sure that it was him there with me. My father was the magic cloak I wore at the battle at Re'im.

⮞

On Shabbat morning I was at home in Kibbutz Beit Kama. An enjoyable Shabbat, good weather, everything's good. My sons had gone to a nature festival a stone's throw from the border. I have two boys: Shaked is twenty-three, Geva is twenty, and they're both known for being party animals. This party was well-organized, with all the proper permits from the police and the state, as it should have been. Until, in a second and a half, it turned into hell.

At seven in the morning, Geva calls my wife: "Mom, they stopped the party. The army called me up; pack me a bag for a week. I'm with Shaked; we're on the way to Kibbutz Re'im." This is what happened: they left the party, and when they reached the road, they could turn right or left. Whoever turned left to Be'eri died – almost all of them were killed – but my boys turned right. There's a small bomb shelter by the entrance of Re'im, and they debated whether to go inside or not, and in the end they decided to move on. Everyone who hid inside the shelter was killed. But they drove on into the kibbutz, where there was this one guy, Simhi, a hero, a real hero! He was walking around there saving people – even though he didn't have a weapon – and Simhi said to them, "Come quick! There are terrorists!" and he ran with them to some safe room there. Later, I heard that he himself was killed.

As soon as she hung up, I got into uniform and drove off in the squad car, speeding like crazy. On the way, my son calls me, whispering: "Dad, there are terrorists in the kibbutz. Call the police; we ran into one of the houses, come save us!" I don't wish a phone call like that on anyone; it was one of the most terrifying calls I ever got in my life. I hear him, step on the gas, and say, "Geva, don't call any more – from now on, just message me. Not one call; I don't want them to hear your voice. Hide." That's what I said to him on the phone, then the messages started coming.

The first message was, "They shot Shaked in the leg. Don't come." He told me not to come so that I wouldn't put myself in danger. What happened was that my sons went into one of the houses with something like sixteen other people from the party. Geva and another soldier from an elite unit, Maglan, found a kitchen knife and a beer bottle and thought that they'd manage to fight off the terrorist. But then they realized that it wasn't just one terrorist – there were dozens and dozens of them. So they went into the safe room, with everyone, and just seconds after they shut the door behind them, the terrorists start shooting in the house and throwing grenades. They're in a safe room, sixteen kids from the party, including Shaked and Geva, and Geva and another guy take hold of the door handle and hold it shut. So when the terrorist gets to the door, he tries to open it, but Geva's a strong guy, and he holds it so tight that the terrorist can't even move it – if he would have been able to move it, the terrorist would have realized that there was someone inside.

And then, out of frustration that he can't open it, the terrorist just sticks the barrel of his gun right up to the door and shoots two Kalashnikov bullets – they're armor-piercing bullets – and they go through the door and hit Shaked, my older son, in the leg. But Shaked doesn't cry out; he doesn't make a sound – he understood that he had to be quiet even though he was hit by two bullets, even though it feels like his leg is exploding, he realizes that he can't make the slightest sound or the terrorists will know they're there.

The terrorists were sure there was some kind of problem with the door, that something's caught, and they begin to go through the house. Meanwhile, Geva takes Shaked's belt and makes him a tourniquet. And the terrorists come to the door from time to time and keep trying to open it, but they don't succeed.

Me, from my perspective at this stage, I have no idea how big the thing was; I thought that there were three or four terrorists in the kibbutz, and that was it. I didn't understand what was going on. On the way, I figured it made sense to drop off Geva's bag at his base in Urim to make room for more people in the car, but when I got to the base there was no one at the security gate. Looking back, I had a miracle there, because when I was there – you can see it on the security cameras – when I was there, the terrorists were already inside the base murdering everyone who crossed their path. There was a massacre in the base while I stood there for a few minutes, waiting at the gate. I had no idea, and when I saw that no one was coming I turned around and left.

From there I drove to the police station in Ofakim. I had my revolver, but I wanted to get a rifle, and I figured that I'd ask another cop to come deal with the terrorists with me, no big deal. On the way, I see all these cars standing at the side of the road, but from my perspective they were just parked on the shoulder; I didn't see any terrorists or bodies or anything. So I go into Ofakim Station and see blood at the entrance. I see a cop with a head wound and ask him, "What happened?" and he says to me: "What's the matter with you? Don't you listen to the news? There are terrorists here in Ofakim, battles in Ofakim, in Urim, in Be'eri, and in Sderot." Suddenly, the enormity of it hits me. We'd done police training for scenarios like that – terrorists infiltrating towns or taking over intersections to block reinforcements. At that moment, the sky seemed to turn black.

I said to the cops there, "Guys, I have children in Kibbutz Re'im; I'm going to go save them. Any chance someone'll come with me?" and they said to me, "Sure, but let's first see what's happening here in Ofakim." So I said to someone there, "Fine, so give me a rifle," and he says to me, "Sure, you can have a rifle, but there are no bullets; there are no bullets or cartridges left; the policemen who are fighting in Ofakim took everything we have. If you want, wait a little; the guy in charge of the equipment's coming soon." I said to him, "There's no time to wait."

Now I – the other cops think that I'm a little obsessive because I always keep a helmet and spare cartridges in my car. I'm prepared. They always said to me, "Why do you carry all that stuff around?" – well, here you go. As I left Ofakim, I saw a police car on the way, Deputy Superintendent Davidov, the Rahat Station commander, a good friend, and he asked me, "What are you doing here?" I said to him, "I'm going to save my boys; they're in Kibbutz Re'im," and I saw from the look in his eyes that he couldn't come with me. He has lots of trouble here, terrorists everywhere, so I said to him, "Go to your men. Good luck!" And I understood that that was it, I was on my own with this; no one else is going to help me. So I set out alone for Kibbutz Re'im.

⤙

On the way, I see – it was terrible – I'm driving on the same route that I was on before, with all the cars at the side of the road, only this time I see them all from the front, and I see all the bodies, the blood, and I start to drive slowly, with a bullet in the barrel waiting for a terrorist to surprise me. It was like some horror movie, a totally apocalyptic sight. Some of the bodies were people who tried to run away, and some were burnt, and I'm driving between the corpses, and in the meantime the kids are corresponding with me, sending me pictures of Shaked's wound, asking me when I'm coming.

At about nine in the morning I get to Re'im, to the back entrance to the kibbutz, and at the intersection I see a cop motioning me to stay back, and the moment I see him, I realize that there are terrorists shooting at me from every direction, even before I braked, so I park the car on the side and open the door and start shooting back at their direction, without seeing them at all. And then they fire two RPGs at me, that's a kind of anti-tank missile, and one missile hits just five meters away from me and explodes, and the other one hits about seven meters away, and I realize that if they shoot a third one then I'm a goner, so I lock the patrol car and sprint toward the kibbutz. And they shoot at me. Bullets go between my legs, over my head, I hear them whistle next to my ears, dirt flies up from the impact, but I just run. And as I run, I curse every cookie I've eaten lately– I mean, I'm fifty-three, not young, and not exactly thin, and I have to move forward as quickly as possible.

At the entrance to the kibbutz, I meet another four cops, and one of them says to me, "Do you have a cartridge to spare? I'm out of bullets," and I say to him, "Here, take a cartridge." I knew I was on my way to my boys, but I couldn't say no to him. They had just evacuated a wounded cop, and they said to me, "Come, wait outside," but I ran into the kibbutz. They didn't understand why; they thought I'd gone nuts, but a few of the policemen came with me, they joined me. By the way, one of the cops that joined us – his whole backside was covered in blood, and I said to him, "You're hurt! You're dripping with blood!" but he said to me, "Yeah, I was hit by a grenade in Ofakim, but my legs can move, my eyes can see, and my finger can pull the trigger, so we keep going."

⁂

So we start making our way through the kibbutz, slowly, carefully, because there are terrorists around, and then I suddenly hear, "Don't shoot! Police!" and I see a man in police uniform, light blue, with a police cap and insignia. He's standing in front of me without a weapon, without anything. He's smiling at me and says, "Take it easy, don't shoot!" No accent or anything; he sounds completely Israeli. And my head begins working: where do I know him from, maybe from Ofakim, or from Arad, or from Rahat? As he approaches me, I say to him, "Don't come any closer!" and his smile starts to fade, and I tense up, and I look at him, then he notices the four cops behind me who have reached me, and suddenly his smile completely disappears.

I ask him, "What station are you from," and he answers, "Special Reconnaissance," which doesn't make sense because they have different uniforms, but I wasn't quite sure because there were some cops who worked security at the Nova Festival. So I ask him again, "What station are you from," and he repeats the same answer, but by then I can see a green Hamas bandana peeking out from under his cap, then I spot more terrorists in camouflage in the shadows behind him, and I shout "Terrorist!" and I shoot. I hit him first, and then everybody joins me. Only later did I understand that this was actually an attempt to kidnap me.

Then a gunfight breaks out there at very close range, and once again, they have an RPG and machine guns, and we kill three terrorists there – some died and some ran away. The moment I understood that the gun battle was over, I continued moving forward into the kibbutz, making my way to the location that my boys sent me. I walk the whole time between bushes for cover. On the way I meet an old man who must have been eighty years old, a kibbutznik – only kibbutz types can speak like this – he says to me, "Hey, dummy, you just dumped three bodies on me here! What am I supposed to do with them?" So I say, "Don't do anything with them! Run back fast into the safe room; there are a lot of terrorists here!"

On the way I also called my commander to update him about what's happening, but while I was talking with him I heard someone shushing me from one of the houses. It was a young man holding a tiny baby – teeny tiny, about a month old – and the man says to me, "Don't wake up my baby – either come in and be quiet or go away." He was holding his hand over the baby's mouth to keep him from crying – with one hand he held the baby and closed his mouth and with the other he held a gun. I just apologized and kept going.

When I was finally close, so close to where my boys were, I was creeping across the gravel when a small box suddenly flew out of the bushes. I looked at the box, the box looked at me, and boom, it explodes. I realized that it was an explosive charge, someone must have heard or seen me, and I started backing away. And then I stopped and waited for the terrorist to move, and when he moved, I shot him from a range of four meters. It all happened just a meter away from where my boys were.

It took me two and a half hours from the moment I got to the kibbutz until the moment that I got to the house, the safe room where they were. I make my way toward the house, get there, take cover, and carefully enter the house. My heart is pounding – and the house is empty. Just sand. Bullet shells. Blood. The safe room is empty. What a feeling that was. I was sure the terrorists had kidnapped them; I was sure that I had missed them. I sat myself onto the couch, laid my rifle on my lap, and buried my face in my hands. I said to myself, What do I do, what do I do now? That's it. I'm in the lions' den. I missed my moment, I failed, my mission had failed.

But after a few minutes there, suddenly I said to myself, Maybe I missed something, I'll send them a message; maybe they ran away. So I send them a message, and they reply! They're alive! I feel a rush of energy like I'm recharged – I see that the location was slightly off, that it had sent me next door! So I stick my head out of the door and see ten terrorists, twenty, setting the house opposite this one on fire, trying to force the shelter door open. I send Geva a photo of that house. He sends back, "No, we're in a different house," and describes it, and I realize that they're in a house right near where I am. Really close.

I make my way out, taking cover in the tall bushes, and wait for just the right moment to sneak inside without being seen. Then I see all the terrorists going into that very house; the house where the kids are. I see their commander come with a map, and he spreads the map out there under the pergola, and his terrorists go inside the house and come out to the pergola with cookies and coffee, and he gives them instructions; he talks and explains, talks and explains and I see his map is divided into command zones: you go here, and you go here, and I can see and hear everything because I'm barely two meters away. And I send a message to my son, "I'm right across from the house. There are twenty terrorists at the entrance. Stay quiet." My son said to me that when he got that message, he almost had a heart attack.

Meanwhile, I sent a message to my station's deputy commander, Tal Zarhin. I sent him my location, and I wrote to him that twenty terrorists are preparing for deployment here; send everyone you can. That's what I wrote, and he understood the message. As I finished writing him, I suddenly heard a burst of gunfire right next to me. Some terrorist was probably shooting in the air for no reason, but my kids, who were inside and knew that I was outside, were sure that I was dead. That's what my son told me, that when they heard the gunfire – they thought that their father was dead. That was it; the story's over. So I went back into the empty house and took a selfie and sent it to them. I didn't smile in the first photo, but then I took another one, and I smiled in that one.

I was sure that would be my last photo ever. I couldn't see any way in my mind's eye that I'd make it out of there alive. I saw how many terrorists there were; I heard the pickup trucks coming, and I realized that that was it – there was no army, no police; it was the end. I said to myself, I've smiled my whole life – I'll smile in my last selfie, too.

I was there in the bushes for about an hour, until an IDF special forces unit arrived! They must have received my message with the location. I started to hear them coming closer, giving orders, "Turn right, cover from here, cover me from there." The terrorists heard them coming too and started running away from the house. They left the pergola and ran off. When the soldiers reached me, I said to them, "Police!" and their commander, Colonel Roy Levy, patted me on the shoulder and says to me "What are you doing?" I said to him, "I've been here; I was the one who sent the location." I warmed to him right away, that Roy. He's no longer with us; he was killed in that battle.

Roy said to me, "Crouch down," and I said to him, "I'm old, I can't bend down, I have a tear in my meniscus. If I bend down, I can't get back up." He starts to laugh and says to me, "Forget it, just give me a situation report." So I told him, "Listen, I'm here because of my sons. I'm trying to get them out of here; they're in the last house on the right. I have to get them out. There are dozens of terrorists around, something like forty or fifty." That's what I said.

Roy says to me, "Got it. Listen carefully. You and I will go to the front of the house and distract the terrorists. I'll send a team round the back to get your kids out." So I said to him, "Okay, great. But there's another house here with kids in the safe room, and they've set the house on fire, the kids could suffocate." The path was clear because the terrorists had run away, so I ran with the guys to the other house, the one that was on fire, and we got the kids out of there. There were about fifteen youths, with soot on their faces, soot in their nostrils. They had breathed in so much smoke that they weren't doing well. We brought them to a safe place, then the battle began.

The firing near me intensified, but it's hard for me to lie down or kneel, so I took cover behind some tree and fired from there. The terrorists kept moving around and attacking from different places; it was major chaos, and they threw a lot of grenades. At a certain stage, I began moving forward, and as I moved the soldier beside me shouted, "You have a grenade on your foot!" I looked down and saw a grenade resting against my heel – but it didn't explode.

At some point I started moving forward, and as I left my spot I saw a terrorist maybe ten meters away from me. He came out of the bushes and positioned himself across from me and began to shoot; he must have shot six bullets, but none of them hit! He aimed right at me and shot and I just stood there, frozen, not moving, and he kept shooting. At some point his gun jammed, he lowered it, and as he lowered it three of us shot at him at once and he fell. And the officer there with me said to me, "Tell me, man, are you wearing a magical cloak or something?"

At that point the guys from the police special reconnaissance unit knocked on the window of the safe room where the kids were, and one of the policemen went in through the front door and brought all the kids out of there – fourteen youths came out, everyone but my kids, the guy from Maglan, and the medic who was with them. They brought Shaked out through the window. They couldn't lift him up, so they put him onto a sheet and carried him out with the sheet. Meanwhile, more soldiers arrived, bringing a stretcher, and they transferred him from the sheet to the stretcher.

Just then, while they were arranging the stretcher, the terrorists who had spotted the rescue operation came and started shooting and throwing grenades again, and I remember that I saw Geva walking along carrying Shaked's stretcher, and a grenade was thrown right next to them. Geva threw himself on Shaked and tried to protect him; he lay there on top of Shaked with his back to the grenade, and the grenade rolled right next to his head. If that grenade had exploded, they would have both been killed on the spot. But it was a dud, and it didn't explode.

Roy Levy hadn't forgotten about me, and he sent one of his officers to look for me – in the heat of battle, fighting for his soldiers, fighting for his life, he still thought about me. I went up to him, and he said to me, "Listen, your kids are at the infirmary, we rescued them, they're safe and sound. We have the Negev Recon Unit here, we have the Masada Tactical Unit, and Sayeret Matkal commandos just arrived at the kibbutz – go to your children."

On the way to the infirmary, on the way to the kids, I went into some house – I had to drink, it had been over five hours, so I went into some house. The house was wide open, a complete mess; there was no one there. I found a cup, filled it up with water, and took a sip. But it caught in my throat. I couldn't drink, I couldn't swallow. Here I was, in someone's house, and the people who lived here might have been murdered; they might have been taken captive. I just couldn't. I poured out the water, washed the cup, and moved on.

>❧

I was very lucky that day. God was watching over me. So many of my friends were killed before they even had the chance to fight. A good friend of mine was murdered in Ofakim before he had time to shoot a single bullet. He was murdered, and I'm still here. It's simply Divine Providence; it's all up to God – and my father sitting next to Him, persuading Him to let me live. He was a persuasive guy.

A month or so later I went to visit my father's grave – I had to thank him. I truly believe that thanks to him, I'm still alive. I visited his grave, spoke with him there, then we went with the kids to synagogue and recited *Birkat HaGomel*, the gratitude blessing. From there I went to Jerusalem, to visit Roy Levy's grave. I had to thank him as well. He didn't forget me. I could have waited there on the battlefield for hours, and no one might have come, but in the midst of all the chaos, in the midst of the carnage, he remembered me.

When I met his wife and told her what happened and told her about our conversation and the jokes he made and how he remembered me in the heat of battle, she understood perfectly. She said, "Yes, that's him; that's exactly what he's always like; that's him." I think it was good for her that I told her.

>❧

My friends are always asking me what motivated me, what kept me going, what saved me from losing hope even when everything seemed hopeless. And I want to say that today, whenever I see my boys – when I get back from work, when I eat lunch or dinner with them, when I see them, the answer's clear – my children are still alive today.

I don't know if this is optimistic or not, but ever since that day, at every funeral I've been to – and I've been to funerals – I imagine myself in the family's place, standing at my own son's funeral. I see the hostages' families, I see their agony, and I think: Wow, I was nearly in that situation. That could have been me. The country is in a sad, sad place right now. No doubt about it.

On the other hand, I keep reminding myself that I should be the world's happiest person. I was there, I made it out, I won; I won my boys' lives, I won my own life back. It's always with me, always, always – the thought that I was fortunate enough to succeed, to survive. So many others weren't given that gift; they never came back. For me, that thought leads only to one place: a place of gratitude. I'm grateful for my life; I understand that my life and my sons' lives are a gift. It's a gift we cannot, must not, waste.

I Can Sense Daddy All the Time

Denis Belenki's Story

Age 47

As told by Denis's daughter, Paulina, age 14

⚲ *Sderot*

My dad loved music very much, and in his spare time, whenever he wasn't working at his job in the police, he would sit and play guitar. Once, when I was eight, he introduced me to a singer he loved, a Russian singer called Monetochka, and I got really into her. I loved her songs so much, and whenever we drove somewhere together, we'd play her songs and sing along, like karaoke and stuff. About a year ago, that singer came to Israel for the first time! So obviously we bought tickets and went, and it was just, wow, an amazing concert; I was like going crazy up front, and he like got me a Coke and was guarding me from the back, but when I looked back at him, I saw that he was singing along too! Ha!

I'm fourteen now. That's about how old Daddy was when he came to Israel. He met my mom through some video game! She moved to Israel for him. I have an older sister and a younger brother, but my sister lives in Tel Aviv so I'm kind of like the oldest. My dad's been a policeman for years now, and policemen work very hard. So he's only home like half the time.

He was a really fun dad, a happy person; he made everyone happy wherever he went. He knew how to light a place up; he knew how to talk with people. We have a little garden, and he really loved to grow flowers there; he took care of the plants, planted fruit trees, and even grew strawberries with us.

He also loved dogs. When I was eleven, my mom and dad got me a sweet little dog I named Pepsi; she's this orange-brown color. And my dad was just crazy about her. He always played with her and took her running; he would take her to the vet for every little thing, and he would really go wild with her; he'd mess around with her and be silly.

He really was kind of nuts, and very funny. During the holidays, like Novy God (the Russian new year), he'd tell all these jokes and stories at the table. And he was always there for me, for anything any time. He was always proud of me and everything I did; there aren't even words to explain it. Really, there aren't enough words to explain how amazing my dad was.

On Saturday morning all these sirens started, so my mother and brother and I went straight to the safe room. My dad was finishing up a night shift in Sderot; he was supposed to come home at around seven. In the safe room I turned on my phone, and my WhatsApp was full of all these videos of terrorists here in Ofakim! There was a clip of terrorists shooting at a police car, and I was really scared that it was my dad. So we called him, and he said that he was going to be held up a little, and I was so relieved that he was alive.

Around the same time, a missile hit a house in Sderot, and he drove over there with his team to check out the situation, then a few minutes later he called and told us that they were shooting there and asked us not to call him anymore. That was early in the morning. And that was it; that was the last time we talked to him.

What happened was that, as they drove to check out the missile, they got reports about terrorists in the Sderot police station. So he decided with his team that they should turn around and go back there. He also decided that it made more sense to go on foot than in a car because a car is such an obvious target for terrorists; it was much bigger, and you could see it coming. So they started to make their way toward the station where this big battle took place. You can see in the photos what was left of the police station after all the fighting there.

As they reached the station, they could see that there were terrorists inside. There was one policeman outside who didn't have a gun; he had come to the station to sign out a gun or something, and my dad stopped him and told him not to go in because there were terrorists inside. At Dad's funeral that policeman came up to me and said that if it wasn't for my father, he'd be dead now.

After that, my dad and his team went inside; there were four of them. The terrorists started shooting at them from the top of the stairs, trying to kill them as quickly as possible. But my dad didn't give up and didn't run away; he stood there with his friends and shot at them; the four of them kept shooting, they didn't stop shooting. At some point he split from the rest of his team, and that's when he was shot.

We heard that whole story from police officers who were here a month ago; they visited us and told us everything. One policewoman told us that she's alive thanks to my dad because he protected her from a grenade. The terrorists also threw grenades at the policemen. Another policeman told us that even after they shot my dad, even when he was already on the floor, he kept fighting; he kept shooting at the terrorists. That policeman also told my mother at the shiva, "I was the last one to see Denis. He just saved my life there," and my mother and I were stunned.

I still don't feel like I know everything, every detail, and I'm not sure I want to know; it might just hurt me more, I don't know. I know that my dad saved people. I know that he was brave and that he fought really hard until the end. I'm proud of him for doing that, but it's sad because I wish he had saved himself as well.

Recently, a lot of people tell me I look like my dad. People always told us we looked alike; we both have the same nose – haha! – but there are other things we share as well. For example, I feel like I can also click with anyone the way he could, find a way to connect with anyone. I also feel the same joy that he did. He was a happy guy. Even now, even though he's not with us, I can still feel his joy inside me, as if the joy I got from him is watching over me.

I remember all the things my dad and I would do together, all these fun times we had, and when I remember them it makes me happy, but then I remember that he's not here anymore, and that I won't have any more memories like these. I remember how I once tried this new kind of makeup, and I showed him and said, "Isn't it gorgeous?" He gave me all this advice, like, "Look, you should use more red here and add more there," then it actually looked much better. It was really surprising because he's, like, a dad! Like, how come you know so much about makeup, haha!

It really hurts. It's hard, really hard, and I try to cope. You can't really cope with something like this. But I'll cope with it little by little. I know we can get therapy for free; I don't go because I'm not really comfortable with it. Maybe I'll go in the future. Some of my friends do. I have a few friends whose relatives were also murdered on that day, so we support each other. We're getting stronger. Mom is also having a really hard time; my brother and I try to support her as much as we can. When we're home, we try to be with her as much as we can, that kind of thing.

I can sense Daddy all the time. Sometimes I dream about him at night. I dream that he's trying to communicate with me, that he tells me he's so proud of what I'm doing now: going back to school, going back to my robotics course, going back to volunteering with special-needs kids, and starting new after-school activities.

The week it happened, I dreamed that he, like, came to us, and he hugged us and told us that it was just a drill. He had to pretend that he was dead but he wasn't really dead. And in the dream he hugged me, and I felt it so deeply. I'm still holding on to that hug.

I'm so happy that my dad is going to be in this book. It's really important to me. Really. I was so excited when I got the message asking me to tell his story. And I know that someday my kids, though they'll never meet their grandpa and never get to know him, at least they'll be able to hear about him. And they'll know that he was a good man, and happy, and funny. So thank you; it's really important to me that he'll be remembered for generations to come.

Adrenaline Helps, and So Does Dad

Ofek Livni's Story

Age 27

○ *Nova Festival*

I don't know if this is related, but my girlfriend and I broke up a few months ago, so I got back to business a little bit: parties, messes, everything. And my friend Gilad – the kind of friend who parties as it should be done – said to me, "Bro, you must come to Nova, you must," so I said, "Let's go." I convinced my childhood friend Ori to come, and we ordered tickets.

I'm a second year MBA student at Bar-Ilan University, and the semester is going to start in like a second, so we come psyched – ready to party, to have fun.

We got there at midnight, but the main stage opened at three a.m., so we had some time to pass. We all sat under a shade canopy. Gilad came with his girlfriend Noam, who came with her sisters Inbal and Netta, and the four of them joined up with Ori and me. There was a group of cute girls next to us. There was good energy – like a love vibe. Nova has it all – all types of people, every variety, and everyone was like in bliss. We got up to dance, we sat back down, we danced again, sat again, trance in the background. It went on like that until the first missile was launched.

✺

We heard a boom and looked up at the sky. It was a serious boom, louder than the trance. One boom, then another one and another. We're all good Israelis, so everyone instantly throws themselves onto the floor with our hands protecting our heads. Suddenly there are a million missiles in the air. Dozens. Hundreds. The first feeling is anger – "Why are they ruining the party for me?" After a few minutes like that they turned off the music, and the policemen told everyone: That's it, wrap it up, go home.

Then everyone started packing up, and I told the gang with me, "Let's wait until everyone who left first gets on their way so we don't just sit there in a traffic jam for no reason; that's dangerous with all the missiles." Meanwhile I'm like calming people down from the explosions – I have this helper kind of trait; I know how to hug people and calm them down, get their blood pressure down, so I help when I can. Suddenly we hear shooting. Real shots. And I tell Ori, "We are out of here."

We started to run to our car, me and Ori. We told the rest of the gang to get into their car and leave in the direction of the police. People got out of their cars, then came back in; it was chaos. But I stayed in our car – a car gives me a sense of control over the situation, a car gives me cover; it's an attack vehicle, it's an escape vehicle. In the end, though, I got out of the car and join them on foot, and we all manage to get to the road at the exit. After some gun battles there, this policeman comes and says, "Run!" I mean, the moment a policeman tells you to run, you know that they've lost control. Which is legit because there were so many terrorists there. But the moment that I get that they've lost control, from that moment on, I listen only to myself. That's it. I don't care what they tell me; I decide what I'm going to do because I'm getting out of there alive. I let my adrenaline shoot up like to the max; I say to myself: Excellent, I need the adrenaline hit; I want it to help me. What's running through my head is "Everything can go to hell, I'm not about to die here because of some lame Hamas guy – it's not happening. I'm not a sitting duck."

We all started to run together, but then I understood that I'm not giving up on the car. I went back alone to get it. They're shooting at me non-stop, but I don't care; I'm determined to get out of there alive and save my friends. I get to the car and go to get my friends out. The whole time bullets are flying over our heads, but I'm in mission mode – I tell myself, if any terrorists come I'll run them over; if there are a lot, I put the pedal to the metal. I get to my friends who are hiding in the trees behind the car, and now we're all in my car – Ori, Gilad, Inbal, Noam, Netta, and me – and I continue to the next phase, getting us out. The group that was with me are not fully with it; they start screaming and all that. But I was focused, I took responsibility for the situation, I calmed them down. At that point I'm still getting stuck there – there was crazy chaos where the party was: people, cars, traffic, and we're all crammed into the car, two in front and four in back. We drove around for about half an hour trying to find the way out because there was traffic or shooting all over, and there was a lot of hysteria in the car, a lot of shouting – "Drive the other way," "Why are you going south?!" – but between me and myself, I am in this place of like: "Let me do it, this one's mine, okay, it's my show, this is my money time."

I called my father on the speaker. He's this old farmer, practical, task oriented; I knew he would help me in this situation. He quieted everyone down, made sure they'd be quiet, and began to direct me using the phone's GPS signal. "Go onto this path now," "Turn right here," "From here you go up to Patish." After a long time we found this road, and they shot at us again, round after round, so we tried a different road again and again until we found a quieter path. We drove east on this dirt road when we saw another two girls, Shelly and Nitzan; we told them to get in, and they got in the back and like sat on laps; it was crazy packed. After that we met another two guys who were walking on the road. We told them to get into the trunk; like, I stopped the car and threw everything out of the trunk and had them sit there. We were ten people in a Hyundai Tucson, and they were all stressed, and we tried to calm them all down, me and my dad.

Bottom line, most of what I did there was driving carefully and calming people down. The adrenaline helped. That's exactly what it's there for; it helps you do what the body in the day-to-day doesn't know how to do or want to do. It tells you, "What do you want? Let's go, you got it! You want to be strong? Here you go, be strong. You want to see better? Here you go, see better. To hear better? Hear better."

The adrenaline helped, and my dad helped too. He knew how to explain to me where to drive; he gave me confidence. We speak the same language, the two of us. Hours of working in the garden together or out in the fields on the tractor; motorcycle rides and bike rides; or just out walking the dog through the fields; going to the basketball court together to shoot hoops. Those are things that build a connection. Every kid fights with his dad, right? Of course my dad and I had our disagreements, but the bond itself was built strong. It's the same way with my mom.

We drove through the fields, on the roads; we ran red lights, and in the end we got to Ofakim. Ten people in the car. We thought that was it, that we could calm down, that we could stop, but suddenly there was a siren, and another siren, and another; we threw ourselves onto the floor, and there were these terrorists on hang-gliders above us; it was insane. We all went back into the car and kept driving; on the road there were lots of policeman, army special forces, counter-terrorist units, all these patrols, crazy chaos. In the end we reached Beit Kamah; there's a shopping center there full of people who came from the party, with a lot a lot a lot of soldiers, just like a movie, utter chaos, but they're singing: *Am Yisrael Chai*, the People of Israel Live. From there, I drove like crazy to Modi'in. I dropped off some of the guys there; we took a photo together and parted ways.

I don't like it when people say I was lucky. There was no luck there. Maybe there was some divine protection; that I'm willing to accept, but I worked very hard to get us out of there alive. I didn't improvise, I didn't go wild; some people might have pressed too hard on the gas and flipped over the car, but I know how to drive fast off-road because I've been doing it for years, in jeeps and ATVs, and I know what adrenaline is. There's this concept in Judaism called *hishtadlut*, making an effort. I made an effort, so I had that divine protection.

The guys that were in the car with me, they're all like, "He saved us, he's a hero." I don't like the word "hero." I just did what I could. And there's something else that hurts me about the whole story. At one phase there's this group of people running, and there are people I'm passing next to, seeing them in the cameras of the car, and as I pass them I offer them the chance to get in, but they didn't get in, and since then I'm a little bummed about that. It was a complicated situation and everything, but in the party area, even with all the craziness, if people would have asked to get in, I would have squeezed them in one on top of another; I would have grabbed them and brought them in one after another. My heart aches for the people I couldn't save. The heart aches, it aches.

Me, my status on Whatsapp is, "I'm not right-wing or left-wing – I'm just a true Zionist." People have called me a Bibi-ist, a leftist, a right-winger, because I think differently about every subject. Because I'm not this or that, I'm a true Zionist. That's who I really am. My family is Zionist to the bone, to the core. I'm here, and this land was mine way before it was anyone else's. I have no problem sharing it with other people if that's what they really want, but leave me alone and let me live in peace.

Me, ever since the party, ever since that story, it's been important to me to hear a lot of music, more trance, and to just dance a lot, just to be happy, to smile. So many people were murdered at that party. People who sat with us under the canopy there never came back. They're the angels of Nova. And the angels of Nova are dancing up there, and they want us to dance down here, too.

What's terror? Terror is meant to spread chaos and fear. The minute that I'm scared, and I'm not dancing or having a good time – they've won. So my victory is that I'm alive and I smile, I dance and I'm happy. I really feel that. Right now I just want a crazy trance party. I want to dance for them, just dance. Sometimes when I dance I want to cry and to scream, to unload the whole crazy thing happening now around us. Everyone who went there – they were people who wanted to dance and to be happy, so I'm dancing and being happy for them because they can't do that down here anymore. They're dancing with me up in heaven. I'm here for them, dancing away. Dancing for me and for them.

Just Afraid Someone Would Realize I Didn't Belong There

Eran Masas's Story

Age 45

⦿ *Patish, Nova Festival*

The name "Eran" usually starts with the letter *ayin*, like *erani*, which means "alert," "aware." But my birth certificate has Eran with an *alef*, which has no meaning. I used to think it was more special that way, but wherever I went, everyone would misread it and call me "Oren." Even my parents couldn't really explain why they had spelled it that way; no one could give me a good answer! I'm a Virgo, a perfectionist; I like to get to the bottom of things. So, a few days before it all happened – right before! – I went and legally changed my name to Eran with an *ayin*, for spiritual reasons. Really. I went to consult with a rabbi and said to him, "Rabbi, help me get my life together! What am I?" and the rabbi said that I should be Eran with an *ayin*, so that was it; since then I'm Eran with an *ayin*.

Until I was eighteen, I was a complicated kid. A big trouble-maker, kind of wild, very problematic, going my own way. I was an outsider in my family and never fit well into the system. So I was really scared before my enlistment because I had a history and I had issues – I was sure that the army wouldn't go near me, that they wouldn't take me at all. But I had one teacher, my homeroom teacher, who said to me, "Go try out to be a parachuting instructor!" which was at the time considered elite, and I said to her, "Are you kidding me? They'll slam the door in my face!" but she said, "Go, I have some friends there who'll 'work things out' and get you in." "Working things out" was my middle name, ha! So I went to the tryouts, I gave it everything I had, and I passed. When I told my teacher that I got in, she took me aside and said to me, "Listen, I have to tell you something – I don't know anyone there, I have no army connections. What you did, you did entirely on your own."

When I told my family that I got in, my father kind of gave me this look, like he just didn't believe it was true. Until then, I was basically a constant disappointment to my father. But when he saw me in uniform, going to a special course in a combat unit, he got this spark in his eye, like he had finally gotten the son he had always dreamed of and hoped for. And to see my father so proud of me – that gave me faith in myself. It gave me hope.

And that was it. That was when my life turned around. Everything changed. If I hadn't gotten into that parachuting instructors course, chances were high that I'd find myself in the world of crime one day. I owe a lot to the army, a lot. So I enlisted into the parachuting instructors course and went from there to the Egoz commando unit and from there to the officers training course. And I served in the army for twenty-five years. In those years I married Maya, and we had four children – Malachi, Benaya, Romi, and Arbel. After that, I was discharged from the army at the rank of lieutenant colonel; I was the head of the logistics branch of the officers training school when I retired. It's a tough business, retiring, leaving the military. The first year is the hardest – it's like a year of mourning, because you suddenly need to understand, at the age of forty-five, who you are and what your story is. So I was discharged, and I tried different jobs, and today I have a position in the Kiryat Ata municipality near Haifa – I'm Director of Municipal Beautification. That's what I do for a living.

❧

The Sabbath, October 7th. I'm at home at the end of a completely normal week. I'm already discharged, not in the headspace of the army at all, and suddenly I begin to get calls from my older brother, who lives in Eilat, at seven in the morning. I answer, "What's up?" and he asks me, "Where are you?" and I say to him, "I'm at home, asleep." And my brother says to me, "Turn on the TV; the country's done for." That's what he said.

I got up, went to the living room, and turned on the TV. The first thing I see there is the picture of the Hamas pickup truck in Sderot, and my first thought is "No way, no way this is actually happening!" and my second thought is, "If they're over there, then get up, get your handgun, and stop them!" It was so childish, so stupid, so not thought out, but I just said to myself, "Eran, get up and do something! Go to that truck! Go there!" I mean, I'm out in Kiryat Ata; it's clear that by the time I get to Sderot, it'll all be over, it's more than two hours away. The police and the army will take care of it. It'll be over.

But still, I started walking around my house, looking for my uniform. I get the gun and my wife comes and says to me, "What is this, what are you doing?" and I say to her, "They called me from the army, I have to drive there," which isn't true, ha!, no one actually called me. So I finished getting ready, I kissed the kids goodbye, and I left.

⤬

I started driving south, speeding like crazy, and on the way, I hear the news. At that point they still didn't know what was going on. They knew there was a mess, but they didn't really understand anything; they didn't understand the magnitude of the attack. The whole way down, I tried to work out where I'm driving to, who do I know in the south, who should I call, and then a friend of mine from my officers course pops into my head, a guy who lives in Patish, next to Ofakim, so I called him. I had no idea what was going on in Patish – I just called and he picked up. I say to him, "Liel, what's up?" and he says, "Don't ask, what a mess," and begins telling me his story. He's related to Rami Davidyan, from the family that saved young people from the festival; they went back and forth picking people up, he tells me, and I say to him, "I'll be with you in Patish in twenty minutes," and he says to me, "But how? You're from

Kiryat Ata, what are you talking about?" and I say to him, "I'll be there in twenty minutes." So I drove, no Waze, no GPS – the last time I was at his house was twenty years ago, but I still made it there, no problem.

When I got to Patish, I drove up to the gym, and all these kids who escaped from the festival were there. There was total hysteria; I saw policemen and some locals, so I sort of snapped myself into authority mode; I tucked my Golani Brigade beret into my shoulder strap, so that people would think I was still in active service, and I went inside. I still didn't know what happened, I still didn't understand the situation, but I went into the hall, and there was crazy panic, so I started shouting, "Listen, everyone go inside, everyone go inside," and I grabbed a few soldiers and this officer who was there and said to them, "Listen very, very well; you need to make lists, I want everyone here on the list, with phone numbers, so we can start helping them get ahold of their parents, so we know who's here."

It was crazy chaos there, totally insane, so I started shouting again: "Listen up, we're assessing the situation, trying to understand what to do. We're in control, the army is here, the army is on its way. I'm here to help you." And some journalist jumps on me with a camera and says, "We have a representative of the Home Front command!" and I'm like thinking, oh no, I'm not a representative, I'm not even on reserve duty, I just want to get things sorted out.

After a while, I understood that there wasn't much for me to do there. I didn't come just to make lists; I came to make a difference, I came to fight. Someone there had the location of someone who was still at the festival who needed saving, so I decided to go to him.

If you ask me what I was afraid of there – I wasn't afraid of terrorists, and I wasn't afraid of dying – I was just afraid someone would realize I didn't belong there, that I had exceeded my authority. When I set out that morning, I took out my handgun and loaded the chamber because I understood that there were terrorists on the loose. I didn't understand that there were hundreds and thousands of terrorists; I thought there was a terrorist or two, not more. I didn't understand what was happening yet.

After driving for a while I see a police jeep that had crashed into a white pickup truck, and I realize that there's a body there, left lying next to the jeep, and at first I'm still thinking it's an accident, but then I suddenly see a terrorist getting out of the truck! He starts moving in my direction, kind of limping, and it hits me that he's a terrorist. I just freeze up for a second; I say to myself, "Eran, kill him! Kill him!" Then my mind is going back and forth, like, "Am I even allowed to kill him, am I not allowed to kill him?" all within a fraction of a second.

In the end I shot him and killed him. He drops to the ground. Then another terrorist jumps out from behind him, and I shoot him too; I empty out my clip on him and kill him, too. Then I went back to the car, and I began to drive with my weapon actually sticking out of the window and head to the location I had recorded. I speed like crazy, and on the way, next to the entrance of Kibbutz Re'im, I see loads of burnt out cars, bodies left lying there next to them, and dead terrorists. Then I got to the festival grounds, to where the festival had been. There, I see in front of me burnt cars, bodies everywhere. It's a sight that I'll never forget my whole life. My whole life.

So I got out of the car and started making my way through the festival grounds on foot. There was this silence, and I took out my phone to film it, even though that isn't my thing – but I thought I had reached the end, I was about to die. The phone like gave me some sense of security, enough to walk around; it gave me the feeling that I wasn't alone. Then I started talking to myself, and as I got closer to the festival grounds I shouted out, "IDF! Police! IDF! Police! Does anyone here need help? Anyone?" and there was silence, an inexplicable silence, a hellish silence. I'm shouting and no one is answering me, no one answers, and the whole compound is full of bodies, dozens of bodies, hundreds of bodies, masses of people. Only then, I think, only there did I understand the magnitude of the onslaught.

I walked around there for a long time; I combed the area, and after a while I saw soldiers coming in, so I stopped filming because I didn't want to look stupid, like this lieutenant colonel sitting there and taking pictures. What's up with that? And I said to myself, Okay, what's my mission now, what am I doing here? At first I was in combat mode but there was no one there; the terrorists weren't there anymore. Afterward

I said maybe I'll go into medical mode and evacuate the wounded, but everyone there was dead; everyone had died already. It was terrible. And then I thought, Hamas also abducts corpses, so I decided that I need to collect all the bodies into one place before it gets dark. The bodies were scattered everywhere.

There was a big white tent there; it had been the evacuation point from the festival, so I said, okay, it seems big enough, we'll bring everyone there. Later, it turned out that it wasn't enough for all the bodies there. In the meantime, another three officers who were there joined me, and together we tried to work out how to gather the bodies.

In the end we found this Mule, like a small tractor, and got it started, and we attached a big cart to it and started driving around. We decided to start at the far end of the grounds, and there were burnt bodies there in the bushes, and I understand that I have to film, I have to document it all, so that it will exist for history; that's how I saw it. I felt that it was the Holocaust; that's how I saw it, that's how it felt. I took a few photos, then I started to lift up the bodies, but I was suddenly terrified that they would fall apart when I moved them. I was afraid to touch them, so I moved on to bodies that were more intact.

There was this one body of a girl that I picked up; I don't want to go into too much detail, but it was clear that she had been raped. I will never forget her. I asked for her forgiveness for what they had done to her, and I covered her with her clothing. When I tried to lift her up, the ground was kind of uneven and I toppled over, it was so hard to carry her, and I fell down with her, and I say to her, "I'm sorry, I'm sorry," and I put her on the cart gently, and realize that I'm not up to it. After what she'd been through, after what the others had been through – I just won't be able to do it! I can't handle it! But then I decide that there's a mission here, there's nothing to be done about it, there are so many bodies, so I decide to detach myself. And that's what we did there for hours, long into the night. We went around and loaded the bodies – from the ground, from cars, from mobile shelters – we loaded them onto the cart and unloaded them in the tent; loaded, unloaded, loaded, unloaded, for hours.

There was one moment in the middle of the nightmare with the bodies when we found three kids who were hiding; they were alive! It was the happiest moment that I had. I took them to my car, and they were in this state of terror, and I said to them, "I'm here with you, I've got you, everything's okay, I'm taking you to Patish," and the whole way I held the hand of one of the girls that was there; she grabbed my hand really hard, digging her nails in, like, *Don't leave me*. It was insane. I brought them to Patish and went back to the festival grounds to keep gathering the bodies.

At four in the morning, we had collected two hundred and forty bodies. I carried about eighty bodies, something like that. And I began to feel really exhausted. And I'm trying to think, what's next? There is still fighting going on, but I don't know that. So that was it. When the sun rose, I drove back to Patish, where I see that the situation has stabilized a little – it's hard for me to use that word, stabilized. Only then do I tell myself to calm down, and I decide to drive home.

When I got home my wife didn't really understand what I had been through there, what I had experienced; she didn't understand how much death I had seen that day. It's not like I can understand it myself. In general, ever since I got out of the army, my parenting, my marriage – it's all very complicated. But that's already a different story.

I don't really know why I did what I did. I remember that in 2006, in the Second Lebanon War, there was the story of the deputy battalion commander who threw himself on the grenade. Roi Klein. I took a lot from that story. And I can say with complete certainty that if I hadn't done it, if I hadn't gone down south, if I had sat at home watching the news, acting like some kind of victim, I never would have forgiven myself. Never! So much so that I would have seriously considered leaving the country, just because I wouldn't be able to show my face in public. No way! I would never have been able live here.

I think about it a lot, what would have happened if I had gotten there earlier, even by half an hour – maybe we would have found more people there at the festival who were still alive. Maybe if I had gotten there earlier, I would have taken part in the real fighting. I can really picture myself getting hold of someone's rifle, putting on a vest, and going out to fight. I don't know, it's just beating myself up, but I think about that a lot; those thoughts keep me up at night.

In the very end, I think about my kids. I just want life to be good for them. I don't care if they're great students, I don't care about their grades. I just want them to be happy, I want them to smile, for them to be content with simple things. I want children who take pleasure in the simple things, who feel joy from the simple things in life. And I really, really just want things to be good for them here. In this country. I look at what's happening here. I don't know about this place's future, I see all the hatred, I see what happened on October 7th, that the army didn't come, the police didn't come, and I feel that there's so much to fix here, so much to fix.

Really, I think about our country a lot, the country and its future, Israel's future. It worries me, especially now, after what happened. I'm not a political person at all, but I'm always thinking to myself – when will a real leader come along already, someone who'll tell us, "Guys, stop fighting, I know what to do; this is what will bring us to a good place." A leader who'll talk like that, who'll take us to a good place. And I really don't care if we get there by war or by peace; it doesn't matter to me. What matters is for it to come from a clean place, not special interests. I just want the situation to get better. Better than it is now.

My Purpose Is to Bring Life into the World

Michaela Koretzki's Story

Age 45

Kibbutz Alumim

I've always had that adrenaline bug ever since I can remember; that must be why it was always my dream to work in an emergency room. When I finished my nursing studies, I asked the head nurse to assign me to the ER, but she said, "There are no positions right now; try somewhere else," so I said to her, "I'm not giving up! I'll come back to you next year, and you'll assign me to the ER!" A year later, I went back and said to her, "Hi, you promised me, remember?" and she said, "I don't have room in the ER, but there's a midwife position available if you like." And I've been there ever since; it's been eighteen years.

There's always plenty of action in the delivery room, especially in Soroka Hospital – suspense, adrenaline, you're always on, full Energizer mode. There are also plenty of emergencies, so I often get the chance to make that switch into action mode, hyperfocus, figuring out what has to happen next, how to deal with a situation, how to save a life. I think that's what probably prepared me – to some extent – for what happened that Shabbat.

୬

At six-thirty in the morning, I was the first one to wake up from the sounds of the Iron Dome. In our kibbutz, we hear the missile interceptors even before the Red Alert siren – it wakes you up, you realize what's happening, okay, and you run to the bomb shelter. We're used to it. You stand in the shelter, you don't even bother sitting down; you wait until you hear a boom or two or three, and then it's over, you leave, and that's it, you get on with your day.

But this time, we quickly realized that this was something else. We counted the booms – ten, twenty, thirty – crazy numbers, and started wondering what's going on. At one point, my husband Tzviki said that the Iron Dome had stopped intercepting, that it had reached its limit. And we kept hearing booms, missile after missile, and then Tzviki said, "It must be a diversion; something bigger is going on."

Tzviki's parents were staying with us for the Sabbath, in the kibbutz guest house, and my daughter said, "Wait, I don't think that Grandma and Grandpa's place has a safe room!" So as soon as there was the slightest lull in the booms, Tzviki hopped on his bicycle, rushed over to the guest unit, and brought them back. They don't move very fast. His father, Yefim, is seventy-five years old and was injured in the army; he walks with a cane. He fought in Tel Faher in the Golan Heights; that's where he was injured. They finally made it over and came inside our shelter.

When Tzviki came back, he went straight to the safe where he keeps his gun. He understood what was happening right away and called his brigade commander, who was on vacation in Eilat. Tzviki says to him, "Listen, something big is going on here," and the commander says, "Thanks for letting me know, I haven't heard anything, I don't know anything about it." By now we had already brought our phones into the shelter. And the booms kept coming, and the kibbutz started sending messages to lock doors to our houses and remain in the safe rooms because terrorists may have infiltrated the kibbutz.

Then the rumors started flying. My friend, a midwife from Moshav Yesha, half an hour away from us, sends me a message: "I just got off the night shift, I can't get home, my husband says there's fighting in the streets." Our doctor, Dr. Dan, messages me asking what was happening in Alumim because there are casualties in Mefalsim, which is only fifteen minutes away from us. Slowly, I begin to realize that it's closing in on us, and then we get a message: they're here; there are terrorists in the kibbutz.

⤭

We were in the shelter for hours, and the stress definitely affected our bladders because we all kept needing to use the bathroom. And every time we went, Tzviki would accompany us with his gun. At around nine-thirty I went to the bathroom, and all of a sudden there was very loud gunfire right next to the house. I found myself bending down, crouching actually, worried that a bullet might get me through the bathroom window. I finish quickly, and when I get back, I find a voice message on my phone from our neighbor in the civilian first response team, asking if I'm home. Before I could even call him, he's already knocking at our door, "It's Eran, open up!"

So Tzviki and I leave the safe room, open the front door, and Eran is standing there saying, "I'm bringing you a patient." He asks Tzviki to help him bring him over, and they go outside, and there's really loud shooting outside. It's not the booms of missiles anymore; it's all gunshots.

The moment they leave the house, I run inside, get two first aid kits I always have with me, and look for more equipment. I'm the kibbutz nurse, so people often come to me to get bandaged. Kids come when they split open their chins or foreheads; I have all the stuff for that kind of thing. And of course the kids know that whenever they come, the first thing they get is a piece of chocolate.

I also found an IV kit; I always keep one at home for pregnant neighbors who get dehydrated; I've had them at home for years. In fact, it probably seemed almost natural to them to bring me someone who needs treatment, but at the time no one knew what was about to happen next.

⤭

Moments later they come in with the injured guy, and I see it's our neighbor Amichai, who's also in the first response team. My first thought is that blood is dripping on my floor; I didn't really get what was happening yet. They bring him in, and he's covered with blood, and he touches the wall, and I see that he's getting blood all over the wall, too, and in that very moment my brain switches to emergency mode. I regain my composure and say, Okay, let's see what happened to him; let's see where his injury is. Eran goes back to the fighting, and Tzviki stays to help me, and I'm still barefoot, still in my pajamas. And I can't be barefoot; there's no way I'm working barefoot.

So I say to Tzviki, "Listen, I need you to bring me my shoes; I need to stay grounded. I can't feel grounded when I'm barefoot!" It must be psychological. Tzviki brings me this flimsy pair of flats, and I shout at him, "No! I need something stable! I need my sneakers!" and my sneakers were just outside the house. We have a shoe closet by the entrance, and Tzviki says to me, "I'm not going outside to get your shoes! Just wear what's here!" and I say, "I have to feel grounded!" so Tzviki runs outside where the bullets are flying and brings me my sneakers. I put them on, and I finally feel a little more stable.

We take off Amichai's helmet, we take off his vest, I check him for injuries, and as I'm checking we realize that we need to crouch down and hide because bullets might come through the window. We lay Amichai down on the kitchen floor and move the table over him, then the three of us are there under the table with its white tablecloth like we're characters in a children's book, hiding from the world.

At that point Tzviki's father comes out of the shelter to help us. He tosses the eggplants out of some bowl on the counter, fills the bowl with water, dips a towel in the water and starts cleaning all the blood and dirt off so that we can see Amichai's wounds. Then I can see that Amichai has this kind of hole in his arm; something must have exploded right against his arm. So I wrap it tightly with bandages, as tightly as possible; I kind of improvise with these elastic bandages I have. Amichai shouts in pain; it hurts him like crazy, and I say to Tzviki, "Give him three Advils," that's all we have at home, and I hook him up to the IV, hang the IV on a nail in the wall, and text Dr. Dan in the meantime. I describe it all to him, I've never treated bullet wounds before, and he writes back, "You did great. If he's stable, just wait until they can evacuate him." So we wait.

❧

Suddenly Eran knocks on the door again and says, "We have another casualty." I look at Tzviki and think to myself, *I've used up all the bandages, what do I do?* There's a WhatsApp group of all the ambulance drivers, nurses, and doctors on the kibbutz, and I type, "Guys, I need help, can anyone come over?" But no one can get here; the fighting is right outside our house. Then Tzviki remembers that Amichai brought the first response team's two-way radio with him, so he picks up the radio and shouts into it, "We need more bandages over at Michaela's house! We need more bandages!" and in the meantime they bring in the second guy; he's a big guy, barely able to walk, very pale. They're supporting him, practically carrying him inside, and it's our neighbor Ayal.

Ayal looks at me and gasps, "I can hardly breathe; I'm wheezing," and I can actually hear the wheezing. But I can't see any obvious wound, so I say to Tzviki, "Get me scissors!" We lay him down next to Amichai and cut off his shirt, but I can't really see anything, so we turn him over, and I identify three bullet wounds in his back. Amichai, lying wounded next to him, is an ambulance driver, and he says, "It's a collapsed lung; he needs an Asherman!"

A lung collapses when air fills up around it through an open wound in the chest, which prevents the lung from expanding. An Asherman dressing has a valve that treats that kind of wound, but of course I didn't have one at home. Later, we found out that his chest cavity was filling up with blood, not air; he was bleeding into himself, which was why we couldn't see bleeding on the outside like with Amichai.

So I bandage Ayal up as best as I can, and I hook him up to another IV and he's lying there on his left side, facing Amichai. I remember how Ayal strokes Amichai's head and they speak softly to each other, and Ayal says, "Amich" – that's what he calls him – "Amich, how you doing, where were you hurt?" and Amichai says, "I'm okay, don't you worry, stay strong," and they kind of keep each other going, and they check in with each other every few minutes. It was very moving.

⤔

Ayal is very badly wounded; he keeps spitting blood, and I keep wiping it up and encouraging him, and Amichai and I keep saying to him,

"Ayal, stay with us, breathe." At one point Avi, a member of the kibbutz, suddenly comes into the house. He saw that I was begging for help on WhatsApp, that we urgently needed oxygen, and he had an electric bike, so in the middle of all that madness, he got on his bike and brought us oxygen!

We hooked Eyal up to the oxygen, but it only bought us so much time. He just keeps repeating, "I can't breathe, I can't breathe," but we know that the ambulance isn't allowed to come into a firing zone. He's clearly living on borrowed time and has to get to the hospital, and there's nothing else I can do, and I feel this black hopelessness starting to weigh down on me, and that very moment, Gilad walks through the door.

Gilad is a volunteer ambulance driver, and I tell him, "We have to evacuate but they won't let any ambulances in; what do we do?" and he thinks for a moment and says, "We'll do it ourselves!" He picks up Ayal's rifle and tells Tzviki, "Come on, I'll cover you, go get the car," and Tzviki puts on Amichai's helmet and goes outside, and Gilad and the guys from the response team cover him. They fire a whole burst of gunfire, and Tzviki runs to the car, and after another burst of gunfire, he keeps going. He reverses right up to the front door and folds down the backseat.

And Ayal says, "I can't breathe, I can't stand up," and we realize how complicated it's going to be to get him in the car. So the three of us try to lift him, and we take maybe three or four steps, and then we reach the front door, and he suddenly says, "I'm falling, I'm going to pass out," and he collapses by the door. So we lift him up together, and we shout at him, "Ayal, you have to help us, Ayal, you have to!" and we try to keep him with us. We manage another five steps, but then he falls down again, right next to the car, and then Gilad yells at him, "Ayal, open your eyes, get yourself into the car; you've got to help us!" and he just opens his eyes and throws himself into the back of the car, into the trunk, and lies there.

Tzviki asks Gilad, "Who's driving?" and he answers, "You drive; it's your car," and Tzviki looks at me, and I look at him, and I say, "Are you sure you're leaving now?" and he gives me his handgun and says, "Give this to my father so he can take care of you," and gets into the car. And Amichai gets into the car as well, and Gilad sits in the back too, with his rifle aimed outside to cover them.

To avoid the gunfire they drive out across the kibbutz lawn, through the internal paths where cars don't usually go, and just before they leave the kibbutz Gilad says to Tzviki, "I'm going back to help. You drive as fast as you can to Netivot; Magen David Adom is waiting for you there." And Tzviki is left alone with the two injured guys, no armor on his car, no gun, no nothing; he just roars off to Netivot as fast as he can. There are a few checkpoints with soldiers along the way, and when they see the car coming so fast they aim their rifles at him, so he has to slow down each time and open the window and shout "Wounded, wounded!" so they let him through.

He reaches the Netivot Junction, where the ZAKA search and rescue people try to stop him, but he just keeps going, driving like a madman, and comes to a brake-screeching stop in front of the Magen David Adom station, where two guys run out toward him with fire extinguishers. He says, "I'm not here for the fire brigade, I have two wounded guys here!" and they say to him, "Yeah, but your brakes are on fire." He literally burned some rubber!

Our kibbutz has packing facilities for avocados, carrots, oranges, and potatoes, and a lot of migrant workers live next to the packing house. While we were in the shelter that morning, terrorists broke into their place, led them to a hangar in the kibbutz, and simply massacred them. Only a few days later did we find out that twenty-two of them had been murdered, and two were taken hostage. The horror. The sheer horror.

Around one p.m. Eran calls me again. I see his number and think, *God, no more patients, I have no equipment left, I have no IVs left, no disinfectant.* I pick up and he says, "They told me to come to you. This time it's me." He comes in, and I see that his leg is all bloody. Once again I find myself on the kitchen floor, next to cushions that are already soaked with someone else's blood, and I peel all the layers off of Eran and see that his leg has already been bandaged, and I cut away the bandages and find two gunshot wounds. I try to bind it up, but the bleeding just won't stop. I have no bandages left so I improvise with torn up clothing, and I bind it with a towel, but it just keeps bleeding, and I ask him, "How long has this been going on for?" and he says, "Since Ayal got hit." Four hours. He's been fighting for four hours with two bullet holes in his leg, and if they hadn't insisted that he come here, he would have kept losing blood. Fortunately, another evacuation vehicle left the kibbutz soon after, so he was taken to the hospital.

After Eran leaves, the kitchen feels kind of empty, and I lean against the wall and catch my breath for a moment, then I look at my phone and see a message from Dr. Dan: "Ayal is in surgery now; he made it to us at the last second. Another moment and there would have been no one left to save."

Two weeks later we all went back to Alumim to see our house. It looked like a movie that had been frozen. It was just as we'd left it: the candlesticks and the memorial candle; the holiday food with the stuffed cabbage and cheesecake, the white tablecloth on the table, the blood-soaked cushions, the bloodstained doorpost, Amichai's blood smeared across the wall. As if time had stood still. We sat outside on the floor, with two cats that had stayed behind, and we tried to process it all. And I thought about how my purpose in life is to bring life into the world, and that's what happened that day as well. I mean, we managed to save three people; it's like they were reborn.

Who Falls in Love on the First Date?

Netta Epstein's Story

Age 22

As told by Netta's fiancée, Irene Shavit

⚲ *Kibbutz Kfar Aza*

At first I refused to go out with Netta. I tried to brush him off elegantly, but he didn't give up; he just wouldn't give up! We first met at the pub in Nir Am – the Green Pub; it's a well-known place. He thought that I was with someone there, so he didn't have the guts to introduce himself. But later he got my number from a mutual friend and started sending me messages: It was really fun to see you, I hope we'll see each other again, I hope we'll have a chance to get to know each other. I understood what he was getting at, and at first I just brushed him off.

But then he started sending me more messages, still not giving up, like: How was your day, how's it going in the army, how are you doing? He was really persistent, and then he asked directly, "Let's go out; let's go out just you and me." I ghosted him for almost twenty-four hours before I finally answered. And in the end I said yes. From there it all went really, really fast. On the first date we had ice cream in Gan Yavne; it was cute. And let's just say that Netta's not the best at delayed gratification, so we definitely kissed on the first date. Ha!

I remember how I came home and said to my mother, Uh oh, Mom, I fell in love on the first date; I'm going to get my heart broken. Who falls in love on the first date? Big mistake. Big mistake! Like, just a second, take some time and get to know someone well before you fall in love; don't fall in love after two hours! But it was real, and it all happened so fast after that – two weeks later I was already having Friday night dinner with his family.

He was a goofball, a real goofball, one of the funniest guys you ever met. He would laugh at his father's jokes, real dad jokes, but they weren't funny no matter how hard his father tried, haha! And every time we went somewhere on the train together, he'd start talking to strangers sitting across from us, and I'd be going crazy, like, Netta, shut up! Let me sleep. Why are you talking to people you don't even know? But that was him. Going with him to the kibbutz dining room was horrible. Horrible! I'd stand there with the tray, and it would get heavy because it was loaded with food, but he would chat with every old lady there, every kid, and every old man; he had to stop and talk to everyone he saw there, and in the meanwhile the food would get cold; it was a nightmare! He loved everyone.

We were supposed to get married in April – April 24th. Netta wanted to study coaching; he wanted to be a soccer coach. It was the love of his life. That and beer. He would brew his own beer, and I hate beer, it's the most disgusting thing I ever tasted. It's gross! And now the whole Israeli brewing community has started brewing special edition beers in his memory, and they all send me tons and tons of beer. I still hate beer and don't know what to do with all that beer!

On October 7th we were in Kfar Aza in "The Young Generation" neighborhood. There was supposed to be a kite festival that morning – we were going to make kites and fly them high in the sky as an expression of peace and co-existence. Funny that they decided to attack on the day we had planned to celebrate co-existence. Everyone had come out special to the kibbutz in honor of the occasion; there were loads of guests, loads of kids. We had planned to go to his grandma for breakfast before the kite festival because his grandma made this Yemenite pastry, *jahnun*, from scratch – *jahnun* was her specialty.

At six-thirty in the morning we woke up from all the noise, the sirens, the Red Alert, then Netta gets a message that we're supposed to lock the doors, and I was like, "What? They never tell us to lock the doors; that never happens," and he said, "I don't know, they said to lock the doors." Fine, so we locked up the house and went into the safe room, like everything's fine. And then, at around seven, someone sends him a message that his grandma has been murdered. She was one of the very first victims that morning. She went outside because she had forgotten her phone in her mobility scooter, and they shot her out there. That's how we realized that something bigger was happening, that this wasn't just a regular Red Alert or siren, but something more extreme.

About two hours later we started to hear them, right in the houses right next to us. Shooting, explosions, screaming. Endless sirens, the sounds of war. We heard it all. And within seconds they broke into our house. We heard them smash the kitchen windows, we heard them closing in on the door. We heard them opening the safe room and screaming, "Where are you! Come out!" in this heavily accented Hebrew. Then they started throwing grenades at us.

The first grenade they threw exploded on the other side of the room, and nothing happened to us. Then they threw a second grenade, and it also exploded, and I got burns. Netta, I have no idea whether he was also hurt by that one. I think he was. But then they didn't throw the third grenade – they rolled it, and I remember watching the live grenade rolling along toward us. I just, I couldn't, my instinct was to squeeze my eyes shut and curl up into a ball as tightly as I could, but his instinct was the complete opposite of mine. So I closed my eyes, and suddenly I heard Netta shout, "Grenade!!!" and I look up, and I see him throw himself on the grenade, and as he jumps I see them letting loose with a burst of gunfire, then he lands on the grenade, and there's an explosion.

His body was right at the entrance to the safe room, and he's this huge guy, he's a meter ninety, something like that, so to get inside the safe room they'd have to jump over him, over his body. So they decided not to do that, not to come in. They just threw another grenade into the room, a fourth grenade, and that grenade started a fire. And I'm sitting there in the corner, and they're in the living room, and from their tone I can tell that they're arguing but don't understand what they're arguing about. So I take out my phone and send a message to Netta's father: "Ori, Netta's dead, and there's a fire in the safe room. What do I do?" It was clear to me that he was dead. I don't know why, I don't know how. But I could tell.

And Ori writes back, "Put out the fire, find a way to put out the fire," and I write to him, "How can I put out the fire? They'll hear me, they'll see me," and right then the smoke started to get much thicker, so I took my leggings and held them to my nose so that I wouldn't breathe it in. And I listened; there was nothing else for me to do but listen. I heard them opening the fridge; I heard them opening a bottle of beer, then I heard them leaving, stepping on the broken glass and moving on to the next house.

As soon as they left I ran out to the living room to get away from the smoke, to breathe the air, and I started sending messages. I told my parents what happened, and that I love them, and that I'm sorry for everything if anything happens to me, and that they're the best parents I could have asked for. I was sure that this is it; it's okay, I'm going to join Netta, it's all good. It was clear to me. Then I remembered all the soldiers who had been murdered, then their bodies were kidnapped, and I was sure that they'd take his body away too because that's what happens. Hamas hold on to dead bodies. I was sure they would come back for the body, so I had to hide.

So I took my body spray, which is water based, and I went back into the safe room and began to spray it on the fire to put it out, and I got under the bed with Netta's body hiding me, and I took an old duffle bag and covered up my lower body. And that's how I lay for hours, hours. I was there for hours facing Netta, watching him lying there with his gorgeous body, with his sculpted buns – I always teased him that he spent far more time toning his behind than I ever did – and I lay there across from him, thinking to myself, What amazing buns Netta has, what an amazing body; he's really the most gorgeous guy in the world.

Then a few hours later the terrorists came back into the living room. There was a gunfight; they shot at the soldiers from the living room, and they didn't see me – Netta was blocking me, and they had no idea I was there, and that was the second time he saved me. Then a few hours after that, around five in the evening, I suddenly heard Hebrew. The soldiers threw a grenade into the living room, and the explosion shook the whole safe room. This grenade was really powerful and I realized that it's different than what the terrorists had before. Then I saw them going into the house, dressed in a uniform that looked familiar, with weapons that looked familiar to me, so I said to myself, "Okay, let's go; what do I have to lose? I'm going outside."

And I started shouting to them, "I'm here! I'm here under the bed!" and they said, "Come outside with your hands up," so I went out to them, and I asked them to take Netta, to bring him with us, but they wouldn't; they said that they first had to save everyone who was still alive. Just then the terrorists started firing at us. It turns out that there was a sniper on the rooftops who started shooting at everyone who came, at all the soldiers who came, so the soldiers covered me and led me outside. There was a Red Alert on the way, incoming missiles, and all the soldiers lay down on top of me, and I went along with them and kept trying to find reception so that I could message my family that I was still alive. I realized that I had to go up to the gas station further up the road because there might be reception there, so I shouted out to the soldiers, "If the terrorists didn't kill me, then the Red Alert won't kill me – I have to tell my mom and dad!"

At eight that evening I met up with my father. I had a ride north with the army, and my father came and picked me up. They only took Netta's body out on Tuesday afternoon. And the funeral was only a week and a half after that, with a temporary grave in Kibbutz Einat.

Time passes slowly now. I'm still stuck in October 7th, still in shock. I'm done with making plans because God just laughs. I live each day as it comes, each week as it comes. We'll see. I don't know. We'll make the best choices we can. But Netta is inside me; I can feel him living inside of me. He always hoped that I'd see myself the way he saw me. He would always say, "If you would only love yourself like I love you." I always had a hard time with self-love; I would always say, "I can't do that, I don't want to, I'm not good enough," but ever since he died his voice echoes through me. He's not here anymore, so I have to believe in myself, I have to love myself. That's what Netta wanted me to do.

I had this thing with him that I believe in white butterflies – that if I saw one it meant that I would have a good day, that someone was protecting me. Whenever we went hiking, I'd say to him, "Look, a white butterfly; it's a sign that today's going to be a good day," but I'd almost never see them; I rarely did. And ever since he was murdered, not a day goes by that I don't see a white butterfly. I saw a white butterfly today. Yesterday I took his sister out to eat. I said, "Let's get away from it all and be alone," and all these white butterflies kept flying past us, circling us. Really.

I know – I know with all my heart that he's here with me. And that thanks to him, I'm going to live the best life I can live. I know that the moment I learn how to really love myself, to accept myself as I am, he'll be so proud. And that's what's going to be. If he made a choice for us not to die together, then I will make him proud. I want him to look down at me from above and say, "That's Irene, and she's mine, and she'll always be mine."

I Have a Wild Stallion at Home

Yehonatan "Barnash" Tzor's Story

Age 33

As told by Yehonatan's wife, Reishit

◉ *Tzomet Ma'on*

Yehonatan and I met on a blind date. We never set eyes on each other beforehand, nothing. A mutual friend just threw it out to us, "Maybe you should meet," so we met. On the date I thought he was a real show-off; he was like, "I'm in the Shaldag unit, I'm from Shaldag." Ha, I had no idea what that was; I did Civilian National Service, not the army, so what would an elite air force commando unit mean to me? He started to get enthusiastic: "I have an ATV, I have a motorcycle, I have a VW Beetle, I'm this, I'm that." I think he was kind of offended that I wasn't too excited. But in the end, to humor him, I said, "Okay, if you have a Beetle, then I have to see it. Let's go; take me out for a ride."

So thanks to the Beetle we went out for another date, and it progressed from there; we would drive around in that Beetle, and it would break down all over the country. That's how we started out. That whole first stage of dating was with that Beetle; he would always go on about how well it drove, that we could drive it to Ein Gedi, sure, why not, Eilat too. Yeah, right – each time we'd get stuck somewhere, and there'd be some story; we'd start rolling down into some chasm or get stuck on some cliff, then we'd have to sleep in the middle of nowhere, or he'd try and free the car himself by reversing out and just get stuck again, then he'd call some friend to rescue us from the middle of the desert. Something always went wrong. Every date, something else would go wrong for us.

But I went along with it. He had me under his spell. He wasn't an ordinary guy. I was captivated by his charm. He had this charm to a degree that you just couldn't resist. Everything he did, he did in his own very special way. If he wanted something, nothing would stop him. With him, the feeling was that there were the laws of nature, and then there was Yehonatan. The laws of nature sometimes yield, you can fool them because fundamentally, anything is possible. That was the feeling – that with him, everything was possible, really everything, and there was no obstacle that you couldn't surmount, no dream that couldn't be realized, and no problem that couldn't be solved. That was how he became a leader; that was why his soldiers would always follow him through hell or high water. He gave people this deep, strong sense of security.

Yehonatan grew up in Yitzhar when it was first starting out. His family was among the very first to move there; first they lived in a tent, an actual tent, and a kind of grocery truck would come once a week. From a young age, he was already deeply connected to the earth. He was a nature-loving kid; he had horses, and he'd ride all over the hills of Samaria. The guys from Yitzhar nicknamed him "Barnash," and it stuck – they say it in this deep, masculine voice, like, *Bar*nash – and from then on everyone called him Barnash except for me. To me he wasn't "Barnash," to me he was Yehonatan.

When he was growing up, he was also exposed to the more complicated side of life in Yitzhar. He lost a few friends to terror attacks; there was a time when it got to the point that he slept with a knife under his pillow every night. It was a difficult time for all the kids who grew up in that area. Later on, the disengagement from Gaza shook him deeply. He was one of the fiercest protestors there; he was arrested a few times at demonstrations. He had a whole criminal record from that period.

Later, when he tried to join the army, the army didn't even want him; he had to resolve all of his files first and do community service. He would always joke that he single-handedly planted the whole boulevard of trees in Yitzhar during all that community service.

He showed up at the tryout for Shaldag with long hair, a cowboy hat, and hiking boots. All the others at the tryout were these clean-cut kibbutz guys; they looked at him and didn't know what to make of this strange kid, but he left them all in the dust. A few days ago I received a message from some reservist from Shaldag; he was on the team that ran the tryout back then, and he wrote to me, "Half of the psychologists there wrote that he was a dangerous settler, a 'hilltop youth' who was wholly inappropriate for the unit, and the other half wrote that he had exactly what they were looking for in the unit." It was always like that. There were always those who completely misunderstood him, who couldn't see where his daring, his chutzpah, and his creative thinking came from. He was not the kind of person that just toes the line. Throughout his army career, every time he was up for promotion there was always a debate; there was always someone there who said, "What are you talking about, he's not right for the role, he's rebellious, he has too much chutzpah, he's wild, he's too nonconformist," and there were always those on the other side who said, "What's with you? He's a leader, he thinks out of the box, he does it all his way, and that's exactly what we're looking for." That's his story.

During the Covid years he and his friend bought an old Berman Bakery delivery truck and turned it into a camper trailer. Starting from nothing he turned it into this cushy camper. Then we took it all over the country with the kids for six weeks – we drove around, hiked, went climbing and diving; it was incredible. Later on, there were years when he was studying law, and even then, he would get up at six every day and sign up for all kinds of competitions – Iron Man and triathlons – and I'd say to him, "Take a break, take it easy!" But that wasn't his thing, taking it easy. He had this compulsion to swallow life whole.

He would describe himself as a wild stallion; that was the title he gave himself, and he really was like that. I realized that it was true: I have a wild stallion at home, and I don't want to break him in; I want him to fulfill himself. But on the other hand, we have a life to lead together, so we had to work it out together – gradually, wisely, and that's how my wild stallion discovered that he was a bit of a domesticated horse as well.

We live in Kedumim, in a neighborhood called Mount Hemed. It's a little bit isolated; it's on a very beautiful hill with a breathtaking view. I grew up in Kedumim, and once I took him up to this hill to watch the sunset, and he said to me, "Tell me, are you crazy; how come you never told me about this place?!" and I said to him, "I don't know, it's just Mount Hemed, it's nothing special," but he walked around as if he were nuts, saying, "Wow, what a view! I can't believe it, it's insane! This is where we're going to live." And we actually built our house here, right on the cliff. On the edge. And after we moved here, I saw that something in him settled down a little. It really was his life's project: to build our house with his own two hands, to stop wandering and searching, and to finally find what he had been looking for.

At six-thirty on the Shabbat morning of Simchat Torah, the phone calls started. Our three kids and I were still sleeping, and he wakes me up saying, "Listen, the brigade commander called me, something's up." He tries speaking with the commanders under him, who are in the field with his company commander and his deputy battalion commander, and they both told him they were in the middle of fierce combat, and they both shouted to him under fire, "It's war, come!" So he came; he got ready in seconds, took his rifle, and left the house. And before he left he took a box of cookies from the fridge and said to me, "I hope I'll be back before the end of the holiday."

He wasn't stressed; truth is, he never got stressed; he was always very level-headed, and this time I didn't get the feeling from him that this was anything out of the ordinary. I'm used to those kinds of call ups; when you're the Commander of the Nahal Reconnaissance Battalion, you're always getting called up, so I said to him, "Okay, let's go, good luck!" Like I didn't make a big deal out of it; the kids were also like, "Oh, Daddy's going again." Great.

Only a few minutes after he started driving, I think, he started to realize that there's trouble, that it's a catastrophe. At this stage he started conducting conversations with all the commanders under him in the field; with all the security response teams in the region; with all the local security heads. He also reported to the brigade commander, who was also called up from his home, and together they basically try to make sense of what's happening. And the soldiers from all the bases along the border are shouting on the phone, "Listen, we're up against dozens of terrorists, and we're out of ammunition; if no one comes right now, we're dead, we're going to die here." So he starts moving forces around, all while he's speeding like a madman. He's racing at like two hundred kilometers an hour and giving orders at the same time: "Come from there; don't go from here. We know that there's a band of terrorists over there, so come from a bypass road," and he really keeps moving all the troops around there. As he's speaking with his people, he learns that his deputy battalion commander, Ido Shani, has been killed, and so has his company commander, Roey Chapell. He realizes that he's driving straight into the hellscape of the war.

When he reached Ma'on Junction, where he and his brigade commander had arranged to meet, his commander wasn't there; he had already gone ahead inside. There was a soldier there, a tracker, blocking the road – his job was to prevent people from going through because of the terrorists in the area. He also tried to stop Yehonatan, but Yehonatan said to him, "It's okay, it's okay, I'm with the brigade commander." As they were talking there, they suddenly hear shooting just past the junction, and Yehonatan realizes that the brigade commander is already there in some kind of skirmish just a few kilometers away. He breaks through the tracker's barrier and races onto the road. Moments later he sees the commander's car by the roadside, and he realizes that his commander, Yehonatan Steinberg, has been killed. And at that moment, he encounters there by the roadside dozens of terrorists who spray bullets at him. I think that right then – that's what we gathered later, based on what they found there – at that moment he realized that he didn't have a chance.

So he just decided to use his car as a weapon. He takes his car and just begins to go wild there on the road. He manages to run down a terrorist motorcycle and kills another terrorist and slams right into their pickup truck with all his might. The terrorists parked their truck there in the middle of the road to block everyone coming, so that they could shoot them, and he just hit them at breakneck speed so that their truck flew off to the side of the road, taking some terrorists with it. And in the end he was actually killed in his car from a bullet to the neck; he died instantly.

Later on, his friends went down to the scene to investigate, to try and understand exactly what happened to him. There were a whole bunch of cars there on the road because so many people had been killed there. They barely managed to identify Yehonatan's car; it was completely smashed up, and they said, "It looks as if someone was fighting with this car, wait, it could be that it's Barnash's car." The car was so wrecked that it was barely identifiable.

Afterward, they realized those terrorists weren't able to move ahead because they had no more vehicles to keep going; Yehonatan had wrecked their chances of moving on. The Urim IDF base was just a few meters away, but that group of terrorists never got to the base; many of them actually went back to Gaza, and some of them were killed on the spot.

People are still coming to my home to visit; masses of people stream in every day. They come in waves: wounded soldiers that have been released from the hospital; his replacement battalion commander; and all kinds of people he spoke to that day, and they all say to me, "Listen, he saved our lives. He told us what to do; we didn't understand what was going on, and he told us which route to take, he warned us to stay away from certain areas, he told us where the terrorists were, and he told us to drive back." People come to me and say, "Listen, if he hadn't told me to retreat, I would be a hostage today." He saved so many people there that day because as soon as he realized that there were ambushes everywhere, and hordes of terrorists, he said to everyone, "Wait a minute, don't run into their traps, turn back."

I was angry at him. You told everyone else to retreat, so why didn't you turn around; why didn't you turn back? But after you start to understand what was going on there, I realize that at the time, he wasn't thinking about himself; he wasn't thinking about his family – not about me it seems, and not about the kids. He was one hundred percent totally inhabiting his role, his mission, what he had taken upon himself when he committed to being an officer in the IDF, when he committed to being the commander of the Nahal Reconnaissance Battalion. He didn't really have any other choice. He realized that his brigade commander was engaging terrorists; he realized that his soldiers were in their base in an impossible situation, so he charged ahead to fight.

I think a lot about what went through his head in those moments when he understood that he was entering into the lion's den, into a place crawling with terrorists. He understood that he was in a hopeless situation, facing dozens of terrorists firing away – yet he still pressed on the gas and galloped ahead and went wild. It's not human to do such a thing; why should a person take his life with his own hands? But Yehonatan wasn't a private individual there. He was a commander, and he had a mission. It was his final mission. And he charged into that mission like a wild stallion.

⁂

On October 6th, the day before Simchat Torah, Yehonatan gave our youngest son a little puppy as a birthday present. Our youngest son's birthday was just before Simchat Torah. The kids and I named the puppy "Hope" in English. Yehonatan, who didn't know any English at all, asked, "I don't get it, what's 'hope'?" I said to him, "You know, hope, *tikva*," and he said, "I don't know; the name doesn't really speak to me."

When he brought the puppy home she was tiny, really tiny, but since then she's somehow grown like crazy. The truth is that, I don't know, he was always like that – there was always this feeling with him that he'd thought of everything. And this gift, too, this little puppy – there's that same feeling: "How did you know, Yehonatan, how did you know that she'd be just what we need," this sweet little creature that brings us so much joy during this time; that'll grow along with us. How did you know to leave us here with this wild little creature, so wild and unruly and vital and alive.

A Woman in Command

Or Ben Yehuda's Story

Age 35

📍 *Sufa Outpost*

Inever thought I'd be a commander in the army. When I enlisted, I was very shy, and when they asked me to train as a squad leader, I was sure there was absolutely no way that I could handle it, that I could command a dozen soldiers. I thought it was beyond me. But there were always commanding officers around who kept telling me, "Do the squad leader training, do the officers training course, you've got to do it, you'll be good at it!" so I went along with it even though I didn't really believe in myself.

At the end of my tour as a deputy company commander, I decided that's it; I'm leaving the army. I felt it was too much for me, so I went back to civilian life. I founded a scout troop, I took the college entrance exam, I hiked the Israel National Trail, and I was really out of the army. And then, after eight months as a civilian, I suddenly got a call from my brigade commander to rally me to the flag. He asked me to go back to the army – just for one year – to show young female commanders that it can be done, that a woman can command a company. He knew how to press my buttons. The truth is that I really did want to be a company commander, but I just didn't believe it was possible because until then there were hardly any women in that position. So I decided to go back to the army and be a company commander.

It's a thing, that question of how much I believe in myself. It's still there. Even now, before I became a battalion commander, I kept going back and forth asking myself so many times if I'm good enough and fit for the job. And I think there's something positive about that kind of deliberation. Confronting self-doubt pushes me forward. The fact is, time after time I say yes. I am good enough and I am fit for the job.

×o

My name is Or Ben Yehuda. I'm thirty-five years old and the commander of the Caracal Battalion, a coed infantry battalion. I have three children: Erez, who's seven, and six-year-old twins, Netta and Ella. My family is my light and the air I breathe; they're the most important thing to me in the world. Even before the war, I only saw them every other weekend. Now, since the war started, I can count on one hand the times I've hugged them, and I miss them so much it hurts.

People often ask me what keeps me going in this role. Because it's not an easy job. I think that what keeps me here, what keeps me going at this mission, are my amazing soldiers. Even now, when I'm the battalion commander, my office door is always open to my soldiers – I invite them in just to listen to them, to stay grounded, to stay part of it all. I also go out on missions with them and fight by their side. They're my strength; they're my oxygen. Without them I am nothing.

Whatever I demand of my soldiers, I demand of myself as well. If they have to get up at five each morning to be on call at daybreak, which is the most sensitive time of day, then I'll be there alongside them – with my vest and helmet. I'm the first to get down with them to a kneeling position. In the boiling heat, in the freezing cold, no matter when. My job demands tremendous mental strength and stamina. The soldiers are looking for that and really appreciate seeing it in me.

I remember, when I was a company commander, we had a visit from the Head of Southern Command. He came to one of our outposts and gathered together representatives of the enlisted soldiers for an open discussion. We commanders were outside, and he asked the soldiers all kinds of questions. And when he came out, he looked at me and said, "You – I think you'll go far." I looked at him and said, "That's a high compliment coming from a general!" and he replied, "You have a soldier here who told me that you wash the steam pans with them in the kitchen, and you raise the flags with them at roll call." I hear him and think about it for a moment. Out of everything I do – all the ambushes and combat operations and intercepting terrorists at the fence – out of everything that I do, that's what she told him? That I wash the pans with them?

I said to him, "I'm a little surprised that that's what she chose to tell you." Then he said: "On the contrary, it's the highest compliment she could have paid you. It's no big deal to be with them when you're armed to the teeth, out to stop terrorists. The secret is also to be with them doing the challenging everyday tasks. That's when they really see who their commander is." And then he added something that I was a little shocked to hear. He said to me, "You command as a woman."

I was a little offended by that, I didn't understand the comment. But then he explained, "Many women in traditionally male positions, in tough positions, try hard to play it tough. They put on a sort of 'tough commander' disguise – they speak in a deep voice and change their walk. But you manage to stay who you are and don't hide your feminine side. You show them the real you, with no disguises, and that real you is very important to your soldiers." That's what he told me, and his words will stay with me for the rest of my life.

I've thought a lot about what I bring to my position as a woman. I'm putting aside for the moment the fact that I'm a mother. I have this thing that when people ask me how many kids I have, I answer, "Five hundred and forty-three! Three of my own, and five hundred and forty kids in my battalion." And that's really how I look at it. But even before I became a mother, if there was something I could say I was good at – and I never compliment myself about anything – but the one thing that I've always been sure of is my emotional intelligence. I have the ability to sit across from the toughest soldier, the most hardened fighter, and to break through all their layers of defense and have a real conversation with them, heart-to-heart.

Many of the soldiers in my battalion come with a lot of baggage, from difficult homes, with tough stories. I often ask myself, "How would a male commander in my position react to this situation?" And I really don't want to generalize; clearly there are guys with a very high EQ, I know many myself. But I feel that something different happens with me.

There's that special moment, it's a sacred moment, when a soldier sits across from me – and in the day-to-day, they're real powerhouses, machine gunners, sharpshooters, they go out on crazy missions – but in my office, they open up, share the difficulties they're experiencing, what's going on at home; and we really talk, and sometimes we end our conversations with tears and a hug. That's something that I don't think happens with every battalion commander. I was just laughing about it with my deputy commander – he'll be promoted soon, so sometimes I'll describe a situation with a soldier and ask him, "How would you respond," and he looks at me and says, "Uh, I guess I'd bring him a cup of water or something." Haha!

I went through a long story with one fighter. I realized something wasn't quite right with him. For over a year he avoided the routine home visits that commanders make to check that their soldiers have everything they need at home. The commanders wanted to visit him, and he kept giving them excuses. So it turned out that for almost a year and a half they didn't conduct a visit at his home – he would always meet his commanders in some park. He was an excellent combat soldier, but one day he went AWOL for a few days; he just didn't show up. I understood that I had to speak with him one-on-one.

So I brought him into my office, and I said to him, "Tell me, why do you disappear whenever they send a commander to visit you at home? What's the deal with evading it every time?" At first I played it a little tough. So he replied, "No, I just had something…just then I got stuck with a problem with my phone…." I could tell he was just leading me on, so I said to him, "Listen to me, that story's not going to work with me. In this room, you're going to tell me what's really happening. Because, when you didn't answer your commander, my mind started racing because I've seen it all. I've been a commander in the army for seventeen years. I've fished soldiers out of trash cans in the middle of the night, I've seen soldiers in fist fights with criminals…. I've seen it all. So when you disappear on me, that's what starts running through my head. So, if you want me to calm down, tell me the truth."

And he looks at me for a moment, and suddenly he starts crying. Then, after a good hug, I said to him, "Okay, now you're going to tell me what's going on." So he looks at me and says: "Commander, I don't have a home. I live on the street." It turned out that this soldier left home when he was fourteen. He has no family to fall back on – he's not in touch with his parents. He must have gone through a very problematic phase; his parents decided to cut off contact with him. And he'd been living on the street for years.

I said to him, "I'm a mother, and I'm not going to let you sleep on the street because you're my kid too." And he just broke down in tears. And ever since, he has an apartment that we got for him, and we make sure he gets every voucher and social benefit possible. He also sits with me once a week, comes into my office – the door is always open to him – and talks to me about everything. It's one of those things where I ask myself, "Am I worthy of the extraordinary soldiers that we have here?" They are truly amazing, and every morning I ask myself if I'm worthy of them.

I was on base the Shabbat of October 7th. The Caracal Battalion is stationed in Wadi Raviv, on the Egyptian border. Most of what we deal with is violent cross-border smuggling, from both sides of the fence. They come almost every day, and they'll try anything to smuggle their goods across. They often come armed. And I'm there to keep my soldiers focused so they remember how to deal with these incidents. From my perspective, anyone who approaches the border armed is a potential terrorist and will be treated as such.

On October 7th the shifts and patrols in the sector were slightly different from the usual because it was the holiday of Simchat Torah, and people were hiking in the area. This demands of us all sorts of advance preparations, so by six a.m. I'm already out on the patrol route. At one point I get a phone call from my deputy company commander, who is stationed near the community of Bnei Netzarim at Sna'i Outpost, which is the northernmost outpost of our sector. So the deputy company commander calls me and tells me that there is a Red Alert warning of incoming missiles from Gaza in all the nearby towns and the outpost as well. I immediately ask him if everyone is okay, if any of the forces are injured, but he reassures me that everyone is accounted for; we call it "seeing green." But I'd been battalion commander for seven months and had never heard about incoming missiles at Sna'i Outpost before; this was the first time. And so I ask myself what on earth is going on.

As soon as I hang up with him, the civilian security coordinator at Bnei Netzarim calls me and tells me that missiles had landed there in the community, as well as in its greenhouses, and that he has two Thai workers who are wounded. I immediately alert my battalion aid station, which is basically a team responsible for medical care, and we start the drive north. On the way I call the Nahal Reconnaissance Battalion commander, Yehonatan Tzor. "Barnash" – that's his nickname – "tell me, do you have any idea what's going on?" and he answers, "I heard something about terrorist infiltration. All our forces are on high alert. I'll call you as soon as I know more."

Okay, I take that in – "terrorist infiltration," what could that mean? – and I say to him, "No problem, I'll handle the towns for you so that your forces can deal with the border fence. I'll take Bnei Netzarim, Yated, Shlomit, Naveh, Yevul – all those places are on me, and you deal with the fence with your people." We hang up with a "Good luck, love you!" and keep going.

When I reach Sna'i Outpost everyone is waiting for me outside with their vehicles ready to go. I stand the soldiers in a half-circle and explain to them what's happening, even though I don't really have any idea myself. I tell them, "There's a Red Alert throughout the Gaza Envelope, terrorists have infiltrated into Israel, and our mission is to protect the communities. We are focused only on that mission." I divide them into fireteams, tell each team which vehicle to take and who's going to which community, and I say to them, "Run! Assign all of your combat roles now, which forces are with you. Bring every possible weapon you can – grenade launchers, heavy machine guns, assault rifles, grenades, everything you can bring – and good luck to everyone." And that's how I send them off.

Then I get another call from Barnash. He basically tells me that Sufa Outpost has been overrun and that some of his soldiers are there. I say, "Sure, I'm on the way to your people," but when I hang up I say to myself, "What did he just tell me? They overran the outpost? What does that even mean?" I can't even fully understand the words coming out of my own mouth.

So I get on the radio, I tell the deputy company commander of the auxiliary and the platoon commander, who was still with me, that our mission has a change of plan: the three of us are going with our forces to Sufa Outpost to help the fighters there; terrorists have attacked them, and they are engaged in intensive fighting. I also warn them to be ready and alert because we might encounter terrorists on the way.

So that's how we set off, three military vehicles, a dozen soldiers total, and I'm navigating with Google Maps in my hand because I don't know the sector at all. As we drive, Barnash sends me on WhatsApp his contacts at Sufa Outpost, along with a voice message: "Or'chka" – that's his nickname for me – "watch out! There are terrorists all over the area; take care of yourself. I'm doing two hundred kilometers per hour to get to you – see you soon!" And I'm like trying to understand what this means, how we can contend with something like this, why there are so many terrorists, what are the implications.

I reach Sufa Outpost, and the first thing I see in front of me is an Achzarit; it's a type of heavy APC, an armored personnel carrier. The Achzarit is caught on a concrete barricade, and soldiers are lying around it on the ground with their weapons down, all of them with varying degrees of injuries. Lots of fighters. When I see this I immediately call my medical team, the one I had directed to Bnei Netzarim for the Thai workers, and I tell them there are a lot of wounded here and ask them to join me at my location. Our medical team is an all-woman team made up of a paramedic, a nurse, medics, and a driver, and they get into their ambulance and begin to drive to me.

I approach one of the wounded Nahal soldiers next to the APC and ask him for a situation report. And he says that a lot of terrorists have infiltrated Sufa Outpost, and he doesn't know what's happening inside. I call the sergeant whose number Barnash sent me, and he says to me, "We're by the gate, come quick!" I say, "We're coming!" and I start advancing on foot with my forces, weaving between the barricades.

When we reach the gate, I spot the sergeant standing in the guard booth and I rush forward toward him, shouting, "IDF! IDF! IDF!" He shouts back to me, and I cut across the square between us, it must be a hundred meters. I run across to him, and he shouts at me, "My God, what are you doing!!!" and I shout back, "I'm coming to you! I'm coming to help you!"

I reach the guard booth and look inside – and he's there with three other soldiers, each of whom has been shot in a different place; he's the only one who isn't wounded. And he tells me that about thirty soldiers have barricaded themselves in the mess hall in the base. And that he's out of ammunition. Now I – I have learned from painful experience about running out of ammunition, so I say to him, "Just a second," and I get on the radio to my command team and ask them to bring me an ammunition box, because I always have an ammo box with me in case someone runs out. So we brought the ammunition box to the guard booth, and the soldiers filled up their clips. It was like they could breathe again.

❧

In the meantime, my medical team arrives, and I can hear them in the background beginning to treat the wounded Nahal soldiers outside the gate, next to the APC. Suddenly, I notice that to the north of the outpost terrorists are walking around the embankments. Hordes of terrorists! But I am focused on the terrorists who have infiltrated the base.

I tell the armored vehicles we came in to advance, to come through the main gate, and suddenly the vehicles come under crazy fire, and grenades, and an RPG that barely misses us, skimming the roof. One of my soldiers gets out of the vehicle and is immediately shot in the foot, and the terrorists inside the base start running in our direction! We draw them out to us, and there I am, standing out in the open.

It is only at this point that I realize for the first time what we are up against. These are trained bands of terrorists with machine guns, anti-tank missiles, RPGs, fragmentation grenades – crazy military capabilities. And we see with our own eyes that they have bulletproof vests, uniforms; they're commandos in every respect. Then I understand that the only thing left for me to do is basically to freeze the situation – to make sure that no more terrorists get inside and that they don't take any soldiers out of the base as hostages – and in the meantime to try and call in reinforcements.

I order my vehicles to drop back, and when I confirm that they're all out, I close the gate and call my tank company commander and the company's female tank crews, who are also under my command, and tell them to come as soon as possible. It's a relatively long drive and tanks that do it on treads will take a long time to come, so I know that I have time on my hands until the reinforcements arrive. Okay.

I call a friend of mine who took the battalion commanders course with me. He is a squadron leader at the air force base in Tel Nof. I say to him, "Omer, I need you to bring me an attack helicopter, pronto!" And he hears the explosions in the background and asks me, "What is this? Are they firing at you?" but all I can say is: "Omer, it's urgent! I'll explain it to you later. I'm at Sufa Outpost. Please tell the pilot to call me; I'll direct him," and he says, "Okay, okay, I'm on it. Be available by phone."

And actually, at around ten o'clock, an attack helicopter pilot calls me and says, "I'll be with you in a moment!" I start to briefly explain the situation, where I am, where I want him to shoot, and what I need him to do. But then, just as he's directly overhead, he calls and says, "Or, I'm really sorry, but I have to go to a different town. There are other infiltrations; I can't be with you for this," and he just flies away. And it begins to dawn on me that this isn't just happening where I am – there seem to be other situations, other battlegrounds, because if that pilot is saying that other towns have been infiltrated as well, then we must be in a very, very complex situation. And at that moment, I realize that I can't rely on anyone else, that whatever happens here is on me.

At some point I notice that there's a defensive earthwork, an embankment, to my west, a huge one, and I say to myself, that would be a good position. The terrorists will be coming in from there; it's the closest point to Gaza. I start heading there with my command team, my signal soldier, and my driver. We jump up, run, take cover, jump up again, run, and take cover, over and over until we reach the edge of the embankment. So I turn my head to the side, and see a sight I will never forget as long as I live.

I remember the situation so clearly. I peer, lift my head up, then bring my head back down, then look to the side again – some five pickup trucks are coming at me, and packs of motorcyclists, and terrorists are hopping between the dunes, between the trees, all in combat vests and uniforms and advancing in our direction. I can't even count them; there are hundreds. Hundreds! And in the distance behind them are long lines of people from Gaza who are just marching in our direction, some armed, some unarmed, and I say to myself, "Well, that's it; this is where I'm going to die, right here on this spot. I'm going to die here."

I've been in many encounters and many firefights in my life, but it never felt like this; it never even came close to this. This time I accepted death, I came to terms with death, I understood that's how it is. I remember looking up and apologizing to my children; in my heart I begged them to forgive me – they're so little, and so cute, and I'd never come back to them, never see them again. That was it; I saw this was really the end. And then I said to myself, "Okay, if this actually is the end, then I'll end it well. I'll die standing tall. I'll do the very best I can, and I'll fight until my last drop of blood."

So I turn to my soldiers, a group of twelve brave fighters who are waiting for me to tell them what to do. I turn to them with a half-smile – they told me afterward that I smiled, but I don't remember it – and I say to them, "Let's go, let's take them apart!" and they all shout, "Let's do it!!!" They come to the embankment with heavy machine guns, with whatever they can carry, and we take our place there and start shooting at anyone approaching the outpost; we shoot like crazy people! And at a certain point, we have a light anti-tank missile, so at one point we launch it toward one of the Hamas trucks, and the truck explodes, a tremendous explosion, something extreme – the truck must have been loaded with explosives, and the blast takes with it some motorcyclists who were nearby. As we continue fighting, I suddenly realize that many of the terrorists are beginning to retreat, to turn around and run back, and I suddenly understand that we are, in fact, doing something significant here.

≫

We were there for about half an hour, and then, within all the chaos of the situation, I suddenly hear the chains of a tank behind me. What a crazy sigh of relief! I tell my deputy company commander, "Stay here! I don't know whose tank it is; I'm running to bring it to us!" It's already about eleven a.m., and I start hopping back toward the tank, through the barricades, when suddenly I spot a terrorist jumping me, point blank, almost close enough to grab me. And as my luck would have it – I have a bullet in the chamber and a finger on the trigger; it was just a question of who shoots first, and I shot first.

The terrorist collapses in front of me, and I stop – I just freeze, like, what is this, what just happened here!? I hear the deputy behind me, shouting, "Commander! Commander! Are you okay?" and I take stock of myself and think, I am okay! I turn around to him and signal with my hand that everything is under control, but he rushes up to me and takes a look at me and says, "What, like, what just happened between you two; what's going on here?" and I say to him, "Exactly what's running through your head."

But the tank! I remember, I can't let it get away; we need it! So I ran fast toward it, and because I'm trained in signaling with my tank crews I start signaling to them with tactical hand signals: "Terrorists, over there, behind me. Do it – one shell in that direction!" And they get it, they're with me! For the first time, I have some kind of backup force that linked up to me. We perform some kind of flank, take up a good position, and just start firing in the direction the terrorists are coming from. We shoot and shoot, and they move away, retreating, and I realize – we all realize – that if we don't keep up the fight here and now, these terrorists will pass us and get to all the towns behind us.

At some point, my deputy company commander and my signal soldier are hit by an RPG and fall to the ground. So we take them out of there, and I contact my pilot friends who fly transport helicopters, and I ask them to come and land on the pad beside the outpost, because I moved the wounded there and need them to be evacuated. And it really happens! They come, they land there, and they evacuate the wounded forces for us. And my medical team is still there; they have been treating the wounded nonstop and loading them on stretchers and evacuating them to the landing pad. We also managed to bring the wounded soldiers from the APC to the landing pad, together with the wounded from our battalion and some more civilians we picked up along the way, who fled from Kibbutz Sufa and Pri Gan and all kinds of places. They basically all get care from my extraordinary med team, those amazing women, those angels, and then the helicopters I summoned evacuate them to Soroka Medical Center where they get proper treatment.

Around one p.m., I get a phone call from the Flotilla 13 naval commandos to say that forty fighters are on their way to me by helicopter, and they'll be landing any minute. When they arrived, I spoke with them and briefly explained what was happening; I explained to them that I was primarily occupied with stopping forces coming from outside, but that there are still terrorists on the inside. And the commandos went into the outpost and engaged in battle.

Then, at three p.m., a miracle happens! The doors of the mess hall open and thirty soldiers come out. Some are seriously wounded, some moderately wounded, some lightly wounded; every single one of them has shrapnel wounds all over either from guns or from grenades that exploded in the mess hall – and some are bandaged with tourniquets. They were in the mess hall for over six hours, and for those six hours they fought like madmen. They sat inside and aimed their weapons at the mess hall door so that whenever a terrorist tried to come in they could shoot at him like crazy, and they succeeded. They blocked the entry of terrorists into the mess hall and basically kept themselves from getting killed. Out of all the soldiers that came out of the mess hall, there was a single stretcher with a soldier killed in action. Everyone else made it out alive. And at eight p.m., Flotilla 13 informs us that they have cleared the outpost of terrorists.

At one point, a large group of soldiers arrives in Sufa with a new company commander who has just replaced their company commander, who was killed. There was also a lieutenant colonel that I know there – we once worked together. I come up to him and ask him, "What's going on; what are you doing here?" And he tells me, "I came to replace Barnash." I looked at him and said, "What do you mean? I have to call him in a second and tell him that everything's okay now, that it's all over, and that we're in control. He's the one who sent me here." And he looks at me and says, "Or, Barnash was killed."

I looked at him in shock, and he says, "I know I'm like the Angel of Death right now. But that's the situation." And then I understand, it hits me: if they managed to kill Barnash, who everyone knows is a wild horse of a man – you can't keep that guy down! – if they took Barnash from us, then something truly inconceivable happened here.

There were also a lot of casualties at Sufa. A lot of casualties. And I remember, there was this moment at the end, when it was all over, a few minutes before they came to take the casualties away. There was a moment when they were laid out next to each other, and I went up to each one and touched their faces gently, I caressed them for a moment, and I told them that I'm sorry, and closed their eyes.

And I remember that I told myself at that moment that these people, who are now making their final journey – they were extraordinary heroes. They fought like lions to save Kibbutz Sufa. They fought until their last drop of blood. What happened to them is exactly what I was sure would happen to me when I was there on the embankment.

And to see those strong, noble fighters lifeless is something I will never forget. I never want to forget it. Those dead are basically a reflection of all our fighters. There is no end to their dedication, no end to what they granted this country, to the people who live here. They sacrificed what was dearest to them so that this country can continue to exist, so that we can continue to live here. And the feeling I had there, next to those holy soldiers who gave their lives, the love I felt in my heart – I'll never forget it for as long as I live.

I Wasn't Looking to Be a Hero, But That's How It Turned Out

Rami Davidyan's Story

Age 59

Patish

T he day before Simchat Torah, Friday, was the anniversary of my father's death, so of course the whole family came here to Patish, and all the kids stayed with us for the holiday, and all the grandchildren. There was this festive atmosphere, and we all had the holiday dinner together, we ate, we drank, we were merry, and that was it, we went to sleep.

On Shabbat morning I woke up early, like I always do. Me, no matter what I do, my biological clock wakes me up at five. So I got up early, I showered, and sat down to have tea and coffee with my wife Iris, who wakes up with me every morning. And then at six-thirty we heard the Qassam rockets like everyone else, and it was something out of the ordinary. But I, I have a tradition – every Shabbat morning I go out to meet my friends at Aroma Café, not far from Patish, and we hold our weekly "parliament" session. So I told Iris that I'm going there, and she said to me, "No, what are you talking about, there are rockets!" and I said to her, "Okay, I know, it's no big deal, when aren't there rockets?"

While we were talking, as I was debating whether to go to Aroma, I suddenly get a call from my friend, who says, "Help me, Rami, help me! I need you to get to a certain place to save my son!" He sent me something on WhatsApp, a location, and I said, "Sure, I'm going!" No questions asked. I just jumped into my car and headed off to that location. As I was getting ready, my wife said to me, "What is this, where are you going, look what's going on out there!" But I ignored her.

As I start to drive out of Patish, I see a bicycle lying abandoned on the road. It was an expensive bike, and as I drive past it, I think, what is this, who would do that, how strange. A minute later, I suddenly see a car abandoned on the left side of the road, so I pull up next to it and I see people shot up in the car. And I thought to myself, that must be a Bedouin car, there have been some Bedouin gang hits in the south lately – I still couldn't imagine what was really happening. I didn't understand what was going on. I called the police to report it, and the phone rang and rang, but no one answered me.

Okay, so I kept driving toward the location they sent me, and suddenly, about a kilometer later, I see a swarm of kids in front of me, running in every direction, like the Exodus from Egypt, something crazy like you only see in movies, and they're screaming, "Where are we! Where are we! Help us!" I realized something was happening, something big, but I still didn't quite understand what was going on, so I shouted to them, "Calm down, you're in a safe place! Come here, come to me!" and in about ten, fifteen minutes I managed to gather most of them together, and at the same time I called my sons-in-law, "Come with pickup trucks and trailers, come help me, it's an emergency!" And in the same breath I also called the head of our community council, Katie, and I said to her, "Open up the big bomb shelters, it's an emergency!"

In the meantime, I gave the directions to the young people that were there, so that they could continue on foot toward Patish, and I waited for my sons-in-law to come take the kids. And when they arrived, I continued on my way to rescue my friend's son; I found him about ten minutes later. He was there with like twenty guys – and I, I only had my five-seater, so I had no choice, I told them to get in! They jumped onto the roof, they climbed onto the trunk, they climbed onto the hood. Instead of five, I fit seven kids inside the car, and I started driving.

On the way out, from their stories, I understood that what was going on was very irregular, and I said to them, send my number to people who are hiding, we'll come and get them out, take my number. So the guys that I took out on the first trip started sending my number to their private groups, and then it progressed, within seconds it was spreading like wildfire, "Rami's number" was shared all over the country.

And then I started getting thousands of messages, thousands of calls for rescue, it was insane. And from then I started to work on autopilot. I drove out and came back, drove out and came back, each time to a different location that popped up, I couldn't even choose where to go first, I just drove, and the messages were so horrifying, I couldn't even start to sort through them, I couldn't even answer them. They were full of terror and panic and pleading, it was horrible, chilling. Most of the guys I picked up, I took to my place, some of them I dropped off in the middle of our community. And each trip became harder and more complicated, because each time I went deeper and deeper, closer and closer to the festival grounds.

After a few rounds, I realized that it was dangerous, there were still terrorists there, and shooting, so this is what I did: I would park the car in these low places, like in dry riverbeds, and from there I'd begin to run on foot, find the kids and rescue them, that's how it worked, until two, two-thirty in the afternoon. Some of the kids that I picked up told me terrible things; they told me that terrorists were waiting for the kids outside the orchards, waiting for them to come out, to shoot them down. It was a terrible massacre, horrible things, even in the worst horror movies we've never seen things like that. I don't believe there is any producer who could produce anything like that. It's not – it's just not conceivable, no, not at all.

✌

At one point I got a phone call from this amazing girl called Amit. The first time she called me on WhatsApp she was still full of energy, her voice was strong, but with each new message I felt like she was slipping away, like I was losing her. By the time I reached the location she sent me her voice had become really faint, and I didn't get why. And only when I found her did I get it. There were six armed Palestinians with her, they were holding her there! And I saw her and thought to myself, what do I do now, what do I do?

And then I just started speaking to them in Arabic, it was totally instinctive, I said to them: "What's going on, how are you, what are you doing here, my name is Abu Rami and I'm from Patish, from Rahat. I'm Muslim like you!" And I started negotiating with them, friendly-like, and then at some point I said to them, "You know, we're all in danger here, because the soldiers are going to show up any minute now, so listen to me, I know the area a little. Give me the girl, you run in this direction, and I'll run in that direction, and then maybe we'll meet up somewhere, run as far as you can!" I stood there just two meters away from them, and they were all armed, they could have taken me out in a second, killed me, taken me hostage, abducted the body, and I can't explain it, I don't know why, but they believed me. To this day, I believe that God's hand touched me – it touched me in many situations and in many places there – because they believed me, and gave her over to me, Amit, and minutes later she was in my car and we drove out of there. I did everything on autopilot, I was on autopilot.

And that evening, at seven, I got another call from some kids: that they had made it to some factory and needed rescuing, they begged me to rescue them because they had been there for a long, long time – they were there for nine hours – and the police didn't answer, and the army wasn't coming, for nine hours! So I said to them, "No problem, I'm coming to get you, just tell me what you see, give me some idea of what's around you so I can find you!" And then they said to me, "There's this room here full of televisions, and loads of cameras," and then it hit me that they were in this factory that I know well, so I drove in their direction with my son-in-law, and with someone else, and I'm happy to say that we succeeded in rescuing them too.

I had left my house at a quarter to seven in the morning, and I kept going, we kept going, until the middle of the night, I had a lot of rescues there. And the whole time, there were messages and phone calls and people pleading – that was the hardest, the phone calls, I felt like every one of those calls was from my own children. I hear a girl crying on the phone, "Where are you, I'm begging you, when are you coming!" and I have to go to her, I have no choice, there's no other option.

❧

At first I drove my own car, a Toyota Corolla, but soon after that I switched, I wanted a more massive car, one that could maneuver, so I took my son-in-law's car. And by the end of the night, both cars were full of bullet holes. Looking back, I realize that it was a miracle, I get it now. But at the time I was on autopilot.

Late that night, around ten, I got another location of a kid seeking help. I went out there, speeding the whole way, and when I got there I found him inside this cement pipe, but he didn't make it, he was already dead, they had murdered him. I knew that I couldn't just leave the body there; anyone who knows the area knows there are a lot of foxes and jackals there, and I couldn't just leave the kids lying there abandoned like that.

And that was it, from that moment I began collecting the bodies, kids' bodies. I drove and I found bodies by the sides of the road, and in all these little riverbeds. I took them. I picked them up into my car, and I set them down in a place where they could pick them up in the morning. I had this tree there, and next to the tree was a picnic bench; and that's where I brought the children that died, and I found all these jackets and picnic mats to cover them. And I kept going until the wee hours of the morning.

And on Sunday morning, too, I kept receiving locations from kids, and from parents, and I kept driving out to pick them up, we had a lot, a lot of work. Soon afterward, two guys from the IDF canine unit joined me with tracking dogs, and together we continued pick-ups; by now, we found mostly bodies. And we kept going, I didn't stop at all until Wednesday morning. It wasn't out of a sense of mission. I didn't think anything or see anything or hear anything. I just saw each task in front of me. I felt as if someone was saying to me, "This is your project, man. That's it. Drive!" That's what it was.

I was born and raised in a home where there was a lot of giving, a lot of giving. I grew up without a father from the age of twelve, and my mother needed our help at home, she needed us to give, and all kinds of people helped our family out, I remember it. So just like they helped me in the past, I need to pay it forward. That's what I believe in – giving to others. And I do give to this day; if I can help people out, if I have something to give, then I have to help. And these kids needed help, boy did they need help there.

While it was happening I wasn't thinking about anything – I mean, I knew that there was a massacre going on, and I saw what I saw, there were horrifying, horrifying things there, things you can't even begin to grasp. But in real time I didn't feel it. I didn't think about it. I'll be sixty years old soon, I can barely move, but I ran around there like a gazelle! At first I didn't think about it at all, but it hit me later, a week or two later, when all kinds of people started saying things like, "What's with you, what were you thinking? You could have died, you have a wife and kids at home." Only then it hit me.

And now, I – I have major trauma today. I saw a lot of burnt bodies, and all that. The smells haunt me, they don't leave me alone. When does it come back? When I come home and my wife is cooking me something, and there's this smell, that's when it hits me, it hits me and my heart just – my heart, I feel it all, and my whole body starts trembling.

There's one more thing that won't leave me alone. Something I saw that continues to haunt me. I can't go into detail because it's not appropriate for a book like this; it's just too horrifying. I spoke about it when they filmed me for the documentary "Screams Before Silence"; there I could describe what my eyes saw. Without going into detail, I'll just say now that I collected the bodies of many young women who had been ... sexually abused.

It's clear to me, clear to me, that this will stay with me for years to come. I know that I'll never, ever forget what I saw, I'll never forget it my whole life, there's no way I could forget it. It's already engraved on my heart, it's in my blood. That's it, it's imprinted on me. There's no way.

⁂

It changed me, this story, what happened, it changed me in a lot of ways. Everything got mixed up that day. The day of Simchat Torah, the anniversary of my father's death. And all the kids that were there. Those we saved. And all the bodies that we found. There were so many bodies there, so many bodies. Of terrorists, too. And it's all mixed up.

Today, I meet people in my town who get into arguments about nonsense. Nonsense! And I say to them, "Tell me, is it worth it, what's with you? The things I've seen, I saw things – let me tell you, we are living in paradise! What's with you? Don't you remember where we were just a few months ago?" I try to explain it to them, so they get a sense of proportion about what matters and what doesn't matter. Yes, I've changed, I'm not the same person, that's for sure. I don't know if I'll ever go back to being the same Rami that I was. I've also started therapy now, two sessions a week. I just started a little bit, maybe it will help me. I hope it will help me.

I really saw terrible things there; I saw things that you don't even see in movies. But I don't regret it. No, I never regret things, for good or bad. That's sort of my approach to life – to accept everything, to accept whatever comes. So I have no regrets, and I'm happy with what I did, with the people I saved, I'm really happy about it. I wasn't looking to be a hero, I wasn't, but that's how it turned out.

Daddy, You Are Not Leaving Us Alone

Hadar Bachar's Story

Age 13

Kibbutz Be'eri

The night before October 7th, we were in Yardena Park, this playground in the kibbutz. I was there with two of my friends, and we talked and laughed until late, and we made this clip on TikTok. We didn't post it, we just filmed it, and in the clip me and my friend made it look like we were making our other friend, Alma, disappear. We did it a few times, and at two-thirty we finally went to sleep. Only later, after it was all over, when Alma was being held hostage in Gaza – only afterward we realized that we had filmed a clip of Alma disappearing. And then she really did disappear.

My name is Hadar, I'm thirteen years old, and I live in Kibbutz Be'eri. My mom Dana ran a daycare here on the kibbutz, and everyone really, really loved her. She took care of really teeny babies, and I would be there a lot; we spent a lot of time together there. Ever since I was little I was there with her, holding the babies and changing their diapers. My mom had so much patience for the little kids; she spoke to them as if they were big kids. And they loved her, and the kids' parents loved her too. Everyone in Be'eri just loved her.

I really, really love baking – cakes, cookies, *jahnun*, pastries – I just love it. I have – I had – all this baking equipment at home because I loved making complicated recipes. I love baking everything – sweet stuff, savory stuff. Besides baking, I also love surfing. Just like my brother Carmel, who loved surfing too. I think I got it from him, my love for surfing and the sea. That's it, that's what I have to say about myself.

At six-thirty on Shabbat morning, we hear a lot of booms – boom after boom after boom – so we get up and go into the safe room like we always do. It was my dad and mom, my brother Carmel, and me at home. One of my brothers, Nofar, was in the army – he was on guard duty just then – and our oldest brother Rotem was in India on a trip. So it was the four of us in the safe room. Very quickly, we start to sense that something is off, something is unusual, there are so many rockets in five minutes, we had never seen anything like it before. Red Alert after Red Alert, more sirens and more interceptions. At one point, my mom hears this kind of megaphone; she hears shouts through a megaphone, "There is a terrorist infiltration!" So we checked the kibbutz WhatsApp group and saw this message: "There's an infiltration, lock your homes, turn off the lights, go into the safe room and lock the door!" We were all shocked by that message, including me.

We went into the safe room, and everyone is thinking, like, Okay, how long can it take; should we bother bringing water or food, nah, what for. So we're all in pajamas just waiting in the safe room. And little by little we see from the messages that it's starting to spread all over the kibbutz, and it's getting closer to us. So my brother Carmel runs to the kitchen to get this big knife, an Arcos knife; we even have a photo of him with the knife.

And after sitting there in the dark for some time, we had to pee, and we wanted to go out to the bathroom, but my dad said, "No way are you leaving the safe room!" so we peed in one of the pots we had in the safe room – my baking cabinet is in there. We even put some cloths that we found there into the pot and peed on the cloth so that if the terrorists would pass by right then, they wouldn't hear that someone was there, peeing. We were really, really quiet in there.

A little while after that, really not much time, we started to hear shouting in Arabic, really loud shouts right outside the window, then we heard the terrorists coming into the house, we heard their footsteps, and they came to the safe room, to the safe-room door, and they started shouting there in Arabic, "*Iftah al bab! Iftah al bab!*" Open the door! Open the door! And my dad and Carmel were holding the door because it didn't lock – they were holding the door handle – and the terrorists were pounding on the door and screaming at us, really screaming, and then my dad tells them in Arabic that there are kids here, "*Ruh, kulahn walad!*" Go away, they're all children! And the second he says that, they shoot at the door. The bullets go through the door and hit Carmel in his arm. His arm just flew out of place from the terrorists' gunfire.

Because my mom takes care of babies, she did a first-aid course, so she knew how to make a tourniquet, so we went over to Carmel together and made him a tourniquet, and the whole time the terrorists are shouting at us to open the door, and they fire at the door again, and they hit again. This time they hit Daddy, they hit his legs, and my dad is thrown to the floor, and the terrorists come right up to the door and try to open it but they can't; they must have somehow hit the mechanism and can't open it at all. And my dad, his hands were still okay, so he managed to make himself a tourniquet. And as he was treating his wounds, they started setting our house on fire, from the inside.

They started gathering things from the house, all kinds of stuff that could burn – chairs, furniture – and they set the entrance to the safe room on fire and made sure the fire kept going. Each time it went out, they lit it again, and the whole room was filling up with this black smoke. We couldn't see anything, there was so much smoke, and we couldn't breathe either. So we took out the cloths that we had peed on from the pots, and we put them over our faces, and that helped us filter out the smoke. We were there until three in the afternoon, something like that, with those cloths on our faces.

At one point, the terrorists decided to come at us through the safe room window. They started trying to blow up the window; they put these blocks of explosives on it, big ones. They were determined, those terrorists; they put down one block, and then another, and by the second explosion there was a hole in the window, and then they started throwing grenades inside through the hole. They threw three grenades. They couldn't see where we were because the whole room was full of smoke. So the grenades hit the couch – I got shrapnel in my leg, Daddy got some in his stomach, and Mommy got some in her arm, but it wasn't serious.

Then one of the terrorists stuck the barrel of his rifle through the hole and shot a few bullets inside, and one of the bullets hit Mommy; it hit her in the lungs, and she fell to the floor and was kind of folded over. All four of us were wounded, but I was in the best shape, so I took everyone's phones and started sending messages to whoever I could. I sent recordings to the whole kibbutz; I still have that message: "We need someone to come save us, we need help, we need it; Carmel can't breathe, please, someone, come."

And I called Magen David Adom, and they said that they can't go into the kibbutz. I called the civilian security head but he didn't answer – I didn't know that he was already dead then. I got a phone call from Magen David Adom, and they said, "Take the clothes off your mom! Check where she was hit!" so I tore off her pajama top and looked for a wound, but I didn't see anything, and she and Carmel kept saying goodbye to us – they kept saying, "I love you," "I love you all," and they slowly kind of faded. Carmel asked us to bury him with his surfboard, and that's what we did; we buried him with his surfboard.

At this point we were lying on the floor; the whole room was still full of smoke, and our nostrils were all black, but it was easier to breathe on the floor, so we lay down sort of on top of each other, and I'm trying to clean the black off of Mommy's nose, and I see that she's not able to breathe anymore, and she starts whispering, "I have nothing against anyone, I have nothing against anyone," that's what she said, and then she just died. And I call Magen David Adom, and they say to me, "Check her breath," and there's no breath. Then my dad says, "Mommy isn't suffering anymore, it's okay. Now let's focus on Carmel."

At some point I made myself a tourniquet on my leg. I took off my shirt and had nothing but my underwear on, and I made myself a tourniquet. I lost a lot of blood from all the shrapnel. Then they came back and started burning us again; they started another fire. At this point I got burns on my legs because they were close to the door, so I said to Carmel, "Come on, we have to move," so we moved to another part of the room. But then Carmel and my dad kept passing out, so I kept saying to them, "Wake up! Wake up! Stay conscious!" and I sent tons of messages, I called everyone I could, and I asked them all to come and save us. At some point Carmel started wheezing; his breathing was weird, and I tell him, "Carmel, listen, you can't wheeze now! There are terrorists outside, if they hear us, they'll come in and take us away and kidnap us, or they'll throw a grenade and we'll all die." But a few minutes later, his breaths got shorter and choppier, and he died too. I tried to pick him up so I could do CPR on him, but I didn't have the arm strength. I was really weak from all the smoke I breathed in. And Daddy said to me, "Hadari, Mommy and Carmel aren't suffering; now let's focus on ourselves."

So then I sent more messages from everyone's phones, and I sent a message to the kibbutz from Mommy's phone: "It's Hadar, we're all wounded, they're shooting here, come now. They blew up our house, Mommy and Carmel are dead, I don't want to die, please come now." And every time I heard a noise, I hid under this suitcase so that they wouldn't see the light from my phone. And I kept sending messages. Then one of the messages actually had an impact on someone; someone sent a tank to exactly where we were. We hear soldiers in the house, and my dad calls out to them, but he can barely shout anymore, he was in really bad shape, he kept passing out, so I shout to him to wake him up: "Daddy, you are not leaving us alone, we won't be able to live like that!" And he kept coming to and passing out again. Then I heard the soldiers, and I shouted to them, and they came to us, and they saw blood all over the room, and the soldiers were sure that we were all dead.

☙

It was like seven in the evening. We were there for about twelve hours with the smoke and the wounds. The soldiers couldn't open the door from the outside, so we had to squeeze ourselves out somehow, so I climbed out of the window, but I couldn't put any weight on my foot. And the soldiers brought me something to cover myself with because I was only in my underwear, and I told them that I need water, and they brought it to me, I drank a liter and a half in one gulp, in half a second.

Then they carried me in a chair and my dad in a stretcher. They took us to an exit of the kibbutz, and from there to an army ambulance, and from there to ambulances to Soroka Hospital. When I got to the ER the orthopedists came and cleaned up my leg and took off the tourniquet, and one of them said to me, "If you had kept that tourniquet on for another half hour, you would have lost your leg." They took my dad for emergency surgery; he was really in critical condition. They tried to save his leg, they tried to reconnect the main artery, but they saw that too much time had passed, so in the end they had to amputate it. But at least he was saved. At least me and my dad are still alive.

I don't know what to say about this story. I just don't know. I have nothing to say. I have dreams of going back to the kibbutz. I have dreams of becoming a pastry chef. But I don't dream much now, and I don't really know what to wish for myself. My friend Alma, who was held hostage in Gaza, was released in the hostage deal. Now we're together again; we sit together in the park and we talk. But something has changed. Everything has changed. Even when we're laughing, it's just not the same anymore.

My Dad Really Was the Strongest

Avi Amar's Story

Age 55

As told by Avi's daughter, Stav

◉ *Kibbutz Be'eri*

I was my father's prize jewel. He was always showing me off; he would always bring me along with him, even when I was a little girl. At every gathering with friends, at every horseback ride that was supposed to be just for the guys, just men, I was there with him. And he'd bring me to his police unit, and he was always so proud of me. He was this suntanned guy with the bluest eyes – not just blue, a blue that you could drown in, a sea of quiet, of joy, of life. As a girl, I was this pale blonde with blue eyes just like his. And he'd always bring me along and brag: "Yup, that's my girl, looks like me, huh? Came out just like her dad!"

I'm my father's oldest child. We're six siblings – soon to be seven. My parents are divorced, and my dad remarried twice, and his current wife – his widow – is due to give birth soon. Really any day now. Whenever people hear my family story, it seems like it must be complicated, but my dad made sure that everyone was on good terms, that everyone would get along well and love each other – that was his life's work, that we'd be a family. And he also always had a special bond with my mom;

even after they divorced they stayed good friends. That's definitely not something to take for granted.

When I was in school, he'd always make a point of coming to every event and every parent-teacher meeting, especially because he and my mom were divorced. I remember that once there was this day when they invited all the fathers to fix up and paint the kindergarten. He was given a small job, painting the fence, but my father decided to build a whole pergola! He came with his tools and started working there like crazy, fixing up the playground equipment, too, and all the fathers are looking at him, like, Hey, you're making us look bad! But that was exactly him. He was the *man* in any room he entered.

Right, little kids in nursery school argue with each other, like, "My dad is the strongest," "No, my dad is stronger than your dad"? Well, my dad really was the strongest. Always, always, no matter where I was, I always knew that I had this big strong guy for a father; I really felt safe wherever I went because I have my dad, and he is the strongest, and nothing can faze him. No matter where I went, what I did, or what I went through – he was always there for me, he always gave me that feeling that everything was going to be okay just because he was there for me.

He never raised his voice. I don't remember ever hearing him shout in my whole life! Not from stress; not if I was about to run into the street and fall; not even if I did something that angered him. He never shouted at all. When I was in high school, I even started to feel like insulted by it. "Dad, why don't you shout at me, why don't you even get, like, mad at me?" And he would laugh and say, "But why should I? You're really okay." He always said that he didn't need to raise his voice to show me what was right.

I remember when I brought my boyfriend home for the first time – I'm the oldest daughter bringing a boyfriend home, and my boyfriend was trembling with fear! He was scared to look my father in the eye, like, hey, Stav, where did you bring me, how am I supposed to face this guy? My dad had this strong, masculine presence. But as soon as my dad could tell that my boyfriend was a good guy, and that he'd look out for me, he loved him like a son; he hugged him and joked with him, and he'd always say, Where are there more guys like Itai; I want all my daughters to find someone like him!

My father was a sabra, a native Israeli, the quintessential Israeli. I always think of him in his sandals or barefoot. Actually, he was almost always barefoot; it was like he had an extra sole attached to his foot. He could walk on bizarre surfaces – thorns, heat, boiling pavement, freezing snow; he didn't feel a thing. And he would always have all kinds of scratches on his arms and legs that he'd never even notice. I'd meet him, and he'd have cuts that were bleeding, and he was not aware of them, and I'm like, "What is this, Dad, what happened to you? Come here, I'll bandage it for you!" and he'd be like, "Oh, that, I didn't even see it." He really was a hero like the heroes of old, of legends. He was that kind of hero.

Shabbat morning, October 7th. I woke up early that day because the whole family had planned to meet up for my birthday. My birthday is in September, but we hadn't managed to get the whole family together until then, and it was really, really important to me – and also to him – that all the siblings would be celebrating together. Everyone together. That rarely happened, of course. At six-thirty that morning the sirens began, and already then, he sent a photo of himself in uniform to the family group with a message: "I'm going in!" He was always going in somewhere. Whenever there was anything going on, any security incident, we'd receive a message: "I'm on my way!" On your way to where, Dad?

In the meantime rumors started flying about all kinds of terrible things in Sderot, and instead of writing, "Take care of yourself!" like everybody else, I just called him, and he answered – he always answered my calls – but later I realized that it was crazy that he answered because there were already gunshots in the background; he was in the middle of a battle then in Sderot. There was actually a horrifying bloodbath there, masses of terrorists, crazy numbers, and in the midst of it all he answers me! I ask him what's happening and start talking, chattering away, and my father interrupts me and says, "Stavi, I'll call you back later, okay?" That was when I got suspicious. My father was never too busy to talk to me; he would always drop everything that same moment to listen to me. So I say to him, "Okay Dad, take care of yourself; we'll meet later at the birthday party," and my father said to me, "I love you, I'll take care of myself, we'll see each other later."

And this is what happened, this is what we understood later. My father went first to the battleground in Sderot; at first the police thought that that this was the central arena, so he went there to fight together with the district commander, who was his commander. There was a crazy mess there; they were trapped in the police station, and there were snipers there. On the way there one of them took down like six policemen from my father's squad. They were killed right in front of him, and he kept fighting. As he was fighting there, reports came in about people taken hostage in their homes, about massacres in the kibbutzim and at the festival. People keep calling the police and sending them locations, and he understands the situation and says, "I'm not staying here." You can hear him on the police radio recording, again and again – "I'm going out to save civilians" – though the district commander tries to calm him down: "We'll send other forces there; you're a high-ranking officer, so come take over this sector here in Sderot," but my father insists, "No no, this sector's under control; I have to go save civilians."

And that was it: he started going from kibbutz to kibbutz, from place to place, based on the locations people were sending the police; each location was another person who needed saving. At one point he got to Kfar Aza, and he started fighting there together with Keter Tzoran, his friend from the unit. They fought there until the army came. What you need to understand is that the police were basically a human wall that day. That's what they did. It was easier for the police to be first on the scene, so while the army was being pushed back, the police went everywhere as reinforcements. And they just kept fighting wherever they went. Heroes.

As they fought, his policemen were all getting really thirsty, and my father realized it. No one knew where to get water, so my father said,

"No problem, no problem, it's on me," and he called the manager of the nearby gas station – he knew him, somehow – and told him, "Bring out all the six packs of water that you've got!" and within minutes he comes back to them with plenty of water, and all the policemen there are in shock, "What is this? Where did this come from?!" and my father laughs, "It's on me!" And of course, it was critical to pay the gas station manager – in the middle of the battle, my father transfers money to him to pay him for the water! That's my father for you. That's my dad.

And there, in Kfar Aza, someone takes that famous photo – a photo of my father holding a soldier, hugging him tight. It's the final photo of him. The story of that photo is that there was a soldier there, a kid who got shell-shocked, when he saw all the bodies and the burned houses, when he saw everything that was there, he just went into a state of shock! No one there knew what to do with him, and someone took his weapon away, and someone else took off his vest, but everyone just kind of stood around him and didn't know how to respond. My father takes this in and goes up to the soldier, pulls him aside, finds a place to hide with him between the cars, and bends down and hugs him. Some-one happens to be there and see this hug, and takes the photo, and that's how we have that amazing photo of his last hug.

That hug – you can really see how his fingers are grabbing hold of him tight – that's the hug I know so well; that's the hug that, if you're inside it, you can't be afraid of anything. That's the hug that he gives me when I'm going through my hardest times – that's how he hugs that sol-dier, as if he's his own son. He manages to calm him down. He manages to envelop him in this protective bubble. That's what he knew how to do best. Because my father, if you feel him beside you, if you feel that he's with you, you know that nothing can happen to you.

From Kfar Aza he returns to Sderot, responding to a call for help from some family; from Sderot he drives to Sa'ad; from Sa'ad he reaches Be'eri, and he's doing it all in his own car, not in a bulletproof vehicle or any-thing. He reaches the road where the festival was, and the road is lined with burnt up cars and bodies. There was another policeman with him in the car, and he filmed my father driving with one hand and shooting his handgun with the other hand, like some kind of Rambo.

They drove around the Gaza Envelope for hours, he and his guys; wherever they went they waged battle and drove off the terrorists. They killed dozens of terrorists on that day, dozens. The guy who was with my father in the car told us that on that morning, every time they killed terrorists, my father would stop the car, gather up all the terrorist weapons, take them apart, and toss them into his trunk so that they wouldn't reach the wrong hands. How did he know how to take apart a Kalashnikov? I have no idea, but he knew. And after everything, when they found his car, they saw that the trunk was chock-full of terrorist weapons.

When they got to Be'eri, a policeman there told him, "Avi, we're going to die here! Wait!" He understood from his commander, over the radio, that special police forces are supposed to go in soon, so he waits at the entrance, and every five minutes he calls the special force on its way to check where they are. When the unit arrives in their armored vehicles, he asks to go in with them, and the policemen say to him, "There's no room," and he just looks at them, and they understand that they need to make some room. The policeman who was in the car with him sees him going in and says, "Avi, we're going to die here; it's a deathtrap, and we have families," and my father says, "You take care of yourself; wait for me here; I'm going in."

The first stage of their mission was to get inside the kibbutz and go all along the fence to assess how many terrorists were there. Their intel was that there were thirty terrorists, but there were actually more than three hundred terrorists. They drive into the kibbutz; as soon as they go in the terrorists start shooting at them, but they just push on and pass them, and keep driving. After that they reach the breach in the fence on the side closest to Gaza. They see the opening, and they see the terrorists escaping, presumably running away from them, and at some stage they see some of the terrorists coming back inside, so they stop, and turn toward them to fight them, to shoot them, but when they stop, they suffer a direct hit from an RPG. And the vehicle was bullet-proof but not rocket-proof, and the jeep that my father is in takes the first hit.

From what I understand, my father was killed instantly. It was important to me to hear that; to really get into the details, to know that he didn't suffer, that he died on the spot. It's also important to me to say that my father was killed at the height of the battle, at the height of adrenaline, and that he didn't see it coming. He didn't have time to be afraid or suffer any pain; he was killed in battle after engaging and neutralizing dozens of terrorists. He was killed while performing the mission for which he got up in the morning every day for years: to protect civilians.

The army only got control of Be'eri on Tuesday; there were three days of battles there. Even then, we didn't have any information about my father. We heard rumors that there was an incident with police jeeps, but we didn't know anything. I called the police the next day. I tried to get a grasp of the situation, to get details, and I learned that he was considered "missing." On Friday night, at three in the morning, a full week after the seventh of October, a police delegation knocks at the door, and the officer stands there, and he's all trembling, and he says to me, "Your father was identified through DNA." I say to him, "Tell me if he's dead; I need you to say those words to me: 'He's dead,'" and he says them to me. I sit myself down, and I don't cry, I don't say a word. I sit down, and I take a sip of water, and they look on, waiting to see my reaction. I look at them and say, "I was a Casualty Officer, so I know more than anyone that there's life after this, and that we'll be okay. Thank you for coming; thank you for telling me in such a respectful way," and I hug them when they leave. And that's it.

This past year we suddenly started talking about my wedding and about having kids. It's still far off, but my father kept bringing it up. Kept talking about it. And once we had a really open conversation about it, and I said to him, "Wow, Dad, what does it even look like, having a grandfather and grandmother who are divorced, what does it mean? Your generation invented it, after all. I'm scared that my kids won't experience you the way I did." And my father laughed, "Ah, nonsense, what are you talking about; it's nothing like that! They'll come visit every Shabbat, and Pazit" – that's his wife – "will make them food, and we'll take them on trips, and we'll build a pergola with them, and we'll do silly things with them, exactly like it was with you!"

He really promised me that he would be the best grandpa in the world; he promised me that he would always be there for my kids, just like he's always been there for me, and it moved me so deeply. I was happy that my kids would grow up like I did, with this hero at their side. I was happy that my kids would get to feel what I felt, what his policemen felt, what that soldier in Kfar Aza felt. I was happy that my kids would go through the world with the feeling that there's this big strong hero watching over them, everywhere and at all times.

A few weeks after the funeral I went back there, to the place where he fell. My commander, who's originally from Be'eri, took me there; she showed me where he was killed. At the very corner of the kibbutz. From what I understood, their jeeps were left to burn there for a long time, a very long time, because the IDF didn't get near there. And that fire actually formed a sort of firewall around the two houses in the corner there. And my commander, she showed me those houses, and she said that in all the houses on the outer perimeter of the kibbutz, barely any people survived, but somehow all the people who were in those two houses survived. It seems that the terrorists didn't approach them because of the jeeps; so actually, even in the final act of his life, my father managed to save people.

That same night, when they knocked on the door and informed us that he was no longer with us, I went to wash my face. And when I looked up into the mirror, I suddenly saw him looking back at me. What I actually saw were my own eyes. Our eyes. But at that moment, I think I understood that something from him is still here with me, wherever I go. And at that moment, I decided that whenever I miss him, whenever I want him to be here with me, I'll go to the mirror and look into it, and I'll look for him inside of me.

Note: The photo referenced in this chapter can be found here:
https://bit.ly/aviamar

David Also Beat Goliath with a Stone

Yonatan Elazari's Story

Age 19

As told by Yonatan's mother, Miriam

◉ *Ofakim*

On Simchat Torah, when we started to hear about everything that happened, we weren't worried about Yonatan at all. We weren't worried because he wasn't supposed to be out there, he wasn't supposed to be fighting at all. He had barely been in basic training for two months; he didn't even have his own rifle yet. But then, on Sunday night, after twenty-four hours in which he was thought missing, we were informed that they found him on a rooftop. They found him there in his Shoresh sandals, alone on the roof, with a rifle, empty bullet casings, a knife in his belt, and a smile on his face. They found him smiling. And when we heard that, we said, Okay, that's him, that's Yonatan. He died exactly as he lived – on the roof, in his sandals, with a smile.

❧

Yonatan was a rooftop kid. That's what we called him. Ever since he was tiny, he was always climbing on anything he could. Climbing walls. Boulders. Everything. We always teased him that the song "Little

Yonatan," about a mischievous boy who climbs a tree, was about him. When I look through the photo albums now, I see so many photos of him on rooftops – even in the Torah day school where he studied, that was his unofficial job, to bring the balls down from the roof when they got stuck there.

At the end of twelfth grade, he started climbing seriously. He worked hard at it. His name was saved on my phone as "Yonatan the little monkey." He would climb on things with such ease, with such dexterity, as if there were no gravity. In general, it always seemed to me that Yonatan felt his physical existence was hemming him in. He wanted to stretch his boundaries. He wanted to be taller, he wanted to be stronger. He was climbing, always climbing. And when I look back over his life now, I truly feel like his whole life was one perpetual upward climb.

His physical capabilities were truly remarkable; he really had some sort of gift. He had confidence in his body; he felt secure in it. Later, after it was all over, we received footage from the security cameras on the street there, in Ofakim, and you see him running into the street where the battle was; you see him running there, before he went up onto the roof. His team commander saw the footage and said to us, "That's not something he learned in two months of basic training. That capability is entirely his own."

For most of his life, Yonatan was physically small – really tiny. A short kid, fair, with mischievous blue eyes and a smile you just couldn't miss. There are people like that; you just can't think about them without imagining a smile on their face. And Yonatan, that was his trademark, that smile of his. That smile just came with the package.

He was a child who loved nature, a sort of jungle kid. As long as I can remember, he had a connection with animals; he was also a vegetarian. It drove him nuts that people eat animals. And because of him, we had every possible kind of domestic pet – everything except for a donkey. He drove me crazy, begging for a donkey, but that was where I put my foot down.

When he was eight years old he started going to a wilderness survival class, and he was in it for five years. The guide would teach them how to build a shelter, and even on the stormiest days of winter they would go inside the shelter, light a fire, and cook. It was fantastic.

Survival also meant knives. He had a thing for knives. He always had some kind of knife in his pocket. In his teenage years, it took a more serious turn. He bought himself knives; he would carve them, make them, collect them. It made me a little tense; it seemed too much like a weapon, tending toward cruelty. I wanted my sweet Yonatan back, gentle Yonatan; what was this; where did he go?

He had three hard years in high school. The teenage years were very rough. His grades plummeted, he was glued to his smartphone, he stopped being vegetarian – he became tough, too tough. It was strange – it was like he put up this gruff, aggressive facade; like he was training himself not to be gentle, not to be sensitive. It was rough. We just didn't understand what was happening.

Looking back on it later, when my husband and I discussed it with him, and analyzed it together with him, we came to understand that this was his way of coping with a feeling he couldn't shake back then, the feeling that he was too small. He was very short at the time, and also very small for his age. And it suddenly made him insecure, his low height. He would actually cry about it, about how short he was. Because he was physical, athletic, healthy, masculine – and he felt that his appearance didn't match how he felt. He wanted to be strong, so he shunned everything that seemed weak to him, and he perceived anything delicate and sensitive as weakness. So he lived for three years inside this shell, inside a disguise. I cried then, and I prayed for him, and when he finally came out of that shell, it was like a butterfly emerging from its cocoon.

At the beginning of twelfth grade, he heard a lecture in his school about how social media companies manipulate people, and he was utterly shocked by it. His reaction had nothing to do with being religious; it was more about the kind of person he was, the king he was inside. He realized that he was enslaved to his phone, that he was being manipulated. So he took a hammer and broke his phone. Just smashed it to pieces.

He said to me, "Mom, I wasted three years of my life. Three years!" and suddenly it started happening for him, getting back to himself. He went back to all the things he used to do when he was younger; he went back to them as he was, without the costume, without the knives. And he just started gulping life down, swallowing it whole. He did everything possible: skydiving, climbing, mountain biking; he took his siblings on hikes; he went biking with friends from the Sea of Galilee to the Mediterranean; like he just remembered who he really was. And I could breathe easy again. And I marveled at the brave journey that my Yonatan had made.

Yonatan never faked anything. He never did anything just to please others. If he chose something, it was one hundred percent out of his inner desire. And that's also how it was when he chose Torah. He loved the Torah, Yonatan; he loved it with this love that's truly difficult to describe in words. In the final year of his life, he devoted himself to Torah. He was completely captivated by it. One of the last mental images I have of him is from the last Shabbat, the week before Simchat Torah. There was some kind of celebration in our community, and in synagogue they gave him a Torah to hold. And Yonatan didn't just hold the Torah – he embraced it. And that image is really burnt into my mind.

In August, Yonatan enlisted into Duvdevan. Duvdevan is a commando unit that specializes in urban warfare. It was his childhood dream, and he got to realize it. During his two brief months of army service, he just blossomed. His whole personality blossomed! He'd always had this sort of self-image as a fighter, and suddenly he was embodying this image, and he was just happy.

On Simchat Torah Yonatan was in Ofakim, spending the holiday in the religious school where he had studied Torah the year before – it's called Mekhinat KeAyal – and celebrating the giving of the Torah together with all the other students. He told us beforehand that there was no way he was going to miss Simchat Torah there; he knew what kind of dancing there would be! Later, his friends told us how he danced that night; how wildly, whoa, how he danced. He danced in a kind of frenzy. He danced barefoot; he didn't even wear his sandals.

In the morning, when the sirens started, all the students went into the safe room. But when they started to hear shooting in the street, he decided that he was going out to help. He went out into the street and saw that there was a gun battle going on. So he started picking up stones to have something to fight with. He didn't have a weapon, so he took stones. And that's how he went around at first, with two stones in his hands. David also beat Goliath with a stone.

And when he was outside, he saw a soldier fighting there; so he ran up to him and asked him if he had a knife. The soldier says to him, "Yes, but what are you thinking, bro, this isn't the time for a knife," and Yonatan said to him, "I'll work with what I have," and took the knife. At one point, he and the soldier started treating the wounded, and that was where he met Tali Hadad, who was also going around, trying to help, right in front of the terrorists.

Tali Hadad is a truly courageous woman from Ofakim. She evacuated the wounded there, under fire. And her son, a soldier, was also wounded there, so she evacuated him to Magen David Adom, and took his weapon from him. Yonatan sees her there, evacuating the wounded; he sees that she's going around with a weapon, and he goes up to her and asks her for it. She wouldn't give it to him at first – she sees this young religious kid in sandals; what could he do with a gun? But then he tells her that he's a soldier in Duvdevan, so she gives him her son's gun, and Yonatan takes it and runs off to fight the terrorists.

At this point, Yonatan joined two residents of Ofakim who were fighting there outside. He joined them and didn't leave their side. They didn't know who he was; they didn't understand who was this kid who hooked up with them and went with them from yard to yard, searching for terrorists. And as they were fighting, in one of the yards, he suddenly sees a dead terrorist. He jumps into the yard and takes away his weapon, and a battle begins right there. They realize that a band of terrorists has entrenched itself in one of the backyards there, and they're shooting in every direction and killing people. And Yonatan and the two guys with him realize that the only way to bring them down is from high up; they need to find a good, high vantage point. So they go up to the roof of a house opposite that yard, and Yonatan climbs onto the rooftop, climbing as only he knows how to climb, climbing as if he was born to climb, and he takes up a position there, and just fires away. And then, after a few minutes of fighting, he gets shot from below and is killed on the spot. With a smile on his face.

When Yonatan was in second grade, the rabbi told me that he was daydreaming too much in class. I came home and said to Yonatan, "The rabbi said that you're daydreaming in class." And he said, "That's right." And I look at him, and smile, and then he asks me, "Do you want me to tell you what I'm daydreaming about?" and I say yes, and he says, "I'm daydreaming that I'm a king." And he was a king; he was really, truly a king. But not a king who feels that everyone owes him. Exactly the opposite – a king who takes responsibility, a king who looks out for everyone, a giving king. I remember how, a month into his basic training, he told me excitedly that he was going to be a sharpshooter. I asked him what that was, and he said to me, "Mom, the sharpshooter is the one who dies first."

Just before the funeral, we got a message from Tali Hadad. She's fantastic. She heard that they found him on the roof, and when she heard, she recorded this message for us:

"Yonatan's mother and father, I want to tell you about your amazing, courageous child. A child who died for the sanctification of God's name, a child who chose to fight of his own free will. Yonatan could have sat watching the battle from the sidelines, but he chose to take up a weapon and fulfill his calling.

"I met him in the field, and he asked me for my injured son's rifle, and I looked at him, and I saw his amazing smile, and his big eyes, and his white shirt and his tzitzit – he looked like an angel. And he really was an angel. He was an angel who loved his country and his people. He was an angel who entered the field of battle, an angel who chose to fight against terrorists without any commander, without laws, without rules, out of joy and humility.

"And I want you to know that your son, Yonatan, fulfilled his purpose in this world. Be proud of him! He departed this world like an angel, dressed in white, with a smile and a glimmer in his eye. My oldest son is also named Yonatan. To me, it's a great name. It means: the Lord has given. 'The Lord gave, and the Lord hath taken away; blessed be the name of the Lord.'"

We were recently talking about it with the kids; about how now that everyone knows our Yonatan and his story, it feels a little like he's been taken away from us. And now, he belongs to everyone. None of us was surprised that Yonatan finished his role in this world in this way. None of us was surprised that Yonatan acted with such inconceivable courage. That was Yonatan.

But Yonatan was not a perfect role model. He could do stupid stuff, and he had struggles and weaknesses. And together with that, he had courage and inner strength that were expressed through his choices, and through the process he went through, his personal development. His courage reached its height at that moment of truth on Simchat Torah, but really, it had been there all along at every moment that he chose to keep climbing upward. And if there's one thing that we want people to take away from our Yonatan's story, it's that insight – that everyone has power inside of them. That everyone can take hold of themselves and raise themselves up. Everyone has the ability to make the right choice at the moment of truth and to turn himself into a king.

I Took Them Both Down from the Bathroom

Eliya Lilienthal's Story

Age 24

⊙ *Kibbutz Sufa*

I'm originally from Gush Katif; I grew up in Atzmona. I was six and a half in 2005 when the disengagement happened, so I remember it a little. I remember our house a bit; the synagogue, not too much; the kindergarten a bit. From there we moved to the town of Naveh, so I'm from Naveh. That's also here in the Gaza Envelope. In the army I was in the Armored Corps – I was a commander of new recruits, a sergeant for basic training. After the army I started working; first I worked in farming – I packed carrots and potatoes. After that I went to work with sensors at the Gaza border. I installed sensors in the new fence.

When I finished there I heard that they were looking for a new Head of Security in Kibbutz Sufa. I heard it from my girlfriend Yael's mother. I thought about it, I weighed it, and in the end I said: "Why not, I'll go check it out." So that was it – I started the job last August, a year and two months before the war, but I resigned even before the war started. I don't know, I didn't find that job fulfilling, I didn't make headway with the first response team or with the army; everything was sort of stuck, and I had done as much as I could. So I took an online investment course and started trading a little, learning the ropes. At the end of October, I was supposed to finish my job and leave the kibbutz.

In the months before the war we were always talking among ourselves about how there was going to be something big, there was going to be a war; it was really very clear that things in the area were heating up. It was in the air; everyone who lived there could feel it. We didn't think it would be anything like this, though; we didn't think that the army wouldn't be there.

The night before, I was at my parents' in Naveh for the holiday. We drove back late at night, and at six-thirty we woke up from the sirens like everybody else. At around a quarter to seven they called me from the battalion's operations room; they told me that there were serious terrorist infiltrations along the border with the Strip, between Holit and Kerem Shalom. But I didn't understand at all the scale of what was happening. I ran with Yael to the safe room; I called up the first response team and told everyone to take out their weapons and gear up. There was still a directive not to leave home because of the Red Alerts, so I told them not to go out yet, that I would come pick them up. My vest and helmet were still in the car.

Already at 6:55 I started to hear gunfire inside the kibbutz. I called the army's company commander for our sector, and he didn't answer. I called the battalion commander. He told me that the company commander had been killed, and so had the deputy battalion commander; that all the forces in the area were engaged, so we were on our own. That's a moment I'll never forget. We were left on our own. I decided to run to the car to get my gear – my helmet and vest – but as soon as I open the door of my house, I see these four terrorists right across from me, fifty meters away, and they see me.

I went back to the house, opened the shutters, and updated the first response team and the local council that Sufa has a confirmed infiltration. I could hardly breathe. A few minutes later I hear gunshots in front of my house, and I see two terrorists messing around with my neighbor's car – it looks like a security car, and he has cameras in front of his house, so they must have thought that he was the Head of Security for the kibbutz, and they started shooting up his car. So I ran to the bathroom, which has this small window, and I waited until they got a little closer, and I took them down. I shot through the screen so they couldn't see me – it was a great position because the screen kept me hidden – and I took them both down from the bathroom.

About fifteen minutes later, my neighbor calls me and says that she hears Arabic in the front of the house. So I went back to the bathroom and saw two more terrorists, this time a little further away from me. I took down one right away; the second managed to hide behind some safe room. We had a little exchange of fire; in the end I took him down, too.

After that I left the house. First I went and brought the terrorists' weapons inside so that the other terrorists couldn't use them; then I went to my car to get my vest and helmet. I said goodbye to Yael, who was in the safe room, and I started to pick up members of the first response team, who live at the other side of the kibbutz. First I went to my deputy's house because he was already injured – not from that day; he hurt his back at work – so I picked up his rifle for another member of the response team who was with us, Ido Hubara of blessed memory. In the end, we were six guys total.

A few minutes later, the guys tell me that they hear Arabic to the north. I couldn't hear anything that day anymore; when I shot from the bathroom, my ears got screwed up. So I didn't hear it, but they heard. We started heading north, and then, just outside the fence, in the corner of the kibbutz, we saw about fifteen terrorists trying to breach the fence. There was a ladder on the fence, and they had made a hole as well. We started shooting at them – we were a little far, and we wanted to get into closer range, so I told the team to cover me. I ran toward them, heading for this mobile shelter, really just a cement block. I wanted to get inside to get a good position, but as I was about to go in, I saw a terrorist right in front of me, behind the shelter!

It was only then that I understood that aside from the terrorists outside the fence, a ton of terrorists were already inside the kibbutz. A scary battle began – shooting, grenades – one grenade exploded next to me, just three meters away, but nothing happened, thank God. A few of our guys managed to take down two terrorists there, and Ido Hubara of blessed memory got a bullet in the head. A neighbor ran to pull him back out of range, and his father – Ido's father – came to pick him up with his ambulance; he's the kibbutz paramedic. He came to pick up his own son. A sad story.

At that point, after Ido had been shot, we realized that we were in lousy positions. We started to back up to find higher ground. I took up a position from the second floor on one side of the street, with Michael on the other side. Yuval went to the rear – he took down two terrorists there – and one guy stayed below on street level. That was how we made sure that no terrorists could come in. The whole time, motorcycles were driving up to the fence, and there were non-stop explosions and munitions charges from there, a non-stop exchange of fire. We stayed in position until one in the afternoon when some fighters from LOTAR, the counter-terrorism special forces unit, finally arrived.

The whole time I keep calling – the army, the local council, whoever I can. I tried to summon help. I heard on the radio that there was a mess in the kibbutzim, but I didn't understand the scale of it. Just in our kibbutz there must have been something like fifty terrorists. It was also important to me to be available to people from the kibbutz, to answer everyone on WhatsApp, to post updates – I wanted to give them the feeling that someone was out there watching over them. It was important to people. There was this twelve-year-old boy, Alon, who kept writing me; he sent me messages, and I calmed him down. I kept telling him that everything was okay. Even though it really wasn't.

At around two in the afternoon, a helicopter arrived. We guided it to the orchard, and they took down like thirty something terrorists there. In the afternoon I began to search the kibbutz from house to house with the guys from the special forces, to make sure that there were no more terrorists. By six in the evening, loads of forces had arrived: a tank, hundreds of soldiers, jeeps, helicopters, and they started taking people out of their safe rooms.

❧

I don't know why I did what I did. I had never been under fire before. I don't know. I mean, first of all, it was my job as Head of Security. As soon as I understood that we were on our own, that the army wasn't there, I knew that if I didn't go out, no one would, and we'd all be finished. What can you do? That's the job.

My mother says that it's all thanks to my video games. When I was a kid, she would always tell me that those games with all the shooting were chipping away at my soul. But today she says that maybe my soul was "honed" to get it ready for a real battle; that there was a guiding hand that helped me complete this mission. That's what she says. Maybe she's right; I'm not ruling it out.

The day after the battle, they evacuated the entire kibbutz to Eilat. I only joined them two days later, and the whole kibbutz gave me a hero's welcome, the whole kibbutz. I understood then – I felt – that I was here to stay. Even though I had already resigned, even though I had already officially left the job, even though we had already started packing. Yael and I decided to stay here. We reconnected with the place, with the people. We'll make a little money on the stock market, and we'll keep watching over the kibbutz. That's the plan.

I'm Going Out, There Are Terrorists

Moran Tedgy's Story

Age 41

◉ *Ofakim*

I was always the strange bird in the house. We're eight siblings, I'm the seventh. And I was always the strange bird, the one who was different. First of all, I was opinionated; my father, may he rest in peace, would always get into shouting matches with me – he was opinionated, too, and my son's the same way. And second, I always worked hard in school, I always excelled, and my whole life – really from earliest childhood – I would set myself goals and achieve them.

After the army I joined the police. It wasn't my dream, it certainly didn't come from home, but my whole life I had wanted to be a fighter, and in the army, in the unit I was in, they didn't want to let me sign on for longer, so I joined the police. I enlisted in the Special Reconnaissance Unit, I was a fighter for a year and a half, and from there I worked my way up. I joined at twenty; today I'm forty-one. I've been in the police for twenty-one years. Time flies, it's crazy.

One of the things that really kept me going as a kid and as a teen was playing sports. I played everything: basketball, volleyball, netball, track and field, shotput; I stuck with it for years. To this day, sports are a part of me. You have to understand what it does to a girl to be part of a team, to travel to competitions, to compete against other kids. Sometimes she experiences what it is to give her all, absolutely everything, and win, and sometimes – many times – she experiences what it is to lose.

And learning how to lose – that's also learning how not to give up. To learn how to lose is to learn that even when all seems lost, you can always practice, get better, stretch your boundaries, push yourself to the limit, and extract every last drop from your body and soul. That's something that's stayed with me since fourth grade, when I fell in love with sports. And that day, that Shabbat was that kind of day as well – one when I had to extract everything I could from myself, to the absolute limit.

At thirty, I came out of the closet. It didn't happen until then because I just didn't know that about myself, I honestly didn't know. I didn't get it. Girls would always hit on me, they could always tell, but I didn't get what they were talking about or what they wanted. And then, at twenty-eight, I wound up with a serious girlfriend, so I saw that it had to stop, I had to tell my parents, my family. I hired a therapist to help me deal with my parents; I was scared of their reaction. My whole life, they had been so proud of me and happy with me, and I was scared, I was so scared of disappointing them. The truth is that I also had to go through a process of my own. I had to learn to love who I was, and it wasn't so simple for me either. It wouldn't help for my parents to accept me if I didn't accept myself. So I hired a psychologist to prepare me for that, and at the fifth session, I'll never forget it – I decided that that was it, I was going to tell them.

First, I wrote them a letter, eight pages long, so that they'd have it to read afterward. Then I met with my parents – I told them I wanted to talk to them, I'll never forget it! I told them, "I'm in a relationship," and then they smiled, and then I continued, "with a woman." My mother's first reaction was to give me a hug. And then she started to cry. My father was silent.

It took them about another month to accept me. During that month, my siblings kept showing my parents videos of parents who distanced themselves from their children, and what it did to them, and in the end my mother came to me and said, "I'm not giving up on my daughter." Later, when my partner and I decided to get married, I went to my father and told him that I wanted a wedding, and then he said to me, "What? Just make a party for your friends! What do you need a wedding for?" and I cried, and went outside, and he came out to me and I said to him, "You think I chose to be this way, you think it's under my control?" and he understood, and then he was with me full on, all the way to the wedding.

And that's it, we got married, and we had two kids, a boy and a girl. Lavi Asher, who's six and a half, and Eldar Hallel, who's four. May God bless them. Lavi Asher was named for my father when he was still alive, and my father was insanely proud. They were very much alike – not just in name, but in personality too. And my son was close to my father on a different level; to this day, two and a half years after my father died, my son still dreams about him and asks about him and says to me, "Mom, I miss Grandpa."

We were together for eight years, but then it didn't work out, and we divorced. Now we're co-parenting, and we get along. Today I live in Ofakim with my partner, Stav. We're together a year and a half. Stav is also a policewoman; we actually met at work when I moved here.

> ❧

On the Friday night of Simchat Torah we were at my mother's in Beer-sheba. We had a meal with my family and Stav's family; we ate and laughed until the middle of the night. We only got back to Ofakim at three-thirty in the morning, together with Stav's family, and we went to sleep. And at six-twenty Stav wakes me up and says, "There are sirens." We go down to the safe room, I look at my phone and see the news: missile launch, interception, launch, interception, launch, launch, and I say to Stav, "Listen, war has broken out." That's what I said, in those words. I have no idea how I knew that.

I have a police radio at home – it's always with me – and I have a bulletproof vest. I went upstairs and got on the radio and I had a shock; within moments I started hearing the reports: terrorists in Ofakim, wounded policemen, casualties, chaos. I start calling my officers up to the station and getting in uniform. And Stav says to me, "What is this, what are you doing?" and I say to her, "What do you mean, I'm going out, there are terrorists," and she says, "You're not going out!" and I answer, "What do you mean, not going out?" and she says to me, "Wait, get a better sense of the whole picture, there are terrorists out there." Exactly then we see the first clip that went viral, a clip of a woman driving in Sderot and the terrorists are shooting at her – I see that and say to myself, "Okay, enough, I have to go!"

It's not that I wasn't afraid. I had this abnormal sense of pressure inside my body. And my body was shaking, shaking! I knew that I was going out into a firestorm. Into a sea of terrorists. Stav stayed home to protect the family, and I thought: Okay, I'm not going out by myself. I need someone else with me. I called a policeman here in the neighborhood, Gitai, and I said to him, "Gitai, get ready. I'm coming to pick you up." I went out, cocked my gun – just a Glock pistol, a personal firearm, not serious enough, and I went and picked up Gitai and said to him, "Come on, let's drive to the police station and get assault rifles."

On the way to the station I see a street completely full of Ultra-Orthodox residents of Ofakim in prayer shawls, on their way to synagogue. They didn't have phones with them on the holiday, so they didn't realize what was going on. So as I drove by, I shouted to them, "Get inside! Get inside! There are terrorists." And then, on the way to the station, we pass near where the action is, so I said to Gitai, "You know what, let's go there!" I didn't really understand that there was a major infiltration there. I thought it was something limited, a few terrorists, that's it.

I left the car on the side of the road and advanced toward the action. There were some policemen there, but I was the only one with a radio, so I automatically took command. I started radioing in reports and one of the policemen on the scene gave me a situation report: three policemen had been killed and there was a gun battle going on across the street. Terrorists had barricaded themselves with hostages. And the terrorists had the upper hand.

And suddenly we're caught in a barrage of fire. Boom! I was in shock, I said to myself, God! Where am I! What did I get myself into! It was crazy – and suddenly there were grenades, and RPGs flying toward us, and I run behind a truck and radio in reports. I realize that this is an extreme situation; that there are hostages; that we need a negotiating team here, a counter-terror unit, more forces – I reported everything over the radio.

Then a civilian comes up to me and says, "Listen, on the next street over there are three terrorists, holding four members of a family hostage in their own home! The terrorists are inside, inside the house!" so I say to him, "Okay, we'll respond soon," but he doesn't let up, he shows me photos! And then Effi, a commander who had arrived in the meantime, says to me, "Go take charge there. Take whoever you want with you and go!"

I turned back, saw who was around, and then I said to the ones I felt most sure about, "You, you and you, come with me!" We started running between the houses, taking cover, until we got to HaHita Street; on the way, we saw a man's corpse that had been flung out of a window, and I got that we were close. I come closer, and on the ground, I see empty magazines that the terrorists had left there, and I know that this is the house.

First I tried to view the house from every angle. I went to the side and I understood where the family was, and where the terrorists were – they had barricaded themselves in some kind of guest unit – and there was a sukkah hut left up from the Sukkot holiday that was in between them and the house. And thanks to the sukkah, the terrorists didn't see the family that was there. The sukkah saved them. And then, a moment before we went in to fight, I felt a need to take a moment and call my kids. I stopped and dialed. I needed to hear their voices and tell them that I was okay, that they should take care of themselves and that I love them. I called and spoke with them. After I hung up, my ex wrote to me, "Don't forget that you have kids. Take care of yourself."

After that, we brought the family outside. That was the first thing. I sent a policeman from an angle that the terrorists couldn't see, and he opened up the door for them and brought them out. He was lucky that they didn't see him. After that, I split up our forces and began to conduct a crazy gunfight with the terrorists. Crazy! There were three terrorists holed up there.

Their first volley of fire hit the officer next to me in the stomach, and I got shrapnel in my face. My whole face felt hot; I touched it with my hand and saw blood. We fell back for a moment, just to regroup, and then grenades started flying at us. And I realized, okay, we have to get organized here and bring in more forces. I reported on the radio, we kept up the shooting, and we waited for reinforcements. Two hours went by like that, with crazy shooting, and there were missile alert sirens blaring the whole time, and we kept firing at the terrorists, closing in on them, and never budging.

In the end, ten soldiers and a few more policemen got there. One terrorist tried to get out of the house and was hit. After that, we killed the others as well; all three were neutralized. When we went inside, we saw that they had not a small amount of explosive charges and a map of the synagogue. They came to the house to get into the synagogue; they thought they'd be able to kill people there.

From there, I went back to where I had been before, where the hostages were, and I see that the counter-terror unit has arrived and a battle is raging there. At the same time, I receive reposts of other incidents in Ofakim. This isn't my sector, I'm not a city cop. But the station chief had been wounded, and another commander was abroad, so I took it upon myself to take charge of responding to the incidents. And every minute there was shooting from another direction; every minute we hear the scream *Allahu Akbar*, and we need to respond. So many policemen went out to fight there to protect the civilian population.

I was out there for hours; I was responsible for the outer area of the city, with a bleeding wound in my cheek, ha! At one point, I found myself in a situation assessment with the mayor. It was utter chaos. And as the day went on, we started hearing about more and more friends who were killed in battle, so many friends – Itzik Buzukashvili, who did the officers course with me, and Jayar Davidov, who was the commander of the Rahat police station. They were good friends of mine.

I remember I saw a policeman sitting there on the ground, crying, falling apart, and I said to him, "What's with you, what are you crying for, get up!" and he points to the corpse of a policeman there, and says, "That's my brother!" and I realize that I'm not too far from falling apart myself, but I keep myself from crying, I keep it together.

Around six in the evening, I was in some part of the city, and I felt like I was about to faint. I had been running around fighting since the morning and I hadn't eaten anything or had coffee. And there was a detective with me and I asked him if he could do me a favor and go up to some civilians there and ask them for a square of chocolate. I felt like I was going to collapse, to break down physically and emotionally. So he went and came back with these bags of popsicles; the civilians there were so sweet.

I remember sitting there eating this funny, elongated popsicle, getting sugar into my system, and as I'm eating this popsicle I'm seeing messages about friends. I read that Devora Avraham was murdered at the party in Re'im, and that was when I broke. I couldn't keep it together. I had been holding it together all day, until that moment.

I went to the side and broke down sobbing; I don't know, like, it hurt so much. She didn't have children, and she was a unique, wonderful soul. I had been her commanding officer for three years – I had helped her develop. We had a deep bond, and we had such admiration for each other. I knew how to see the best in her, and how much she had to give. And she was a top gun; it was clear to me that she wouldn't leave the party, that she would stay there to fight. I just fell apart completely. A nervous breakdown.

Just a few minutes after that, they called me. A policeman calls me and says, "We need help." What kind of help? To inform the families about their loved ones. That's usually left to a welfare officer who's been trained especially for the job, but, to my sorrow, we had lost fifty-nine policemen. So I got a list of names and addresses and I went – without any prior experience, nothing. I just went to tell the families.

I informed three families. Those were insanely hard moments. Moments when I look them in the eye, and I don't understand what I'm doing. I don't even understand what I'm saying to them. There was this one girl, about fourteen, and when I told her, she just couldn't understand me, she just didn't understand. It was a family of Russian origin, I think, and they had this little red-haired dog in the house, and it kept barking, and there was a little boy trying to calm it down, and when I saw that boy it gave me a flashback to my son, and right there I just turned around with my back to the girl and started to cry.

I was out on the job for forty-eight hours straight. After forty-eight hours the body starts to react and does weird things; my hand suddenly started twitching by itself, and all these little tics, from the pressure and exhaustion. And I saw surreal things, just surreal. Trucks came to Ofakim loaded with terrorist corpses. Truckloads. And they also brought terrorists they had captured alive. We guarded them until the middle of the night. There were some unreal things there.

For the first two weeks after that Shabbat, I did endless shifts, twenty-four-hour shifts. The kids were at my mother, and I would drive over to them from Ofakim, and the drive was terrifying for me. Every time I'd come into the house, after a shift, I would search room to room with my handgun. And only then could I calm down.

It was a hard time, very hard. Another funeral, another family, another missing friend that we first thought was taken captive, but then we'd find out that they had been murdered. And we have to repress a lot just to cope. I'm still repressing so much, so so much. I know that to have survived is like the greatest gift. And I try to hold onto that. To wake up. God gave me my life as a gift. And I know, I'm sure, without a doubt, that my father was there with me that day. He watched over me as I fought there in Ofakim.

So many police officers fought on that day; so many police officers gave up their lives. People need to know that as police, we are sworn to serve and protect. And yes, to serve is to give out traffic tickets and to maintain order at protests. But we are also sworn to protect. And during those battles, the police went out and fought. In the end, it was the police who were the first to respond on that day. And I'm proud, proud to be a policewoman in the Israel Police.

This war is a completely just war. It's a fight for our very existence. And I swore that I'd keep working with all my strength, and doing whatever is necessary, until we win. There are still hostages over there; there are families who lost their children in that horrific disaster, and we owe them victory. Our children will grow up with this as their history; we, as a country, will teach them this history. And I truly believe that if we win, our children won't have to fight any more wars.

I Didn't Just Stare Death in the Face; I Embraced It

Mickey's Story*

◉ *Kibbutz Nahal Oz*

Never in my whole life did I think that the idea of killing my wife and my daughter would ever cross my mind for even a fraction of a second. But there was a point there – when the terrorists were at the door of the safe room – a point when we realized that this was it. My wife and I look at each other in total silence when my daughter isn't looking, and my wife makes this sign of two fingers walking like legs and shakes her head "No." She's basically saying, without words, "We're not going with them."

Then she points her fingers like a gun and points it at herself, then at our daughter, then at me. That's basically her way of telling me, "If they come in, kill me, then Netta, then yourself." And I nod. And I put my hand over my heart, signaling her, "I'm sorry; forgive me." She signals that she's sorry, too, and she smiles. A sad, sad smile.

I'm Mickey. I used to be a member of the security forces; now I work in agriculture. I'm married and the father of six-year-old Netta and ten-

---

* For security reasons, Mickey's full name cannot be published.

year-old Ofri. I was born in Ramat Aviv and grew up in the noise and anonymity of the city. No one knows you; I liked that. I never thought that at the age of forty-five I'd be a farmer, in love with kibbutz life. My wife was born in Nahal Oz, so when we looked for a place to start our family, I said, "Let's go, let's try it." It took me two years to understand that this was where I wanted to live. We've already been here for twelve years now.

When we came to Nahal Oz, life here was already complicated, with all the mortar bombs from Gaza. It's a tough way to live; it's tough to raise children knowing that at any moment something might fall on them from the sky. Nahal Oz is a very pastoral place, and this contrast between, let's say, the green of nature and the Red Alerts was very difficult for us at first. It was difficult for us to deal with that disparity. But gradually, somehow, we accepted it; it didn't frighten us quite as much. Not that anyone should get used to a situation like this or accept it, but the good outweighed the bad. And life was good for us.

On that Shabbat morning we woke up from the sounds of explosions and sirens. Our little girl Netta was with us at home, and our older daughter Ofri was with her friend from the kibbutz – they camped out in tents with some other families. As soon as the sirens started I jumped out of bed, called Ofri, and ran toward the tents. She didn't answer, and when I got to the campground I didn't see them there. I started looking for them in all the shelters, but they weren't there. I went back home and kept calling, and she finally answered. She said that she was at the neighbors'. She was tired so I told her, "Go back to sleep; it's just mortar bombs, it's okay." That's how it is with us: we're used to it, we don't get worked up.

So I'm in the safe room with my wife and our little girl, and I remember asking myself, after running to the campground and the shelters, I ask myself, "How long has it been already?" It suddenly hits me that it's been a long time; this wasn't the regular rate of mortar bombs. In those seconds, I realized that this must be a terrorist infiltration. And before I can even process that, we start hearing gunfire. At first it was at the perimeter of the kibbutz; I still thought it was the army or something. Maybe some incident at the border fence – it happens sometimes. But then I realize that the shooting is getting closer and closer to us. It sounds louder and louder, Kalashnikov shots. At the same time, we started receiving WhatsApp messages that there are terrorists in the kibbutz, and that they are entering homes.

At this stage the terrorists were only entering homes toward the back of the kibbutz; that's what the messages said. We live in the front of the kibbutz, and the neighbors where Ofri was are also in the front. But I realize that it's only a matter of time before they get to us as well. I call the Head of Security and all kinds of people who live in the back area of the kibbutz. No one answers. I call Ofri, no answer. Then I see that I can't send or receive messages either. The network has crashed. In the meantime, we start hearing screams in the distance.

Suddenly we hear Arabic everywhere, and we hear tons, masses, of terrorists outside. They're shouting with megaphones in Hebrew and English, "We're Hamas! We are Izz ad-Din al-Qassam! The kibbutz is ours! The IDF isn't here! Whoever is in the houses, come out and surrender! If you do not come out, we will come in to get you!"

At this point, we had no network and no electricity. I tell my wife and daughter to stay completely quiet, and I sneak out of the safe room. I have a Glock pistol; I had one magazine already loaded, and I had another one on me. I understood that I would need all the bullets I had. I have this whole stash of magazines at home, so I open it, arm myself with as many as possible, and prepare to fight.

After that I went outside. There's a small patch of woods next to my house, and I see soldiers in olive-green uniforms. For a moment I thought it was the IDF, and I felt this sense of relief that the army had come. But then they started shooting in my direction, and I realized that they were terrorists – a lot of them. I rushed back into the house and took off my police hat and shirt – I didn't want them to know that I had anything to do with security. I open the safe room to check that my wife and daughter are okay, I tell them to keep quiet, and I go back to the living room and wait.

Suddenly I hear them right by the wall outside our house. They're breaking the shutters, tearing the window screen, and starting to smash the glass. I run to our bedroom, which is right next to the safe room, take up position at the corner behind our bedroom door, and aim the gun at the window. A few seconds pass. One of them starts climbing in. I shoot him in the head – a single bullet and he's dead; he drops outside to the ground and dies. A second later, another one climbs in, I shoot him in the neck, and he falls outside. Two seconds later another one comes in, I shoot him too – a single shot in the shoulder – and he falls. All from point blank; they're that close. I remember their screams, their frustration.

Moments later, I hear glass breaking on the other side of the house. They're breaking that window too. I run there, find a corner in the corridor across from the window, and again, three of them try to climb in, one after another, and each of them gets a bullet. There's quiet for a few minutes, I get ready, then I hear more of them coming from outside – a serious number. I realize that they have it in for my house; I begin to think that they're specifically targeting me. I hear a jeep pull up next the house. Their forces are climbing out and shouting – they're very, very restless. Then there are a few moments of silence, then – boom! – an RPG explodes at the front door.

The door flies off its hinges. I pull myself together right away, get up, take up position in a corner between the bathroom and the corridor, and hide. They enter the house, and we begin to wage battle. They want to reach the safe room, but to get there they have to go through the corridor, and I'm basically waging a battle with them over the safe room door. Each terrorist opens fire on automatic before he turns into the corridor, but I just wait; as soon as they come into range I take them down with one or two shots, and they fall, wounded. Sometimes dead.

We spent two and a half hours there non-stop shooting. I have my Glock pistol, they have their Kalashnikovs. Some of them use armor-piercing bullets, but they don't take me down. That riles them up. As time goes on, I notice that their level of military competence is changing. The first teams of terrorists are well-trained, well-equipped; they know how to fight. But gradually, those who arrive are simply undisciplined;

they display less thought, less composure, just charging in wildly, shooting in every direction.

❧

Suddenly I see them throwing grenades at me. Two grenades. I manage to take cover behind the bathroom door. One grenade doesn't explode, but the second one blasts the door, and the shock wave throws me to the floor. I'm in shock for two seconds, but I pull myself together right away because I realize that now they can enter the hallway. So I decide to go back into the safe room to protect my wife and daughter from in there. I back into the safe room, close the door almost all the way, and wait behind it.

They come up to the door, and we begin to wage battle right there; they shoot at the door, and I shoot back. They start burning things outside, and smoke starts coming into the room. At one point they stop for a moment, so I immediately run to shut the door and hold the handle closed. They realize that I'm holding the handle, so they step back and fire at the handle; they try to hit me but miss. One of the bullets grazes me, but I keep holding the handle.

There are a few moments of quiet, then once again, a crazy boom. They had attached an explosive charge to the door, and it flies wide open. One of them reaches his hands into the safe room, but he doesn't get past the door – I shoot at them, and they can't enter the saferoom. My wife and daughter are huddled together in the corner, and I realize that it's a matter of minutes at most. I have one gun that fires one bullet at a time; I have to change cartridges every so often, and they have RPGs and explosives and grenades and automatic rifles. It's over. It was clear to me that they'd make it inside. And that's the moment when my wife and I silently decide that we won't go with them, that if they come in, we'll shoot ourselves and die together, free.

So they shoot inside, and the room fills with ricochets, shrapnel, smoke. A serious battle. Suddenly I hear my daughter shriek, "Daddy stop! Daddy stop! Daddy, come here! Come back to us!" When she shrieked, I screamed back to her. My screaming must have made them think that I wanted to surrender or something. So they stop shooting, and one of them suddenly starts speaking to me. He says, "What's with you? You don't have a chance. Just surrender, don't be stupid."

I answer him in Arabic. His eyes open wide; he doesn't understand where this Arabic is coming from all of a sudden. I address him and his comrades and tell them that I'm an Arab, and I know the Koran, so they shouldn't kill me. That throws them off. They say to me, "But there's a different name on the house." Suddenly, I know for certain that they want me. They've come especially for me; they must have intelligence to come specifically to me because they know that I'm in the security forces, and they want either to kill me so that I can't resist them, or take me to Gaza.

At this point they go away for a moment, so I jump right up to close the safe room door. The door is riddled with holes so badly that you can see through it. But when it's closed, you still can't get in. Two minutes later, they come back with their commander – the Hamas commander who carried out the entire massacre in Nahal Oz.

So the leader comes in, and everyone falls silent. From behind the door I can see him – I see him through a hole in the door, and I can see that he's holding a shoulder-fired missile, an RPG, and it's pointed at me. He asks me, "Do you surrender?" and I said, "Yes, I surrender, I'm coming out, let's end this." But I don't come out of the safe room. I tell him that I surrender on the condition that he won't hurt my wife or daughter. When I say that, his men leave, disappear, move on to another house. Now it's just him and me.

I realize that I'm about to be taken hostage, so I try to buy time. I start talking to him. I ask him for a cup of water, and he says to me, "Come out, I'll even make you a cup of coffee." Later on, I heard that that's what he did with the neighbors, the ones who were taken hostage: he went into their homes, spoke to them nicely, reassured them that nothing would happen. An intelligent guy, very slick, very clever.

I ask him in English, "Why are you doing this? It's against Islam to kill women and children," and he answers me in English, "Of course not, we're not killing women or children; we're not doing anything like that." We keep talking for five, ten, fifteen minutes. I'm playing for time – I'm behind the saferoom door; he's pointing the RPG right at me. I know, I just know, that I'm going to be taken hostage. I'm sure of it. Suddenly, he says to me, "That's enough. Come out of the safe room now and come with me." So I say to him, "Just two more minutes, give me two minutes to say goodbye to my wife and daughter."

Another two minutes pass, and he shouts to me, "Your time's up!" I start asking him another question, and he shouts, "No more talking! Now I'm beginning a countdown!" I say, "What do you mean, a countdown?" I see him standing across from me, across from the door of the safe room with the RPG, and he starts to count: "Ten! Nine!" I ask him, "Why are you counting?" and he says, "Because if you don't come out, I'm shooting inside and finishing you off!" and he continues, "Eight! Seven!" When he gets to three, I shout to him, "Stop! I'm coming out!"

He says to me, "I want you to come out with your hands up. Leave the gun on the floor. Open the door and kick the gun over to me." I say to him, "Okay, that's what I'm doing, okay. I've been injured; let me just put the gun down, and I'm coming out." I'm behind the door; he can only see a small part of me. I begin to rattle the gun and the cartridges so that he'll think that I'm putting them down.

I'm standing in front of the door and say to him, "But you promised me that if I come out, you won't shoot my wife and daughter. I'm coming out now, so you have to keep your promise. Put down the RPG; why do you have to stand there aiming the RPG?" He says to me, "You're right." In that fraction of a second when he says "You're right" and starts lowering the RPG, and his eyes move – I open the door, charge forward with my gun, and shoot him. In the groin.

After he went down, no one else came into our house. We waited inside the safe room until they came to rescue us. We waited for hours. As soon as the army came and we were rescued, I ran to find out what had happened to my Ofri. I ran the hundred meters to our neighbors' house, and she was there with them in the safe room; the terrorists hadn't hurt them. When I see her there, when I got to her and saw she was okay – I can't describe how it felt to hug her; it's something you just can't explain.

✒

I don't feel like a hero. It's hard for me. My friends, my close neighbors – they were killed, some of them were taken hostage. All I did was protect my family; if only I could have done more. Not a day goes by without thinking about my friends from the kibbutz who were taken hostage. I'm sitting here with my wife and my two daughters, and my friends are hostage, alone, separated from their wives, from their children. It's hard. Sometimes I can't even eat, knowing that they might not have anything to eat or drink.

Many families in Nahal Oz, many of the households, didn't even have a gun to defend themselves with. We were lucky, or maybe it was destiny. My wife isn't usually a believer, but even she says that maybe there was someone watching over us here. But what about all those people who didn't have that happy ending? It's hard, very hard.

But there's something else in this whole story that gives me strength. There's that expression, "I stared death in the face." Me, I didn't just stare death in the face; I embraced it. I made my peace with it. I even thought of helping it along. What would have happened if my wife and I had given up – if after they blew up the door to our safe room we had just given up? To tell you the truth, it terrifies me, it terrifies me to think about it. I was certain that we weren't going to make it; a few times I was convinced of that, absolutely certain.

But somehow, I got through the whole story, and my family is still alive, and today, I can say with absolute certainty: *Ein ye'ush ba'olam,* There is no despair in the world. That's a very strong feeling of mine. There's no despair. There is no such thing as giving up. Even when you see the end, even when you're sure that it's over – don't give up. Never, ever, ever give up.

Everything He Did, He Did to the Fullest

Yaakov Krasniansky's Story

Age 23

As told by Yaakov's mother, Zvia

Kibbutz Nahal Oz

Our home is Ultra-Orthodox, so Yaakov grew up in an Ultra-Orthodox home. I grew up in a religious home, Religious Zionist, then later became Ultra-Orthodox. My husband grew up in a kibbutz, Ein Carmel; after the army he left the kibbutz and became religious. We have four children: Miri, Shmuel, Or-Tamar, and Yaakov. Yaakov is the youngest. He was enveloped in warmth and love from the day he was born.

He was a special boy, really special; everyone felt it. He excelled at his studies in the Talmud Torah primary school near our home in Jerusalem; he was an exceptional, smart, brilliant, beloved boy, the leader of the class – but in this quiet way, not aggressive, always calm. From there he went on to a good yeshiva where he did very well; they called him "our *mizrah*," which loosely translates to "our lodestar." That's what they call the top students. He would leave home at five-thirty each morning, on the first bus, he would get there before everyone else and sit and learn, and the rabbis loved him. All the students wanted to be friends with him and loved him deeply. You couldn't help but love him. That's how it was when he was an Ultra-Orthodox yeshiva student, and that's how it was in the army. That's what we heard: he was a tough commander, very professional, but then he'd always be there for his soldiers. He was attentive to all their needs; he'd do their duties alongside them – he'd wash dishes with them, clean the toilets with them, no ego, no nothing. He was a champ at *ahavat Yisrael* – loving the people of Israel. He just loved everyone.

After the Talmud Torah school he moved on to the Or Yisrael yeshiva in Petach Tikva. There he was simply an *ilui*, a prodigy; that's how they all saw him. But Yaakov, even though he really loved the yeshiva, felt that he was looking for a different kind of Torah study, and one day, he decided to leave. The yeshiva couldn't believe he was leaving; they just couldn't believe it! They saved his room for him, and his bed; they tried to get him to come back, but he had already moved on. Every decision Yaakov made – whether it was to change his yeshiva or to join the army – we supported him wholeheartedly. We trusted him completely; what he said mattered to us. We wanted to know what he was thinking – his opinions were very important to us. Our Yaakov was a source of pride, whether he was in yeshiva or in the army. Always.

At a certain stage, Yaakov realized that he wanted more from life. He decided to complete high school matriculation exams instead of spending all day solely on religious studies. So he moved to Yeshivat Nehalim, a Religious Zionist high school where they offer secular studies, and he studied there for seven months. He had never learned mathematics or English before, but nevertheless his grades were excellent. Excellent, but not enough for him, so he stayed on for another six months and retook all his exams. He took the highest-level math exam, the highest-level English exam. That's Yaakov – everything he did, he did to the fullest, all the way.

❧

Before the army, Yaakov decided to get in shape. Fitness was important to him; he really got into it and started working out – all day, every day! He never missed a day – no matter what, even after he enlisted, he would come home from the base and go to the gym, come home and go for a run.

After he enlisted in the army – he joined what's called the Border Police – I said, "Oy, for God's sake, what now; he's definitely going to want to leave home." I was really sad about it. In our Ultra-Orthodox neighborhood, drafting to the army is unusual. I didn't say anything to him, but inside, I was really sad that he might feel more comfortable moving out. But in the end, what happened is that he didn't leave home – even in the army, throughout his regular service, he stayed at home. He wasn't religious by then, and we're an Ultra-Orthodox family, but we still got along. We had a lot of love here. We have a two-story house; downstairs there are two tiny bedrooms, and on Shabbat, he had the whole top floor. He didn't bother us, and we didn't bother him. We never bothered him. If you have love and respect like that, then there's room for everyone.

It didn't bother the neighbors either – it's an Ultra-Orthodox neighborhood, but everyone knew him and loved him and respected him; they told me that every time he would go out of the house and go down in his shorts to work out, he would lower his eyes and look down so that no one would feel awkward. They all loved him and appreciated him. Even here in our neighborhood.

He finished his army service about half a year ago, but then he went back to serve – he signed on as a career soldier. In between, he took a few months off and got his driver's license, and he studied for his college entrance exam and got a 770 out of 800. That was the kind of person he was. He was a person who did things to the fullest.

❧

On the morning of Simchat Torah I woke up very, very early and went to *vatikin*, the prayer service at dawn. Something happened to me at the prayer service that I think had never happened to me before. I just couldn't stop crying; I cried from the beginning of the prayers to the end, for no reason; I didn't feel any pain or sorrow or anything, but I cried. I can't really explain it. After that, I left prayers quite calm and went home, and as I'm slowly making my way up the stairs, I see my Tamar waiting in the stairwell, which is unusual, and I'm like, "What happened?" and Tamar says, "What? Can't you hear the sirens?"

That Sabbath of Simchat Torah, Yaakov was on duty at Kibbutz Nahal Oz, right next to the Gaza border. He was on call there, the commander of eleven fellow fighters, all guys from the undercover police unit. They weren't part of the IDF – they were police, not army. Everything I can recount about the day that Yaakov was killed is based on what his fighters told us. A fighter named Yoni came to visit us during the shiva week of mourning, and Yoni was with Yaakov during his final moments. Thanks to Yoni, I know what happened.

The story really began the night before, on the eve of Simchat Torah. Yaakov's group was stationed in the kibbutz and made themselves this "fun night" in their rooms. They played all kind of games there – board games, soccer; they joked around, made some noise, had a good time; it was fun for them.

The kibbutz's head of security, Ilan, was outside on the porch with his wife. It was already one o'clock in the morning, and they heard the racket that Yaakov and his guys were making. Ilan's wife says to him, "The guys here are awfully noisy; maybe try and get their commander's number and ask him to quiet them down." So Ilan makes a few calls and manages to get hold of Yaakov's number. But a moment before he actually calls him, he says to his wife, "You know what, forget it; let them have their fun," and she agrees, and they don't call him, and they go to sleep. But because of that noisy soccer game, it turned out that Ilan the security head had Yaakov's number on his phone.

Yoni told me that after they played soccer, something happened that he'll never forget. It turns out that after the game, when they were all preparing for bed, Yoni says to Yaakov and a few more guys there that he feels frustrated, that he's bummed out by his service. Yaakov asked him why, and Yoni said to him, "I feel like I'm not doing what I was trained to do; I want more than this." That really shook Yaakov up, and he said to him, "I don't get you. We're posted at one of the most sensitive locations in the country, and they're counting on us to do the job. Wherever we go, we bring security; that's our job, that's what we're about."

What happened after that is that they talked until four in the morning! A truly amazing conversation. Yaakov basically explained to them what it means to be a fighter; how a fighter needs to conduct himself, how he needs to be alert and prepared for whatever's liable to happen. In that conversation, he basically went over military doctrine with them – as if he had some prophecy, as if he knew that in just a moment they would need to put it into practice. Thanks to him, this is what Yoni said, thanks to Yaakov, "When we went out to battle in the kibbutz, we had two things going for us. First, we were ready. Second, we knew at every moment that we had a commander that we'd follow through hell or high water."

At six-thirty in the morning, Yaakov and his men wake up to a Red Alert and an endless barrage of rockets – two straight hours of sirens. The number of rockets falling was just not normal. So at that first moment, the whole group, all eleven fighters, woke up and went to the safe room. They were there for a few minutes. Then they started hearing gunshots, all different kinds of shots at the same time. Rifle shots and anti-tank missiles. Very, very unusual.

What Yoni told us is that, while all the guys there were still getting themselves together, Yaakov was already in touch with the Nahal Oz Outpost. He called their operations room and spoke to the surveillance soldiers there. They told him that terrorists were attacking the outpost! At that very moment they were infiltrating it! So Yaakov immediately plans to set out with his guys to fight at the outpost, but a moment before he goes off the radio, the surveillance soldier shouts to him, "Now they're infiltrating the kibbutz too!"

As soon as he hears that, Yaakov decides that their first duty is to fight in the kibbutz instead of the outpost. He figures that the outpost already has soldiers, so they have someone who can fight and ward off the attack. Of course, unfortunately, it turned out that that wasn't what happened at all; there were far too many terrorists, the outpost was overrun, and a lot of soldiers were killed there. But in the kibbutz, if Yaakov and his fighters hadn't fought there, it would have ended up far, far worse. What happened was that Yaakov's decision to stay and fight there with his force basically saved the kibbutz.

Yaakov called up his guys, and they all got into uniform and got ready. As they were getting ready Yaakov got a message from Ilan, the civilian security head. It was a lucky that he had his number. Ilan updated Yaakov in real time, when the terrorists were breaking into the kibbutz through a breach in the fence near his house. He sent his location; there were already dozens of terrorists there.

It turned out that Ilan was murdered just a few minutes later. Ilan Fiorentino, may the Lord avenge his blood. The terrorists purposely went there first because they knew he was the head of security. Unfortunately for us, they had good intelligence, and they wanted to murder him first so that he wouldn't interfere with their murdering other people in the kibbutz. But even though Ilan was killed, his message had already been sent. Yaakov received his location and said to his fighters, "Listen, there are terrorists just a few meters away from us. We're not getting into vehicles; we're going there on foot."

I don't know how he came to that decision, but it was very clever, and it saved his guys. If they had gone in armored vehicles, one of the fighters told us later, then the vehicles would have drawn fire, and the terrorists had special rockets for that purpose. It would have been a deathtrap.

❧

So Yaakov and his force start advancing toward Ilan's house. Within seconds, they already encounter terrorists, but Yaakov keeps running forward. He left a few fighters there and ran ahead with the rest. He realized that if they didn't get there fast, the terrorists would enter the kibbutz and start killing civilians.

On the way heavy fire is directed at them, really heavy! There were so many terrorists there, and so many snipers; they just shot at them from every direction, and Yoni told us at the shiva that "Yaakov just ran forward! I've never seen such determination to make contact with the enemy!" All the soldiers there saw Yaakov and his bravery, and they followed him. Yaakov's bravery helped them overcome their fears. That's what Yoni said.

At a certain stage, when they're really close to the location that Ilan sent, Yaakov encounters a terrorist just a meter away, and before he shot him he made sure that he wasn't a civilian from the kibbutz or something like that – he said something to him in Arabic, I don't remember what, and the terrorist turned around, and that was how Yaakov knew he wasn't a civilian. So he shot him and killed him. He shot him only when he was certain that it wasn't anyone from the kibbutz; he didn't want to harm any innocents, God forbid. That was Yaakov's heart; that was how he worked.

At that stage a very big battle began. It was fierce, and Yaakov and his selfless fighters fought there bravely! They killed terrorists and put a halt to the massacre right at the start. In that battle, after a while, Yaakov gets shot in the leg. He goes to the side for a moment and takes care of it himself; he applies some kind of tourniquet to stop the bleeding, and he returns to the fight.

Then – it's hard for me even to think about it – he gets shot again, in the same wounded leg. Even then, he doesn't give up. He keeps shooting, keeps on killing terrorists. The third bullet that hits him fells him to the ground. But even then – even after three bullets! – Yoni told us that he was lying down, but he kept shooting and killing terrorists. He fought like that, wounded; sometimes he lost consciousness and then would regain it and go back to fighting some more. Then, when his body couldn't contain his soul any longer, the Holy One, blessed be He, gathered him in.

⁂

While this was happening, all that day, I was at home, and I was really worried. I went back to the synagogue and prayed and cried and worried, and I couldn't eat a thing. We read the whole book of Psalms that day, word by word, and we prayed and wept, and then at 4:30 in the afternoon, there was suddenly a knock on the door – I'll never forget it my whole life long – these strange knocks, and my husband didn't want to open the door, but I said to him, "Open up, open the door." And he opens the door and sees a Border Policewoman there with four more behind her, then one of the officers asks me, "Do you know anything? Has anyone spoken with you?" and I said, "No, I don't know what's going on," then he says to us, "Sit down." That was a difficult moment, very difficult. They explained to us what happened; they told us that they had the body and that it was in good condition – many of the bodies there couldn't be recovered, many of them were burned, and there were many people missing – but thank God, it sounds awful, but we were happy that at least we knew what had happened. That's what happened on that Simchat Torah day.

We found out afterward that more than a hundred terrorists went into Kibbutz Nahal Oz. Even so, the scale of destruction was significantly lower there compared to the other kibbutzim. It's the closest kibbutz to the border, closer than Be'eri, and it should have been hit worse than Be'eri. But in the end, in Kibbutz Be'eri there were over one hundred casualties and thirty-three hostages. In Nahal Oz, where my Yaakov fought, there were sixteen casualties and six hostages. But beyond those victims, four hundred and fifty residents of Kibbutz Nahal Oz were saved.

‎֍

Yaakov always said that he had a mission, a mission for the people of Israel. He always talked about it; he could feel it all the time. He talked about it from age sixteen, that he had a mission. Recently, just before Simchat Torah, something came over him. He ate much less – on the Sabbath he would always eat without leaving a crumb – but he suddenly stopped eating. And a friend of his from the army told me that they were at the Western Wall a week or two before the war, for *Selihot*, late-night penitential prayers, and he suddenly saw Yaakov with a cigarette although Yaakov never smoked. I think that he sensed something. He sensed that something was about to happen.

He was such a beloved child, so very loved; wherever he went they loved him deeply. I always thought that he was something special. I remember how, when he went to the army, I would pray every night that he would thrive there as he'd thrived in yeshiva because they always respected him at the yeshiva and admired him. But he decided to leave that world; he decided to go be a Border Policeman, and I was afraid that he wouldn't do well there. I would stand by the window and pray, and say to God, "That's my son, and he's Your son too. Please help him so that they will love him there; help him succeed, help him thrive there." Oy, had I known what would happen, I wouldn't have prayed like that.

But that's what happened. My Yaakov was killed as he was trying to save innocent people, to save other Jews. He told his soldiers, "We're going to save the kibbutz!" And they followed him past all the terrorist pickup trucks and motorcycles. They followed Yaakov, and they fired, and fired, and fired! And the kibbutz was saved, and Yaakov was killed. That was his mission. That was his purpose in the world.

Each One Taking Their Bungee Jump

Shachar Butzchak's Story

Age 40

📍 *Ofakim*

I n tenth grade, I had this friend who wanted to go bungee jumping. I have no idea why people go bungee jumping, but that's what he wanted. So the instructor fastens him into his harness up there on the bridge. He connects the harness to the cord, and my friend jumps; the second he jumps, the second he's in the air, the instructor shouts to him, "Wait, wait, I didn't connect the harness!" and the guy is falling, falling, falling and hears him and knows that it's over, it's all over – then suddenly the rope catches him. Turns out that this is a trick that the instructor always plays on everyone who jumps – as soon as they're in the air, he shouts out, "I didn't connect the harness!"

I think that that jump is a good example of how faith works. Bungee jumping is having faith! I mean, this person is about to jump off a bridge and knows that he's fastened into a harness; he does it and it's scary, right? But he knows that he's tied to something, that it all means something, that something up there will catch him, and in the end he's going to make it out alive. Then you have someone else who does the same jump, but he thinks that he's not tethered to anything; he thinks that nothing's holding things together; he falls through the air just like the other guy, but it's a million times more terrifying, a million times harder. From his perspective, that's it, life is over. Even if he discovers in the end that he actually *is* connected, the experience of the jump is harder and scarier. It's much easier to make that bungee jump when you know that you're connected to something that in the end is going to catch you. That's what faith gives you in life.

That's what kept me going that whole time, I think; that's what kept me going when they were shooting at me, when I fell – I felt, I *knew* that I was connected to something bigger. That's what gave us all, whoever was there, the courage to come out to fight. Sixty residents of Ofakim got up on that day and ran outside while a terrible massacre was raging; they knew that they had to do it – not for themselves, but for their city, for their people, for their country. They were attached to something from above that held onto them. Thanks to that faith, sixty residents saved an entire city.

My name is Shachar Butzchak. I'm married to Avishag, the best woman in the world, and we have six children. After the expulsion from Gush Katif in 2005, my wife and I wanted to get out of our bubble, so we went to live in an ultra-secular cooperative community, Ein HaBesor, in the Gaza Envelope. We came for a year and stayed for seven; we grew so close to the people there that at the end of the seven years the community applied for me to become their official rabbi. In the end it didn't work out in Ein HaBesor, but we moved to another town in the same area, Mivtahim, where I did become the rabbi. We now live in Ofakim; I'm the rabbi of the new religious community in the city. My wife is originally from Ofakim, so for her moving here was coming full circle.

On Friday night, Simchat Torah eve, there was a major celebration here in Ofakim; the students from the religious pre-army program KeAyal came here to dance with the community, and that group knows how to celebrate! We danced together for hours with great joy; some of them even danced barefoot. That was the taste in our mouths when we went to sleep that night. Before it all began.

At six-thirty in the morning, like the rest of the south, we woke up to an unusually fierce barrage of rockets. Unusually powerful, unusually frequent compared to the standard Red Alert. It was practically continuous, one after the other. We go into the safe room – my kids grew up in the Gaza Envelope, so they're used to sirens – but half an hour later we suddenly begin to hear gunshots coming from the street.

Our neighborhood is right near the entrance to the city, on the side closest to Gaza – it's just a twenty-minute drive, something like that. So the terrorists come here bloodthirsty, and they see a couple in front of them, a husband and wife, sitting on the grass with their morning cup of coffee, and they simply open fire at them. Can you imagine just sitting there having your morning coffee and suddenly getting gunned down by a Kalashnikov? That actually was the terrorists' first mistake: that they started shooting right away. That helped us understand what was happening immediately, within minutes. By the way – that couple is still alive today, thank God.

The terrorists came well prepared; they had maps of Ofakim marking all the synagogues. In one of the terrorist's pouches, for example, the name "Beit Menahem" was written down with "9:45" next to it; Beit Menahem is a synagogue, and 9:45 is when it's the most packed, and when the kids are there. They clearly had a lot of inside information; they came prepared.

In short, we're in the safe room, we hear shooting, and suddenly I get a message from Dan Assouline, the head of security for Mivtahim. When we lived there, I was in the first response team, so I still get their messages; I see that he writes "Terrorist infiltration, possible raid. When the rocket barrage ends, everyone get into their gear; we'll start sweeping the area." I read the message out to my wife, and she says to me, "Raid? Who's raiding whom? What's happening here; how can this possibly be happening?" I write back to Assouline privately, "Listen, I'm in Ofakim. I'm coming to you, but I'll need to drive on Shabbat, so just confirm that this is really serious." He writes back, "It's serious."

I go out to my car to drive to Mivtahim, but even before I can get myself organized, we begin to hear shooting. I take my handgun – a personal firearm with fifteen bullets, put on my first response team hat from Mivtahim so they can identify me, and say to my wife, "Okay, I'm going." I leave the house in my sandals and start running in the direction of the shooting, something like three hundred meters. I'm all alone, no one else is in the street, everyone is holed up in their homes – which is only natural; there weren't even any policemen around. That Sabbath, there almost weren't any policemen in Ofakim; a lot of them had gone to secure the Nova Festival. So what happened is that a random bunch of civilians and off-duty cops left their homes spontaneously to fight with whatever they had. That's all there was.

Our neighborhood has older homes and newer homes. The old houses don't even have safe rooms, and the terrorists knew it; that's why they started off in neighborhoods with older houses. In those kinds of neighborhoods, when there's a Red Alert siren everyone runs outside to the mobile shelter in the middle of the street. So the terrorists just stood in the middle of the street and shot in every direction and killed the people who were running to the shelters. Or, for instance, they would go to a four-story apartment building, the older type that didn't have a shelter, where the residents gather in the stairwell during Red Alert sirens, and the terrorists simply went inside and murdered nine people in the stairwell. It was terrible, just terrible.

So I'm running and reach a narrow alley, and I see two of our guys taking cover. One of them called Shilo had a handgun; the other one, Nehorai Sa'id, is a soldier who was home for the Sabbath; he had his assault rifle with him. Nehorai isn't even from our neighborhood; he lives on the other side of town, but someone had called him and said, "There are terrorists here shooting right outside our neighborhood," so he just takes his parents' car and drives here to fight. Can you imagine that moment, the parents giving their car keys to their kid and saying, "Go do what you need to do"?

Nehorai shouts to me, "Three armed terrorists!" which is one of the first things they teach in basic training: first update the forces. As soon as he finishes shouting that to me, three armed terrorists start shooting an automatic burst at us with their Kalashnikovs. So I duck my head, take cover, and cock my gun. It's the first time in my life that I'm under live fire. I hear the bullets whistling over my head. The street is thick with dust; bullets are hitting walls, smashing windows. It was insane.

A few seconds later the terrorist's magazine was empty so he stops for a moment to reload. I lift up my head and see Nehorai and the other guy breaking right, so I shout to them, "Let's stay in formation," and they listen to me. I run to them, then we start moving ahead toward the terrorists. We knew that with every second that passed before we killed them, they could kill another family. So we ran toward them through the narrow streets; we ran like crazy people, moving from cover to cover – from trees to cars, anything. I got there first, ready with a bullet in my chamber. I couldn't see the terrorists yet, but I knew which direction the shooting was coming from.

Suddenly, suddenly I see this figure in front of me with olive drab clothes, an IDF uniform, and a brown vest. The air is thick with dust, and I'm pointing my gun, trying to make out who it is – a terrorist or one of our forces. In that moment of hesitation, he shoots first and hits me with a burst of gunfire. A Kalashnikov bullet hits me in the leg, the left leg, and I manage to hop on my right until I make it to cover.

I remember myself hopping on one foot, holding my gun and shouting to the fighters, "I've been hit! I caught a bullet in the leg! I'm hit!" I remember reaching cover and lying down on my stomach and aiming the gun forward as the terrorists keep shooting. They shot like madmen. Only later did I discover that that was when Nehorai fell; he was killed just a few meters away from where I was. A hero of Israel.

The bullet hit me at the top of my left thigh and went out the back; later, in the hospital, they told me that it made a big mess there; it tore nerves and broke the bone in two. But back there, in the field, I lie on my stomach and feel my blood flowing out of my leg, warm blood.

I take my phone out of my pocket and place it on the sidewalk; with one hand I keep my gun aimed toward where the terrorists are, and with the other I make four calls. The first was a voice message to our community WhatsApp group: "Friends, there are terrorists in the neighborhood. I've been shot in the leg for real. Everyone get into a safe room!" The second was to Dan Assouline; I say to him: "The terrorists aren't on the way; they're already here." The third call was to my wife; I say to her: "Avishag, I've been shot in the leg but I'm okay. There are terrorists; get into the safe room, shut the doors, windows, everything." The fourth call was to Magen David Adom. I say to them, "I've been shot by terrorists in Ofakim. I've been shot in the leg and need to be evacuated."

The Magen David Adom operator explains to me over the phone that they can't come into an active combat zone until the fighting is over, and in the meantime, "put pressure on the wound and bandage it up." I explain to him, "I can't, bro; I have to keep my gun pointed," and he says to me, "Hold the gun in your right hand and stop the bleeding with your left," and I say to him, "You don't understand what's going on here; I have to stay focused!" Right then I hear the Kalashnikov fire coming toward me, getting louder and louder, and I hear the terrorist coming closer. I don't know if he's coming to finish the job and kill me off or if I'm maybe about to surprise him now. So I whisper to the operator, "Be quiet; the terrorist is coming." And I hear the operator whisper to the operator next to him, "It's the Yom Kippur War, bro. Terrorists are running through the streets of Ofakim."

The terrorist is coming closer and closer – when suddenly everything goes quiet. To this day, I have no idea if the other guy in our makeshift formation killed that terrorist, or if the terrorist suddenly decided that this whole street was already dead and went on to somewhere else.

❧

A few minutes later, someone suddenly reaches me; he runs up to me from behind and says to me, "Rabbi, it's Itamar. I'll help you; I was a medic!" and he starts carrying me, kind of dragging me into a nearby house. The family is barricaded up inside. It's an old house with a wooden door – which means that if the terrorists break in with their Kalashnikovs, they'll tear the place apart in seconds.

Itamar takes a few strips of cloth to make an improvised bandage, tries to stop the bleeding as much as he can, brings one of the older kids there and says to him, "Press here where it's bleeding so the bleeding will stop," and immediately goes back out to fight. A minute after he goes out, some civilian comes in with an empty handgun and says to me, "I'm out of ammo; I need your gun to keep fighting," so I give him my gun. Then I realize that we're waiting here in the house without any way to defend ourselves at all. I tell the family to close the windows and turn off the lights so that the terrorists will think that the house is empty.

I lay there for about an hour and a half before they came to evacuate me. People don't know what it means to have a gunshot wound; it's difficult to describe what it feels like. All I can say is that it's very, very painful; the pain doesn't stop; it's a strong, constant pain. I'm lying there, and the boy there next to me starts reciting a psalm by heart, psalm 91: "*Yoshev beseter Elyon*, He who lives in the shelter of the Most High dwells in the shadow of the Almighty," which is a psalm you recite at funerals when the deceased is being led to the grave. It was very ironic. I'm lying there, and he's reciting it again and again, then he turns to me and asks, "Rabbi, is that a good psalm to say?" and I say to him, "It's an excellent psalm; keep going; it offers special protection! Afterward, you can add in the funeral rites for me if you like," and we both cracked up. It was just one of those moments.

The whole time, I was sure that there were only three terrorists total, three terrorists with assault rifles. I had no idea that there were over twenty, armed with huge amounts of firepower, RPGs, grenades, blocks of explosives – enough for a whole army to face, a whole army! But what actually happened, according to the municipal authorities, is that the army didn't arrive until two in the afternoon, meaning seven whole hours after it all began! Most of the terrorists were eliminated by civilians and policemen. Their last stand was in Rachel's house, where she staved off the last five terrorists in the city with tea and cookies. But besides the ones in Rachel's house, by eleven in the morning all the other terrorists had been wiped out.

We now know from the Shin Bet's reports and from what the local division commander said that more than a hundred terrorists were supposed to arrive in Ofakim after the massacre at the Nova Festival; Ofakim was their next stop. But the terrorists here called their friends and told them that there was too much resistance here, that they shouldn't come. Not only did we fight off all the terrorists who attacked Ofakim, we prevented the attack of a hundred more as well. It's a heroic story of people who saved their own city; forty thousand residents were saved thanks to sixty civilians and policemen who left their homes to fight.

I feel that a special trait of our people emerged on that day, a special trait of the soul that we inherited from our forefathers Abraham and Isaac, one that rises to the surface in times of trouble. For example, Dan Assouline, the head of security from Mivtahim, and Tal Maman from his first response team – both good friends of mine – I found out later that both of them were killed in that battle; both of them sacrificed their lives to save the community of Mivtahim. There are so many other stories, countless extraordinary stories about ordinary people.

There was a seventy-something-year-old bus driver who went out during the fighting; he left his house alone. He heard "*Itbah al Yahud*, Slaughter the Jews!" and decided to go out to help the wounded. When the police yelled at him, "Hey there, go back inside!" he said to them, "You're not letting ambulances in; you're busy with the terrorists, so who'll take care of the wounded? Let me pass; I've taken the bus driver's first-aid course!" and he went through the fighting, treating more and more people, checking their pulses, bandaging them up – over seventy years old in a knit cap and slippers, walking around under fire and saving lives. That's one person. I'm another person. And there are more and more people like us, countless people who went outside, who went out to fight, to help, each one doing what they could, each one giving what they could, each one taking their own bungee jump. Together we saved an entire city.

That Community Becomes My Own

Nasreen Yousef's Story

Age 46

 Yated

My husband Iyad and I got married late, when we were twenty-eight, which is not really accepted in the Druze community. But we both came to our relationship with the same mindset: we were picky, looking for someone good, because marriage isn't just for a day or two – we wanted someone to spend the rest of our lives with, and thank God, he found me and I found him, and we're good together.

When we had just met, Iyad saw how much of a Zionist I was, how much I love the country and the people of Israel. So, soon after we started dating he bought me a gift, a Star of David necklace of white gold, with inlaid jewels; each stone symbolized something different. When our relationship got very serious, he said to me, "If it all works out, with God's help, we'll get married and move in next to my base," because at the time he was serving in Kerem Shalom before they built the base in Re'im. So I agreed, and we actually did get married and live in the Gaza Envelope. But the first year was tough for me – I'm a Druze woman from the Carmel, with forests and mountains; what do I have to do with this pale yellow desert? I really missed the sweet smell of pine trees, but I slowly, slowly got used to it; what else could I do?

And that's it; it's already fifteen years that we've been living here in the Gaza Envelope, and we're truly in love with the area and with the community here. All my children were born here. We have four really sweet children. Our youngest son is named Amit Yisrael – Amit is for the hero Amit Ben Yigal, of blessed memory, who was his parents' only child, and Yisrael is because he was born on Israeli Independence Day, and the State of Israel is our country.

Okay, so this is what happened. Friday is a day for cooking, for cleaning; the whole house has the delicious smell of challah bread. That night we watched a TV series together about the Yom Kippur War. We finished the first episode, and I was torn up, sobbing, and I said, "Start the next one." We watched a few episodes. Then at ten-thirty we suddenly heard this really loud boom that made the whole house shake, and I asked my husband what was going on outside, and he said, "They've gone back to making disturbances at the fence; they're bombarding our forces." "So what do we do?" I ask him, and he says, "Don't worry, Hamas has been deterred. And if they dare rear their heads, they'll get socked."

After that, at night, I was just about to put my head down when suddenly I heard another loud boom. I picked up the phone and messaged the civilian security head. I wrote, "Good evening. How are you? I'm sorry about the hour, but I wanted to ask what's going on outside," and he answers, "Good evening. I don't know of anything unusual outside. Everything is in order," so I wrote back, "Good night."

The next morning, at six-thirty, the first Red Alert sounds. I pick up my head – what is it now? – and I look and see only my two boys next to me, Omri and Amit Yisrael, and I knew that my husband was sleeping in the living room because of his leg. He was on sick leave from the army at the time because he had broken his leg. So I run to him. "Iyad, get up! Red Alert! Let's take the kids to the safe room." We begin to transfer the kids to the safe room, one at a time. The Red Alert doesn't stop; there are loud booms, unending, and our safe room – which is the boys' bedroom – is really small; two beds and a desk hardly fit in there. When we were there I suddenly remembered our new neighbor from Kerem Shalom; I remember that she told me that her husband was away on duty that Shabbat – he's a policeman – and she's all alone with her three little girls, and they don't know anyone here yet. So I said, "Iyad, the neighbor is all alone; go bring her here with us," and that really did happen: Iyad ran over to the neighbor, Chen, with his broken leg, and he brought her – he carried two girls, and she picked up the third, and they came to us. We all crowded into the safe room.

A few minutes after she came, there was suddenly this loud boom! and the power went out. I'm like, What, a blackout now? How am I going to prepare Amit Yisrael's bottle with the water machine down? It was dark so we opened the safe room window a crack just for a little light, and when we opened the window and looked outside, we saw that there were terrorists out there.

And that was when it really became chaotic. Iyad got into uniform despite his broken leg, called his commander, and said, "Listen, there are terrorists here; I'm getting into uniform." The officer says to him, "No! You're on sick leave; you have a broken leg!" and Iyad says, "Listen, I'd rather die in uniform than cowering in the safe room like a mouse!" and hangs up.

At that moment, I decide that I'm fighting together with him; I'm not staying at home. I gave two knives to the neighbor in the safe room with the kids to have inside there, I went back to the kitchen, and I saw that outside our house, a minute away, the security response team had caught a few terrorists. They were talking to them, trying to interrogate them, and I realized that I could help.

I went outside just like that, in a blue shirt and flip-flops, and I went up to the terrorists there, and I started talking to them. I started hitting them and shouting at them in Arabic: "Where did you come in from? Who sent you? Where did you come from? How many are you?" One of them, I see from his eyes that he's dazed, that he's on drugs; his eyes are glazed over, and I shout at him and grab him by the collar until he points at the greenhouse and says, "There, there's an opening in the fence," and I said, "How many are you?" and he said, "A lot." So I immediately tell the guy from the security response team that there are a lot of terrorists in the greenhouse, and that they're coming in from there.

They were all in shock, and I found myself taking charge of the mess there, like in some movie. I started tying up all the terrorists that were there; I brought cable ties from our shed, and duct tape, like they have in the army, and ropes; I even took my kids' shoelaces, and we tied the terrorists up there with all the ropes, and we tied kitchen towels over their eyes as blindfolds. And the head of security comes at that point and says to me, "What are you doing outside?!" and I say, "I'm helping here!" There was one wounded terrorist, and he kept saying to me that they're good people, that they deserve sympathy, that they're running away from Hamas, and I shouted at him in Arabic to stop trying to fool me, I shouted, "Liar! Liar! I see you, I'm standing in front of you! I'm not afraid of you!" until he quieted down. And there's a Red Alert the whole time, and explosions, and black smoke in the sky, and we have no internet, no power, and no water, and the time drags on and on and on. God, it was terrifying.

My husband Iyad knew what was happening out there; he knew that the whole sector was full of terrorists, but he didn't want to tell me. My neighbor Chen's husband, the policeman, came then; on the way he'd neutralized like ten terrorists by himself, and he told the response team what was really going on in the sector. Meanwhile, I went to bring food for everyone who was there; we had some soldiers and officers with us, so I went into the house and cut up some fruit and vegetables and brought it out to them. Iyad says to me, "Nasreen, fill up a bottle of water for me," and I ask him, "Is it for you?" He says, "No, they want to give the terrorists some water," and I say, "No way! I'll put bleach in their water," and he starts shouting, "Don't you dare say that! We're the most moral army in the world. We're human beings. We're not like them; we're humane." And I shut my mouth, I went and filled up water for him, and I said, "Great, but if you give them water, I'm filming it. I want the whole world to know what we're like and what they're like."

Suddenly a phone rings. Everyone looks around to check whose phone is ringing, and we realize that it's one of the terrorists' phones. The terrorist gives me the phone, and I look at the screen and see that it says "The Nest" in Arabic, like a bird's nest. I explain that to the officer there, and he says, "Answer it!" So I answer in Arabic, "Hello." And the guy on the phone says, "Mohammed?" and I say, "It's not Mohammed, it's Nasreen." He says, "Who are you?" and I say, "Don't worry, I'm an Arab, I live next to the fence. I'm on your side, the gang is here with me," and he shouts, "Who are you?!" and I answer, "I can't shout, my name is Nasreen, I'm an Arab, my house is by the fence, I'm hiding everyone here; we're sitting in the dark because the Israeli army is looking for everyone who came in here from Rafah." He asks me, "Where are you located?" I explain where I am and ask, "Where are all of you?" and he says to me, "We're on the way; we're coming in from Rafah; we're very close."

I translate everything he says, word by word, to the officer there, and every time "The Nest" answers, I put him on mute for a second and translate for the officer. Then I ask him, "How many of you are coming? I want to get ready for you," and he says, "Hundreds" – hundreds he tells me! And then he asks to speak with one of the guys there, so I ask him, "Who do you want to speak to? There are a lot of them; lots of guys are with me," and he says, "Give me Mohammed Wadia." So I ask, "Who's Mohamed Wadia?" and that was the wounded one, and I grab him by the shirt and say to him, "Listen, Wadia, I swear on my honor that I'll finish you off if you don't say exactly what I tell you," and Wadia says, "*Tayib*, Okay," and I say to him, "Talk!"

So he talks. He says to him, "We're with Nasreen; she's a good woman, one of us. We have a place – we've been hiding with her all morning. The army is searching for us, and she's hiding us. She gave us food, water, drink." I'm translating everything into the officer's ear, then I hear the man on the phone say, "Great, there's another squad in the community you're in; there's a big battle next to the monument, and we're on our way too. *Inshallah*, God willing, today we'll conquer the State of Israel!" When I heard that, when I heard that there was another squad of terrorists in Yated and that they wanted to conquer the whole country, I really felt like I was choking, choking, and I hung up and said to my husband, "I can't take it anymore," and I went back inside, to the safe room, to the kids.

❧

Meanwhile, darkness had fallen, and I'm in the room with the kids, and only I know what I heard. No one else knows what was going on out there except for me and the ones who were there next to me, next to the terrorists; no one else knew that there was another group of terrorists in Yated, and that there were more on the way. No one else knew that we might be about to die, or that they might take us hostage. I kept it all to myself.

The officers took the car and went out on a search for the terrorists, together with the response team. I stayed behind to keep guard over the terrorists. We kept guard over them all night, Iyad and I and our neighbor; we kept the car's headlights on them all night until the morning.

After that, at night, our oldest daughter, Shiran, comes over to me, and she's crying so hard, and I say to her, "Sweetie, what happened," and she says, "Mommy, I'm so sorry that I didn't listen to you, and that I used to go to my friends without asking, and I'm so sorry that sometimes I was rude to you and annoyed you, I'm sorry, Mommy; please forgive me!" I said to her, "What's with you, what did you get into your head? You're my girl. When was I ever angry at you, sweetie; I'm not upset about anything." She really thought it was the end. It was all so terrifying.

At one point I got a terrible message, just terrible, that two of my friends from Kerem Shalom had been murdered. They were in the security response team. It just broke me; I was so broken. Then another horrifying message came: Ido Hubara from Kibbutz Sufa had been murdered. We had a special connection, Ido and I; he had a special family, he was like a brother to me, and he was always there for me, hugging me and calming me down with that shy smile of his. When I heard that, I tried not to cry, but I couldn't control it. I got into the shower – I told the neighbor I was going to shower – and turned on the water, sat down and started crying, kicked at the walls like a madwoman, and screamed like a madwoman until I calmed down.

❧

By three-thirty in the morning we were completely exhausted. The kids were asking for food, but I had nothing left in the house; it was all finished. I went to the snack cupboard and took out some snacks and brought them into the shelter so they'd eat something. We had no real food left. Suddenly I hear a helicopter, and I say to my husband, "What's that?" and he says, "I have no idea!"

We only found out afterward that it was the Air Force coming to rescue us. The officer had passed on everything I had translated to the army, what the terrorist had said, and the helicopter came to Yated. They found terrorists inside the town, and there were lots more terrorists near the monument, and they shot at them and neutralized them. There was this soldier in the battle by the monument, a guy that I knew, and he came to my house sobbing; he lost a friend in the battle there, and I hugged him. And he said, "You're a brave woman. You're a hero; you don't realize what you did, but people will speak your name." And I told him that I didn't do anything, and he said to me, "Nasreen, you're talking nonsense."

Afterward, we found out that the terrorists had maps, and they had our home address. They knew where we lived, and they came to us, to Iyad, because he was a military man. They knew that we had dogs at home; it was no coincidence that they came to us specifically here. They had plans.

We evacuated ourselves from town the next morning. I told the kids to put on their shoes, and we took them to the car – first Amit, then Omri, and Sivan and Shiran. I took Amit's diaper bag, and we went on our way. The whole time, I told the kids to keep down, not to lift their heads up. All the roads were blocked, so Iyad drove through the fields at a crazy speed, and the whole way I see burnt cars, cars flipped upside down, the corpses of soldiers, the corpses of terrorists, and dead civilians inside the cars. The whole way I was screaming out, "*Shema Yisrael*; Hear, O Israel!" I couldn't even feel my legs from all the screaming, and I couldn't breathe. When we got to Beit Kama, to a safe place, I realized that I had lost my voice. I was completely hoarse, and for two months I couldn't speak from all that screaming.

Afterward, I received a lot of criticism. What I did didn't suit certain Arabs. I was in Eilat recently at a PR event, and the amazing

Yoseph Haddad was there, the one who does amazing PR for Israel. I stood next to him at the entrance to the event, and all kinds of Arabs came and surrounded him and started to attack him a little. They saw that I was on his side, on the side of the state, so they attacked me as well, and actually tore off the Star of David necklace that Iyad had bought me. I had planned to give that necklace to my daughter when she'd join the army, but that was it, now that won't happen. The necklace was torn and lost. It's so sad for me that there are people trying to tear me away from my country.

When they tell me that I'm a hero, I tell them that I'm not. I just protected my home, my family, my community. As a Druze woman, when I live in a Jewish community, that community becomes my own. I'm Druze, and I'm Israeli. I believe that there's only one God and that He created everyone. I truly believe in Providence, and I believe that it's no coincidence that the Holy One, blessed be He, sent me to this community, to this place, to these people whose lives were saved.

I want to be optimistic, to believe that there won't be any more shooting, any more terror attacks, any more Red Alerts. I want to believe that we'll be able to come back, to rehabilitate the community, to show the other side that we're stronger. True, you came into our homes; you beheaded, you raped, you murdered babies, but you won't break us. You'll never break us! And I feel that the souls of the friends I lost – their souls give me strength at this time.

Hamas, in my opinion, didn't get its strength from its ammunition. Hamas got strong from the divisions within our people, from all the baseless hatred that festered here, that formed among us. That's where Hamas got their strength. I say that all the time. If we love each other, we'll win. If we keep going out to the streets to protest and hate each other, then we'll go back again and again to October 7th. Our whole lives will be October 7th. That's my opinion. I grew up in a completely Israeli home. And I know, and I believe, that we're all one people, truly one people! I hope and dream that my children will wear their uniforms proudly, like my husband. I want to see them all in uniform! I say that with pride. I have a great love for this place. If we succeed in being together, united, we'll be unbeatable. Simply unbeatable.

Two Things Kept Me Alive

Yadin Gellman's Story

Age 30

Kibbutz Be'eri

There are moments in life when you're facing an amazing view and you just have no words and no need for words. You don't even want to take a photo; you don't want anything else. You just want to contemplate that view, to be there in front of it. The moment I met Adva was that kind of moment for me. Of amazement. A moment without words. It happened at the premiere of the first movie I acted in, "Image of Victory." That was my first ever premiere. And Adva was there in a red dress – beautiful and delicate, but powerful. I saw her and just fell in love, I just fell in love right away.

I hit on her that first evening, I asked for her number, but she hesitated. So I began a brief campaign to persuade her. I sent over female friends of mine; I messaged her on Instagram. It took a long time for her to agree to go out with me, but I was persistent until she was convinced. And our first date – I don't want to get into too much detail, but it was perfect. We went on a twelve-hour nature hike; we had deep conversations; we went swimming in a freezing river. I remember going back to my apartment after that date and telling my roommate, "She's the one I'm going to marry."

✒

My story begins on October 6th, at the surprise party Adva threw me for my thirtieth birthday. She organized this whole production, and I didn't have a clue! We drove south to the Ramon Crater, to this "glampground" called Selina. When we got there, my whole team from the army and all my friends from home were waiting for me. It was just amazing. Amazing.

The plan was for us to be there from Friday to Sunday and just have fun. That's what we did. We played volleyball, went in the pool, had a barbecue. Then, toward evening, at sunset, we started like a party and danced, and at eleven at night we turned the music off – we had to because it was a nature reserve. Then we sat together around the bonfire, my whole army team and all the friends I grew up with, and got into this beautiful, deep, emotional conversation – seven of us in the crew turned thirty that same week, so we all took turns giving each other blessings, and we all just opened up; we'd never opened up like that before.

That night, just before we went to sleep, I held Adva and kissed her and thanked her for the happiest, most joyful evening I ever had in my life. Then we went to sleep.

In the morning, she wakes me up and says, "Yadin, I'm sorry, but there's a war; look at your phone." I didn't understand what she was talking about; it came out of nowhere, no one had any intel. So I turned on my phone and saw a message from my commander: "Everyone come as soon as you can."

We woke everyone up, the whole team, and everyone packed up their things and rushed to their cars. It was still early in the morning. We all started driving from the Ramon Crater to our unit. On the way, at some point, I said goodbye to Adva; she drove out to report from the field – she works on the TV news – and before we went our separate ways, I thanked her again for the best day of my life.

By the time we reached the unit, we had already seen all the clips on Telegram; we saw clips of terrorists in the streets, in the bases, in the kibbutzim, and we understood, we all understood that this was something different, something that was out of control. We got to the unit and began to get ready; we split up into our usual teams and forces and started driving in the direction of Kfar Aza. I sat in the front seat with my rifle loaded and pointed out the window. Yes, it was war.

When we reached Route 232, we passed the police barricade and saw what's now known as the "Road of Blood." The whole road was lined with cars and bodies; there was a crazy number of people who were murdered there, lots of burnt cars. Lots of missiles falling to the right and to the left, and we're all on high alert with bullets in the chamber.

At the entrance to Kfar Aza we saw dozens of cars that people had abandoned there; people just ran outside and fled for their lives. That's what it looked like. Inside, in the kibbutz, we had a team already in the heat of battle. They didn't answer us on the radio so we didn't know where to join forces, and we weren't allowed to go in without making contact because of the risk of friendly fire. We really wanted to join the fight; we were going crazy from the noise of the explosions and gunfire. Meanwhile, we set up a medical aid station outside of Kfar Aza, at the kibbutz entrance, and started to bring out the wounded. There was an armored vehicle from the Duvdevan unit, and it drove in and out a few times evacuating the wounded.

At one point a civilian car suddenly shot out of the kibbutz at breakneck speed; we spotted it and shot at the tires, and it stopped. We ran up to the car and saw a terrorist at the wheel with two girls in the trunk – he was attempting to kidnap them. So we apprehended him, tied him up, and sent him for interrogation. We evacuated the girls to Soroka Hospital; they were wounded and in shock – they had almost been taken hostage – so we bandaged them up as fast as we could and made sure they were taken to the hospital. We saved them from being taken captive.

About an hour later we were called up to Be'eri. At the entrance to Be'eri, I met up with my "battle buddy" David Meir; in battle you have a partner whose side you never leave, and from that moment on, we kept together. We led the force – I went first, he was second. David had enlisted a year before me; he's religious, a right-winger, a real Zionist, a big smiler, and a righteous guy. Gung-ho. We had known each other for ten years. At the entrance to the kibbutz we see our unit commander, who says to us, "Just go in; we're not waiting for anyone to get on the radio. We have a team fighting inside – we're going in there and linking up with them!"

We piled into this small armored vehicle called a David. Right near the kibbutz entrance we saw this kind of convoy of Thai agricultural workers; we found them there – they had hidden, terrified for their lives. We rescued them from the kibbutz, poor guys, and went right back in. This time, we joined a serious battle there; this sounds as surreal and screwed-up as it gets, but there was a battle raging in the kindergarten.

There was a team there from our unit; and the terrorists, as far as I could tell, were everywhere, vast numbers of them. Terrorists in every direction, 360 degrees; I even saw one hiding behind the blue slide in the playground. I remember that I suddenly saw the barrel of a Kalashnikov sticking out of the kindergarten window; it hit me that the battle had begun; it was time to fight. Sometimes it's all a matter of minutes, even seconds. Within seconds, really, that episode was behind us; the terrorists were dead, and we moved on.

At the same time, our second team flanked the kibbutz to come from the other side. There was a crazy massacre in the kibbutz dental clinic. So the other team worked on that, trying to get there. After we finished, after the two teams had wiped out all the terrorists both in the kindergarten and in the clinic, we started going from house to house in the kibbutz to rescue people.

That's what we did for hours. We really went from house to house to house. If there were terrorists inside, we wiped them out, then brought out everyone who was there – everyone who was still alive. It was very rough fighting there – the thinking was that terrorists could be hiding in any corner, but we couldn't just throw grenades inside because we were worried about hostages. So we went inside each house with our weapons to track the terrorists down with our own eyes.

Each time we found someone, we called our commander, who was driving around the kibbutz in the armored vehicle, and he'd pick up whole families in the car and bring them out. That was the drill all day long. We saw some difficult scenes there; I'd really rather not get into it. There were people there who they burnt, families hiding in their safe rooms when their father was already dead. There were horrifying scenes there. I remember that in one of the houses we drank water, and the family there saw us and asked to drink; they had been hiding for hours without water. So of course we gave them all our water. That was the moment we understood what they had gone through there in their own homes.

It went on for hours until it grew dark. At about seven in the evening, we got a directive to go to the house of Pessi Cohen; we understood that something serious was happening there, a major incident with hostages. So we were on our way there, advancing in that direction; meanwhile we continued to mop up each house in the kibbutz.

So that's how we moved forward until we had one last house left to search before we reached the kibbutz dining hall. This house was raised up a little aboveground on these low pillars, about four steps up. We advanced toward the house. And suddenly a terrorist sticks his rifle out of a window to the right, fires a whole burst of gunfire at me and David, and misses us entirely – except for one bullet that hits my trigger finger. So I switch fingers, zero in on the gunman, start shooting, and charge at him.

There was another guy there, let's call him M., he's a lieutenant colonel, and M. and I charged at the terrorist together and killed him. We were fighting right next to the house, that last one, and I figured that if there were terrorists in the house, there must be hostages there as well. That's what I concluded. So I ran toward the door, and just as I'm about to go inside, a terrorist sticks his rifle out of the window right above me and fires a whole burst of gunfire right at me and David.

That round hit us as intended. I fall to the ground along with David. Then I realize that since the house is a little raised up off the ground, there's a space beneath it, so I push David inside and crawl after him, turn to the right, holding my rifle, and aim it at the steps. My thinking was that a terrorist would come out any moment to finish the job – he'd come and throw a grenade at us or shoot another round – so I said to myself: When you see his legs, shoot and he'll fall. Then shoot him again when he's falling. That was my plan.

So I have my Negev, which is this big, powerful automatic weapon, and I had a lot of ammo on me. And I was pumped full of adrenaline, so I don't even realize yet that I had been shot in the shoulder – I mean, it really hurt, but I didn't know what condition I was in. At that moment I remember that I have a radio on me, and I try to push the button, and I realize that I can't lift up my hand – my left hand just like wasn't working. So I pulled out the radio with my other hand and reported to them, "This is Gellman. David and I are seriously wounded; we're under the house." They got my message and told me that they were preparing for the rescue.

At this stage it was still quiet. But a few minutes later I hear a lot of gunfire overhead, right above me, burst after burst of gunfire, then quiet again. I realize that we're in a much worse situation than I thought because there's a serious number of terrorists right above me, and I know that it'll take time to get us out of here. So I tell David that it's time to examine our wounds, and I check myself. I see that my legs are okay, and my stomach is okay; I have a little bit of shrapnel near my eyes, okay, but then I touch my chest, and I feel an actual bullet hole. I lower my arm, and I realize that I have no arm; my whole arm is this huge open hole. No arm. That's what I concluded, that I'd lost my arm.

And David tells me that he's wounded too; he has a lot of bullets all over his body, in his back, stomach, chest, arms; he's badly hurt. In the meantime, I hear on the radio that the team that's on its way to rescue us has taken casualties; they have three wounded, and I know that there are terrorists right above me and behind me and to my right – everything is terrorists. There's no way out, and I realize that David and I are stuck here, maybe for eternity.

Right then, I remember, two thoughts went through my head. The first was that I have to survive. That is, I have to keep holding my gun; I have to stay alert. And the second thing I was thinking about was Adva.

Suddenly, Adva popped into my head – to be specific, I was regretting that I hadn't married her yet, and that I hadn't had kids with her yet, that we hadn't started a family. That's what I thought about, that's what was in my head as we lay there. That's what kept me alive.

We were there for about forty-five minutes. We lost a large amount of blood. I kept telling David that it would be okay, and we'd make it out of there, and that he shouldn't worry, but I knew it was bull. At a certain point, I was sure that it was all over. I got on the radio with a friend of mine, someone who's also friends with Adva, and I asked him to tell Adva that I love her and that I'm sorry. And that was it. Then David asked me to pass on to his wife Anat that he loves her, and to tell his son Shaked that he loves him and he's sorry. That was our report over the radio, and that's how we said goodbye to our loved ones.

About fifteen minutes later, something like that, my friend contacted me on the radio and said that he was coming into Be'eri with a tank. When I heard that, it gave me this jolt of energy; it totally woke me up and motivated me to survive. Then suddenly I hear the tank coming, and I see it in front of me. His team had staged this major rescue operation, the tank was advancing, and they came from behind it and attacked the terrorists. The tank shot at the house and the whole house shook above us and all this shrapnel rained down on us. But from my perspective, it was an amazing feeling; I felt like hope was raining down on me.

The team crawled under the house to get to us, and they pulled David and me out, then they took us out to a first-aid point. They cut all my clothes open. I was sure that I'd lost my arm, but my arm was still connected to me; it was just completely smashed up and wide open. My friend who was there tied it to my vest so it wouldn't fall off. That was a crazy moment.

From there they took us out to the first-aid point outside of Be'eri and treated us there next to each other. I saw a doctor there who's a good friend of mine; he's the one who drained my lung right there in the field – he really saved my life; he saved me. If he hadn't done that, I would have died the moment I went into the helicopter. As they were treating me there I said to my friend, "Take my phone out of my underwear, I have to call Adva," and I remember telling him the code to open the phone, and telling him how to spell Adva because I knew he'd search for it with the wrong spelling – haha!

So he called her, and she was reporting from the site of the Nova Festival – her team was reporting from Netivot, but then she made the call on her own to drive to the Nova grounds. She was one of the first to arrive on the scene. At first she tried to treat the wounded there, but it was hopeless, so she started going around the fields there to rescue whoever she could. She just drove through the fields shouting, "I'm Adva from Channel 12 news; come out!" She saved dozens of people; that's what she was doing when I was in Be'eri.

Adva was about to go on the air, but she happened to see the phone ring, and she picked up and said, "Sweetie, I'm going live in thirty seconds; is it urgent?" and my answer was, "I'm okay, everything is okay, go back to work. We'll talk later, I've been shot in the chest." Then my teammate took the phone and explained to her that I was in critical condition.

In the helicopter on the way to the hospital, right after we take off, I suddenly have this feeling like my whole body is being cleansed; suddenly everything is just falling away from me. I don't feel any pain, and I feel like I'm being drawn out of my body. I think I died for a moment. Luckily, my friend from the team noticed and slapped me on the face. He grabbed my head and said, "If you close your eyes one more time, I will kill you myself." I woke up.

The helicopter was supposed to fly to the hospital at Tel HaShomer, but because they weren't sure we could survive such a long flight, they evacuated us to Soroka Medical Center in Beersheba instead. When we got to Soroka, Adva was already there. The doctors who admitted me told her that I'd survive but that I was going to lose my left arm, that they'd have to amputate it; they were completely overwhelmed by casualties. So Adva decided to get me out of there to save my arm and my life. She started looking for ambulances and found one, and they drove me to Ichilov Hospital in Tel Aviv. The whole way, she kept talking to me from the front seat. At Ichilov the doctors were already waiting for me; they put me under and saved my arm. Angels.

I woke up the next day after the surgery. I called my unit commander and asked him, "What's going on with David," and he told me that everything's okay; I should focus on myself. After that, they put me back under for more surgery, and when I woke up I asked again, "What about David?" And the same thing happened again on the third day; each time they kept avoiding answering and wouldn't tell me what was happening with him. Finally they told me that he had died when we were in the helicopter, when we lifted off into the sky. As we took off, both of us drifted away from our bodies; he died, and I came back to life.

Ever since October 7th, I've been in serious rehab. I've been through seven surgeries, and I'm in physical therapy. While I'm in rehab I read the news, and I see on Instagram what the world thinks about us, and I'm freaking out, just freaking out. I can't fathom how it makes any sense, after everything we went through on that day. I understand that there are two fronts to this war: one on the ground, physical battle, and one on social media, for public opinion. So I decided that I have to work on public opinion.

I started on Instagram, and I continued with the help of my friend, who was involved with some major fundraising event in New York. From there I just moved from place to place, I spent about a month in the US appearing at universities, rallies, all kinds of conferences. That's what I've been doing. Everything in our country is so fragile right now. I can't fight so I found another way to help, to tell the world how things really are.

The days go by. I feel like every day is a new October 7th; I've been in this war for far too long. This whole thing has changed me. I don't know, I walk down the street with my dog, holding him with the arm that they managed to save, and think that none of it should be taken for granted. Little things don't feel so little anymore. To stand on my feet. To brush my teeth. Above all, this ordeal clarified how I really feel about Adva.

Not many people can say that their partner saved their life. In my case, it's true twice over – first in my head, my love for her kept me alive under that house, when I was struggling to stay alive. Then with her decision to transfer me to Ichilov and to save my arm. Even before that day I felt how much she meant to me, but afterward – it became clear as day. All doubts melted away. Now our relationship is different; it's bound up with life and death. She kept me alive, and she's also what I live for.

A Hero Is Someone Who Can't Stay on the Sidelines

Noam and Yishai Slotki's Story

Ages 31 and 24

As told by Noam and Yishai's parents, Tali and Shmuel Slotki

⦿ Kibbutz Alumim

We have seven children, thank God. They spent a significant part of their childhood in nature, connected to the land, in Kibbutz Ein HaNetziv in the Valley of Springs, where we lived for a number of years. They were constantly hiking there together, and they absorbed the values of hard work, responsibility, Torah, service, love for nature, and love for people.

Later we moved to Jerusalem, so they became more city kids. They discovered the magic of tall buildings, of busy streets, of the intermingling of the people of Israel in all their variety. From there, each child charted their own path in life. On this path, somehow, three of our children made their way to Beersheba: Noam, our second; Shifra, our fourth; and Yishai, our fifth. All three of them live in Beersheba, and all three of them live near each other, within a small radius, next to the university. They went through life together; they were always getting together. Yishai and Noam formed a very close bond there, a sweet brotherly bond. They would hike together, work out together, eat Shabbat meals together; and sometimes they'd get together for a beer in the park and talk about life.

>৯

Our Noam is thirty-one years old. He was such a hyperactive kid! Smiley, happy, rambunctious. He never did well in formal settings – he couldn't stop moving – so basically by twelfth grade he decided to enlist in the IDF early, before he even finished high school. He first joined the Egoz commando unit, and from there he went on to the 13th infantry battalion in Golani, where he served for three years.

After the army he went on to earn his academic degree. He still found it difficult to sit and learn; he still found it hard to sit still, but he succeeded in completing his degree like a pro. Along the way he married his wife Adi; they were married for seven years, and just last year they had a baby, a little boy, Netta Yehuda, who's named for Noam's uncle Yehuda, who was killed. Yehuda was also in Egoz. Now Noam and Yehuda are buried on Mount Herzl, not far from each other. That's Noam.

Yishai is twenty-four and the identical twin of Yonatan. They were born half an hour apart, but they have different Hebrew birthdays because one was born before sunset and the other just after. It's funny – they're twins, but they don't have the same birthday! They were always very, very close to each other: as brothers, as twins, they were very, very good friends their whole life. Yishai was also kind of hyperactive, full of joie de vivre; he had a good heart. He spent a lot of time volunteering; he volunteered at "Lev Binyamin" for children with special needs; our Yishai really had a good heart. So young.

Even among the members of his team in the Golani reconnaissance unit, he was known as the guy who raises everyone's spirits; at times of crisis, he was always the one who would offer encouragement and reinvigorate the team, always with his wide, shining smile. About two years ago he married Aviya, and they had a baby girl, Be'eri Shahar. She was named Be'eri Shahar before the war, of course, but now we feel that her name has taken on a deeper significance, a new meaning. Her name has become our prayer: a prayer that a new *shachar*, a new dawn, will rise again over Kibbutz Be'eri and all the communities of the Gaza Envelope.

⮞

On that morning, when the first sirens began in Beersheba, Yishai and his wife Aviya and their baby Be'eri Shahar went out to the stairwell. They don't have a safe room in the apartment, so they went out to the stairwell during the sirens because it's the most protected area in the building. That's where they heard from neighbors about what was happening near the border, what they knew then. Yishai and his wife keep the Sabbath so they hadn't turned their phones on, but the neighbors told them that dozens of terrorists had infiltrated the Gaza Envelope and that they were murdering people there, that people there were begging for help but no help was coming. That's what they heard.

And at that very moment Yishai simply went into his home, put on his uniform, took his handgun, dropped off his wife and baby at Noam's house, said goodbye, and went on his way. When Noam understood what was going on, he immediately did exactly the same thing: got into uniform, took his handgun, and went out after him. Both of them drove toward the Gaza Envelope, to the heart of the inferno. Each in his own car. On the way, they called each other and met up so that they could drive together and fight together, side by side.

We didn't know what was happening at all; we didn't know anything. That Sabbath we were in Kfar Etzion with a group of soldiers in the process of converting to Judaism. When the sirens began and people were called up to reserve duty, we understood that something had happened, but we didn't really know what. Only after the Sabbath did we learn that Noam and Yishai had driven out there; it was only gradually, over the next few days, that we began to piece together the puzzle of what happened to our children during those hours on the Sabbath.

What became clear to us from all the images and stories that we pieced together was that they had many opportunities along the way to stop, turn back, and go home. The drive from Beersheba to the border takes about three quarters of an hour; we assume that that they saw very many vehicles fleeing in the opposite direction, signaling to them that it was dangerous, that they shouldn't come close, but still they kept going.

There are video clips that show them arriving and entering into the battlefield; you see cars on fire there, you see wounded people there, things that are really not simple, but even then they didn't turn around and go home. Instead, they got out of the car and began to attack. They could have changed their minds at any moment, but nevertheless they charged ahead – because they understood that they could help, that they had a role to play.

What happened was that they reached Kibbutz Alumim; we don't know why they went specifically there of all places. But we have the footage from the kibbutz security cameras. And in the footage you see how they drove up to the bus stop at the entrance to the kibbutz. You can see a whole row of cars, burnt out, perforated with bullets, on fire. They get there to an actual combat zone. They park the car and get out. As soon as they get out, they're under fire. Bullets from every direction. In the video clip you actually see the sparks from the shooting. There's this ditch there at the side of the road, this drainage ditch, and you can see them running into the ditch, crouching down, and assessing the situation for like a minute. Then they just go charging out of the ditch with their guns drawn, in the direction of the terrorists. At that point, they leave the camera's field of vision. From then on, you can't see them anymore.

Before they entered the kibbutz – you can see in the footage – there were two soldiers from Golani there, and one of them was wounded; later he ended up losing his leg from that wound. That soldier told us that our Noam, who was a medic, spoke to him, shouted to him, asking if he needed help, but the soldiers told him that they were okay, so Noam and Yishai continued on toward the kibbutz.

Later on we heard – not firsthand; this we heard from a soldier who apparently was fighting on the other side of the road at the same time. He told us that he saw them, both of them, fighting with incredible courage, in perfect sync with each other, covering each other, flanking, shouting. At a certain point, they ran out of ammunition in their handguns, so they grabbed the Kalashnikovs of the terrorists they had killed and kept fighting. For about forty minutes, they managed to keep the terrorists at bay; they fought against them and blocked them from entering the kibbutz. Until the battle was over. That's how, at the entrance to the kibbutz, they were killed. They fell together, side by side.

That's it. That's basically all we know; that's everything we managed to uncover. We don't know if we'll ever know with certainty what precisely happened there at the entrance to Alumim. When we observed shiva, the week of mourning, a paratroop officer who had been there with them came; he had had the assignment of collecting all the bodies. He told us that when he reached that area, they saw Yishai and Noam. He said that both of them died in fighting stance, with bodies of dead terrorists all around them. He said that when the soldiers saw them they understood – they immediately understood that these were two great people. They realized that these two fighters they now saw lifeless, had actually saved – had played a part in saving Kibbutz Alumim. He had all his soldiers stop their mission for a moment to recite a chapter of Psalms next to their bodies. They prayed over both of them together without knowing that the two had any connection; he found out only later that the two men who had died there were brothers. Our sons. During the shiva, he told us that when his soldiers stood there next to Noam and Yishai, he said to them: "I don't know if heaven has a scent. But if it has one, then it's the scent of these two holy men."

For almost five days, we didn't know what happened to them. We had no idea. Only on Thursday morning were we informed that their bodies had been identified. The identification process was difficult; there were so many unidentified bodies there. I still had a sliver of hope that they might be in one of the hospitals. We knew there had been a fierce battle there at Alumim, but still, I had hope. But on Thursday night they were buried at Mount Herzl, side by side. Two brothers.

Tzviki, our youngest son, recently printed bumper stickers with a powerful phrase, one that perhaps encapsulates the entire story. He wrote, "A Hero is Someone Who Can't Stay on the Sidelines." That is, a hero is someone who sees that someone else is in trouble and doesn't stand to the side; doesn't lower his eyes, doesn't just look away; he tries to help. It doesn't have to be with guns drawn and charging into battle; it can be anything. If you notice a classmate struggling in class and you help them; if you see someone out in the street who needs help and you stop to help them even though you're in a rush, that's being a hero, too.

Noam and Yishai – they realized, they felt, that their brothers were crying out for help. They got emergency call-ups to reserve duty, but they understood that it would take hours before everyone was mustered together, so they just got up and drove. They didn't know anyone there personally. They just felt the need to go out and do whatever they could to save their brothers.

They asked us recently, in one of the interviews: Tell us, if your sons had called you on their way and asked you what to do – to turn back or go on – what would you have said? It's a tough, tough question. I think that we would have told them to go on. If you feel skilled enough and confident enough, if you think that you'll be able to help people, to save lives, then go on. That's what we would have said.

Noam and Yishai aren't the only heroes from that day. There were so many heroes, and they're now part of the pantheon of heroes of Israel's history from time immemorial. We now know that the terrorists had grand plans; they had plans to reach the center of the country. They had detailed plans, with maps. It was only those heroes who went out to battle, who detained them until the army was able to respond – it was only thanks to heroes like those that their plan failed. So Noam and Yishai weren't the only ones. There was brutal fighting inside the kibbutz, too, waged by Alumim's first response team. So many heroic individuals rose up that day and took action. Noam and Yishai are among those great heroes to whom we owe our lives.

Since they were killed, our lives have changed. Life is harder now. We have a gaping hole; there are widows, there are orphans. We all miss them terribly. On the other hand, we have great pride in how their lives ended and in the legacy they left – not only to their own children but to everyone. Their heroism, their concern, sensitivity to others, unity, mutual responsibility – this is truly their legacy; this is the last will and testament that they left us. A legacy of unity.

We have taken this upon ourselves as a mission for our family and nation – to try and change the national discourse in Israel; to try and lead Israeli society to a different place, to one of mutual respect and unity. We want to make the change from divisive language to a language of unity, of fraternity, and of mutual responsibility. We have the right to speak about this and to promote it because we are part of this mutual responsibility. Our two sons were killed saving their brothers, their people – brothers they didn't even know – because of their awareness that we are all responsible for each other, that we are all brothers.

He Did It All in Flip-Flops

Ido Harush's Story

Age 21

As told by Ido's father, Yaniv

◉ *Yiftah Outpost*

Ido tried out for many, many pre-army leadership and volunteering programs. He was absolutely set on attending one. He went to many different tryouts and open weekends; in the end he was accepted to the MiNesharim Kalu program in Ma'agan Michael, and he was happy – it's considered a good pre-army academy, one of the best in the country. To tell you the truth, I was less pleased. First of all, it's up north, very far from our home here in Mitzpeh Ramon; second, it's an ultra-left-wing, super-secular program, and our home is traditional: we go to Friday night prayer services, we have a Sabbath meal with *kiddush* over wine. I don't know, I had hoped that he'd go somewhere that was a little closer to God. In the end, what actually happened was that he became the "religious guy" in his class – he'd organize the prayer service every Friday, read the Song of Songs, make the *havdalah* blessings at the end of the Sabbath, put on phylacteries. That's how it is; you never forget where you come from.

He received a summons to try out for the IAF pilots training course. I, of course, was excited, but he said, "It doesn't interest me." I said to him, "What do you mean, you're not interested? Just try to pass the first stage." So he goes and passes the first stage, second stage, third stage, but as he passes each stage, he becomes more and more adamant that he's not interested in any of these elite units. They don't interest him at all. When it's time for the final stage, he writes a waiver to withdraw, and I say to him, "What's wrong with you? Just try to get selected; in the worst case you'll get sent to a different elite unit," but then he says to me: "Dad, we all decided together – Room Seven in the academy – that we're going to enlist together in the Armored Corps: the 7th Armored Brigade, 77th Battalion." That's what he said to me! It was an institution, that Room Seven of theirs – him, Yoni, Segal, and Adir. The four of them decided together to go to the Armored Corps, and that was it. Once they'd made their decision, nothing else interested them.

Speaking of of unity in Israel: Yoni and Ido are a real love story. Talk about unlikely friendships! Yoni comes from a very left-wing home and joins anti-government protests on Kaplan Street, and Ido is very much our kid. So all day long they yell at each other, "You're a leftist!" "You're a crazy right-winger!" – they scream but they adore each other. They would travel all over the country to go out together hiking, having fun. It was something special.

That's it. After the pre-army program ended, they had this graduation ceremony, so we drove up. Ido was the star of the show and did all these hilarious impressions. He was a joker like that. After the ceremony, we met Muki Betser, one of Israel's legendary commandos who was a key figure in Operation Entebbe in 1976; he founded this pre-army program. Muki says to me, "Listen, your son made my life difficult this year at the academy! He didn't back down on anything. He challenged me, he asked tough questions; he was always playing devil's advocate, always opening up the conversation." Basically, Ido forged his own path.

In the end, Ido joined the Armored Corps according to plan and rose swiftly through the ranks – it's called "the star track." The most hardcore guys in the Armored Corps are called "tank freaks," and Ido got the bug. On every leave he'd come home black with grease full of gunpowder. As soon as he'd get back, he'd rush off to the hardware store to buy all these specialty brushes to maintain his tanks more expertly, and he was always talking about tanks and telling us about exercises that they did. In the beginning of his service, when he was posted on the northern border in the Golan, he'd put on this happy music every morning when the guys would clean their tank, and they'd all sing along as they scrubbed. He was a real tank freak!

In the months leading up to the war, he served on the Gaza border at the Yiftah Outpost in the Zikim area. He was the head of the battalion commander's crew; the battalion was spread out along the border, at every outpost there were tanks, and his team would rotate between them. During the month leading up to October 7th, he was always telling me how frustrated he was; that he was constantly dealing with disturbances at the border fence, that there was craziness and chaos. He felt something was coming.

Just before Rosh Hashana, one of the soldiers came down with Covid, and Ido didn't want to have to deal with finding a replacement, so he volunteered to stay on the base that weekend. He didn't come home for nearly a month because of that whole story! I tried to pressure him; I said, "Rosh Hashana isn't just another Sabbath!" but he says to me, "Drop it, Dad; it's nothing, everything's good." So after a month he comes home for the first day of the Sukkot holiday, and we really have such a wonderful weekend. Just wonderful. His friend Uri came over too, and we all sat in our huge sukkah drinking wine and laughing. There was a real holiday feeling, a sense of joy. On Sunday I take him to Beersheba; I drive him to the central bus station. When he gets out of the car, I feel this pang, this pang they talk about – I don't know how to explain it – and I go out to him from the car and hug him, kiss him; that's also not typical for me. That was it; we said goodbye.

On Simchat Torah, in the morning, I wake up at six-thirty and hear my wife talking to Ido on the phone. I can hear sirens coming from the nearby Air Force base, but I'm not worried – okay, things must be heating up again in Gaza. I go to synagogue, but on the way I hear these muffled thuds in the distance, and I realize that this is something different, so I go back home, get into uniform, and rush to the base. When I get to the war room there, I see that famous photo of the terrorist pickup truck in Sderot. Only then did the penny drop.

From that moment, I keep trying and trying to call him, and I call my wife Shalhevet on the phone to see if he called, but he doesn't answer, doesn't answer. At around twelve noon I begin to feel that something no good has happened. I have this ominous feeling: there's no information, no one really knows what's happening, and things don't look good. I stay at my post in the war room and keep a book of Psalms right next to me; in between duties I recite some chapters of Psalms and make all kinds of bargains with God. That's it. By four in the afternoon I figure it out on my own, and I drive home and wait for the casualty notification officers to come. They came at half past midnight, and there was no need for them to say anything. It was all too clear.

When we observed the mourning week of shiva, so many people were there. Suddenly this friend comes over and shows me a photo with writing on it: "Harush came to save me." It's a famous photo now, and I identify him there in his shorts and flip-flops, in combat. That's how I come to understand that there was some kind of story there. Then more testimonies came in, and more testimonies, and more visits, and I slowly, slowly begin to understand what happened. Then, about two weeks later, the mother of Naama, a friend of his from the base who was also killed, calls me, and she says to me, "Listen, I got Naama's phone back, and there are video clips on it, videos of the final battle; I think you need to see them." And thanks to those videos we know what we know.

‎⤳

This Naama, who guarded at the post at the entrance to the base, was a friend of Ido's in the battalion. During her final moments she was in touch with her family, and she filmed the whole thing. Five short videos show how Ido comes to her at the guard post with his rifle, barefoot and in shorts. You can hear his voice screaming, and you can see him shooting and directing the forces in the base. He's calling out – I don't know who he's calling to – "Come to me! Come to me!" It took us a while to understand the story, to understand what happened.

It all started with sirens in the base; mortar bombs, explosions. Everyone ran to the shelter; they were already used to that, the guys there. It was only afterward, when they heard the shooting of assault rifles at the guard post, that they realized that something else was happening. Then chaos broke out; most of the soldiers on base were still in bed or taking shelter under their beds. When Ido hears the shooting, he immediately decides to leave the mobile shelter – together with one of his soldiers, Yuval – to fight.

The mobile shelter is far from the entrance to the base, about three hundred meters away, and already on the way, as they run, Yuval falls down dead. Ido passes him and keeps running, shooting as he runs; you can see it in the videos. He reaches the entrance to the base where Naama is and where two guys from Golani are. They put in serious work too, those Golani guys. Ido fires and screams like a madman, trying to direct the fighting.

When the deputy brigade commander for that sector came to visit us, he saw the videos, and he was in shock. He said to me, "Listen, you don't realize what your son is doing here. You may not know how a battle is waged. Your son, I've seen a lot of fighters in my life, but how he's standing there in the heat of battle – no fear, no helmet, no nothing, no hesitation – that's something else." That's what he said. Again, Ido wasn't in any kind of commando unit; he wasn't a pilot. Like, I wouldn't have expected that kind of soldiering from a regular soldier like him, to battle in that way, because he wasn't really a fighter; he was a tank guy. He never took advanced firearms training, but still he stood there under fire, directing the fighting, shooting down at least six terrorists, and keeping them out of the base – all this when he was practically barefoot. I don't know how to explain it, where he got that energy from, I swear I can't even begin to explain it.

⤗

Everyone who fought there in that battle was killed. Naama was killed, and Ido was killed, and the guys from Golani too. But what I understood from an officer who was in the war room – what he revealed to me was that Hamas didn't succeed in getting into the base. We were sure that they got into the base; that's what happened at nearly all the other outposts, but at their base – Ido's base – they managed to keep them out; they actually stopped Hamas from coming in. Thanks to that, all the people who were there were saved; they weren't murdered or taken hostage like in the other bases. Even the battalion commander's family, who were staying there, were saved – his wife and kids. It's all thanks to Ido and the soldiers who fought alongside him. That's the story.

Last week, my older brother hired someone to replace a door in his house, a reinforced steel door. When the installer came in, they talked about the war, and when he heard the name Ido Harush from Mitzpeh Ramon, he asked my brother to call me so he could speak to me. I answer the call, and the guy says to me, "Ido! Am I speaking to the father of Ido?" and I say, "Yes," and he says to me, in tears, "My son is alive thanks to Ido! My son was a bulldozer operator at the Yiftah Outpost. Ido saw him coming out of his room, and he shouted to him and his friend to go back in because of the terrorists! They're both alive thanks to him!"

I told my wife a few days ago that I'm sure that Ido died with a smile on his face. He's definitely in heaven flying high because of what happened, because of all the people he saved. But it doesn't comfort me that he died like a hero; it doesn't reduce the pain at all. In his room there's still the smell of tanks, the smell of dust and motor oil and grease. His shoes are still there, too, and his coveralls. It stinks, but we're not cleaning it for now. It's still hard for us. The Sabbath is the hardest. Once the Sabbath in our place was tumultuous – laughter, eating, drinking, shouting, arguments. Now it's quiet. Now it's very quiet.

A Box of Sliced Vegetables

Yitzhar Hoffman's Story

Age 36

As told by Yitzhar's wife, Zohar

♀ Kibbutz Be'eri

My first date with Yitzhar was out in nature, with a camping coffee kit at a nice lookout point. I remember he called me from the road and asked, "Do you have any cookies at home?" I found something even though we're not really cookie people, he made us coffee, and we sat and talked and had a great time. From the very beginning, I could tell that he was something special. First of all, he was incredibly good-looking! But besides that, from the start, I saw that he had these contradictory qualities. On the one hand, he was a manly man, all tough and macho, a fighter, but on the other hand, he was so gentle, so modest, so sensitive and considerate.

When we first started dating, he was still in the army; he'd only get out every other weekend or so. On Saturday night, instead of going out with me or with friends, he'd often stay a while longer at his parents' house to wash their floor and clean up, then we'd meet up later. It didn't matter that he could have gotten out of it easily – I mean, you're an elite fighter on a two-day leave; why are you staying home to mop the floor for your parents? But that was Yitzhar; that's the kind of person he was. He was sensitive and considerate toward everyone.

Our relationship developed slowly. Very slowly. We're very different people. I'm pretty shy, and short; part of me always kind of wanted to disappear. He's the exact opposite – tall, charming, charismatic; wherever he went, he was always the center of attention. We went out for four years before we got married. By then, he was an officer in the army. Sometimes he'd only come home once every three weeks. It wasn't easy, but I knew that he was totally worth it; I was completely in love with him.

&

After seven years, Yitzhari finally left the army. He wanted to start a family already; he wanted to raise kids. His parents were quite old by then; he was the youngest, and it was important to him to be a young father. He was so happy when our oldest son was born. Yitzhar chose his name, "Be'eri." He loved how rooted and how Israeli it sounded. He loved that name. When I think about it today, it gives me chills that we named him that. Be'eri.

Adjusting to civilian life wasn't easy for him. It's no simple feat, starting all over again after being a revered officer in an elite unit. He studied for his college-entrance exam and dabbled in carpentry for a while, building wooden decks, that sort of thing. Then he studied structural engineering and worked on all kinds of projects. He was ambitious: he wanted to move up to a senior management position, something serious, something meaningful. That was his life plan.

When Covid hit we were living in Jerusalem, and it was terrible. Most of our friends left the city and moved to small towns; the whole city shut down, we didn't have any kind of community, and we were very lonely. So we started spending a lot of time visiting his sister in Eshhar, a small community up north; we really liked the energy and the people there, but it felt too remote for us. At some point, Yitzhar said to me, "Let's try; we'll give it two years, think of it as a relocation. Worst case scenario, we'll go back to Jerusalem, no big deal." He always made me feel so safe and secure. So I took the plunge and followed him here.

It was an amazing time. Magical. We both quit our jobs, moved up north without any plans. I was pretty nervous about it – like, what were we going to do? We had to find jobs. But Yitzhar said, "Zohar, we have a once-in-a-lifetime chance to spend half a year together without having to work; we'll never get another chance like this." So it began, this sweet, sweet time. We'd wake up every morning and say, "Okay, what should we do today? Where should we hike, where should we have coffee, where should we have lunch?" It was a magical time. Yitzhar knew that it was a once-in-a-lifetime chance, and he was right. It was amazing.

⁂

Yitzhar always led a double life – a civilian life and a military life. He always had two roles: his role as a civilian, and the crazy project he started in the reserves. It was his and his friend's initiative – that friend is now the head of their unit. The idea was to start this attack unit of elite reserve fighters with very special capabilities, with a level of competence you don't usually get in the army. When I would see him working on things to do with that unit, I'd ask him, "What are you up to? What are you always working on?" and he'd always say, "The next time there's a war, you'll find out."

He would work their butts off; they'd go for weeks of very intensive training. Most reservists spend half the time sitting around, preparing food with camping equipment, but Yitzhar's reservists never stopped to rest. He didn't cut them any slack. Instead of "Yitzhar," they nicknamed him "It's hard" because he really worked them hard and took it very seriously. He believed in it with all his heart. He wanted to make sure that when war broke out, they'd be ready. In that sense, he was kind of a prophet.

He was an army man through and through, even after his discharge. He loved his unit; he believed in that project of his with all his heart. Every time he came home from reserve duty, I'd see that twinkle in his eye. I could see how happy he was.

⁂

On Shabbat morning, just before we set out for the synagogue, Yitzhar saw that he had loads of messages and missed calls. I remember how he sat on the bed and said to me, "Zohar, war! It's war!" He was dressed for the synagogue, so he quickly changed into his uniform, got his bag ready, and left right away. At two in the afternoon, I sent him a message, "What's happening?" and he wrote that they were on a helicopter headed for Be'eri. By two-thirty they were already in Be'eri.

When he got to his unit, his soldiers weren't ready yet. But there was a whole team of young soldiers in their mandatory service that he didn't know. They were waiting for a commander to lead them, so he just took charge and set off. He fought there with them in the kibbutz for three days straight. He told me that they introduced themselves by name only after three days.

From what I understand, in Be'eri there were a lot of different forces, and there was utter chaos, pandemonium, and very high risk of crossfire. When I asked Yitzhar what he was actually doing there, he told me: thirty percent fighting, seventy percent evacuation. They fought the terrorists there, and at the same time, they went through the houses and rescued people who were hiding there. The soldiers who were with him told me at the shiva that he was very calm and collected and that he refused to give up even on what seemed like lost causes. For example, there was one house with a few wounded Matkal soldiers trapped there, and it was very dangerous and complicated to get them out. But Yitzhar decided to go for it and managed to save whoever could be saved. I think that Yadin Gellman was involved in that story as well.

Another example: at one point someone reported that a certain neighborhood had been cleared out, that there were no people left there, and Yitzhar asked him, "Are you sure?" and the guy says, "I think so." That obviously wasn't good enough for Yitzhar. So he went back to the neighborhood to check, went through all the houses, and found another fifteen people hiding there. Fifteen people!

At the shiva, more and more people from Be'eri just kept coming, and they all told me that Yitzhar had saved them from their safe rooms. I didn't know about it. I didn't know that he had saved so many people! He didn't even mention it! All he had told me was that there was complete chaos there and a high risk of getting hit by friendly fire and that he was frustrated, because he thought they could have saved more people there. I understood only at the shiva what they really did in Be'eri.

From Be'eri, they moved on to Kissufim, to Holit, and to Kibbutz Re'im. For three to four days they fought all over the area; that was the beginning of the war. Later on, he and the unit he founded fought in Gaza, and they led the craziest, most dangerous operations. He and his unit fought in Gaza for more than one hundred days.

Yitzhar had always said to me, "When there's a war, you'll find out," and during the war in Gaza, I really did find out. He and his guys were one of the most effective, potent forces there was. They did crazy things there. I think that their most famous operation was the takeover of Shifa Hospital, but there were so many more. When they came out of Shifa I remember asking him, "How come you guys are there? You're reservists! Why don't they use regular soldiers there?" and Yitzhar told me that no one else in the IDF had their capabilities. They had been training for a decade for this very situation.

He was always explaining to them why they were fighting, what they were fighting for, and he gave his soldiers a real sense of confidence. That's what I heard from everyone at the shiva; even before the shiva, whenever I happened to meet his fighters, that's what they said. They all wanted to fight with Yitzhar; they wanted to fight by his side. I remember saying to him, "How are you not scared to go into those tunnels? Aren't you scared that suddenly, I don't know, you'll be ambushed by some terrorist, that they'll try to blow you up?" And Yitzhar said, "We're scared, but we remember what it's all for." He truly believed in what he was doing. He truly believed that this was their moment; this was their time to give whatever they could for our country, for our people. He often spoke about how right now, what mattered was the collective; he truly lived that belief. That's what gave him the strength to go on fighting. And that's what drew all those men after him.

There was a tough incident with the Givati Brigade; there was a skirmish with terrorists in some building and a real concern that three of them had been taken hostage – three soldiers were missing in action. Yitzhar heard about it on his radio and showed up minutes later with his soldiers, divided them up into two squads, and made some amazing decisions on the spot, incredibly cool and collected. They started fighting the terrorists there in the stairwell. Fighting in a stairwell is very dangerous; there are very poor odds of success. And at first, one of his soldiers was wounded in the arm, and Yitzhar was shot in the thigh.

He stepped aside, lowered his pants, and asked the soldier next to him, "Do I need a tourniquet?" The guy said, "No," so Yitzhar just went back and kept fighting with a hole in his leg! He led the battle there for about fifty minutes until it was all over; they eliminated the terrorists and found the missing soldiers, who had all been killed. The guys in the other squad didn't even know that Yitzhar was hurt; they though that he was fine – he kept giving them orders, explaining who was supposed to shoot where; he ran the whole thing like a surgical operation. And he was wounded the whole time. Unreal.

After that battle, they evacuated him to the hospital. It was a muscle wound, which is relatively light. The next day, just one day after he was wounded, he asked me to drive him from the hospital back to his unit. He wanted to do a thorough report of the incident. During the report, everyone was showering him with praise, saying how effectively he ran the whole thing, but he insisted on going over his mistakes, reviewing everything that wasn't perfect. He wanted to learn and to improve. For the next time.

That was his third injury in Gaza. Before that, he had been hit by an exploding wall; he had sustained bad injuries in his knee and his shoulder. But a week later, he was already back inside Gaza, fighting, commanding more and more operations. Many people told me that when he was injured, they were relieved, thinking that now he could finally go home. But I knew that he'd go back; I knew he wouldn't stay home, no way, not when his guys were still fighting.

One day during the war, Yitzhar and the soldiers who had been with him in Be'eri went to the Dead Sea to meet the people they had saved. They were about fifteen guys, and when they walked in everyone stood up and clapped and cheered for them, and they held this whole panel there, where they asked them questions. Some of the questions were uncomfortable, like, "How come it took you so long to rescue us," and

Yitzhar answered them honestly, with real empathy, and said he was frustrated about that too, and asked for their forgiveness. He asked the people of Be'eri's forgiveness for not managing to save everyone they had wanted to save. It was a kind of holy moment: in the middle of a war, a commander, a reservist, who had saved so many people on October 7th, apologizing to the people of Be'eri. It was unique, poignant, special. It's not easy to come and apologize, to take responsibility. But he had this sense of responsibility that accompanied him wherever he went, all the time. It was a natural part of him his entire life.

After a few months of fighting, Yitzhar held an evening of appreciation for his fighters' wives and partners. He arranged this big event; I was there too. There was this standup performance by Hanoch Daum. And they screened a short movie from the operation in Shifa. He made us all feel really connected to that operation; he helped us all understand how important, how crucial it was, what they did there. And he awarded a kind of medal to each and every one of us; the medal said, "thank you," and each one was engraved with the woman's name – it wasn't just a generic medal, he'd had them all personalized.

At the end of the evening he spoke; it was a very short speech about our goal, about how justified this war was, about how every one of us deserved to raise our children without a fear of rockets, and about how we all had the right to grow crops without fear of being hit by missiles. He spoke with such passion, such proud Zionism, that I grabbed his speech after he finished, and said, "I'm keeping this!"

He was such an idealist. He really believed in these ideals, and really lived them: the country, the collective. In the later months of the war, his faith grew even stronger; it grew so strong that Yitzhar realized that he would never go back to civilian life afterward. All those operations, they were so important, so meaningful, he could never go back. He could never go back to working in a construction company. He felt that his special forces unit was putting into practice everything they had been working on for the past ten years, and he soon understood – so did I – that he was going to sign back on as an officer in the unit. That was his destiny; that was his true calling in life. It's what gave his life meaning.

Yitzhar was killed in Gaza by a sniper's bullet. Just one bullet, but a very powerful one that penetrated his vest, went through his back, and traveled into his heart. They evacuated him right away; he was in the hospital within half an hour. But the wound was fatal. When they came to tell me, I wouldn't believe them. I didn't believe it until I spoke to the unit commander himself. I didn't believe it was real. Even now, right now, as we speak, I feel like it's just impossible. It doesn't make sense.

He fought without end, without a break, for one hundred and ten days. He was so proud of his unit, he was so completely fulfilled, he was truly so happy to fight together with his soldiers; he admired them so much! He was so proud to fight by their side. On that evening he organized, he took me from guy to guy and said to me, "Zohar, this is an amazing guy, this guy is unbelievable, there's no one like him!" He just adored them, and they loved him too. It's a special bond, a commander's bond with his fighters.

If there's something I want everyone to remember about Yitzhar, besides all the insane operations he ran over the last four months of his life in Gaza – I want people to remember what a down-to-earth guy he was. Every time he came home – and it didn't matter if he had come straight from Shifa, or straight from some special op – he would mop the floor, do the dishes. He got shot in the leg then came home and played tag with the kids.

I would say to him, "Yitzhari, go and lie down for an hour, go and rest," and he would say, "No, no, no." It didn't occur to him to slow down when he came home. He wanted to help me at home; he wanted to make things easier for me. Even in the heat of war, he could see my needs, too. Each time he'd go back to the unit, early in the morning, he'd make me a box of sliced vegetables. And he'd stick a little note on the box, with sweet, simple words. I mean, what kind of person does that?! Hello! I should be baking you cookies to bring the guys in the army! But no, he was always the one who took the time to slice vegetables for me before he left. That was Yitzhar. That was so Yitzhar. It's a perfect example of who he was.

Alongside everything he did in the army, alongside all the important battles he fought, he was also a wonderful father and a wonderful husband and a person who just loved to be joyful and a father who loved his children endlessly. We always told each other that this was it, we were going to be together forever; we really thought that we'd grow old together. We talked about it. In the end, we had fourteen years together. Fourteen short, beautiful years. I feel like I was given a gift. The gift of living with him, the gift of loving him, the gift of raising children with him.

The Writing Was on the Wall

Shay Ashram's Story

Age 19

As told by Shay's father, Dror

○ *Nahal Oz Outpost*

On October 5th, Shay posted a video on TikTok of this, like, funny dance she did with two of her friends from the base, Noa and Ori. All three of them were surveillance soldiers, beautiful souls. It's such a cute video, so nice – they're all laughing, making faces, these little girls in IDF uniforms; so proud of themselves, having a good time, so happy.

Right after the massacre, people started commenting on that video: "That's what you were doing instead of watching over us – making a TikTok?" It turns out that that video was their last dance together. Our daughter Shay was murdered; Noa Marciano was taken hostage alive and later murdered in captivity, in Shifa Hospital in Gaza. She was murdered in cold blood! By a doctor! Ori Megidish was taken hostage and rescued a month later by the IDF. I so, so hope – I pray – that at least dear Ori, precious Ori, will have more dances like that in her life; that she'll dance all the dances that my daughter and Noa never will.

꙳

When Shay got her placement as an IDF surveillance soldier, she flat out refused to accept it. She said, "No way! It's not interesting, it's not special, and it's not what I'm going to do in the army. Period." She went to the doctor and began to play up some old injury that she had in the lower back, so that the army would see that she couldn't serve in a position that demands hours of sitting. The doctor examines her and discovers that she actually has some minor fracture in her tailbone. But it doesn't help her; the fracture is too insignificant. So she enlists to become a lookout after all.

During the training course she insists on doing more and more medical tests to prove that she isn't fit for the position, but slowly, slowly, she unexpectedly comes to realize that she's beginning to fall in love with the role; she suddenly realizes that she does want to be a surveillance soldier! Suddenly she understood how significant it is to be "the eyes of the country." You're sitting at the border with Gaza, you have a screen connected to a magnifying camera whose moves you control. With one glance you can thwart terrorist infiltrations – or, God forbid, miss them if you look away at exactly the wrong moment. You can prevent terror attacks; you can activate the whole sector! One word to your commander and she immediately sends a remote command to the weapon connected to the camera above the operations center, to open fire at the point that you identified! It's non-stop action. Especially at the Nahal Oz Outpost, where Shay was assigned, which is the outpost closest to the fence with Gaza. She loved action, our Shay; she loved it so much.

But then, just when she enthusiastically completes the course and is excited to get started, her latest medical results come in, and they show that she actually has a more serious issue. When she arrives at her base at Nahal Oz, they say to her, "There's nothing we can do – medically, you can't be a lookout; you can be a driver or join the artillery." So she starts to fight for the job.

You have to understand, Shay is a girl who just doesn't give up. If there's something she wants, she'll never give up on it. There was this one time we wouldn't let her fly to Rhodes with her aunt, so she gets up – this fifteen-year-old girl – she gets up, buys a plane ticket with her own money that she saved, and informs us that she's flying to Rhodes all by herself to meet her aunt. So we gave in – we had no choice. Because if Shay wants something, she'll fight for it until it happens.

So Shay hears that they're taking her out of the surveillance role, and she fights like only she knows how to fight. She tries to speak with anyone she can; she goes for all these checkups until she finally finds one doctor who gives her medical clearance for the job on the condition that she continues under medical supervision. And that's it.

During her service, when she would come back home every other weekend, we felt like she was taller. She was the same girl but older, more mature. She would return home on Friday with a twinkle in her eye, "Wow, you don't understand what crazy trouble there was on the fence – and how I handled the incident and activated the troops!" She felt she was doing something significant. She always said to us, "We're on the fence; we see everything, hear everything – we hear the interceptions, we hear the Iron Dome. You can't believe how many incidents there are at the fence." She really felt, Shay, like she was saving the lives of civilians every single day.

Shay was a very professional surveillance soldier. Even when everything on the monitor looked unclear, she could tell whether it was a cat, a soldier, or a terrorist trying to cross the fence. She knew when to alert forces and when not to, when something was a non-event. One time she called me, crying, "They're going to put me on trial!" It was a day with poor visibility, and the cameras were a little fogged up, and they didn't see well, and some sort of figure passed in front of the camera. Because visibility was so poor, Shay called her commander and said to her, "Ma'am, I see something here, but I don't think it's anything unusual. It looks like some kind of cat or animal; I don't think we need to alert any forces." Her commander said, "I trust you. Whatever you say, you know the sector. It's your call." And, in fact, Shay didn't alert any forces.

But a few days later, they told her that she's going to have a hearing because it seemed that there had been something there after all, and they were now sending troops to survey the area and check what it was, based on footprints and other signs. So she cries to me that they're putting her on trial. And we ask her, "Who do you think is right?" and she says to us, "I trust myself a million percent; there was nothing danger-ous there!" And then Shahar, her older sister, says to her, "Okay! You go with your truth, Shay! Go to the hearing and say what you have to say; you don't have to apologize for what you know is true!" Shay really went on trial, and it ended with them saying to her, "It turns out that it really was just an animal; excellent work, well done."

At one point they wanted her to do a squad leaders course, but she said, "No, not yet; I want a few more months to get more expertise in surveillance." She wanted to be able to be a better commander, to be con-fident of her knowledge, so that when she would teach her soldiers and they'd ask her questions, she'd know how to give them proper answers. But her commanders said to her, "It's now or never," so she answered, "So never. I don't want to be a second-rate commander."

In the end they went along with her. They gave her a few more months because she set the rules for them. She made it clear that she would only go to the commanders course when she had mastered two full "cameras." A "camera" is a military zone, a part of the sector. Then she really began to learn another camera zone, to become skilled there, too. She was really thorough with this. She was absolutely devoted to her job.

Shay never got the chance to go to her commanders course. If she had started the course at the original time they suggested to her, if she hadn't insisted on staying there in that base, in that deathtrap, she would still be with us today. We can't stop thinking what could have been, what if, but how do those questions help? They don't help at all; they won't bring Shay back to us.

At first Shay enjoyed her job, but slowly, slowly, for those last few months, there was this added layer of mystery, of secrecy, as well. She was always saying, "I'm not allowed to tell you; it's confidential." But there were some things that she did tell us. During those last months, she started telling us – at least me personally – she began to say that she's worried because she sees what's going on at the fence, and she thinks it's lead-ing to something. She was always saying that there was going to be real trouble. Serious trouble.

In the weeks before to the massacre, she kept telling her commanders, "They're making a lot of noise; they're coming all the way up to the fence and throwing things and setting tires on fire and trying all kinds of things and checking what works and what doesn't work. It's constant." I remember her telling me that she saw two people next to the fence who didn't fit any usual kind of description at all. That's the most suspicious. They weren't farmers working the area, they weren't regular people, but she sees them there, she kept saying that it's suspicious, that something's happening. But her commanders insisted on calling them "disturbances." That is, something basically ordinary. But it wasn't something ordinary. They were planning something bigger. And Shay understood that. And told her commanders.

She felt that something about the term "disturbances" wasn't right. She felt that they always related to her reports like they were distinct problems, like each time it was one small fire that needed to be put out. She would say, "I don't know if they realize that they need to connect the dots." Because what Shay identified there was a trend. She didn't want to just report, "This happened today, this happened yesterday." She wanted to actually influence the way they understood the totality of all these incidents. She wanted them to understand that someone was planning something there by the fence.

So she said, "Fine, disturbances, no problem, I'll call them 'disturbances.' But I'll report on the frequency of these disturbances, then they'll see that this is all moving in a certain direction, they'll see that it seems to be building up to a bigger operation." So she reported that the disturbances were becoming increasingly frequent; she showed them how all summer long it happened mainly on Fridays, but by September it went up to twice a week, and by October it was almost constant. And she wasn't the only one who reporting on these things; it was all the girls. They sensed it. Because they sat there and saw what was happening by the fence every single day.

She and her surveillance soldier friends were always passing on that there was going to be trouble. They were also able to say when it was going to happen. They'd say, "During the holidays." Her friend Aviv Hajaj, a lookout who was with her on the same rotation and was killed together with her, sent her mother a message just a few days before the massacre: "Mom, there's going to be a huge operation here, and I have this feeling that it's going to happen on my shift." Just like that, word for word! It wasn't just the lookouts; it was their commanders too. One of the officers in Nahal Oz said that there was going to be a terrorist incursion, and she had a gut feeling that it would happen in her own base.

Shay was very vague with us; she didn't really share exactly what she saw there near the fence. But later, after she was murdered, we talked to her friends, and we also saw interviews on TV conducted with the only surveillance soldiers who survived that massacre and other surveillance soldiers from Nahal Oz who were off duty that weekend, and I can't describe, I can't begin to describe how I felt. My jaw just dropped! I banged my head against the wall, I screamed, I couldn't believe what I was hearing.

One of them said on the report that she would see them counting steps next to the fence, digging there, and whenever she reported it, they'd always say to her, "No, it's farming, it's farming." They would see the Nukhba there, the Hamas special forces units; they would see how they were training! They would drive up in their vehicles and charge out, running very fast and timing themselves, how long it took, how long it took them to run up to the fence. But the surveillance soldiers' superiors kept telling them, "That's not a threat; everything is fine." They'd see them practice coming out of tunnels! They practiced how to raid a tank! They practiced gliding on paragliders! They saw it all, all of it, the surveillance soldiers; they saw everything! But their superiors would constantly reassure them; they'd keep saying, "It's nothing, it's nothing; everything's fine."

There was one surveillance soldier there who said that one day this whole group came. It was really something, this unbelievably huge number of people, like two hundred Hamas fighters, and stood a hundred meters away from the fence! She's thinking, she's saying to herself: if they want to, if they decide to charge the fence now, we're dead. And they also knew what the attack plan was; they just worked it out logically. They knew that first Hamas would take out the cameras from the "see and shoot" system, the cameras that controlled weapons the commanders could fire remotely, and that's exactly what happened; that was the first thing that the terrorists hit before they came in.

To be clear, the reports didn't stop at the commanders. Their immediate commanders took them seriously. One day, one of the surveillance soldiers noticed that the terrorists came with maps, and they were looking to the right, to the left. She reported it to her commander, who was impressed and said, "Well done, catching that," and passed it on. The commanders took it seriously, but it was held up somewhere higher along the chain of command. It's not clear to us exactly where it got held up, where it became just dismissive – dismissive of the enemy, dismissive of the surveillance soldiers.

There was one report with such shocking testimony. I don't know, I'd rather believe that it was wrong – but it was from a reliable source, and reliable reporters, and it was shocking! It said that there were some lookouts who decided to warn more senior commanders, and one of them responded, "I don't want to hear about this nonsense again. If you bother us one more time with these things, you'll be court-martialed."

In the weeks before it happened, Shay felt the need to reassure us – perhaps to reassure herself, too – and she said to us a few times, "Okay, even if there's trouble – and there will be, we know that there will be – even if there's a Hamas attack, for sure the army will get it under control. Because if surveillance soldiers sitting in Nahal Oz know that there's going to be trouble, and all of them are saying it, then of course the big army knows! Of course the top commanders know! That's obvious."

They told themselves that in terms of their personal safety, it would be okay. They didn't feel that they personally were being abandoned. They were so sure that they would be safe in their own base, that they were so well protected there, that a previous surveillance crew had scrawled on the wall of the outdoor bomb shelter where most of them were murdered: "Look at her, strolling by without a care, as if

Gaza isn't right there." That's what was written in the shelter where my daughter was murdered. In the shelter where my daughter was murdered, the writing was on the wall. It's unbelievable! I catch myself; I wake up in the morning and I catch myself, and I say, "The writing was on the wall."

>❧

Shay was in the base that Shabbat. When it all started, she wasn't in the operations center with the surveillance soldiers; she was supposed to go on shift at seven. But at six-thirty, when the sirens started, the girls in the operations center told her to stay in the shelter. She went with all the rest of the girls into the outdoor shelter near the girls' dorms, and that's actually where they were, hiding from the mortar bombs. And they waited for something to happen. For someone to come and save them. At eight in the morning, something really did happen. At eight in the morning, not a single one of them was alive.

That morning, when the sirens started, she called me; I was just about to leave for synagogue. Previous times when there had been sirens, she had always sounded calm on the phone, but this time she was really panicked. She told us to go to the safe room in her Aunt Carmit's house because something serious was happening. She really yelled. She said, "I'm going to the shelter here, and you're going to the safe room! It's serious!" We were saying, "Okay, what's a few sirens, what's the big deal," and she was like, "You don't get it!! There are terrorists, terrorists! There's a terrorist infiltration; there's a crazy situation here. Go to Carmit, go to the safe room!"

In the cousins' WhatsApp group, she sends a voice message to all of them – they're like her brothers and sisters – "I love you so much, more than anything! Always remember that! Tell my parents to come to you; scream at them to come to your safe room, I'm not kidding!" She was so anxious, and it was so unlike her, so my wife Sari calls her, "You just get into the shelter, don't worry about us!" and Shay answers her, "Mom, a shelter isn't going to help me; they've landed here with paragliders inside the base." The second we heard that, we got to our feet and ran to Carmit's bomb shelter.

We kept messaging her – me, her mother, her sisters, her cousins, all begging her to get back to us, to keep us posted, and at some point she messaged Sari: "I love you, you're the best parents in the world, take care of yourselves!" and she wrote to her cousin, "Hug my mom and dad for me, tell them that I love them very much." She had very quickly realized that it was the end.

At a quarter to eight on Saturday morning we lost communication with her, but it was only on Monday, at eight-thirty at night, that they came from the army to inform us that she was no longer alive. Looking back, we know enough to say that by 7:55 she was gone. Looking back, we know enough to say that at eleven o'clock that Saturday morning, her brother saw a video clip of her corpse. But he couldn't, he just couldn't bear to tell us. Looking back, we know enough to say that our entire extended family had seen that footage by Saturday night. You see Shay there lying on the floor – perfect, beautiful, fast asleep. And surrounding her are fifteen terrorists.

We waited for sixty hours to hear what had happened to her. Maybe that sounds like a long time to wait to know what's going on. But given everything that was going on, the crazy mess over there, it was very quick. Because Shay had been inside the shelter, they identified her relatively quickly. But most of the surveillance solders that were in the operations center were murdered, and those girls went through things I don't want to describe, things that I don't even want to think about.

Her best friends, the ones who were in the shelter with her, are still being held hostage in Gaza. Seven of those girls were taken hostage, and as of now five of them are still in captivity. After she was rescued, Ori Megidish came to us and told us what happened there. She told us that the terrorists just came right into the shelter, and the girls started running away. The outdoor shelters have this narrow opening, and we don't know if Shay deliberately let the others go ahead of her or if that's just what happened, but she was the last to make it outside. Five of the girls managed to escape, and Shay was one of the girls the terrorists murdered. Right there inside the shelter.

No one knew that three hundred terrorists would attack the base, which had maybe forty armed infantry soldiers, tops. The army's obtuseness – it wasn't with malicious intent; no one there dreamed, no one could have imagined what was about to happen. But there was hubris on the part of the senior commanders. That's all. The higher the rank, the greater the hubris and the greater the obtuseness. That's what it was.

Those girls, they were murdered in cold blood. They didn't have a single rifle, not even a gun. They couldn't save anyone, definitely not themselves. And even so, even though they were murdered unarmed, those girls are heroes. They're heroes because they spoke up, and they made their reports, and they shouted, and they gave warning. And even though no one – no one! – took them seriously, they never stopped insisting on the truth. In the end, it turned that that they were the ones who paid the price.

Shay was a charismatic girl. You couldn't miss her. She would walk into the room, and everybody knew she was there; she had this presence. She was someone that you'd see, someone that you'd hear. She wasn't someone you could dismiss – she was strong and opinionated, and if she wanted to be heard she knew how to bang on the table.

Shay was our youngest, after three much older siblings: Erel, Tehila, and Shahar. After seven years, when we were sure that we wouldn't be blessed with more children, we suddenly received her as a gift. *Shay* means "gift." She was the heart of our family, and now that heart is crushed. We're just torn apart by love and longing. When I think about how her life came to an end because someone, because a lot of people, because a whole system of people just didn't see her, didn't hear her, didn't listen to her and her friends – it's not just infuriating, it doesn't just drive me out of my mind, it's also just – I don't know – it's just insulting. It's an insult to who she was. It's an insult to us, as her parents. It's an insult to our army. And it's an insult to the country.

We Won't Surrender, No Matter What

Yohai Dukhan's Story

Age 26

As told by Yohai's brother, Yehuda

○ *Nahal Oz Outpost*

When Yohai was in high school, his class had this teacher they didn't get along with; it was a real clash. The teacher understood that the situation was complicated, so he asked all the students to write down suggestions for improvement. They all wrote very harsh things to the teacher – the feedback was anonymous. So Yohai takes his friend aside and says, "Listen, you and I are writing only good things to him, and we're signing our names on it." And that's what they did. That created a big commotion, and Yohai just stood up there and argued with the whole class, the whole grade, something like fifty guys who didn't agree with him. He stood up to them in a measured way – he wasn't violent or anything – and he said to them, "Guys, I disagree with you, you're making a mistake." He was stubborn, Yohai, but it was the kind of stubbornness that always comes with truth.

Yohai was a person who went all in. Anyone who knew him knew he was really into the whole "being ready for anything." Ever since he enlisted, he always had his rifle with him, all the time. At family events we always teased him for ruining the photos with it. He even went to synagogue with his weapon – who does something like that?! Who comes to synagogue with a rifle?! But he'd say, "The day I put down my rifle is the day when the enemy will decide to attack."

He also would teach himself a lot of things that an officer in his position doesn't have to know. I remember how he'd come home with all these booklets about the art of warfare, and he'd sit and read and make notes – what he thought was incorrect, what needed improvement. He would just think big. He was always looking for where he could do more than what was demanded of him.

That's how he was at home, too. You'd expect a tired combat soldier to come home and rest, but Yohai, as soon as he got home he'd immediately attack the household chores, helping my mother with whatever was needed; fixing things, straightening out a doorhandle, sealing up a hole. And the whole time, he'd be talking on the phone with his soldiers – a soldier who was in a jam, a soldier who needed this, a soldier who needed that – and Shabbat would be about to start, and he'd still be in the middle of helping someone.

Then when Shabbat came in, he'd go to the synagogue service, and come back from prayers, and we'd eat the Shabbat meal together, and after the meal we'd all be talking and laughing. He'd sit and talk with us and play a little with the nieces and nephews, and I'd see him like leaning against the wall, struggling to keep his eyes open. And I'd say to myself, *nu*, enough, that exhausted, worn-out soldier should go to sleep already. But no way, because now is the stage when Yohai would learn Torah. He'd always sit down to study Rabbi Zvi Yehuda Kook's writings after the Friday night meal; that was his routine. Of course, he hardly managed to get through a paragraph; he'd read a passage, doze off, wake himself up, read another sentence, and fall asleep. I'd wake him. Finally, after a few rounds of falling asleep over the book and me waking him up, he'd give up and go to bed.

Yohai was twenty-six when he fell; during the final hours of his life he was a hero – a hero like in books, like in movies, a sort of superhero. But I think his heroism began long before that, really. The heroism of seeing how you can be of help even when you're dead tired; studying military materials, learning Torah, not giving up on talking with your family, and never wasting a single moment, so that every moment counts – that's day-to-day heroism. Yohai was, first and foremost, a hero of everyday life.

Maybe it sounds like Yohai was sort of a serious type, heavy, but the truth is that anyone who knew him was surprised to discover how funny a guy he was. He had a refined sense of humor; humor on a high level, humor that could also be critical but never went low. Yohai never came down hard on anyone.

He would make fun of the army, of how it was so square and into procedures. For example, there's this thing in the army that when anything happens that wasn't supposed to – let's say, a soldier got a little injured, he fell somewhere, or if there was any kind of safety incident, you then write an incident report. And that report has to precisely describe exactly what happened at each stage and at every hour, and it would drive Yohai nuts that you had to do that for every dumb little thing.

So I remember that one time Yohai was on base, and he wanted to make himself coffee at four in the morning before some mission, and the lid of the Taster's Choice wasn't fully closed, and almost all of the coffee spilled on him. So as a joke he wrote up an incident report about it. I still have that report. He warmly commends "the commander" – namely, himself – who acted swiftly and decisively to prevent the spilling of the entire jar. Under "Initial Lessons Learned" he writes, "From now on, the cafeteria commander must be present at each closure of the jar."

I'm Yohai's oldest brother; I'm three years older than him, but in some sense I've always been more than just a big brother to him because we lost our father when we were little. Our father, Alex Dukhan, of blessed memory, fell in a very serious terror attack along the Worshippers' Route in Hebron. He was a member of the first response team and arrived on the scene and waged battle with the terrorists. Afterward, the alley where the terror attack took place was named "Heroes' Alley," because there were eleven other fighters who fought alongside him with great bravery and were killed. Our father fell as a hero of Israel; twenty years later, his beloved son joined him in the heroes' alley.

First of all, it's critical to understand how it was that the Nahal Oz Outpost was hit so badly, but also how the stubborn, heroic fighting of the soldiers inside it actually saved many communities nearby.

The Nahal Oz Outpost sits on Highway 25. Highway 25 is a sort of corridor with communities along its entire length. It's not some miserable dirt road; it's a major route. This highway starts at the Gaza border and continues due east. The first town it passes, the closest to Gaza, is Kibbutz Nahal Oz, which is three hundred meters away from the Nahal Oz Outpost. After that, if you continue three kilometers east to Kibbutz Sa'ad, and then to more communities, and at the end of the corridor, thirteen kilometers away from the outpost, is the city of Netivot.

The terrorists who were killed at the Nahal Oz Outpost had maps with clear plans for the whole Highway 25 corridor. There were terrorists with plans for Kibbutz Sa'ad; terrorists who planned to reach the town of Zameret; others were designated for Tekuma or Kfar Maimon or Netivot and who knows what else along Highway 25. What actually happened was that most of their plans just didn't come to pass; even Kibbutz Nahal Oz absorbed relatively few losses compared to the other kibbutzim. And most of the other towns along Highway 25 were actually saved, including Netivot, an entire city that they never even reached. We now know that the fighters within the Nahal Oz Outpost neutralized, delayed, and disrupted many Nukhba terrorist forces targeting these communities.

On that Shabbat, one hundred and sixty soldiers were stationed in the Nahal Oz Outpost. Most of them weren't combat soldiers, but rather in combat support or Intelligence. Most of the fighters there that Shabbat were from the Golani Infantry Brigade and the 7th Armored Brigade. Yohai's a platoon commander in Golani's 13th Battalion; he'd been serving there for almost three months, and it was usually very quiet. You could hear the crickets at night and the birds in the morning. None of them ever dreamed – even in their worst nightmares – that what happened there could possibly take place. When the enormity of the tragedy started to become clear, we found out that of all the IDF battalions, the 13th sustained the heaviest losses that day: forty-one fighters, may God avenge their blood.

At six-thirty in the morning, Yohai and his friends wake up to booms. They get out of bed as they are, in pajamas, and just run straight to the mobile shelter. Yohai ran to the shelter barefoot and in his boxers – but he also had his ceramic vest, helmet, and weapon. Because he's a platoon commander, his vest also has a communication device attached to it, so he hears everything coming over the radio network. He hears Shilo Har-Even, his company commander who was killed later that day, saying that there's a commotion and he's on his way to join forces with the armored personnel carrier that's right outside the outpost. At the same time, Yohai also hears the surveillance soldiers' reports over the radio.

Later, we heard the recordings of their reports. At first, it's "Four people are coming down in the direction of the fence," and their tone of speech is business-like, even dry. But then, from minute to minute the reports grow more alarming and their voices rise: "Two men are doing something to the fence," "There are five of them, they've blown up the fence!" and after that, "Thirty men on motorcycles have gone through the fence!" and then already really shouting, "Turkish horseman!! Turkish horseman!!" which is the code for a terrorist infiltration into the outpost. Later on, you can hear how the surveillance soldiers' voices get weaker and choke up, how they hold back their tears and report, "They're inside the outpost." According to what we were told by sources carrying out the investigation of this battle, over three hundred terrorists infiltrated the base that day.

At a quarter to seven, about twenty-five fighters were inside the mobile shelter. The terrorists still aren't inside the base, but Yohai hears the surveillance soldiers on the radio and realizes that it's a matter of moments until the terrorists are inside. So he takes command and says to everyone there, "What's happening now is that we're leaving this shelter in groups of four; the first four go out, race to the rooms, get into uniform, vest, cartridges, helmet, water, kneepads, and come back here. Right after them, the next four race to the rooms, get their equipment, and come back here; just like that, one after the other. Go!" He does this for a simple reason: let's say a large amount of soldiers go out at the same time and a mortar bomb falls or there's an encounter with terrorists;

then everyone will be injured at once and we've lost a significant force. But if this type of problem neutralizes only four of our troops, then all the others are still fit for battle.

So everyone, including Yohai, goes out and comes back to the shelter with uniforms and everything, and now, after everyone's come back, there are twenty-five soldiers armed and equipped and ready for battle. By now, they hear shooting and they understand that the terrorists are already there, and at this point, the guys in the shelter begin to get a little stressed. So Yohai gathers the whole group together and says to them, "There are terrorists in the base, but they won't conquer it. We're going to do everything we can, and they won't succeed. You hear? No one's going to capture this base today!" Afterward, the soldiers told us that those words stayed with them; they echoed in their ears all day long. Those words lifted them up and gave them the feeling that this is their mission now, they're ready for it, and they're going to succeed.

Yohai is in the shelter together with Nimrod. Nimrod Eliraz is the other platoon commander parallel to Yohai in the company, and he and Yohai are very good friends. Half a year earlier, they both came to the company together, both of them new officers – you'd call them "yellow" in military slang, meaning that they're good kids, serious, who follow the rules, and now they have to contend with a group of old-timer Golani solders. So they have this shared experience, and they have a connection. And now, when both of them are in the shelter, they turn into an inseparable team. From that moment on, they make decisions together, fight together, go through everything together.

Yohai and Nimrod are now in the shelter and they make a quick assessment of the situation. They realize that the terrorists are coming into the base from three main points and the terrorists want to seize control of the operations center. So if they want to foil the terrorists' plans, they need to split up the force among four locations. One fire-team goes to the pillbox guard post next to the first point of infiltration; that's Yohai's group. Another fireteam goes to the watchtower next to the second point of infiltration; that's Nimrod's group. Another fireteam will go to the guard post at the main gate, the third point of infiltration; and the fourth fireteam will go to the mobile shelter near the operations center. As soon as each group reaches its destination, it starts eliminating terrorists; they spot them and shoot them down and the terrorists fall, one after another.

At a certain point, the two higher positions – the pillbox where Yohai is and the watchtower where Nimrod is – start coming under very heavy fire. They have to come down from the positions. Nimrod's team goes down quickly from the watchtower, and as soon as their boots touch the ground, really within half a second – boom! The watchtower above their head gets hit by an RPG. If they had delayed by half a second, that would have been it, it would have ended there.

Now the terrorists have already reached the outpost fences, and they position themselves in a way that is unfortunately very smart. The base's fence is made up of tall cement barricades, right next to each other. In the bottom part of each barricade there's a hole, about the diameter of a Coca Cola bottle; these holes are something that the manufacturer made, probably to make it easier to transport the barricades. So the terrorists lie behind the barricades and insert their rifles barrels into the holes and shoot. These barricades became a protected sniper position for the terrorists, damn them. Their fire wounds two soldiers, who later die: one of Yohai's soldiers, Naor Siboni, and one of Nimrod's soldiers, David Ratner.

Now a soldier named Itai joins forces with Yohai and Nimrod; all three realize that there's a massive infiltration from another point at the edge of the outpost. They understand that there are no forces there, so the three of them run there like crazy, and suddenly Nimrod spots a parked military jeep. He takes out two LAU missile launchers, and he and Yohai shoot them at the point where the terrorists are infiltrating the base; the terrorists there scream and fall and some of them are killed on the spot.

By now it's 7:20, and the surveillance soldiers' cameras are not functioning; the terrorists used armed drones to take down the cameras and their remote firing system. At this stage, the surveillance soldiers have all gathered in the office of their commander, Shir Eilat, of blessed memory. Shir's office is deep inside the operations center; it's not exactly an office, more like a tiny cubicle, two by three meters, which fits a desk, chair, and laptop. So the surveillance soldiers gather in Shir's office, and the officers squeeze in there as well; we're talking about eighteen soldiers total, mostly women, crammed into this cubicle; most of them don't have weapons, and none of them have been trained in combat.

Yohai and Nimrod hear them now on the radio and realize that the women are alone there inside the operations center, crammed into Shir's office, basically unarmed, and they decide to head there to rescue them. Their goal is to rescue the women, but they ultimately have another goal as well: the operations center is one of the outpost's vital assets; all the cameras and surveillance equipment is there, as well as classified material. That's to say, it's the nerve center of the outpost. A lot of things are there that they don't want the terrorists getting their hands on.

Now they're three fighters with one mission: to save the operations center. The three of them start making their way there, and suddenly they spot a band of about four terrorists rummaging through one of the offices. They eliminate the terrorists, and when they approach their bodies they see the terrorists for the first time up close. They discover that they are armed from head to foot, with army boots, green Hamas bandanas tied across their foreheads, grenades, Kalashnikovs, RPG missiles, knives, and maps. As they examine the bodies, Nimrod suddenly sees that they have syringes on them! Later, it turned out that these were probably anesthetics, intended to neutralize soldiers so they could kidnap them. Unbelievable.

Yohai, Nimrod, and Itai take the terrorists' knives and maps, and when they look at the maps, they can't believe their eyes. The maps are all in Arabic, but they see the markings in red and they understand everything: they are maps of the base. The operations center is marked in red. The bunker is marked in red. The generators – marked in red. The women's and men's dormitories – marked in red.

Afterward, military investigators told us that when they came into the outpost after it was all over, they saw that some rooms had been ransacked by the terrorists, while others were untouched, fully intact, as if no one even set foot there. The terrorists had no interest in anything to do with firearms or ammunition; the rooms they searched were primarily for communications and intelligence. One room had been full of booklets on IDF warfare doctrine; the pages were all laid out in a row; one of the terrorists must have spread the pages out to photograph everything. These terrorists came to get information; they came to kill soldiers; they came to paralyze the base so that they could get into Kibbutz Nahal Oz and then infiltrate all the towns along Highway 25. That's what they wanted.

After that encounter, at about seven-thirty, Yohai, Nimrod, and Itai reach the operations center. The operations center has a few different rooms, and at the end of the corridor is Shir's office, where everyone was hiding. That means that there were a few doors, a few points you had to get through, before you got to where the eighteen soldiers were hiding; if someone were to take up position at each of those points, they could prevent the terrorists from reaching them. Yohai and his team make that their plan; they decide to prevent the terrorists from reaching the soldiers, at any cost.

By about a quarter to eight, the base is crawling with terrorists. Dozens of them want just one thing: to conquer the operations center. And so the battle over the operations center begins. Yohai's team returns fire, and the whole time they take care to reassure the group cooped up in Shir's office: Don't worry, we're here with you, we're protecting you, we won't let them get in. That kind of thing. At eight-fifteen, a fourth soldier joins the team: Ibrahim Kharuba, a Bedouin tracker. And the four of them – Yohai, Nimrod, Itai, and Ibrahim – start to operate in a more organized fashion.

They start making short sorties outside the operations center, twenty-thirty meters, finding a target, shooting for a minute or two, and returning to the operations center. During one of their sorties, they reach the canteen and find six terrorists tearing open snack bags and just devouring everything in sight. So Yohai's team shoots them down and kills them all with the snacks still in their mouths.

Yohai keeps improvising new tactics. At one point, he decides to throw bottles from the other end of the operations center to distract the terrorists, and then to come out and shoot them. Or, for example, when two terrorists get very close, just two meters away from the entrance to the operations center, Yohai kills them and then drags their bodies to the entrance as an obstacle.

They keep up with the sorties to prevent the terrorists from reaching the area, and at the same time, the group in Shir's office tries to help however they can. The officer gives her rifle to Itai, and whoever has cartridges gives them to Yohai's team. One of the soldiers even finds some dry croissants left over from dinner the night before and gives it to them so they have a little energy.

At nine-thirty in the morning, my sister Tehilla calls Yohai. He's deep into the battle for the operations center, but nevertheless, he still answers her! He keeps it very short: "I'm okay. Keep praying. Not just for me, for all the people of Israel."

My sister was lucky enough to hear him speak those words to her. That was the last time we ever heard from him.

By ten-thirty the operations center is under siege. Masses of terrorists are surrounding it and Yohai and his fighters have no way to leave. So they turn over a table and take up position behind it, shooting at any terrorist who tries to come in. At one point, they run out of ammunition. Yohai has only ten bullets left; Itai is down to nothing, and suddenly one of the terrorists manages to break in! They may be out of ammo, but they don't get flustered – they pounce on him, one holds him down, the other chokes him, the other kicks him, and eventually they use the knife they took from the dead terrorists and succeed in taking him out.

By now, all four of them have been wounded; they're bleeding from surface wounds from shrapnel and ricochets. And suddenly, boom – the electricity goes out. At eleven o'clock, the terrorists brought a saw and they sawed away all the cables next to the operations center; now there's no electricity, no air conditioning, barely any reception, and the entire building is dark.

That's when something astonishing happens; something that I couldn't believe when I heard it; like, how could all these things happen to my brother, one after another? It's like nothing is missing from the screenplay. It's impossible to grasp. After they cut off the electricity, the terrorists started dropping grenades inside – into the building. They just rolled them so that they'd explode exactly on the four of them. The grenades explode inside the operations center, but none of the team is hurt, and then suddenly one grenade rolls right up to them and stops right next to Nimrod. Yohai notices it, pushes Nimrod aside, and throws himself on the grenade. He threw himself on the grenade! But luckily, Hamas don't necessarily make very reliable weapons, and that grenade doesn't explode!

Now the terrorists start screaming at them to surrender. Yohai and his force don't answer them, but Yohai turns to Nimrod, Itai, and Ibrahim, and says, "We won't surrender, no matter what. We won't surrender," and all three of them agree. At around twelve-thirty, the terrorists are already desperate to get inside the operations center. They had really tried again and again and again; they understood that it's a very strategic target and they're not giving up. And now they realize: Okay, we can't get in. So they decide: If we can't make it in, let's just burn the whole place down with everyone inside. And that's what they do. Yohai shouts to everyone, "They're burning the operations center; they're burning it down!" He tries to put the fire out with a fire extinguisher, but it doesn't work because it's a very serious conflagration.

Now the terrorists start climbing onto the roof. The roof has vents, and the terrorists cover them with mattresses, lots of mattresses, and set them on fire so that the place will fill up with smoke, like a gas chamber suffocating anyone inside. Months later, when they took us for a tour of the burnt operations center, everything looked like a crematorium; the keyboards were completely melted; everything was black. Not grey, not sooty, but this dark, dark black. Hell.

Now they realize that their only chance is to try and get out through the window. There are no windows in the whole operations center, not even in Shir's office; the only windows are in the two bathroom stalls in the corridor outside Shir's office. Fortunately, the cement barricades around the operations center aren't right next to the bathroom wall; there's about a meter between the outer wall and the barricade, a space where they could hide after jumping out of the window.

Now Yohai and his team start their next mission: to get the soldiers out of the office to the window. Whoever leaves Shir's office has to go through a totally dark, narrow corridor; it's pitch black and thick with smoke, sounds of screaming and shooting; there hasn't been ventilation for hours now, and it's become a suffocation chamber.

One of the officers smashes one of the bathroom windows and they try to get out. Some of them succeed, but it isn't so easy; everyone is on the verge of passing out; some of them no longer have the strength to get up and climb. Yohai and his team really, really make an effort; they do everything possible to get the others out.

Nimrod makes it out of the window; as soon as he touches the ground, he loses consciousness. But Yohai unfortunately collapses while he's still inside, inside the suffocating corridor. As he's still trying to help the others, he collapses. And that's where his journey ends. Itai and Ibrahim don't manage to escape either. Itai Avraham Ron and Ibrahim Kharuba, may God avenge their blood – they'll forever be remembered as two heroes who sacrificed their lives to save others. Out of the eighteen soldiers who hid in Shir's office, six survived. And our dear, beloved Nimrod woke up only four days later in the hospital. He's the one who told us the story of this battle, Yohai's last stand.

Yohai was always ready for battle, but that battle, that whole black day in which 1,200 soldiers, civilians, and children paid with their lives – all of this could have been prevented. The most absurd thing is that what killed Yohai was the very thing he warned against.

That morning, as soon as the sirens sounded, most of the soldiers got to the shelter in their pajamas, but Yohai showed up in his vest. Many soldiers told us about that; they said how unusual it was that he took his vest before he ran to the shelter. You have to realize, we're talking about soldiers who serve in a base where warnings about mortar bombs are common; they're used to running to the shelter, staying there for a few minutes, and after the launches are over, going back to whatever they were doing. There's no logical reason at all to get into your vest before you run to the shelter – a vest won't protect you against bombs; a vest is for combat. When they ran to the shelter, they still didn't know about a terrorist attack. So why did Yohai jump out of bed, ready for battle? Did he know that there was about to be an attack? Of course he didn't know. He just believed in the threat.

Yohai had this saying that he often repeated: "Believe the threat." It's an old army saying about taking the enemy seriously, about never allowing yourself to become complacent, about never reassuring yourself that if nothing happened today, nothing will happen tomorrow either. That's why he always took his rifle with him wherever he went: to family events, to the synagogue, everywhere. He took the threat so seriously that he wasn't prepared to not be prepared.

He was always talking to me about that, all the time – because he felt like he was the only one who was seeing it. He felt that the military system wasn't there at all. As a fighter in the Nahal Oz Outpost, right on the border, he couldn't understand how the army could possibly allow the Gazans to come right up to the fence, to do whatever they wanted there. He was always complaining about it to his commanders. I remember him asking me once, "Tell me, in your time, when you were in the army, was it the same? Were they allowed to get so close to the fence?" I asked him why he kept obsessing over it, why he kept complaining about it – it wasn't going to change, it wasn't up to his commanders, it all depended on much higher-ranking officers. And he said something chilling; when I look back at it, I realize that it was some kind of prophecy – a black prophecy.

He said to me, "Because if we keep complaining about it, we won't get used to it. If we get used to it, we won't be here anymore." He said that the terrorists are purposely getting us used to them coming up to the fence; they're getting us used to ignoring them. They want us to ignore them; they don't want us to be on high alert or to relate to what they're doing as a serious incident. "It's wearing down our vigilance," he said. Oh, how right he was. How right he was.

After all, what happened in Gaza – how did it happen that Hamas suddenly turned into such monsters? How did it happen? It happened just as Yohai said it would – because we got used to it. We got used to this crazy, unacceptable reality. We tolerated it. We tolerated tens of thousands of rockets falling on Israel, tens of thousands! And what do we do in response? We teach our children how to run to bomb shelters! When does the State of Israel ever allow itself to retaliate? Only after they manage to kill someone! That's how it is with Gaza; that's how it is with Hezbollah; that's how it is with Iran; that's how it is throughout the maddening Middle East we're stuck in. It's just as Yohai said. And now I've buried my own brother, just because the powers that be were willing to tolerate everything he warned against. Tolerate, tolerate, tolerate, until there's no one left to tolerate anything, God forbid.

In recent years I was a kind of father figure for Yohai, but the truth is that now I feel like I'm his younger brother. In the sense that now I look up to him. I've always looked up to him really, that's the truth. People tend to glorify their loved ones after they're gone; we tend to forget about their faults and we look back at them as if they were perfect, and this creates a gap between the truth and how their family thinks of them after they're gone. But in Yohai's case, I don't feel that there's any gap. I always truly admired Yohai; we all did.

Yohai is a tall guy, one meter eighty-three; it wouldn't have been so hard for him to climb onto the toilet tank and squeeze out of the window. But Yohai is probably the person who least thinks about himself, in any way, shape, or form. That was the way he lived his life. Both when he was in yeshiva and when he was at home, his whole personality was like that. Running to the shelter in his vest and helmet while wearing boxers; telling his soldiers, "We're not going to surrender, this base isn't going to fall"; racing to defend the operations center from countless terrorists – that was completely him; that's who he was.

It might sound crazy to say this, but I'm not at all surprised that he jumped on that grenade. Nothing he did that day surprises me. And if I ask myself what Yohai would say if he were here now, I think he'd say to us: Come on, guys, get up, get on your feet, hold your heads high; we still have a lot to do here in this country of ours.

If Not Me, Then Who?

Daniel Perez's Story

Age 22

As told by Daniel's father, Doron

◉ *Nahal Oz Outpost*

Once, one of Daniel's friends told him that he was going on a first date that evening. This friend, Elisha, was kind of excited; he told Daniel that there was this girl, and they were going out to a restaurant, but Daniel cuts him off – "Tell me, how do you plan on getting there?" – because he knew that Elisha didn't have a license. So Elisha tells him that he's probably taking a bus. Daniel was horrified! He was a guy with style, with class – he couldn't imagine his friend going by bus to a first date. So he said to him, "I'm going to be your driver." Elisha couldn't talk him out of it; Daniel presented him with a fait accompli.

And that's how it was. Daniel took my car, cleaned it, cleared out all the bags and papers that were in there, took everything out, scrubbed and polished until the car was ready for a first date. Daniel picks this couple up with the car – Elisha sits with his date in the back – and he takes them to the restaurant. Elisha says that they were at the restaurant for four hours, and when they came out at the end of the date, they were astounded to see Daniel waiting for them there in the parking lot! He waited for them in the car for four hours! They felt uncomfortable, but Daniel just smiled and said, "If I'm your driver, then it's all the way." By the way, that couple is getting married soon.

And that's what he was like. That's what kind of friend he was. Whatever he did, he went all the way, including with friendship. Friendship was of supreme value to him. As of now, at least thirty of his friends have told us that Daniel was their best friend. I think that Daniel was the best friend a person could ever have.

When Daniel was thirteen, my wife and I made the decision to immigrate to Israel. Actually, it was coming back to Israel. My wife and I had already moved to Israel from South Africa; we got married in Israel, but then we went back to South Africa as emissaries to give a little back to the community where we grew up. We planned to stay there for three years, but it stretched out to fifteen: I was the CEO of the Mizrachi Religious Zionist movement in South Africa, the rabbi of the Mizrachi community and principal of the Religious Zionist school in Johannesburg. That's to say, all my activities were centered around Jewish and Zionist identity, a love of the people, Torah, and Land of Israel, and at a certain point my wife and I understood that the time had come to go back, that our home was in Israel. Moving to a new country isn't easy for anyone; Daniel has three siblings and it was clear to us that it wouldn't be simple for any of our children, but we were the most concerned about Daniel, about how he would cope with leaving all his friends behind.

We were mistaken. As soon as we got to Israel, Daniel made friends with two guys. He didn't know Hebrew yet, but it didn't get in the way; they just became the best of friends right away. And as soon as he walked into the classroom on the first day of school, he fell right in with this group of boys, and within a few months he was already more Israeli than they were. He would travel alone on buses, hitch rides; he was independent. One of his friends was always saying to us, "If I want to go somewhere, I only go with Daniel." That was how he made the people he loved feel. He would do a lot for them and listen to them, and in return they felt they could depend on him.

But Daniel wasn't one of those friends who just tells you what you want to hear. Not everyone knew how to handle him. He was very determined; he knew how to get want he wanted and had a lot of willpower.

A lot. And he also had the ability to stand up for himself: if there was something Daniel didn't want to do, you couldn't make him do it. If you tried, you'd ultimately lose.

For example, when he was twelve, he came to me one day and said, "Dad, there's something I want to do. I know you're not going to like it, but I'm thinking of doing it anyway. I'm going to cut school for a whole day with my friend, because we're going to go on a hike. I came to tell you so you can choose what punishment you're going to give me, and based on that I'll decide whether it's worth it for me to do it." I said, "What? Say that again?" and he repeated it, without getting flustered: "Dad, I want to cut school and I want to know what the punishment will be so I can decide whether to do it or not."

I thought he was joking, but to my astonishment the kid was dead serious. I said to him, "Daniel, you're not doing it, full stop, end of discussion." Now, you have to understand – South Africa isn't like Israel. In South Africa you don't do things like that, you don't cut school; it's something that's just not done. So he says to me, "Dad, it's not your choice, it's up to me. You're lucky that I'm a good boy and I came to tell you. I don't want to do it behind your back, so I'm giving you a chance here to choose what punishment to give me, and then I'll decide if it's worth it for me or not."

I was absolutely fuming. I said to him, "Okay, you know what – fine! As a punishment I'll confiscate the phone we got you for two weeks! That's it. You won't have a phone for two weeks." So he looks at me and says, "Dad, I'm asking you for real: Do you think that punishment is fair?" and before I could answer, he says, "I know what you're trying to do, you're trying to force me not to do it by giving me a punishment that isn't fair, but it's not your choice, it's mine!" And then he said something that nearly knocked me off my feet: "I suggest, Dad, that you think about this some more, and then come back with a fair punishment." I couldn't believe what I was hearing. I was floored and felt beaten into submission. I went up to our room to tell my wife, and she said, "He beat us." That was it. He was unstoppable.

We had a very real, very honest relationship with him. There was a reason that Daniel told me about his dilemma. This was a kid who was never able to lie. He wasn't manipulative and he didn't have a poker face. He was one hundred percent truth. Put that together with his immense willpower, and you get a kid who was very tough to raise. He put us through a lot, but we saw that this was a kid who couldn't be stopped.

>❧

Daniel's dream was to get into the commando unit of Golani, but that dream was thwarted on the day he got injured. He tore the ACL in his knee, along with the meniscus. He was injured while doing this kind of extreme type of surfing called wakeboarding. He would go boarding every day, and one day he fell badly after one of his high-speed somersaults, and that was it.

The military has a system of evaluating physical profiles, and that injury lowered his profile from 97, the highest, to 45, which wouldn't allow him to serve in a combat unit. He had hope that he'd be able to recover and get back up to a high profile, but after a serious surgery and another nine months of physiotherapy, he only had a profile of 65, still not high enough for combat. I said to him, "Daniel, let it go, you won't be in combat but you're smart – go to Military Intelligence." And he said to me, "No, Dad. Maybe you could go to Intelligence and sit in front of a screen, but I, I want to direct my physical energy, I need to be out there, I want to be a fighter. Maybe I won't make it to the infantry, but I have to get into the Armored Corps."

I say, "How will you do that? Your profile isn't even high enough for the Armored Corps!" But he didn't give up. He went to the medical committee that sets the profile and said to them, "Listen, you based my profile on the medical report from before my surgery. That says I need surgery on my meniscus. But you didn't read the post-surgery report, which says that my meniscus healed on its own, and they didn't have to touch it!" When they heard that, they understood who they were dealing with and raised his profile to 72, which meant that he could be in the Armored Corps. He could fight in a tank.

So that's how he fulfilled his dream of being a combat soldier, by being a tank commander. Who would have believed that that tank, that he fought so hard to get into, would ultimately be his last stop. In that tank he saved so many people; and that tank was ultimately a death trap for him.

❧

Of all his friends, Daniel's best friend was his brother Yonatan, who's two years older than him. Yonatan and Daniel are very different from each other. Yonatan is more obedient, more measured, calmer; he followed our path more, in religious levels also. Daniel, in contrast, was more independent, more of an adventurer, more of a risk-taker; religiously, he chose his own path. But despite those differences, they had this incredible bond.

From when they were little, they would do all kinds of nonsense together. For example, once, when Daniel was thirteen, we went away for a Shabbat hosted by the World Bnei Akiva organization, and there were all kinds of Jews there from all kinds of places. For some reason, Daniel and Yonatan decided that they wanted people to think they were from Spain, from Toledo – God knows why specifically Toledo. So they taught themselves three sentences in Spanish, with the accent and everything, and wherever they went they spoke to each other in Spanish – it didn't matter that it was always those same three sentences. At some point people approached me and asked how it is that my boys, who grew up in South Africa, are fluent in Spanish! They kept that up for twenty-four hours!

They were a perfect pair. They would work out together, play basketball, beat each other up, tease each other endlessly. And they could sit together in Daniel's room for hours; they never ran out of things to talk about. Yonatan would always say that he wanted Daniel to be the best man at his wedding; the best man is usually the best friend, but Yonatan's best friend was his brother.

I don't think it's a coincidence that Yonatan happened to end up on Daniel's base that day; actually – we discovered this only months later – Daniel was killed about a hundred meters from where Yonatan was injured on that fateful day. Daniel and Yonatan were brothers that only death could part.

❧

On the Shabbat morning of Simchat Torah, we started to hear sirens in Yad Binyamin. My wife Shelley and I go into the safe room together with our children – Adina, Shira, Yonatan, and also Galya, Yonatan's fiancée. Everyone was with us for the holiday except for Daniel, who was on duty as a commander in his base in Nahal Oz. At eight o'clock, Yonatan's phone starts pinging – ping, ping, ping, full of WhatsApp messages. At first he didn't really look because it was Shabbat, but then he sees that a lot of messages are being sent in his group of army friends, one after another, with the word "surreal" – surreal, surreal, surreal: his whole screen's filling up with that word. He opens WhatsApp, scrolls down, and sees that they sent a clip of a pickup truck full of terrorists driving through the middle of Sderot.

Before he can even begin to take that in, his battalion commander sends a message to all the officers: "Whoever can, come to Sderot." Yonatan sees that, says to us, "I'm going," and switches into his uniform. He didn't have his rifle with him, so he goes out with his handgun, and I see him taking Daniel's handgun from the safe as well. I'm kind of following him around and I say, "But what do you have to do with Sderot? You're a commander of soldiers in basic training!" And then Yonatan turns to me with a serious look, and he says, "Dad, my commander says, 'Whoever can come should come.' I can, so I'm going."

So Yonatan leaves, but we're not worried. We didn't think there was any real cause for concern. We hadn't heard what was happening; it was Shabbat. We didn't know that while we were at home, our Yonatan was fighting in six different locations, one after another. He started out in Sderot and just continued to wherever he knew the terrorists were, to fight them. He was in Sha'ar HaNegev Junction; he fought against terrorists in the vicinity of Sa'ad and Kfar Aza. He collected proper gear on his way: he took a helmet from a Sayeret Matkal commando who had been wounded; a rifle and flak jacket from a friend of his who was critically wounded; and finally, at around one p.m., he reached the Nahal Oz Outpost.

Yonatan and his friends were the first soldiers to enter the outpost in order to take back the base. A little before they arrived, they succeeded in making radio contact with one of the surveillance soldiers who was able to get out of the operations center; she explained that she was with six other soldiers who survived the attack on the operations center, but they were stuck – they were trapped between the operations center and some concrete barrier. She said that there was a lot of smoke around them, it was hard to breathe, the operations center was burnt, and they were about to be burnt themselves! They couldn't leave the barricade; they had no weapons and they'd be completely exposed if they left there. And Yonatan knows exactly what she's talking about – he knows that there's a concrete barrier surrounding the operations center, and he understands that they were below the bathroom windows there. Yonatan and another three commanders who were with him decide to go into the outpost, to make their way to the operations center, and to extricate the soldiers from the base, to a vehicle that will evacuate them.

Nahal Oz is a large outpost. It has a lot of buildings and narrow passageways; the only one who was familiar with the base was Yonatan, because he had visited Daniel many times. So Yonatan actually plans the operation and explains to everyone there how the mission should be accomplished.

When they enter the outpost, they spot a few terrorists by the entrance, but the terrorists don't notice them. They signal to each other not to engage because their first priority is to rescue the surviving soldiers from the operations center. The four of them make it to the barricade behind the operations center and find seven soldiers there, five women and two guys, who are all totally wiped out, coughing, not in good condition, but – except for one of them who was unconscious – they're all able to walk on their own. They manage to rouse the unconscious soldier; they slap him a few times, but he can hardly get on his feet; he's only semi-conscious, so he makes his way out of the outpost leaning on them, but they succeed in saving him! That soldier lay unconscious for four days after that, but he survived.

After evacuating the wounded from the operations center, Yonatan and his team realize that their mission now is to rescue other survivors and to seize back control of the outpost. At the outpost entrance, they meet an elite Police Counter-Terrorist team under the command of Arnon Zamora. Eight months later, he was one of the officers who took part in the rescue of four hostages held in Gaza – Noa Argamani,

Almog Meir Jan, Andrey Kozlov, and Shlomi Ziv. He was killed during the operation, which was named "Operation Arnon" in his memory. A holy man.

Yonatan and his group give Arnon's force a situation report and tell them where they've seen terrorists. They decide to divide the base into two: Arnon and his counter-terrorism team head to the southern side of the base, where the surveillance soldiers' operations center was, and Yonatan and his ad-hoc team take the northern side.

The mobile shelter from which surveillance soldiers were taken captive is on the northern side of the base; Yonatan went inside and saw the bodies of the young women who were murdered – it was just horrifying. They continue past the mobile shelter to clear out the outpost, room by room. Finally, they reach two locked rooms. They knock on the doors, but no one answers; Yonatan shouts "IDF, IDF," yet there's still no answer. The door is locked, but Yonatan doesn't give up. He says, "I'm Yonatan, I'm a commander in the paratroops," and then both of the doors open at once. Yonatan and his friends are able to get fifteen more soldiers out of there, all of them women – among the last survivors.

At five o'clock on Shabbat afternoon, we get a call from Yonatan and he tells us three things. First, "Dad, I got shot in the thigh but I'm okay, I'm in Soroka Hospital." Second, "I can't even begin to describe what's going on in the south, there are bodies every fifty meters, it's the Wild West out here, it's impossible to fathom." And third, "I've been trying to get ahold of Daniel since this morning, but he's not answering. I was in his base in Nahal Oz and his tank's not there."

We try to absorb this, to understand what it means. Our Yonatan is wounded; there's a crazy war in the south; Daniel's not in his base and neither is his tank. What does that mean? We got to Soroka that evening after Shabbat, I started going from bed to bed, looking for Daniel. There was one moment when I saw a soldier from behind who looked exactly like him. I was about to run to him and he turns around and I see that it isn't him. That was a tough moment. I ask myself what my son is going through right now; where is he? Where is he?

Although Yonatan couldn't feel his leg, we organized Yonatan's release from the hospital, since he had no bed, crutches, or wheelchair there as there were too many wounded, and our family doctor and emergency room nurse in Yad Binyamin advised to treat him at home. For the whole next day, Yonatan tries calling the whole world. He's lying on the living room couch, wounded, and doesn't stop calling friends, officers, this guy, that guy – and no one knows where Daniel is. No one's seen him. Suddenly, at four in the afternoon, I hear Yonatan on the phone, saying, "Yes, yes, that tank!" He tenses up, tries to sit up, presses the phone to his ear and asks, quietly, "What happened to the soldiers who were in that tank?" and a few seconds later he closes his eyes, takes a deep breath, says "Thank you," and ends the conversation.

Yonatan looks at me, and says, "Dad, I just spoke with one of the officers in the Armored Corps. He was in the field. And he says that they found Daniel's tank. There's a dead soldier in the tank, and the other three soldiers are missing. But Dad, the dead soldier isn't Daniel; the soldier who was killed wasn't an officer, so it can't be Daniel." Yonatan and I are stunned. We embrace. Then we call his two sisters, Adina and Shira, and we all go upstairs to our room, where my wife is, to tell them all together. And there – that's where we fell apart. All of us huddled together, hugging and crying. It was a very difficult moment. Very, very difficult.

For the whole week, we're in total shock. The army still hasn't made contact with us, but we made our own WhatsApp group with the parents of the three other soldiers in Daniel's tank – Itay Chen, Matan Angrest, and Tomer Leibovitz. All four soldiers, including our Daniel, are now declared "out of communication." I'm the only one who knows that one of the other three has been found dead, but I don't know which of the three, and there's no way I'm going to be the one to tell the other families as it is not yet officially confirmed and certainly not my place. So I wait for the army to make an official announcement, but another day goes by, and another, and it doesn't happen.

Suddenly, at seven-thirty exactly on Thursday morning, one of the parents writes on the group, "There's a knock at the door." Immediately after that, another parent writes, "A knock at the door," and then another one: "A knock at the door." And I know that it's coming, that it's about to happen here too, and I hear a knock at the door. Four knocks on four different doors, at the same time. One in Kiryat Bialik, one in Netanya, one in Tel Aviv, and one at our home. And I know that today one of them will receive the worst news of all, and the others will receive a message with a drop of hope and a lot of fear.

A few minutes later, each parent wrote what the army told them. I saw that the Leibovitz family didn't write, and I understood. I realized that they'd just received the bitter news: Tomer Leibovitz, of blessed memory, is the soldier found dead in the tank. And the other three soldiers – as we've just heard ourselves – are declared missing. "Missing" is still not "captive"; perhaps they're still alive somewhere; they might even be lying dead, God forbid, somewhere in Israel, and they still haven't been found. And this uncertainty – the knowledge that either way, Daniel's situation isn't good – I can't describe it, it's unbearable torture. Unbearable.

Yonatan and Galya were supposed to get married ten days after Simchat Torah. And our son has been declared missing. At any moment we're liable to hear another knock on the door and, God forbid, to need to start mourning, and sit the week of shiva. But we decide that if the couple want to get married, we'll still have the wedding, come what may. Yonatan and Galya went back and forth, but we saw that they really did want to get married and that they were only unsure on our account, so my wife said to them, "This wedding is happening. Exactly as scheduled. And we'll focus on what we have. We'll focus on your joy, on our joy, and we'll be happy, and it will be very joyous."

I didn't know how I was going to get through the wedding. We knew that it was the right thing to do, but how could I get through it emotionally? I realized that there was only one way: to compartmentalize, to disengage. To put Daniel out of my mind on the wedding day and focus only on Yonatan. That was my plan. During the whole reception I forced myself to think exclusively about Yonatan, and it worked. But at the chuppah, under the wedding canopy, something happened that I hadn't anticipated.

The officiating rabbi, whom we love dearly, burst into tears and said, "We cannot begin this wedding without mentioning the person who isn't here, Daniel." And then I felt the pain just rise up and tear me apart, and we all fell apart. My wife fell apart, and my girls. All of us. And those first three minutes there was awful pain, it hurt and hurt. We recited Shir HaMa'alot MiMa'amakim, psalm 130, a psalm for times of trouble, and we prayed, and we sobbed. But after a few minutes, we said "That's it," and we wiped our faces off and we got into the mode of rejoicing.

And I saw firsthand how it's possible in the midst of a difficult time of pain and anxiety and sadness to make room for joy and happiness, and how you can hold onto both. One of our friends said that it was the holiest, saddest, happiest, most inspiring wedding that she's ever been to. And it really was a joyful wedding, a luminous wedding, with moments of tremendous sorrow. I discovered that you can hold both the joy and the sorrow together.

Two and a half weeks after October 7th, a representative from the army comes to inform us, "We succeeded in triangulating Daniel's cellphone, and it's in Gaza. Our current assessment is that there's a high chance that he's been taken hostage." And from that moment on, my wife's suffering, her suffering – I've never seen suffering like that in my whole life. I actually succeeded in compartmentalizing a bit; I was crushed, broken, but all in all I managed to function. Every time the worries would begin to surface, I told myself – "I'll channel this into action." I gave interviews, I tried to raise awareness, I kept myself busy with efforts to bring Daniel home, trips to unexpected places, meetings with government ministers. But what can I tell you? A father's experience just isn't the same as a mother's. Maybe I'm generalizing here, but that's how I feel about motherhood, about a mother's bond with her child, the physical bond. I didn't give birth to Daniel. My wife shared her body with him. And from the moment he was declared hostage, she could hardly breathe.

Every time my wife tried to eat, she felt like she couldn't get the food down because Daniel might be hungry now. She would talk to him in her heart all the time. "My Daniel, how are you feeling, are you eating, are you drinking, are you hot, are you cold?" Daniel was a stylish guy with class, not just regarding clothing, but also with regard to food. He only liked to eat certain foods – healthy food, fresh food – and he wouldn't touch leftovers that had been sitting in the fridge for three days. And when you think about the half-pita bread that the hostages were given … my wife just couldn't bear it.

The truth is that this wasn't unique to her. From the moment Daniel was declared a hostage, I met almost every day with the families of other hostages, mostly the parents of other hostage soldiers. And I saw that most of the mothers that I met were just the same. Suffering like I've never seen in my life. The parents of hostages go through hell. Thoughts keep going to the darkest of places. Is he still alive? Who's holding him hostage? How are they treating him, what are they doing to him there? And we parents of captive soldiers – we know what it means for Hamas to get hold of a soldier, what they do to them. I think about all the kidnapped soldiers and I don't want to imagine it, I don't want to picture it in my head; I can't.

Five weeks after October 7th, the army comes to tell us that Daniel had been wounded. How did they know? They could tell based on traces of his blood. They said that they found his blood – blood inside the tank, blood outside the tank, and on the shirt of his uniform, which they also found. There were no bullet holes in his shirt which was confusing but blood on the left sleeve and left side of the upper body, but we know for certain that he was wounded.

That moment they informed us that he had been wounded – that was a very difficult moment. There was a greater chance that he had been killed. And if he wasn't killed, then how could he survive with his wound? Until that day, we had kept telling ourselves, "Daniel is a strong guy – physically strong, mentally strong; he'll make it." That's what we were holding on to. But the moment you know that he might be being held in some tunnel, without air, hungry and thirsty, and on top of that he's also wounded … the thought of what pain he's going through, what suffering – it's absolutely terrible.

On the 156th day, the father of Itay Chen, from Daniel's tank crew, calls me and says, "Doron, I wanted to let you know that they just came to tell us that Itay was killed." I almost fell off my chair. I asked,

"What? What? What? How do they know, Itay wasn't even classified as wounded, they didn't even find any of his blood, on what basis do they know this?" And he explains to me that they received footage. They found new video clips from which you can tell that Itay was taken hostage when he had already been killed; he was killed before he crossed the border. But there's no sign of Daniel in those clips; there's no news of him at all. Nothing at all.

Until that moment, my wife was still hoping that Daniel was alive, but as soon as she heard what happened to Itay, she understood that chances were that Daniel wasn't alive either. The balance between hope and hopelessness shifted for us; we start to understand but don't want to understand. At those moments, uncertainty is a blessing, because we could still hold onto the possibility that he was still alive, even as the chances got slimmer.

A week later, at sunset on Sunday evening – day 163 of Daniel's captivity – I get a phone call from the IDF missing person and hostage liaison to our family, Yossi Shemesh. He is a lovely man and would often come over to our home to talk to us, to give us support; he had already become a real part of the family. So Yossi calls me and asks, "Are you at home?" and I'm used to him hopping by, so I ask him, "Are you coming alone?" and he says, "No." "Are you coming over with other people," and he answers, "Yes." "Do you want to tell me what this is about?" I ask, and he says, "I'd rather tell you face to face." I said to Yossi, "I understand. Let me get my wife ready, and get the family together. Give me half an hour."

I came over to my wife, hugged her, and told her about the conversation with Yossi. She immediately started to cry. We both cried. We understood that this was probably it, the awful news was on its way. And then they knocked on the door. A representative from the IDF rabbinate, an Intelligence officer, Yossi Shemesh, and a few others. They told us that based on new intelligence, they knew that Daniel had been killed.

This information was from new footage; they got ahold of some different clips that had been filmed by Gazans from different angles. And these clips show that on October 7th, at around twelve noon, Daniel was on the back of a motorcycle in Shuja'iyya. In one of the clips, they told us, you can see with absolute certainty that the young man on that motorcycle is Daniel and that he is definitely dead.

From the day Daniel was declared missing up until that very moment, the army had been investigating the event from every possible direction in order to understand exactly what had happened to Daniel's tank. Over the course of the shiva, some of the investigators came by. And before they told us what they knew, they said, "What your son and his tank crew did – it will go down in Israeli history." They said that it was a heroic act on a major scale; that their story would become part of the military's legacy as a paradigm of courage, initiative, responsibility, and resolute conduct in battle in an impossible situation. After the shiva, they let us listen to the recordings of Daniel's tank radio. You can hear Daniel there. Two hours and sixteen minutes of our Daniel coolly taking command of a very difficult battle.

And now I'll tell you the story of Daniel and his tank crew's final battle. I'll tell you how Daniel was killed, but really I'm telling about how he saved the lives of so many, purely on his own initiative, without having any obligation at all to do it. Daniel, our precious boy – in your death, you gave so many people life.

Daniel's tank crew had four soldiers. Daniel was the commander and aside from him there were another three soldiers – the driver, the loader, and the gunner. These four, Daniel, Itay, Matan, and Tomer, were called "Team Perez." It's customary in the Armored Corps to name a tank crew after the commander. But Daniel wasn't just their commander. They loved him so much, and he loved them. He was their leader. He would always say to them, "We have to be ready for a day of reckoning."

On October 7th, at six-thirty in the morning, sirens go off at the Nahal Oz base. Daniel and his crew run to the mobile shelter, and even though at this stage terrorists hadn't yet attacked the base, Team Perez got to the shelter already geared up and ready for any situation: uniforms, gloves, weapons, and everything.

Within minutes, Team Perez decides to leave the shelter and get into their tank, to drive to their usual post and man it. There's only one other tank at the base with them, with deputy company commander Ido Pe'er and tank commander Yonatan Golan. Team Perez make contact with them, and Pe'er and Golan's tank decides to do as they do. By a quarter to seven both crews are in their tanks and start driving to their regular posts. Daniel's tank is supposed to take a position next to Kibbutz Nahal Oz, a few hundred meters away from the base; Golan and Pe'er's post is a few hundred meters closer to the border.

En route to their posts, while the tanks are driving, they suddenly encounter terrorists. Not just any terrorists – these are terrorists on motorcycles and in semi-trailers. And they begin a battle with them. Daniel's tank is hit by an RPG or a mine, but it doesn't immobilize the tank. Just like that, within a few minutes, the two tanks eliminate all the terrorists. At this point, Daniel and his friends still don't understand where those terrorists came from. After the skirmish, each tank reaches its usual post and gets into position. And suddenly Daniel identifies two bands of armed terrorists on the other side of the border, coming toward them from Gaza! He shells them and hits them, but still no one realizes the extent of the chaos.

At around a quarter to eight, Daniel listens to the radio and hears, to his astonishment, that there's a serious terrorist infiltration into the Nahal Oz Outpost and that terrorists have taken control of the operations center. When he hears that, he immediately tries to get a sense of the whole picture, but what he can't get ahold of over the radio are orders, guidelines, commands. Nothing. Neither of the crews is able to make any contact with their commanders. At a certain point, Daniel even hears the commander of Battalion 13 of the Golani infantry, Tomer Greenberg of blessed memory, going up on the radio and reporting that he's fighting at Kfar Aza. Daniel and his crew try to get on the radio with him, but he doesn't answer. No one answers. There's no one to explain to them what's going on and what they need to do.

You have to understand that Daniel is only a platoon commander. A junior officer at the rank of first lieutenant is not supposed to make his own tactical decisions. He's supposed to receive from above very clear orders, clearly defined missions, such as "At time A, initiate a tank ambush; at time B, go back to your station." A soldier at this rank is supposed to be told where to go, where to place the tank, where it's most important to be. Soldiers like this have no broader responsibility; only company commanders and above make strategic decisions.

But on October 7th, unfortunately, in many instances, the chain of command had been broken. The company commander was killed, the deputy battalion commander had been critically wounded, and the battalion commander Tomer Greenberg was fighting in Kfar Aza. Pandemonium. We understand that during that morning the Divisional Commander of Northern Gaza was in direct contact with Daniel – this is almost unheard of for such a high-ranking officer to be in direct contact with a platoon commander. This highlights the courage and initiative taken by Daniel on that day and the extent of our forces being overwhelmed. All there was during those critical first hours were soldiers: individual soldiers, lone soldiers, who took responsibility, who gave themselves orders and made their own decisions. Decisions that on any other day would have landed a soldier taking them without explicit orders from above in jail. But that day, there were no orders from above. Only from below. And Daniel decided to take action from below, and to do whatever he could, as best as he could.

So Daniel realizes that the Nahal Oz army outpost is in a very dire situation, and he and his crew decide that they're going back to base. He directs the tank back to the outpost but the tank can't go deep inside; remember, most of the outpost is buildings with these narrow passages between them, and there's no room for a tank to drive there. So all they can do is drive around the security perimeter inside the outpost and locate terrorists. At some point, Pe'er and Golan's tank arrives and does the same; both tanks patrol the edge of the outpost, again and again, but they aren't spotting terrorists. I imagine that the terrorists were hiding, because that's what you do when you hear a tank coming. They patrol for about half an hour, basically preventing any terrorists from coming inside.

During the course of the morning, the tanks have brief contact with Colonel Greenberg, who was still fighting in Kfar Aza. Suddenly, they hear on the radio that terrorists are fighting our soldiers at the entrance to the base. Daniel's tank goes straight to the gate, but when they reach the guard post at the gate, they discover bodies of soldiers there. You can hear them on the radio; you can hear his crew saying, "Oh no, oh no, oh my heart." You can hear their heart breaking. But their spirit isn't broken; this only spurs them on to understand how they must, must prevent these terrorists from having their way.

Right after they discover the dead soldiers, another terrible thing happens: Pe'er and Golan's tank, the one that stayed behind patrolling the base's perimeter, is hit by an RPG. Yonatan Golan is killed, along with another soldier from the tank, Or Avital. Three other soldiers are wounded by that RPG; actually, they were able to reach the mobile shelter and they survived, but their tank was now out of the game. Team Perez becomes the only tank left.

Team Perez encounters a single Namer armored personnel carrier (APC), with no commander and just a few soldiers. It turns out that the fallen soldiers by the outpost gate had first been inside that Namer; Shilo Har-Even, of blessed memory, was its commander; he and his team were responsible for eliminating many terrorists. Some of the terrorists that they eliminated were planning to infiltrate towns along Highway 25; thanks to them, some of these towns were saved. But at one point, the APC was hit by a shell and was damaged, so that it was impossible to shoot from inside it. So Har-Even and the rest of his team decided to leave the APC and head into the outpost on foot, to fight the terrorists face-to-face. And there, by the entrance to the outpost, they were killed. These soldiers chose to leave the protected space they were supposed to be in, and to run, completely exposed, to fight the terrorists. It's just unbelievable how much heroism there is in every aspect of this story.

So Daniel and his team are now next to the APC, just outside the base, and at this stage they can't reach any commander. No one's answering. Daniel understands that the terrorists are doing whatever they want back at the base; and he knows that they'll want to take hostages. He tells his crew and the remaining soldiers from the APC: "Guys, we know for sure that terrorists have overrun the base. That means they'll try and take hostages. Our goal is to stop the terrorists from taking hostages. So we're going back now with the APC to our tank's regular post; we'll take up position there and make sure that no one crosses the border back to Gaza."

At 8:40, Team Perez gets back to their regular post next to Kibbutz Nahal Oz with the tank and the APC. Now they keep watch over the border and try to spot anyone trying to cross the border. They tell themselves that if anyone even tries to go back to Gaza, they'll thwart them; they won't let anyone take any soldiers from this base into Gaza.

But within minutes, they make out a horrific sight just five hundred meters away, right next to the base. A giant wave of motorcycles, pickup trucks, armed terrorists, RPGs, grenades – that whole nightmare – is headed toward the base. The radio starts to crackle with activity; voices from the base report that there's another attack; that it's happening all over again.

Now Daniel is faced with a dilemma and this is a dilemma that he has only seconds to resolve. Should he stay with his tank in its regular position next to Kibbutz Nahal Oz, maintaining defense, or should he do something far more dangerous, something that no one has ordered him to do, something that is by no means sure to succeed: to charge directly at them and to try to stop the attack? If Daniel thought small, or I'd even say, if he thought average, then he would have stayed where he was, in his position, and that would be that. But Daniel decides otherwise. He knows that he's the outpost's last line of defense. He understands that if he doesn't stop them, they're getting into the base.

Daniel tells his team and the remaining team from the APC, "Guys, we're not staying here. We're going to stop them. We're not letting them get in." And they're all with him. They're united in this mission; they're all determined to protect the soldiers in the base. So they speed out of there, and at 8:50 the tank just breaks right into the middle of the throng of terrorists trying to take the base. The APC moves slower than the tank on that terrain. Once again, Team Perez is all alone. But they don't despair. They do everything they can; they shell terrorists, they trample them, they fire with their heavy machine gun; they shoot, they turn around, they aim, and they shoot again.

One of the investigators told us that they found thousands of bullet casings inside the tank. A tank isn't even meant for that kind of thing; it isn't designed for battling terrorists with RPGs at zero range. But that's what they do; they do it, and you can hear on the radio recordings how well they do it, working together, with insane teamwork, working seamlessly like one body, and with each success they cheer each other on, "Great job!" and "Bravo!" and that's how it goes, for eleven minutes straight. Team Perez rages wild there with that tank and overcomes those terrorists, one after another.

At 9:01 and 46 seconds, you hear a burst of gunfire on the radio from very close range; and someone shouts "Aaayyy." It's Daniel's voice. He is the only tank crew member whose head was outside the tank. The only way to operate the commander's machine gun mounted on the tank is to expose himself. He decided to do so for the sake of the battle. The theory is that they shot him in the back of his neck, and probably the blood seeped onto his shirt. That's why there's no bullet hole in his shirt, the only part of his uniform that they found. Right after Daniel's scream, you hear someone shouting, "Perez! Perez! Someone's been hit!" And then the radio cuts out. That's the end of the recording.

Today we know that forty-five minutes later, the third wave of terrorists reached the tank. They kidnap Daniel and Itay Chen's bodies, and they take Matan Angrest alive. Tomer Leibovitz's body is left behind; that's the dead soldier that they found in the tank, the soldier our Yonatan heard about on the phone before we knew anything. The other three are still there, still there in Gaza. Two of them are dead; one, we hope, believe, and pray, is still alive.

When we sat shiva for Daniel, someone came and took me aside. He said, "I'm from the Shin Bet, and I want to tell you something. Listen, I interrogated four terrorists; we arrested some of them inside Gaza over the months of war. I interrogated two terrorist brothers from Gaza, and they told me, 'Our mission was to infiltrate Nahal Oz – not the base, the kibbutz, but there was a tank there that kept chasing us, so instead of going into the kibbutz, we just fled back to Gaza.'" That's what he told me! And I realize that it's not just that the tank killed terrorists, it also deterred other terrorists. And I think about how many more terrorists like these there were, who saw what was happening there and just ran away; how many terrorists didn't get into the Nahal Oz base or Kibbutz Nahal Oz thanks to that tank, thanks to Team Perez.

The next day, two people suddenly showed up at the shiva, a man and woman I don't know, and I see that they're weeping. My wife and I are sitting on low chairs, as you do for shiva, and they approach us, and they're crying, and it becomes quiet around them. Then the man takes a note out of his pocket and reads it. He reads it in a loud, trembling voice, and this is what he says. "We are from Kibbutz Nahal Oz. We came here today in the name of the survivors, and in the name of the one hundred and thirty children who were in the kibbutz that day, to show thanks and appreciation for the kindness that was done for us. On that day, when terrorists ran wild in the kibbutz, every door that was forced open brought another disaster upon us, and every terrorist eliminated meant that many lives were saved. The heroism of Daniel, may God avenge his blood, and of his friends, the protectors of Nahal Oz, saved the lives of hundreds of people from our kibbutz."

And I think about it and I suddenly realize that it could be that Daniel, through his act of heroism, saved his brother Yonatan as well. Daniel and his team killed so many terrorists, and deterred so many more – and these were the same terrorists who would have been waiting to attack Yonatan when he got to Nahal Oz. If Daniel and his team hadn't done what they did, then when Yonatan entered the base, there wouldn't have been twenty terrorists, but a hundred. And then Yonatan, God forbid, might not have survived a battle like that, God forbid.

So what we have here is the story of two brothers who unknowingly fought just a hundred meters away from each other, at the same outpost. One saved hundreds of people and was killed; and one, who wasn't even supposed to be there, got there and fought there and saved many lives, was injured, yet survived. You have no idea what God's calculations are here; you don't know. People ask me, "Don't you have questions for God," and I answer that I don't. For whatever reason, I don't. I don't believe that we can ever fully comprehend God's ways; I don't believe that I have the answer to the question of divine justice in this world. Sometimes you have to know how to live with painful questions, instead of accepting shallow, partial answers. But one thing I do say: If you're already deciding to ask questions, you have to ask all the questions. If I ask why the Almighty took Daniel, I also have to ask why He spared Yonatan. We're used to asking questions about the bad and taking the good for granted; but it could be that every day, every day, we should wonder and ask what we've done to deserve all our blessings. Why is it that I have health, or a livelihood, or a family? So if you want to ask questions, ask, but ask all the questions.

The truth is that Daniel was a child who asked questions; he knew how to ask questions, to test boundaries, but for all the nonsense and wild rides he took us on as a teenager, he was a person with values, and humane, and dedicated. In an exceptional way. We found a diary among the belongings that were returned to us from his base at Nahal Oz; a diary that we didn't know existed. He started keeping it when he became an officer who was responsible for other soldiers. What things he writes there, what things. I read it and I wept and I said, "This is a Daniel that I never knew."

The first question he poses to himself, the question he thought about every night before he went to sleep, is: "Why am I here?" He writes about the price that the Jewish people paid before they had a country, something he saw firsthand on his eleventh grade trip to Poland. He writes about the privilege and duty of defending our home. And he has this sentence there, a sentence he writes to himself: "And who will do it, who – if not me. If not me, then who?" That's the question Daniel asks: "If not me, then who?" I try to remind myself of those five words every day. To take responsibility, personal responsibility, full responsibility, to fulfill my purpose – for as long as my soul is within me.

This Is the Sanctity of Man

Yossi Landau's Story

Age 55

*Sderot, Nova Festival,
the kibbutzim near the border*

Once I was almost killed during a rescue operation. It was in America. I and some volunteers who were with me received a call about a serious accident; a plane crashed into a tower in Manhattan, and the tower collapsed. As soon as we arrived at the scene, we saw another plane crashing into the tower right next to it. Within seconds I realized that it was a terror attack. We started running into the second tower and bringing people out, dragging them out, then the second tower also came crashing down. I was pinned underneath. I was there for seven hours, trapped in the dark, almost buried beneath the ruins. There I made a vow to God: I swore that if I make it out alive, I'll give as much of myself as I can to whoever I possibly can. I made it out; I was saved. There, in the ruins of the Twin Towers, I wasn't killed. But in the kibbutzim of the Gaza Envelope, I was. In those kibbutzim, I lost my life.

My name is Yossi Landau, fifty-five years old, a resident of Ashdod and a Hassid in the Sanz community, married and the father of ten lovely children and grandfather of twenty-two, thank God. Just last week I married off our seventh child, Avraham. In my private life, I run a company – I have an international delivery company that primarily serves the Ultra-Orthodox community. In my other life, I volunteer for ZAKA.

ZAKA is an acronym for *Zihui Korbanot Ason*, "Disaster Victims Identification," but we like to say that it's also the acronym for *Zeh Kedushat Adam*, "This Is the Sanctity of Man." When we arrive at the scene of a disaster, we have two missions. The first is saving lives; the second is treating the dead with dignity. By respecting the dead, we sanctify the life they lived, the person they were, the spark of divinity within them. We also show respect to the families they left behind, who want more than just identification – they also want to know how they died, and they want to know that they were seen and treated with respect. This is the source of our great respect for the body of the deceased.

I'm ZAKA's head of operations in the Lachish region, in the south. In the early nineties I had the privilege of being one of ZAKA's founders, and I've been volunteering for the organization for thirty-three years now, thank God. I've been all over the world in the aftermath of all kinds of terror attacks, like the attacks in Mumbai. Not only terror attacks but also natural disasters like the earthquake in Haiti. Eight months ago, I came back from Turkey, from a terrible earthquake. My team there saved the lives of nineteen Muslims. I've been all over, and I've looked death in the eye; I've sensed and smelled death. I thought I had seen it all; I thought I had already witnessed every horror that the human eye can see. But as a colleague of mine from ZAKA said: If I had known what I was going to see on October 7th, I would first have asked God to strike me blind.

On Simchat Torah, the morning of the Sabbath, many of my children are staying with us, plus fourteen grandchildren, and all the grandchildren are already waiting for that moment during the synagogue service – the moment they get to sit on Grandpa's shoulders, to get candy, and to dance with the Torah scrolls. But at six-thirty in the morning, the siren sounds. We're used to sirens in Ashdod; the children get up, go into the safe room, and I'm standing downstairs waiting, at the ready, to see where the missile fell. If there's a hit, I'll rush over to the site. So I put on my clothing, and I'm on standby. I see the Iron Dome interception come out from behind my house, and in the sky I see twenty, twenty-five, thirty interceptions; everything is getting hit by the Iron Dome. I remember saying to myself, "Something's happening here; this doesn't make sense."

Then I start getting phone calls and radio messages from all kinds of officers and commanders, from the army and the police, and from the Home Front Command, and they all say to me, "Listen, Yossi, something's happening here. There's chaos, we don't know what's going on, but what you're seeing, the missiles, is just cover for an invasion – there are terrorists, and there are victims. We're not sure where to send you yet, but be on standby."

About two hours later I get a phone call from the Southern District Commander, who says, "Yossi, listen. Get in the car now and drive first to the warehouse. Fill your car with equipment. Body bags. This is something totally different from anything that you've seen before. Then head toward Sderot."

I call a few volunteers – because of the holiday, I got hold of only two – and I say to them, "Be on standby; I'm coming to pick you up from our warehouse in Ashdod." I fill up my vehicle with body bags, equipment, gloves, everything we need. I also take a rifle and all the magazines I can find. Usually I just have my handgun on me, but I realized that this was a different situation.

Almost all of us at ZAKA have weapons; we do regular shooting practice, organized by the police, because we're in the field. As a first response team, we're often the first ones to arrive at the disaster scene, and sometimes it's still ongoing, so we're trained. We're not a SWAT team or commandos, but we have weapons, and we know how to use them; we can hit a target when we need to, God forbid.

We encountered the first military barrier at Yad Mordechai Junction. So many corpses lay on the road, so many bodies, and soldiers and special forces were on both sides of the road, fighting against terrorists who had come up from Zikim. The hiss of bullets. I introduced myself, and they said to me, "If you go in, it's at your own risk. Have your guns at the ready because terrorists are constantly jumping out."

When I got to Sderot, I saw a huge war room at the entrance to the city, with a command center. They had also set up a first-aid station there, sort of a field hospital for all the wounded. So my team and I and two other volunteers start combing the city, looking for wounded people. This is the first priority, to save people. While we're searching the area, they suddenly start shooting at us! We see them, the terrorists! Shooting at us! We started shooting at them, fighting, but that's not our job. We got out of there and continued our search. We were trying to save lives, and we found, I didn't know how many were alive, but we managed to find about fifteen people, something like that, and bring them to the first-aid station there. We just picked up the wounded in our vehicle, took them to the entrance of Sderot, and left them there in the field hospital for further treatment.

Then we come to this car there, four hours after the whole event started. We get to this car, and there's a couple inside the car; both have been shot, and we start checking them, checking for signs of life, to see if there's anything that can be done or whether they should be put into body bags. The sun is beating down on the hot car, and we know that every minute counts. Then we hear a little girl crying! The girl was still inside the car, under the seat! That was my first slap in the face on October 7th; that was something nobody prepared me for, something I wasn't prepared for.

The girl is sobbing, sobbing, and I say to her, "We've come to save you," and she asks, "Are you one of us?" and I said, "Yes." And she asks me for a sign, to know that I'm not Hamas, so I say the *Shema* to her with tears in my eyes, "Hear, O Israel, the Lord is our God, the Lord is One." She came out from under the seat, and when I look at her all I can see is my own granddaughters, she was about their age, and I almost passed out right there; I almost collapsed and broke down on the spot, but I said to myself, "This isn't the time for that." I covered her eyes so that she wouldn't see her parents, and I handed her over to some police officer who was in the area. And I said to him, "Please take her, take care of her, because as long as she's here I can't bear to keep going."

❧

Then the bodies started piling up. So many people had been killed. I start counting them, twenty, thirty, forty, fifty bodies, and I started talking to myself out loud, I said, "No, no, no, this isn't what I intended, this isn't why I joined ZAKA, this isn't what it's supposed to be like!" What exactly am I supposed to do now with all these bodies, this huge number of bodies? I looked around and suddenly saw a truck parked there at the side of the road. I broke the truck's lock, opened it up, and said to my team – this is what we're going to use for storing corpses.

I keep yelling into the ZAKA radio that I need more help; I need more volunteers. But all our volunteers are Ultra-Orthodox, it's the Sabbath, it's a holiday; they're in the synagogue, and none of them took their radios with them; no one updated them! So then I scream and yell, "We need help! I'm begging for help!" and gradually, the volunteers start coming.

In the meanwhile, I also called the workers from my delivery company. We have a few trucks there. So I called my drivers, and I said to them, "As soon as the Sabbath is over, start the truck and head toward Sderot and Ofakim!" In Ofakim we had more than fifty bodies, and the same in Sderot, and they needed to be loaded onto trucks – at this stage we didn't even know where to take them. Eventually, the decision was reached to bring them to the Military Rabbinate headquarters at Shura, even though, up to that moment, we had no idea where it was.

That whole time, as we were driving around Sderot, there was terrible fighting going on there – at the police station, there were terrorists holding some policemen hostage, and many courageous, holy policemen went inside to fight them. It was a war there, and I suddenly see a tank right in front of me – this was the first time in my life that I had ever seen a tank, in Israel, driving around in a city. The tank was headed for the Sderot Station, and it just barged ahead, running over everything in its path, trampling parked cars; in short, absolute chaos! Those policemen in Sderot – they fought back down to the last bullet; they were really heroes, but tragically, almost all of them were killed there. Only in the early hours of the morning were we able to come back for their bodies.

From Sderot, we went out to Route 34. There's this stretch of road that's usually a ten-minute drive; we drove it in seven hours. We drove down the road with a bigger team, to collect the bodies. And oy, what awaited us there! I saw people who had been murdered inside their vehicles. Bodies strewn outside cars. I saw families there, little children, young people, people who had just been driving down the road, many of them with extra shots to "confirm the kill." I saw cars that were still on fire twelve whole hours after it had all started – ones that had been hit by an RPG or a grenade. I saw cars that terrorists just set on fire to burn people alive. They made sure, those terrorists – may their names be erased – they made sure that there would be no trace of those people left, simply no trace. We're still struggling with this. To this day, we're still trying to identify people starting from zero, burned to nothing.

From there we went on to the site of the festival in Re'im. We got there at one in the morning, and all we could see there – oy oy oy – we saw nothing there but bodies. Just bodies. Bodies, blood, bodies, blood, bodies – that's what we saw. Three hundred and sixty young men and women, holy and pure, holy and pure heroes, who ascended to heaven; pure souls who are now beside the Heavenly Throne. We felt it was a privilege to care for these sacred martyrs.

When we got there, the soldiers there came up to us and said, "With all due respect, we can't allow you to work here." We didn't understand why so we asked them to explain it to us, and they said, "It's dangerous for you to be here," and we said, "Why, explain," and they said, "There are still terrorists in this sector, terrorists who can come here, and we are still have mortar bombs falling here, and there's nowhere to take cover." I said, "What do you mean? There are plenty of small, mobile shelters here." But then I went into one of the shelters, and I understood. It was impossible to go in because all the shelters were full of bodies.

In the end, the soldiers allowed us to work until sunrise; they were afraid that another band of terrorists would strike at sunrise, so we decided to stay until then and finish as much as we could. We got their approval. I had to bring in one hundred and eighty volunteers. Forty of them – what they did, their job was to separate twenty-one bodies that were burned up in one of the shelters. They had to separate them from each other and place each one in a body bag. It took them three whole hours to do that. All of our volunteers are family men with jobs. The fire that I saw in their eyes – I started crying just from seeing that, what kind of people we have in ZAKA. What heroes. I watched them and knew that when all this would be over, they'd have to return home and be with their families. Right now they weren't even thinking about what this would do to them, how much it would hurt them. No, that didn't interest them; they had a task to complete, and they gave it their all, all their soul and all their might. We worked there until four-thirty in the morning, one hundred and eighty volunteers, and we managed to honor the memory of two hundred and thirty-seven holy people.

By this point in the morning, we were sure that we had finished, that that was it. But then they came to us and said, "Your next task is to go into the kibbutzim, where it's the worst of all." I almost laughed at them because nothing could possibly be worse than what we had already seen. Nothing could be worse than a whole party with so many holy murder victims, so many bodies. But when I went into the kibbutzim, when I went in there, I saw the worst of all. I myself, I personally, still haven't left; I'm still there. For seven weeks, I haven't been able to hold my grandchildren, to pick them up and hug them. I haven't been able to look them in the eye. I don't want them to be infected by everything I saw, by everything I experienced. I don't want them to feel what I feel.

We went inside the kibbutzim and saw horrific things. Horrific sights. I'm not going to describe exactly what we saw. We saw things there – children, families, adults, old people; horrifying things, pregnant women, young women who had been violated, whose bodies had been violated. At one point, we went into one house where there was a whole family and a puddle – no, I wouldn't call it a puddle – a river of blood was in the living room. I went inside, I see the state of the bodies, and I start thinking, I start talking to myself: "The parents – they saw what they did to the children, and the children – they saw what they did to the parents, and they must have pleaded for their lives, and while this was happening, those terrorists – they were eating the holiday meal that the family had set out on the table; am I seeing straight, can this be what I'm seeing?"

We were there for some time, and all the volunteers with me there, they're all experienced volunteers, but one by one they come up to me and say, "Yossi, goodbye, I'm going home; I can't take it." I was left there almost alone. I can't take it either, and I need encouragement too, and I don't have any. But there's no choice. So I call everyone who's still there with me, and we hold hands, and we start singing there next to the murdered, next to the family. We close our eyes and sing in the house of those holy martyrs. We promise the family, we make a promise that we'll take care of them and bring them in for identification. We'll take care of everyone who was desecrated here, everyone who was murdered here. That was our promise.

When I came home for the first time, it was after almost a whole week of work out there with barely any sleep. I had lost seven kilograms. When I got home, my family, they didn't want to look at me. Not my wife, not my children, not my grandchildren. I had to take them aside and explain to them that right now, I was at rock-bottom; there was nowhere lower to go. From here there was only one place to go, and that was up, but only with their encouragement and support; that was the only way I could rise up. And I ask you – this is what I said to them – I ask you to give me that support and encouragement. If not, I'm going to collapse. I'm going to collapse. That's what I said. And they gave me their word. And I got that support from them, and I felt strengthened.

About two weeks after that Shabbat, I got a phone call from a friend I work with, and he says to me, "Yossi, listen, my father is ninety-two years old, he's a Holocaust survivor. He really wants to talk to you, is there any chance you can come?" I said, "Yes, I want to come." I took the car and drove to Ramat Gan to meet this old man who had survived Dr. Mengele's human experiments. I showed him photos of what I'd seen, of what our sisters and brothers went through there, what they did to them; I told it all. And this person, ninety-two years old, started to weep. He took my hand and said to me, "Yossi, I want to tell you. What you saw there, even we didn't see. It's worse than the Holocaust."

Today, our courageous volunteers are going through difficult treatment, psychological treatment. Some of them lost their jobs because they simply haven't been able to function. In the middle of the night, I get phone calls from volunteers' wives: "Yossi, where's my husband, he didn't come home," and I start looking for them and discover them fast asleep in the car or asleep in the synagogue. They can't bear to go home, can't bear to live their lives as normal. Or I get a phone call from one of my volunteer's neighbors at three o'clock one Friday afternoon, and he says to me, "You know that that volunteer of yours – he's got five kids at home, but they have nothing for their Sabbath meals. They have nothing at all for the Sabbath," so I start organizing it all. I start organizing meals for them so they'll have something to eat on the Sabbath. Ever since October 7th, I've had stories like that daily. They didn't just kill 1,200 people. They killed us too.

One evening, I sat on the lawn with my volunteers and asked them to start talking, to share what they saw, what they went through. When it was my turn to speak, I said, "I want to share something personal, and I ask that you keep it to between us, so that no one will think I'm crazy, so that no rumor gets out that Yossi Landau has gone nuts. I want to tell you what I felt that day. I felt that those bodies were talking to me. I felt that they were talking to me and telling me their story." That's what I said, and before I could even finish that sentence, they all of them, all seventy volunteers, say to me, "Yossi, we were afraid to say that to you, but that's what happened to us too, that's how we felt too."

The victims, those holy and pure people – they made sure that we'd pass on their message so that they weren't killed in vain. They told us: "They tried to take away our personal dignity, they tried to take away our identities, they tried to erase us, to leave no trace of us, but you'll tell the whole world! You'll tell them, you'll tell them what happened, you'll tell them what we went through. Your eyes will be our mouths. What we can't tell, your eyes can." That was their last will and testament; that was their final request. I've been trying to fulfill that request ever since.

Thank You, Daddy, for Being Alive

Emily and Thomas Hand's Story

Ages 8 and 64

◊ *Kibbutz Be'eri*

As told by Emily

There wasn't even one nice guy out of all the people who guarded us in the box. "Box," that's what I call Gaza. I don't want to say that word, Gaza, so I call it "the box." Me and Daddy have a few code words. "Olives" means terrorists. "Bamba" means Arabs. "Antibiotics" is blood. Hostages are "cheese." Murdered people are "cottage cheese." I use the names of foods I don't like. Because the real words, they sometimes aren't pleasant for me to say.

We moved to Be'eri when I was two and a half. My friend Hila was seven. When she heard that there was a new kid coming to the kibbutz, she gave me lots of stuff, and we've been friends ever since. And it's really lucky that we're friends because, when I was in the box, Hila helped me there. She really, really helped me.

I really love the kibbutz. I love that Schnitzel and Johnsey can run around without a leash. Oh, and they always know how to find their way home! I love having a dog. When I'm sad she can always tell, and she comes and gives me a kiss.

350

Schnitzel usually barks all the time, and she's always moving around. Johnsey is usually quiet and doesn't move much. He's calm. All he does is watch over me. I like to go wild with Schnitzel, but not too wild because she's sensitive. She's sensitive but she likes to go wild. But with Johnsey, I feel strong. Strong and calm. Sometimes I feel sensitive and strong at the same time. And that's when I feel the most calm. Sort of light, as if nothing happened.

I remember that on Friday night we went to Hila's house, then Narkis came. We danced and played around, and it was so much fun. Then in the morning, at six in the morning, Hila woke me up because of the booms, and we went to the safe room. They said the army was there, but we didn't see anyone. Then the safe room door sort of couldn't close, so she moved all these couches against the front door.

I thought that for sure they would get to me, to us. The terrorists. Because we were the closest to the vineyard, and they were in the vineyard. We heard shouting, so we knew they were in the vineyard. And they did get to us; they knew how to break in. Yeah, they knew how to break in with a hammer or something. And because I was at Hila's, Daddy wasn't with us there.

I'm good at drawing. When I was with Hila there, they sometimes let us draw. I would draw Johnsey and Daddy. Now I draw all the time. I love to paint with different shades. Like, say, light green, then regular green, then darker green, and darker and darker. I like when everything's in order. Whenever my friends come to my room they touch all my stuff. So then I say to them, "No, no, no, this goes here, that goes there." I like it when everything's in order. I like it when things are neat.

Now we live in Herzliya. I like it here. I have all these different after-school activities. I go horseback riding, and I already know how to canter. I was scared at first, but once I got on the horse it was fun, and by the end I didn't want to get off. I just got on the horse and started riding, and ever since, I realized how much fun it is. Like, if I don't even try, how can I tell if it's fun?

Sometimes, on Thursdays, I go to this special kind of activity with this dog, a really trained dog, much better trained than Johnsey. His name is Dao, and I play frisbee with him. I don't know how to explain it, but it's the best thing I do all week. Thursday is my favorite day. I have horseback riding in the morning, then I come back and have Dao, then I go to the Dead Sea to hang out with my friends from Be'eri who are now living in a hotel there.

I was scared that terrorists would come to Herzliya. Because they came to Ra'anana a few weeks ago, so I was really scared. But then I understood that they weren't coming, they weren't going from house to house, they were just kind of walking around in the street there, and that's where they did the terror attack. They don't go into houses here. And in the place where we are, there are security cameras, and at night there are these metal things that come down over the windows. So that's good.

I don't know if I want to go back to Be'eri. Sometimes I do and sometimes I don't. On the one hand, the kibbutz isn't close to anything. On the other hand, all my friends are there. And it's tiny, and that's fun. But the terrorists might be able to take it over again, and that's really scary.

As told by Thomas

When Emily was three, her mother Liat passed away from cancer. I went up to Emily and said to her, "Mommy's dead," and she said, "Okay," but she didn't really understand that meant Mommy would never come back. For a long, long time she kept asking, "Where's Mommy? Where's Mommy?" She was only three, after all, a tiny girl; she had no concept of death.

So at one point I took Emily to her mother's grave. I gave her a hug, I pointed to the grave, and I said to her, "Mommy's here, in this little house. She'll be here forever; she's not going anywhere. She doesn't feel anything anymore, she doesn't feel hot or cold, she doesn't feel anything at all." And Emily looked at me, and I said to her, "Emily, sweetie, listen to me, Mommy is never coming back. She's dead. When someone's dead, they never come back."

Five years later, I found myself in a terrible tragedy once again. I was sure that my Emily had been murdered. For many long days, I mourned her death. But apparently she never fully accepted what I had told her back there at Liat's graveside. After two months in Gaza she came back to me. My beloved daughter came back to life.

I grew up in a Catholic home in Ireland. Every Sunday I'd go to church with my parents, a cute little boy in a smart suit and tie. That was a special time; I was religious back then. Today I joke that I'm a "Catholic atheist." When I was thirty-two I came to Kibbutz Be'eri as a volunteer, and I fell in love. I fell in love twice: first with the kibbutz, and then with Narkis.

The kibbutz was the complete opposite of everything I'd ever known. I came from a place with wet, gloomy weather and suddenly discovered the sun, a sun that doesn't just shine, but actually warms you up! I discovered fields, paths, people, children. I was stunned by the beauty of it all. And I marveled at this thing, this "kibbutz." I'd always been in favor of socialism, but like everyone says, I thought that socialism was a nice idea that doesn't actually work in reality. But here I am in a place where it actually works! The head of the printing press makes the same salary as the woman who does the laundry. No one lacks for anything. Everyone has everything they need.

That was the most beautiful time in my life. I remember waking up before dawn to go work in the fields and coming back home at sunset, utterly exhausted, all my muscles aching, blisters on my hands – and a big smile on my face. I was happy. I'm still happy. For thirty years now, Kibbutz Be'eri has been my home. The members of the kibbutz are my family. I can't wait to go back there. It's where I belong.

I met Narkis in our little pub in Be'eri, very soon after I arrived. We fell in love right away; we moved in together just a month later! I stayed on to volunteer for a year, but my visa ran out, and so did my money – I had planned to stay for only three months, not for so long. So I went back home to work, but Narkis and I kept up a warm, loving relationship. And one day, when she came for a visit to England, we met up, and I asked her to marry me. And Narkis said yes! I was terribly in love with her. After the wedding, I finally moved to Be'eri. Narkis and I had two kids, Aiden and Natalie. We ended up getting divorced, but Narkis and I raised our kids together on the kibbutz. She was a wonderful mother to our children; she was a wonderful woman, Narkis.

A few years later, the kibbutz organized a singles' weekend in Eilat. A few friends and I thought it might be nice, so we went. And there, in Eilat, I met Liat. I liked her straight away, we talked all night, and I fell hard for her even though she lived all the way up in Haifa! We had a long-distance relationship for a while; we lived three hours away from each other. Eventually Liat moved in with me in Be'eri, and we had Emily together. But then my Liat left this world.

And when Liat passed away, Narkis simply took Emily under her wing. She treated her like one of her own, like another daughter of ours! Emily barely got to know her biological mother, but Narkis more than made up for it. Emily had a second mother, and her name was Narkis. But then Emily lost her, too. Emily lost two mothers. Almost one hundred members of our kibbutz were murdered on the seventh of October. Narkis was one of them.

Narkis had a good friend called Raaya Rotem. They grew up together on the kibbutz and raised their families there. Raaya has a daughter, a sweet thirteen-year-old named Hila. For some inexplicable reason, despite the age gap, Hila and Emily developed a surprising and lovely friendship. They go to each other's houses, they love to dance and draw together, with lots of laughter, lots of silliness and sleepovers. They're really good friends. On the night of the sixth of October, Emily went to sleep over at Hila's.

On Friday night we all had a holiday meal together in the kibbutz dining room – myself, Emily, Narkis, Raaya, and Hila. Our older children,

Natalie and Aiden, weren't in Be'eri for the holiday. We had a lovely meal. We had our two dogs with us – Johnsey, Emily's dog, and Natalie's dog Schnitzel, who we were taking care of over the weekend. At the end of the meal, Emily asked if she could stay over at Hila's, and I said, "Of course! What a dream! I'll finally get a chance to watch some football!" and that's what I did.

Saturday morning – rockets, sirens. I go into the safe room, call for Johnsey – he's already used to it, and he comes right away – and we wait inside. Emily is with Hila at Raaya's place; I assume that they all went right into the safe room, I'm not worried. I didn't realize that anything unusual was up until I started hearing gunfire. Gunfire from an automatic weapon and the booms of an RPG. Crazy noise. I start talking to myself out loud and cursing, "What the hell is going on, what the hell is going on?" At first I try to reassure myself that it's just some army exercise, but the noises get louder and louder, closer and closer. And I realize that it must be some kind of attack.

I call Narkis right away and say to her, "You must be in the safe room; close the door! The door doesn't lock, so hold the door handle! If you hear people coming closer, if you hear voices in Arabic, hold the door handle as tightly as you can!" I know I have to tell Raaya as well, but Raaya's English isn't good enough, and my Hebrew isn't good enough, so I call Narkis back and say, "Emily is at Hila's! Call Raaya and tell her exactly what I told you! They have to hide in the safe room and hold onto the door handle!"

In the meantime, I arm myself and try to make a plan. I have a gun, about thirty bullets, and two knives as well; one of them is quite long. I try and work out how to get out, how to run over to Raaya's place to get Emily out of there and hide her away. I open the window a tiny bit, just to see what's happening outside, and right away, boom! Two shots at the wall of my house. I quickly close the window, and it hits me that if I go outside, I might simply die within one second.

I think about how Emily lost her mother at the age of three. I won't let it happen again; I won't let her lose her father as well. So at this point I start debating which risk to take. Should I run over to Emily, risking her losing me? Or should I let her stay in the safe room with Raaya and Hila and hope for the best?

At this point I leave the safe room and get settled in the kitchen with my loaded gun. I'm ready for anything, for any terrorist that may come. I didn't want to hide like a mouse. At about ten-thirty, Emily sends me a message, asking if I'm in the safe room, and I answer, "Yes." I don't want her to know that I'm in the kitchen, I want her to stay calm. And right then, my phone battery dies. The electricity in our neighborhood went out. That was the last I heard from Emily that day. It was terrible.

I was in the kitchen for some time. I was dying of thirst. The sink was just a meter away, but I didn't dare get up to drink – what would happen if they walked in that very moment? I have to stay focused! And suddenly, I hear this kind of scratching noise, as if someone is scratching at the kitchen door. I look through the window and see that it's Schnitzel, Natalie's dog! At that moment I realize something terrible must have happened to Narkis. After all, Schnitzel must have been closed up in the safe room with her; there was no way she would have let Schnitzel out. So someone else must have opened the safe room door. I knew it in an instant.

And that was it: I stayed there for sixteen hours, together with Johnsey and Schnitzel, on a low chair in the kitchen. I didn't get up to drink, I didn't get up to eat, and I didn't go to the bathroom. I just sat there with my loaded gun until they came to rescue me. I swore to myself that I'd make it, that I'd survive, so that Emily wouldn't lose me. And that's what happened.

I can't even describe how brave those soldiers were. At eleven o'clock at night, they knock at my door. There's still fighting going on in the kibbutz, so we're rescued under fire. We walk toward the kibbutz gate surrounded by commando soldiers and armored vehicles, stopping every few minutes. I ask them about Narkis and about the Rotem family; they tell me that they don't know anything, but they send soldiers to check their homes right away. And that's how I find out that Narkis has been murdered. And that the Rotem's house is empty.

For three days, Emily was classified as "missing." For three days, no one had any idea what had become of her. And I'm going mad; I don't even know what to do with myself. I had grasped the magnitude of the event, I had found out about all the horrors, I knew they had taken masses of hostages; I heard how they'd abused them, how those barbarians, those beasts, had abused people.

I heard what Hamas had done in the kibbutz, even under fire; now, in Gaza, without the IDF around to stop them, they could do anything that their sick minds might come up with! They could fulfill their sickest, most twisted fantasies! The barbarians, the monsters! And the thought that there was even a slight chance that my Emily had been taken hostage – I couldn't even breathe when I thought about that. It was horrible.

On the tenth of October some members of the kibbutz came to me and informed me that they had found Emily inside the kibbutz, and she was dead. And when I heard that, I shouted "Yes!!!" I screamed and cried and screamed again, "Yes!!!" because that was better, it was better than her being in the hands of Hamas. To be in the hands of Hamas was a fate worse than death; out of the two possibilities, death was the better option in my eyes.

I go into a dark grief, the darkest, deepest grief. We're all completely crushed. Natalie and Aiden are mourning their mother; now they're mourning their little sister, too. We don't even have her body. Everything is terrible. I agreed to an interview with CNN; I was completely wrecked and hardly managed to speak. In that interview, I told them how I'd reacted when I heard that Emily was murdered. And that interview went viral, it spread everywhere. Every possible channel approached me for an interview, and I just wanted them to leave me alone, I just wanted to stay close to Aiden and Natalie and never leave their side. But I realized that this was an opportunity for me to do something for the country. So I pulled myself up by my bootstraps and sat through all the interviews. To speak out. To let the whole world know.

In the interviews I speak about her, about my Emily, my pure angel. I tell them how Emily was full of light; how she loved to dance and sing and play music. I tell them how she could have done anything she wanted; that if she failed at something, she wouldn't give up! She'd try again and again until she succeeded. And I tell them what a natural leader she was, how she drew others to her from such a young age. And how she spread love, and everyone loved her. I finish by saying that we had to wipe Hamas out completely, completely! I'd shout, "We have to end it now! They started it, and we're going to end it! Full stop!"

⚜

That's how it went on for twenty days. We were far from home, evacuated to a hotel in the Dead Sea with the rest of the kibbutz. Every few days I'd give another interview and talk about my Emily. And then, on October 30th, I suddenly get a phone call from the army: "Thomas, we're not sure that Emily is dead. What they told you about the girl they found on the kibbutz seems to be a case of mistaken identity. We're very sorry."

That threw me back into my worst nightmare. Each victim of October 7th was declared either missing, kidnapped, or dead. Emily was first declared missing, then dead, and now she was "missing" again! It was terrible! That sense of uncertainty was simply unbearable. The thoughts lodged in my head like knives. I kept imagining the worst. I imagined her body tossed in the bushes; I imagined her inside the tunnels; I imagined terrible things.

And then a week later, on November 6th, I'm sitting in the hotel lobby when I suddenly see someone running toward me, flying toward me, someone I know from the kibbutz, and she comes up to me and says, "Tom, listen! Listen!" She's all breathless from running, and she stops to catch her breath; she can barely speak and says, "There's this caretaker from the kibbutz, an Indian woman, and she saw her! She saw her with her two daughters!" and I don't understand what she's trying to tell me, and I ask, "Who saw whom, when, where?!" and she sits next to me and takes my hand and says, "Thomas, Tom, listen! There's this Indian woman who says that she saw Raaya being kidnapped with her two daughters. Thomas! Raaya only has one daughter!"

⚜

Raaya was kidnapped into Gaza with Emily and Hila. On October 7th, at half past noon, the terrorists took them out of the safe room. From what I learned, there was no resistance, no dragging, no violence; they just put the three of them in the backseat of their getaway car and drove them straight to a hideout in Gaza. They were there along with a few other hostages, including Itay Svirsky, who was later murdered in captivity. Horrible.

From that point on, they're moved from one hiding place to another within Gaza, sometimes switching places every day. And Hamas starves them. Sometimes they get a pita a day, sometimes half a pita, sometimes just a quarter, and they're hungry, hungry, hungry. Constantly. The water they were given to drink was bitter, very nasty to swallow. And they aren't allowed to talk; they can only whisper. If they laugh, if they accidentally make a peep, if someone cries just a little too loud, a terrorist comes in with a knife and says, "*Uskut!*" Be quiet, or I'll kill you!

The only things they had there, to pass the time, were sheets of paper and markers that they asked for and got. And they had a pack of cards. And they had each other. Even though it was forbidden to speak, forbidden to laugh, forbidden to breathe, Emily and Hila would make each other laugh. In captivity, they still made each other laugh! They worked so hard to find things to laugh about, to make each other laugh, and they'd laugh together. Silently. Without any noise. Silent laughter.

And the whole time, Raaya cares for Emily as if she is her own daughter. She makes sure she eats, she washes her as best as she can – not with a real shower, but over a bowl or sink, with a rag and some lukewarm water. She also cuts Emily's hair short so it's easier to take care of. She really takes her under her wing. And if you think about it, for those two months, Raaya became Emily's third mother. After Liat and Narkis. It's just mad, really.

When it hits me that Emily has been taken hostage, all the strength I've lost comes right back to me, just like that! Ever since the massacre, I had been completely broken. I lost thirteen kilos; I was weak and ill. But when I heard that Emily was alive, I felt like my light had come back.

From that moment on, I had one goal: to bring her back. I realized that maybe, just maybe I can help make that happen because she has Irish citizenship. If I can make Hamas realize that Emily has Irish citizenship, if I can set off some kind of diplomatic snowball effect, stir up some international pressure, then maybe, just maybe, my daughter will come back to me in one piece.

On the day I found out that Emily was being held hostage, a CNN crew was at the hotel. I asked them for an interview, and I told them that Emily was being held hostage and that she has two passports: Israeli and Irish. So that Hamas would know that they were holding an Irish citizen hostage! And I thought to myself, if Hamas have a television, if they hear this interview, they'll realize that they now have Ireland to deal with as well. But that's not enough; I need to get Ireland on our side. And even that's not enough – Ireland has to realize that it's their duty to bring Emily back! Ireland must take action! So I reach out to media consultants, to an amazing group of people, who take the plunge with me into a massive international project: to bring Emily back immediately!

Aiden and Natalie join the fight at this point. Natalie is our Hebrew spokesperson; I'm our English spokesperson; Aiden deals with the politicians. Within just a few days, Emily becomes the face of all the hostages. I do as many interviews as possible, on every possible platform, and always, no matter how brief the interview, I make sure to mention three things: first of all, we have over two hundred people being held hostage in Gaza! Second, my daughter Emily is only eight, but she's being held hostage! And third, Emily is an Irish citizen! An Irish girl is being held hostage!

Some of the channels that interviewed me were rabidly anti-Israel: they would say that Israel is enforcing "apartheid" and they'd refer to Hamas as "soldiers" or even "freedom fighters." They showed me no compassion when they interviewed me; they were very, very annoying. So I gave it to them: "We're living it! We've been living it every day for twenty years. You have absolutely no idea, you don't even have the right to speak to me! Have you actually been to Israel? Have you ever seen this so-called 'apartheid' you're talking about? It doesn't exist, you fools! It doesn't exist! Come to any city in this country, come to any school, come to any hospital – you'll see Arab patients alongside Jewish patients,

Arab doctors alongside Jewish doctors, Arab women who are doctors and university professors! You have no idea what you're going on about. Those 'educated' students protesting also have absolutely no idea." Oh yes, when I need to, I definitely know how to let it out.

Within a few days, I get a message that there are three people – quite important people – who have heard Emily's story, and they want to meet me: the Prime Minister of Ireland, the President of Ireland, and the Foreign Minister of Ireland. Natalie joins me, and we fly out to meet with them. When I spoke with the Irish Prime Minister, Leo Varadkar, he told me that in the two weeks since it became known that Emily had been taken hostage, he'd been to Qatar twice, and he was soon flying to Iran, Syria, and Lebanon to put pressure on Hamas to release my little girl! I was so moved. I realized that I had achieved my first goal: Ireland was in the picture.

After that, we flew to New York, spoke to as many people with influence as we could, and managed to get Emily's picture on a billboard in Times Square! They put her face on one of the digital billboards there. Usually, the ads only appear for a short time, but Emily was up there for more than an hour! I kept giving interviews wherever I could. To all the shows, all the newspapers; I wanted the whole world to know.

And then one day, when I was in London at a huge demonstration for Israel, I suddenly get a phone call from back home. They say to me, "There's a very good chance a deal is going to be made. There's a very good chance that they'll start releasing hostages soon, including children; Emily might be released soon." At that moment, we canceled all our speaking engagements and flew back to Israel.

After forty-eight days in captivity, the terrorists come to Emily and tell her she's about to be released. I have no idea if she even knew that that was possible. I don't know if it occurred to her that one day she'd actually leave that prison. And the first thing Emily says when she hears that is: "What about Hila and Raaya!" and they say, "They're not getting out; you're being released because you have an Irish passport." But Emily isn't prepared to accept it. Full stop. She won't budge without Hila and

Raaya. And she starts crying, crying uncontrollably, saying that there's no way, absolutely no way that she's leaving without Raaya and Hila.

She wasn't freed the next day either. She simply refused to be freed. And they must have realized that they can't let her out against her will. They can't allow themselves to show the world that image, the image of a girl screaming and being dragged out of a Red Cross van. It's not a good optic. So when they saw that she wouldn't budge, they said to her, "Fine, tomorrow you and Hila are both getting released." It was horrible. They basically forced Hila to leave Raaya; they tore a child away from her mother. It was a violation of the agreement – they weren't allowed to separate children from their mothers. So Hamas just lied; they said they "don't know where Raaya is." As usual, they were lying through their teeth. The beasts.

Emily and Hila came home after fifty days in captivity; in the end, Raaya was freed four days later. That's what happened.

When I drove to the base where I was supposed to meet Emily, I brought Johnsey, her dog, along with me. I brought him because I wanted Emily to be able to hug someone; I wasn't sure she'd want to hug me. I didn't know how she felt about me. I mean, I'd failed her that day; I was the father who had failed to protect his daughter. And I didn't know how Emily felt about me during all those days in captivity. I was afraid she'd blame me; I was afraid she would be cross with me. After all, on the worst day of her life, I wasn't there for her. But I knew that she definitely wasn't cross with Johnsey. A dog is pure love. He wasn't the one who'd failed to keep her safe that day.

But when Emily arrived, she ran to me and hugged me. And hugged me, and hugged me, and hugged me. And I hugged her back, and I wept; I hugged her so hard and wept so hard. I've never cried like that my whole life. And on the way, when we were driven from the base to the hospital, I noticed that Emily never took her eyes off me, not even for a moment. And I ask, "Emily, my love, talk to me, tell me what's going through your head," and she says – silently, for fifty days she wasn't allowed to talk out loud, so she spoke silently and I had to read her lips. I made out the words – "Daddy, I thought you were dead, I thought that they had kidnapped you, I thought that I'd never ever see you again," and I start crying, and I ask her, "You're not cross with me?" and Emily doesn't even understand why I'm asking her that. She looks at me and mouths the words, "Thank you for not being dead, Daddy. Thank you, Daddy, for being alive."

May We Take the Path of Light

Awad Darawsha's Story

Age 25

As told by Awad's father, Mussa

📍 *Nova Festival*

I remember once, when Awad was still little, a little boy, he and his brothers did something at home – they made a mess, there was a racket, and all his brothers and sisters ran away, they scattered, and only Awad stayed behind. So I come and see him there, sitting there all calm, looking at me, and I say to him, "Why aren't you getting up? You must have been the one who made this mess!" and he stands there right in front of me, like a little fiend! And he says to me, "Why are you angry, Dad? If I had done it, I would have run away too, but I didn't do it, so why should I run away?" And I believed him, and I said to him, "You know what? You're in the right, it's true, it wasn't you." He had a good head on his shoulders, that boy. And he had the courage to face me. And he had a good heart.

He had a big heart. In our village, Iksal, they're still coming by to offer condolences to us. His teacher came and told us that he once gave her a birthday present, he gave her a little necklace, and another teacher told us that he once gave her a flower. That was the kind of heart he had. Not every kid remembers his teacher's birthday like that, but he had lists, he would remember dates, his aunt's birthday, his uncle's, his siblings'. And even at work, at the United Hatzalah ambulance corps, even there he remembered everyone, and was friends with everyone.

He wasn't a loafer; he was a diligent kid. When there wasn't work with the ambulance, he would work as a waiter at a wedding hall; when there wasn't work there, he worked as a cook, as a cook's assistant. He knew how to cook, too. He would cook everything – fish, meat, shrimp. He had a good head on his shoulders; he'd go to work at the wedding hall, and the whole evening he'd serve his table, and he'd welcome people, "*Ahlan*, how can I help you, what can I bring you." He'd speak nicely, and they'd tip him, he'd come back home with a thousand shekels. He had a head, that kid. He was a good boy. A good boy.

He started medical school in Georgia. He studied there for a year but then came back; it was a mess there during Covid. But he had plans to go back and finish his studies there and become a doctor. He was always thinking ahead. In the meantime, he studied to become a paramedic and work for "Yossi Ambulance." There's this company, "Yossi Ambulance," and they loved him there; how they loved him! They taught him to be a paramedic and kept giving him more work, and he would work for hours there, hours. I said to him, "You should leave; you're always on the road!" and he said, "It's good for me, Dad." He was a worker.

He was our youngest child, but he helped me the most. He was always helping; he'd come to my work and say to me, "Go rest, Dad, just tell me what to do and I'll do it, explain to me what to do, what to add, what to join together, how to turn it on; you rest." I'm a contractor, and he would tag along; he liked to help me a lot. Sometimes he'd come back from school and make food and bring the food to me at work, and say to me, "Dad, come sit and eat – just tell me what to do."

We were always dreaming together. We wanted to build him a house, to buy him a house and then to make him a wedding; there were big plans. He was the angel of the house, an angel; he was always hugging his sisters and giving them kisses; he was our light. And now we're alone, looking each other in the eye every few seconds. And that's it, it's gone; our life is ruined. Every night his mother and I, we pray that he'll come to us in a dream, but he doesn't come, not even in a dream. *Inshallah*, with the help of God, may he come to us in a dream.

Awad went down south on Thursday; he took his ATV cart with him; there was an ATV there that he parked next to the ambulance. When he left the house, he still didn't know exactly where he was going. Why? Because he had been at a similar event the week before, in the Arava region, where Awad worked as a paramedic, so he thought that he was going there again.

Before he left, his mother brought him food. Awad, he loved bringing food for the whole crew; he brought them home-made *labaneh* with olive oil and *za'atar* and pita; he'd bring everything and they'd love it; he did that a lot. And that was it; he drove off, he said to us, "Guys, I'm going for three days, bye bye, see ya," and he left.

They had an event on Thursday and another event on Friday; he treated a few people there, it was hot, they got dehydrated, and he helped them. And that night – that night was the party. Okay, he was used to it; he worked at a lot of events like that, people come sometimes, they don't feel well, they pass out, nothing serious. That's what parties are like.

The next day, on Saturday, he didn't even talk to anyone; we didn't know anything. I was actually in the hospital. Why? Because I had pain in my lungs, and friends said to go to the hospital and get it checked out. Only later, in the afternoon, we began to realize that something was happening; we called him and he didn't answer, we didn't hear from him at all. And I was in hospital with a pain in my lungs; I couldn't breathe. And I couldn't understand why I couldn't breathe. By God, I understand now.

We don't know much. We still haven't sorted it out, haven't spoken to people. What we do know is that the missiles started, then the first wave of terrorists came and started shooting there, and threw grenades, I don't know what else they threw, and people there got wounded in their arms, legs, everywhere, so they started treating them, and he, the paramedic, and the nurse who was with him started treating people, bandaging them up, helping them. At the beginning they treated a lot of people.

He had an ATV and was driving back and forth to bring the wounded to the tent. He drove up to the party area and brought the wounded back; it was like that. But then the terrorists started coming, shooting there, spraying bullets, and everyone ran away; all the paramedics there ran away, and there was a girl with him there, a nurse, and she started crying, and he gave her a hug and said to her, "We don't have time for that now. Pick yourself up, let's be strong! You'll be blessed! Pick yourself up!" and he said the same thing to the Bedouin guy who was there. He helped them run away from there.

And everyone really was running away, and the second paramedic said to him, "Awad, get up and run away! Don't be stupid; get up!" but Awad said to him, "You run away; I'll work it out with them."

Those were the last words that Awad spoke to him: "I'll work it out with them." He thought that he'd speak to them in Arabic, like, they'd talk about the Koran or something. He thought he could be the angel of that battle. He didn't know that they didn't care – about that or about anything.

So he stayed behind; he stayed where the wounded were. He didn't leave them. Even though he was the youngest member of their team, he was the one who stayed behind to take care of the wounded, all by himself. And from there, he wrote to Yossi, to the ambulance owner; he wrote to him, "There's a real mess here, a battle; we need help, where's the state, there are a lot of people coming here in their cars and on foot." That's what he wrote him at ten in the morning. Then more wounded kept coming to him there, and he treated them, too; he was all alone there but he kept treating them, and some of them, some of the wounded he treated survived. That's why the president of Israel who came here said to me that Awad was a hero of the war.

He was killed there in the tent; they shot him twice in the heart, two bullets right in the left side. When they found his body, they found him holding bandages; he was still running back and forth to bandage people. Only his wounds had no one to bandage them up. When I came to see him, when they brought me the body, when I saw him, he was lying there with a smile on his face! And the people checked him and said to me, He's completely clean, like new; nothing's missing except for two bullet holes on his left side where the heart is. His face was so beautiful, so beautiful. He was an angel, a bridegroom! What a face he had. Anyone who saw him said, I swear, Awad is even better-looking now than when he was alive.

✑

Who wasn't there at his funeral? There were Muslims, Druze, Christians, Jews, Circassians; who wasn't at Awad's funeral. For us, it's forbidden for women to go to funerals, but all the women stood there in the street! They all stood in the street and looked at the coffin. Who wasn't there; who didn't make a prayer? I have a rabbi friend who said a prayer for Awad; I have a priest friend from Nazareth who said a prayer for Awad. Afterward people came to comfort us, people I don't even know! Arabs, Jews, they came from Modi'in; they came from the north, they told me, I heard about your son; they came with hugs, and I welcomed them all, I welcome all guests, all people.

Awad was a child of the village, not just my son. People from the village didn't say to me, "We're sorry for your loss," no! They said, "Awad is our son! He's the son who left our home," that's what they all said to me. And I swear, I got so much strength from these people. I'm a person who cries easily, I'm a sensitive person. But I stood there and welcomed these people. There were thousands of thousands of people. They gave me strength. They blessed me with strength.

Me – that's it; I've had my tragedy. But I pray, I pray that now, after what happened to us, we'll be able to live in peace and quiet. We have to make a change in our lives; we are here together, we need to accept each other and live together. We can have a great country, a great world; I don't know why we are like this. Why life is like this. Why we have to live like this, I don't know.

Why shouldn't there be quiet; why shouldn't there be peace? Why can't we all live together? I mean, how long do I have to live? Seventy, eighty, maybe ninety years – in the end, I'll leave this earth. This earth isn't mine or anyone else's. So come, let's live in peace, let's live like that, loving each other, respecting each other. How did we turn into animals here? How were we created; how does God want us to live? Even animals have hearts that are better than ours.

Really, I'm ready to accept it, to give up on Awad and to say, *Yalla*, let's go; the final tragedy was mine, but from now on it will be better, quieter, brighter. *Inshallah!* God willing, may we walk along this path, the path of the moon. Come, let's start over and make light.

Glossary of Terms and Abbreviations

APC – Armored personnel carrier, a tank-like military vehicle designed
    for transporting soldiers and equipment in combat zones

Ashkenazi – European Jews and their descendants

Bedouin – Arab tribes with a traditionally nomadic lifestyle. Many Israeli
    Bedouin citizens serve with distinction in the IDF.

Caracal Battalion – Light infantry battalion known for being one of the
    first units in which women serve in combat roles alongside men

challah – Festive loaves of bread baked for the Sabbath and holidays

civilian security team (Hebrew: *kitat konenut*) – Volunteer team of armed
    first-responders in Israeli towns. Led by a head of security, also
    called civilian security coordinator (Hebrew: *ravshatz*)

Disengagement – The unilateral Israeli withdrawal in 2005 of all its sol-
    diers and citizens from the Gaza Strip

Druze – Religious offshoot from Islam. Druze speak Arabic, and their
    communities lie primarily in the territory of Israel, Syria, and
    Lebanon. Most Israeli Druze men serve in the IDF.

Duvdevan – Elite IDF commando unit notable for undercover opera-
    tions in urban areas

Egoz – Elite IDF commando unit specializing in guerrilla warfare, mainly
    operating in Lebanon

First response team – see civilian security team

Flotilla (Shayetet) 13 – Elite commando unit of the Israeli Navy (like
    US Navy SEALS)

Gaza Envelope – Southwestern region of Israel bordering on the Gaza Strip

Givati Brigade – One of the main IDF infantry brigades

Golani Brigade – One of the main IDF infantry brigades

Hatzalah – International Jewish volunteer emergency medical response service

IDF – Israel Defense Forces

Iron Dome – Mobile air defense system tasked with intercepting missiles fired at Israel

jahnun – Yemenite pastry

kibbutz – Communal settlement based on egalitarian principles where all resources go into a common pool

kiddush – Blessing recited over wine on the Sabbath and holidays

kippa – Yarmulke, skullcap worn by Jewish males

Lotar – IDF special counter-terrorism unit

Magen David Adom (MDA) – Israel's national emergency service (like the Red Cross)

mobile shelter (Hebrew: *migunit*) – A fortified protective space installed in open areas, designed to provide immediate protection against rocket and mortar attacks when the warning time is too short to reach an underground or indoor bomb shelter

National Service (Hebrew: *Sherut Leumi*) – Performed by some Israeli citizens, including many young Orthodox women, in lieu of mandatory military service

payot – Men's sidelocks of hair, grown long in some Orthodox Jewish communities as an interpretation of the biblical command not to shave the sides of one's head

Purim – Jewish holiday in the early spring celebrating the deliverance of the Jews in the Persian Empire from the plot of Haman to destroy them, as recounted in the book of Esther

Red Alert – Siren and alert system notifying Israeli citizens of incoming mortar and rocket fire. The alerts also indicate how much time one has to get to a bomb shelter.

RPG – Rocket-propelled grenade

safe room (Hebrew: *mamad*) – Reinforced room in Israeli homes to protect from mortar and rocket fire

Sayeret Matkal – IDF's special reconnaissance unit (like US Delta Force)

Shabbat – The Jewish Sabbath

shakshuka – Popular Middle Eastern breakfast dish consisting of eggs poached in a tomato sauce

Shaldag – Elite special forces unit of the Israeli Air Force

Shavuot – Jewish holiday celebrating the giving of the Torah and the wheat harvest

Shin Bet (Shabak) – Israel's domestic security agency (like the FBI in the US)

shiva – The traditional first week of mourning in Judaism

Simchat Torah – A festival following the Jewish holiday of Sukkot; this holiday celebrates the completion of the annual cycle of synagogue Torah reading

sukkah – An outdoor hut used ritually during the harvest holiday of Sukkot

Talmud Torah – Ultra-Orthodox elementary school, teaching primarily or solely the Scriptures and Jewish law

Torah – The Five Books of Moses, or, more broadly, the corpus of Jewish religious literature

tzitzit – Rectangular garment with fringes on all four corners, traditionally worn by Jewish males

vatikin – Early morning prayers

yeshiva – Jewish religious seminary

Yom Kippur – The Day of Atonement, a solemn day of Jewish fasting and prayer, considered the holiest day of the year

ZAKA – Israeli volunteer emergency organization, comprised mostly of Orthodox Jews, specializing in search and rescue operations and in collecting and identifying victims of disaster or terrorism

A Brief Overview of the Events of October 7th, 2023, Their Background, and Their Aftermath

Yonah Jeremy Bob

The Gaza Strip is an area southwest of Israel, approximately the size of the city of Philadelphia, with a population about 50 percent larger. Israel is approximately the size of the state of New Jersey, with a similar size population. From 1948 to 1967, the Gaza Strip was ruled by Egypt, and from 1967 to 2005 by Israel. In 2005, Israel withdrew completely from the Gaza Strip, removing around eight thousand of its citizens from twenty-one towns, handing over the governance of the Strip to the Palestinian Authority (PA), the leading Palestinian governing body at the time, and transferring control over the Philadelphi Corridor (the border between the Gaza Strip and Egypt) to the PA and Egypt. Not a single Israeli was left in Gaza.

In 2007, Hamas, declared a terror organization by many Western countries because of its commitment to Israel's destruction, carried out a coup against the PA and took control of Gaza. Israel responded by imposing a naval and land blockade with the cooperation of Egypt, meant to prevent Iran from smuggling large rockets and advanced weapons to Hamas. At the same time, Israel facilitated trade, travel, and humanitarian aid for Gaza via land crossings subject to security inspections, and, in periods of quiet, also allowed thousands of workers to cross the border daily to work in Israel.

Peace talks between Israel and the PA in 2007–8 and in 2014 made some progress but never resulted in a deal. Hamas consistently rejected the peace process. Instead, Hamas and Israel fought smaller conflicts in 2008–9, 2012, 2014 (at fifty days, the longest conflict until the current war), and 2021.

Islamic Jihad, another Iranian proxy based in Gaza, fought several shorter rounds with Israel during that period, including attacks as recently as August 2022 and May 2023.

Throughout its rule, Hamas siphoned foreign aid money to arm itself with rockets and other armaments and to build an extensive network of hundreds of miles of military tunnels and command rooms underneath civilian areas. Tunnels were also built into Egypt to facilitate smuggling of weapons and other items, as well as into Israel to allow terror attacks, until many of the latter were cut off by Israel's construction of a border fence. Israel high-tech border fence was also designed to enhance surveillance and to enable remote fire, reducing the number of troops patrolling the border.

During the May 2021 conflict, Hamas fired around 4,360 rockets in just eleven days, with Israel counterstriking with around 1,500 aerial and other strikes. Between 2007 and October 7th, 2023, Israel's strategy had been to deter and contain Hamas, but not to topple it as long as relative quiet could be maintained, even temporarily. Israel adhered to this strategy despite fairly regular rocket fire from Gaza on Israeli communities near the border.

OCTOBER 7TH

At 6:29 a.m. on Saturday, October 7th, 2023, on the Jewish holiday of Simchat Torah, Hamas began the worst rocket barrage on Israel's home front in history, showering the area with around three thousand rockets in only four hours. Almost simultaneously, Hamas neutralized the surveillance and firing capacities of the border fence and invaded Israel in over sixty different spots to take over twenty-two separate villages.

Israel's top political and defense officials were shocked by the attack and did not succeed in reestablishing a line of defense and deploying forces to the area until around one p.m., by which time most of the approximately 250 hostages were already taken by Hamas's three thousand invaders, and massive numbers of Israelis had already been killed.

The organized invasion by Hamas's trained fighters was followed by waves of other Gazans who entered the border communities through the breached fences and joined in pillage and murder.

The largest mass killing in any one area was by Hamas at the Supernova Sukkot Gathering, also known as the **Nova Festival**, an open-air music festival near **Kibbutz Re'im**. During the attack on the festival, 364 civilians were killed and 44 hostages taken. Many acts of sexual violence and other acts of extreme brutality were committed at this location and numerous others.

During the invasion, small kibbutz and cooperative farming communities in the Gaza Envelope (the area in Israel bordering the Gaza Strip) were hit hard. Several **army outposts** near the Gaza border were undermanned and overrun by overwhelmingly larger Hamas forces, which disabled military communications.

This led to a number of complete security breakdowns. For example, in **Kibbutz Be'eri**, 134 residents were killed, and thirty-three hostages were taken – of whom eleven are still being held by Hamas in Gaza (as of the time of this writing, July 2024), 150 houses were destroyed, and a mere twenty-odd Israeli fighters were up against eighty to three hundred Hamas terrorists for hours. Larger Israeli reinforcements only arrived in the early afternoon, partly because Hamas terrorists took over the area's main traffic artery, Route 232, ambushing and blocking their path until the Israeli troops eventually succeeded in beating back the Hamas forces.

Separately, sixty-four residents of **Kfar Aza** were massacred by Hamas, nineteen were taken hostage, and five remain hostages of the terror group as of this writing. At the high point of the fighting in Kfar Aza, twenty different IDF units fought there against four hundred to six hundred Hamas forces.

In **Nir Oz**, thirty-one residents were killed and eighty-six taken hostage. Sayeret Matkal and Egoz special forces units were sent to help the Nir Oz residents on a multi-hour delay, not realizing how bad the situation was. Both of those units were ambushed at key junctions on the way to Nir Oz and never got there. By the time two other units – the Border Police and the Flotilla 13 Navy commandos – arrived at around one-thirty p.m., Hamas had already left the village with its hostages.

Cities near the border also suffered. Around fifty residents of **Sderot** were killed, and a small number were taken hostage, while the entire 35,000-plus person city was evacuated for several months.

While most of the invaded Israeli communities were very close to the border, Hamas also killed fifty-two residents of **Ofakim**, the city being the farthest Hamas advanced in Israel – around fifteen miles from Gaza.

IMMEDIATE AFTERMATH FOR ISRAEL

Between October 7 and October 11–12, the IDF, the Border Police, and the Shin Bet had cleared out all of Hamas invaders, having themselves lost around 375 combat fighters out of the total of over 1,200 Israelis and foreign residents killed. Around 1,500 of the Hamas invaders were said to be killed, with significant numbers having also been arrested, while others returned to Gaza with hostages.

By October 13, 1,076 Israeli bodies had been recovered, but only 361 had been identified, with many bodies having been mutilated, torn apart, or burned. Some bodies took months to identify and could only be named after a complex DNA testing process performed by Israel's top forensics institute. For months it was also unclear whether some persons were taken to Gaza dead or alive, as Israeli forces continued to search for body parts and other indications.

Around 130,000 people were evacuated from Israel's south, with rocket fire from Hamas continuing in high volumes until December 2023 to January 2024. Most of them were initially moved to hotels in Jerusalem, Tel Aviv, Eilat, near the Dead Sea, and other areas across the country, while some were placed temporarily in schools and other publicly owned locations.

Within months, the government started to relocate large numbers of the residents to longer-term, if still temporary, housing in a variety of communities. On January 1, 2024, the IDF also cleared six villages for their residents to return home, including three in the Ashkelon corridor, followed by three in the Shaar HaNegev region, but it has taken much longer to return various other residents, while there are some communities which may not be rebuilt at all.

From October 8 and especially from October 12 onward, the IDF started to bombard Gaza, especially northern Gaza, with a large number of airstrikes and artillery attacks to pave the way for an invasion. The full invasion started on October 27, and by mid-November, the IDF had killed another 3,500 Hamas terrorists while entering Gaza City and large swaths of the rest of northern Gaza.

The IDF collected massive amounts of armaments and intelligence, destroyed rocket launchers and production facilities, and set about slowly dismantling the tunnel network and Hamas command structure. The IDF would invade Khan Yunis on December 1, taking control by early February, and would invade Rafah on May 6, completing the main campaign there by mid-June.

Other consequences for Israel of the October 7th invasion and massacre include massive fire of aerial threats by the Lebanese terror group Hezbollah on Israel's north, leading to the evacuation of approximately 80,000 Israeli civilians and escalating cross-border exchanges of fire; the firing of 300 aerial threats by Iran on Israel on April 13–14, 2024; attacks by the Yemenite Houthis on shipping in the Red Sea and on Israel; and anti-Israel and pro-Hamas demonstrations throughout Europe and North America, leading to a wave of global antisemitism unseen in eight decades.

Yonah Jeremy Bob is the Senior Military and Intelligence Analyst of the Jerusalem Post *and author of* Target Tehran *(Simon & Schuster, 2023).*

Red Alerts, Bomb Shelters, and Safe Rooms

Readers outside of Israel may have trouble grasping the details of what happened on October 7th without an introduction to how integral bomb shelters and safe rooms have become to Israeli life, especially in towns near the border with the Gaza Strip.

The 1951 Israeli civil defense law requires that all public and private buildings have access to a shelter. The Hebrew term is *merchav mugan*, which literally means "protected space."

In 1992, the Home Front Command published new technical specifications for designated protected spaces in family homes. These include reinforced concrete floors and ceilings, eight- to twelve-inch thick walls, and airtight steel doors and windows. The safe room can withstand blast and shrapnel from conventional weapons and offers protection against chemical and biological weapons.

Older buildings generally have old, dank, and cramped shelters, though some very old apartment buildings don't have shelters at all. In that case, when a siren sounds, the residents rush into the stairwell for the slight protection that may offer.

In newer homes, however, these reinforced spaces are skillfully designed to function as an additional room in the house, a room with airtight, shockproof windows and heavy metal doors. Many southern residents have turned their shelters into a children's bedroom so that children can go on sleeping undisturbed as the rest of the family rushes in for shelter in the middle of the night.

Rocket attacks on Israeli towns near the Gaza Strip began in 2001. They increased in 2005 after Israel's disengagement from Gaza, and the IDF created an early warning siren system for the region. These sirens are known as "Red Alerts," and they give residents of the Gaza Envelope seven to fifteen seconds to run for shelter before an incoming rocket hits.

In 2008, after the Defense Ministry assessed that most rocket-related injuries and fatalities in the area had been caused by shrapnel wounds received when people were out in the open, the government placed fortified bus-stops and mobile shelters throughout the region (with 120 in Sderot alone), so that people would have immediate access to shelter wherever they were. Even local playground equipment includes concrete pipes for children to crawl through or shelter in.

Since 2001, tens of thousands of rockets have been launched at Israel from Gaza, resulting in extensive physical and psychological damage in the region. Imagine running to take shelter in the middle of a shower or rushing to a concrete bus-stop on the way to school or work. This has become part of daily life in the region.

Many of the stories in this book revolve around shelters. On October 7th, when the sirens began sounding, several participants in the Nova Festival ran to the concrete protected spaces in the area. Terrorists attacked them there, crowded into the shelters, like sitting ducks.

Several stories that take place in the kibbutzim involve families waiting in the safe room (or "home shelter") for rescue. As Red Alerts generally last just a few minutes, families did not store food or water in the safe room, nor do the safe rooms have bathroom facilities. The safe room doors don't usually lock; they are not intended to protect against infiltration but rather against mortars and rockets. This is why most of the families on the kibbutzim had to bar their safe room doors from the inside or hold the handles in an (often vain) attempt to keep terrorists out.

Acknowledgments

*O*ne Day in October is a documentary project that was complex on many levels: logistical, psychological, and emotional. To our great fortune, our team was made up of outstandingly talented, dedicated, and sensitive professionals.

Gal Abdu helped us build our database of heroes with wisdom and keen understanding. Lilach Hachmon located and contacted the heroes with outstanding professional expertise and great sensitivity. Though the two of us – Yair and Oriya – met some of them ourselves, most of the interviews were conducted by our dedicated team of interviewers, who conducted raw, deep, and delicate conversations with great sensitivity and skill: Michal Kurnedz connected with each person she interviewed; Or Menachem, who is a light and a comfort, true to the meaning of her name; pleasant and hardworking Moshe Yehuda Ackerman, who wanted to know everything about everyone; and Gal Abdu, who sees and brings out the best in everyone with whom he speaks. Your professionalism, nuance, sense of responsibility, and deep care for each person you interviewed; the sage advice you offered to help us hone and perfect each story from angles only you were able to appreciate; and your comforting, warm encouragement at every step along the way were an endless source of strength and help. Dear interviewers, each page of this book is steeped in the goodness of your hearts and your life experiences. Thank you.

When we first approached Evelyn Landau about transcription, we were sure that the task was purely technical. We didn't realize how lucky we were that we happened to turn to a professional transcriber who coupled dedication, skill, and efficiency with sensitivity and heart. We would like to take this opportunity to remember her dear brother Corporal Andrey (Diushtamskiy) Landau, of blessed memory, who died at the age of twenty-one, out of love for this country. May he rest in peace.

Deep thanks are due to Leron Bernstein, who managed the original Hebrew project with skill, humor, and devotion. Dear Leron, it was an absolute gift to work with you. We also are deeply indebted to the wonderful Caryn Meltz, who managed the production of the book in English with consummate professionalism alongside her characteristic grace and kindness.

Sara Daniel translated the book with a keen eye, great enthusiasm, and astonishing efficiency, and also contributed the appendix on Red Alerts. Thank you Sara; it has truly been a privilege to work with you on this, as always. As language editor, Dr. Will Lee graced the book with his literary sensibility and decades of experience. Yedidya Naveh and Kate Gerstler made very helpful suggestions that improved the final product. Yardenne Greenspan sensitively edited a number of chapters, checking them against the original. Yonah Jeremy Bob expertly and efficiently authored the appendix on the historical background.

Special mention must go to Laurie Novick. As soon as the book came out in Hebrew, Laurie recognized the great importance of producing an English edition; Laurie then voluntarily threw herself into an in-depth translation review, applying her considerable skills, linguistic sensitivity, and sound judgement to capturing the nuances of the original while adapting the book for a new audience. Laurie, thank you for your wisdom and endless devotion. Your contribution to this book has been invaluable.

We would like to thank the diligent, brilliant, and very patient Dov Abramson for the book's bright, hopeful cover, and Tani Bayer for adapting it for the English edition. Thank you to Tomi Mager and

Rina Ben Gal for the meticulous typesetting, to Efrat Gross for her sharp eye, sage advice, and endless dedication, and to Alex Drucker and Talya Lurie for their commitment and their marketing and public relations expertise. Gabi Rosenthal and Eliyahu Misgav managed to advise and to help even while they were on reserve duty.

The data for the map was collated by Moshe Yehuda Ackerman and Ronni Rachel Greenfeld with astonishing attention to detail, and Shmooel Lasry's visual genius brought it all together. Thanks also to military consultant Sgt. (res.) Ariel Ziegler and research assistant Ayala Meltz for their help.

Heartfelt thanks are due to the team of visionaries at Koren Jerusalem, the parent company of The Toby Press. Editorial Director Reuven Ziegler came up with the idea for this book and accompanied the process from beginning to end with wisdom, sensitivity, and rare humanity. Subsequent to the publication in Hebrew, he also oversaw and thoroughly reviewed the English translation, working day and night with inspiring dedication to achieve the best possible result. We authors could rest assured knowing that the book was in the most expert hands. Thank you, Reuven, for your brilliant work, your concern, your talent, your literary sensitivity, and your infectious idealism. CEO Yehoshua Miller encouraged this project with faith, support, and help, even during reserve duty in Gaza. Publisher Matthew Miller expressed enthusiasm for this project from its inception and enabled us to set up the talented, hardworking team who brought this complex work to fruition. Thank you to Director of Development Aryeh Grossman, who always works hard to transform visions into reality.

Our thanks to Laurence Rapp, and to the members of the South African Jewish community, for their support for the publication of this English edition.

Special thanks are due to our families, our spouses and our children, who kept us sane even when the stories chased us in our dreams. Thank you for the endless support, patience, and generosity that allowed us to devote ourselves fully to the painful, enthralling whirlwind of writing deep into the long, sleepless nights.

Above all, we want to thank each and every hero whose story is told in this book. Thank you for being a hero; thank you for your courage;

thank you for your heart; thank you for your kind, forgiving eyes; thank you for trusting us to tell your story and share it with the world.

Thank you – and thank God for you. Thank you for the warm hug and strength you have given to Israel and to Jews worldwide and to all lovers of humanity in this dark time. Thank you to the families who raised these heroes, who lived their lives with them and helped make them who they are. Thank you for your stories and the comfort, laughter, and tears that each one brings. Thank you for giving us the strength to dream the next chapter of the story we share.